Katherine Sutcliffe
Shannon Drake
Betina Krahn
Linda Lael Miller
Christina Skye

Heart-soaring and eternal romance that crosses the boundaries of time ... Restless spirit lovers united in rapturous, undying passion ... The sweet, breathtaking promise of sensual—and supernatural—ecstasy. Now five premier authors of romantic fiction have presented their magnificent talents in a beautiful, boldly original collection of love stories that will haunt you, touch you ... and remain in your heart forever.

Avon Books
Presents:

Haunting
Love Stories

*Don't Miss These Romantic Holiday Anthologies
from Avon Books*

AVON BOOKS PRESENTS:
CHRISTMAS ROMANCE

Coming Soon

AVON BOOKS PRESENTS:
CHRISTMAS LOVE STORIES

Avon Books
Presents:

Haunting
Love Stories

SHANNON DRAKE • BETINA KRAHN
LINDA LAEL MILLER
CHRISTINA SKYE
KATHERINE SUTCLIFFE

AVON BOOKS ◆ NEW YORK

AVON BOOKS PRESENTS: HAUNTING LOVE STORIES is an original publication of Avon Books. This work, as well as each individual story, has never before appeared in print. This work is a collection of fiction. Any similarity to actual persons or events is purely coincidental.

AVON BOOKS
A division of
The Hearst Corporation
1350 Avenue of the Americas
New York, New York 10019

And I Will Love You Forever copyright © 1991 by Heather Graham Pozzessere
A Certain Magic copyright © 1991 by Betina M. Krahn
That Other Katherine copyright © 1991 by Linda Lael Miller
Enchantment copyright © 1991 by Roberta Helmer
Forever Yours copyright © 1991 by Katherine Sutcliffe

Published by arrangement with the authors
Library of Congress Catalog Card Number: 91-92039
ISBN: 0-380-76659-0

First Avon Books Printing: October 1991

AVON TRADEMARK REG. U.S. PAT. OFF. AND IN OTHER COUNTRIES, MARCA REGISTRADA, HECHO EN U.S.A.

Printed in the U.S.A.

RA 10 9 8 7 6 5 4 3 2 1

Contents

Avon Books
Presents:
Haunting Love Stories

And I Will Love You Forever

Shannon Drake

Prologue

Glenraven
Isle of the Angels
The Land of the Scotia
The Year of Our Lord 897

T HE massive wooden door to her room in the highest corner of the keep was suddenly slammed open and he stood there, the breadth of his shoulders nearly blocking all light from entering. Yet the light glittered behind him. It fell upon his shoulders, making them bronze, making the ripple of muscles on his arms all the more apparent. It fell upon his hair, which was blond like the sun, blazing with hints of red.

The day was not so warm, yet he was not heavily clad for the battle he had fought. Leggings barely covered the length of his thighs; a sleeveless tunic, trimmed in fur, fell to his hip.

His sword, held ever ready at his side, dripped with blood.

His eyes, bluer than the deepest sea and colder than the ice of winter, fell upon her own.

And he smiled.

"The day has been won," he said simply. "I have won it."

Fire seemed to dance upon her. Little sparks of searing fire darted along her spine, sweeping up and down. Her heart began to pound, and she met the blue triumph in his eyes.

Indeed, he had come this far. He had won the day.

"I have won the prize, lady," he added softly. "And the prize is you."

She could scarcely breathe. As battle had waged here between the various factions, as she had seen the contenders time and time again—as she had fought them off!—she had felt that curious sizzle in her heart and blood and body whenever their paths had crossed. Aye, they were enemies, for he was of the heathen scourge who had sailed across the seas, and she had been born here, on the very bed that stood between them. Before, they had fought their battles with words.

And now they would fight with their fists. She *had* to fight him! She could not give up without a battle herself, for she was the lady here, and they called her the princess of the Isle of the Angels. "Nay, my lord! I am not a prize! And you have won nothing, for you've not won me!"

His blue eyes looked angry. "Brave talk, my princess!" And he gave her a deep, mocking bow. "But indeed, you are the prize, and you are won. And this very night, you will be my bride."

"Never!" she promised fervently.

"I am the conqueror, lady. And now the king of all that I see."

"Then I shall blind you, and you will see nothing."

"Too late, lady. For I have seen you. And you are mine. Aye, mine. Now. Tonight."

The door closed behind him with a heavy slam, kicked shut by his foot.

"Don't you dare think to touch me! I will call upon what men I have—"

"I dare anything, lady. And any man knows that to disturb me now would mean his death. Would you still call upon your men, lady?"

She held still. Dear God, she'd have no more men die over this isle!

The cold steel of his sword clattered upon the floor.

And he strode into the room.

She could not let him touch her. Reaching wildly, she found the earthenware water pitcher and hurtled it across the room. He ducked, and it crashed over his head, and suddenly his laughter filled the room. It was deep, rich and husky, and it caused the cascade of fire to leap within her again. He came toward her once more, his strides incredibly long. She leaped on top of the bed, a mattress of down on tight-wound ropes, and tried to escape by way of the other side.

It was not possible to do so. His hands closed around her arm. She cried out, swinging hard with her free hand to strike him, to free herself. Her fingers swept across his ruggedly handsome jawline, touching the red and gold fire of his beard, but doing little damage. She lashed out frantically then, trying to strike him again. She heard the sound as her hand at last caught his cheek with a slap which reverberated in the stillness that was only softened by the rush of their breath.

His eyes narrowed. None dared strike this great Northern jarl in the face. No man, ever, had done so.

And now she . . .

Thunder crossed his brow. Thunder that seemed to shake the heavens; thunder and darkness. There was a great trembling, and it was seconds before she realized that it came from her heart.

"Nay!" she cried, for his hand was raised against her, and she was suddenly afraid.

Afraid . . .

For he towered over her. His thighs were twice the size of her own, taut, rippled, looking stronger than oak. And his shoulders, laden with scars, were so hard, rippling bronze once again as she stared down at him, as still as the air around them for split seconds as her eyes locked with his, the green of the earth locked with the blue of the sky and the sea . . .

"Now, my lady!" he repeated.

And even as she stood poised to flee on the bed, she shrieked out again, for he had jerked her arm and she was falling, falling on the softness of the down bedding. She screamed again as he fell on her, for once he was over her, there could be no escape. Arms of steel embraced her like the bars of a prison. Thighs of rippling, fevered muscle locked her in more securely than any walls of earth or wood or stone.

"Nay!" she shrieked again, her head tossing from side to side. "I am the trueborn lady here, and you, sir, are base and vile, a heathen cast upon the sea—"

"An adventurer my lady, indeed," he responded, his thumb and fingers pinning her jaw still so that her eyes were forced to his once again. "Base, lady? Never. I am the son of a grandson of a great jarl, and born not a morning's swim distance from this place. Someone was destined to take this isle. Someone was destined to hold it. That someone, lady, is me!"

"The isle is mine—"

"But you, lady, are mine, spread now beneath me, and nothing more is fact," he said simply. Then, staring down at her, he smiled slowly.

It was a wicked smile. Full, sensual lips beneath the vivid gold of his beard drew back to display white, perfect teeth. Teeth as strong as the man; handsome, compelling. Fire flashed in his eyes. Blue fire. Tempting, searing fire.

Then his hand was at her breast, ruthlessly ripping the beautiful blue linen of her garment.

"Oh!" she cried out, and she struggled again, furious, terrified . . .

Excited.

"Nay . . ."

She tried furiously to strike him again. His fingers wound around her wrists. His hands joined together, and he held both of hers with one of his.

Then his knuckles moved slowly, sensually over her cheek. His eyes burned into hers, taunting her. And he lowered the mane of his blond hair slowly against her. His mouth closed over one of the full, tempting breasts he had just bared to his pleasure.

She shrieked out again, writhing madly to free herself.

The heat of his laughter touched her flesh where his kiss had just been. His tongue moved over the delicate bud of her breast. The feel of it hit her mercilessly. She wanted to hate him. She wanted to fight him unto death . . .

She wanted to still the fever that he created. Oh, to her horror, she wanted him to find her lips, to kiss them, to touch her.

"I will fight you forever!" she swore to him passionately, tears of fear and fury and frustration threatening to spill from her eyes.

"Fight me, lady, but fight me well." And then his lips did find hers. They found them pitilessly, and with no mercy. They swept down on them, full, hot, openmouthed, and demanding. Beneath the onslaught, her mouth parted; she felt the searing heat and fire of his mouth, of his touch, as his tongue entered into her mouth, deep into her mouth. Oh, so suggestively into her mouth. Sweeping, warming, stirring . . .

And somehow warning her that he would enter her. As ruthlessly and as completely.

She tried to toss her head. She tried to fight the kiss. His free hand held her, forced her to remain. His tongue grew more gentle, more cajoling. More lulling. And then he was still.

And she was suddenly motionless herself. Waiting. Her eyes half closed, her body . . . alive.

Then she opened her eyes once again, and saw his. Saw the triumph within them.

He had won again . . .

"Nay!" she screamed in outrage.

But it was too late. Oh, far too late.

For every warning, every promise, was made good. Ere she could begin to move, he shifted, grasping her slender limbs. She fought, but no mercy was asked, and none was given.

She did not cry out again. His eyes caught hers, and his powerful body irrevocably parted her legs. She felt the brazen touch of his fingers, moving lower over her belly.

Then she felt the pain, and she screamed.

"Nay, lady, nay . . ." It was he who protested then. The sweetness, the husky fever and the moist warmth of his whisper against the sensitive area of her earlobe and her throat. His lips touched her flesh again and again. His whisper continued. Then his mouth found hers and caressed and seduced it, his tongue plunging into her slowly and erotically.

Like the great movement of his body, like the rhythm of his desire. He held her first in his arms, letting her know him, letting her body embrace and accept his own. Then he was slow. Filling her until she thought she would split, until she was certain she would die, until she could bear it no longer . . .

Then slowly, so slowly, he would near be gone. Until he came again. Deeper and deeper, wedging his way into her body. Into her soul. Into her life. Everlasting.

Then suddenly it seemed that the storm within him broke. He cried out himself, some primitive cry of his ancient, heathen gods. Clouds and thunder seemed to cascade upon them. He moved with fierce speed, engulfing her in his great rhythm. The pain was gone, for it could not combat the speed. They might have ridden a dragon ship over a black and tempestuous sea. It did not matter, for his arms held her. Indeed, she no longer felt the pain.

Just the heat. A wave of it. Rippling down on her. Dancing along her back. Entering into the center of her, to that very secret place when his body entered hers, reached up, and touched . . .

The storm exploded, into the heavens, into the fall of the night. It seemed to sweep over her and through her. He shuddered above her, fiercely.

He rose above her, his captured prize. His princess.

His love.

For, aye, he loved her. Loved her more passionately than he had ever loved any land, coveted her more than he had ever imagined coveting a woman.

They had been enemies afar.

But now . . .

She would be his bride. He had won the land. He had

fought his rivals, and he had won. And he would have his love.

He smiled and looked down on her. Her eyes were halfway closed. There was the most curious curve to her lips.

For she loved him, too. He was sure of it. She'd had to fight that last battle. She'd had no choice.

But now . . .

"Now, lady, you are mine," he told her.

By all the gods, she was beautiful. A wealth of blond hair spilled around her on the linens and furs that covered the bed. Her face was pure and beautiful like alabaster. Her high cheekbones were ivory and pink, her nose was fine and straight and perfect. Her lips, swollen now from the force of his kiss, were still the color of a summer rose, while the rich wealth of lashes that half covered her eyes were honey dark. Her brows, delicately arched and fine, were that same deep color despite the golden-blond array of her hair.

Her eyes . . .

They opened now to his. Ah, but they were green! Greener than gems, greener than the earth! Greener, deeper, more beautiful than any shade or hue of life.

Color stained her cheeks. A soft, lovely blush. "I am lady here!" she vowed to him. But her voice was husky and sweet. "I will fight you—"

"And I will love you, my lady, forever." He smoothed back her hair. "Forever, and ever, and ever."

Her lips trembled.

"But you cannot—"

He touched his finger to her lips, then softly stroked the length of her beautiful hair. "I have watched, and we have battled, and I have waited. And as I waited, I dreamed of a day like today. Of touching you. Of kissing you. Of feeling your fair body entwined with mine. Of laying my hand against your breast. I am the man meant to have you, my love, and the time has come. Would you have preferred that dark lord, Egan, or the Dane, Radwald? Nay, lady, I see your smile. I think not. Indeed, I come from the heathens, far across the seas. But, lady, I love this island, as I love you. And come what may, I will have you both. And heathen though they call me, I will love you, and honor you, and cherish you, love, from this day forward.''

She touched his cheek in wonder. The fierce, sweet fire tore through her once again.

''Can it be true?'' she asked him. ''Will you really love me so?''

''Aye!'' he vowed fiercely. He held her close to his heart. ''Aye, I will love you. Forever.'' He laid his cheek against her breast. ''Forever. No storm shall ever sway me, no man, no woman, no beast or creature of any heaven or any hell shall stop me. Indeed, not even death shall sway me. I do love you. And I will love you forever.''

Her fingers curled around his. She smiled the rose-sweet smile that truly captured his heart.

''Forever,'' she agreed softly.

And forever it would be.

The Fortress Glenraven
Isle of the Angels
1746, after Culloden

I T was her birthright, but she had not wanted to come here.

It was beautiful, men said, but surely that was their interpretation of beauty, for to Marina, this was not beauty.

This was darkness, this was foreboding—rugged and sparse. This was bare rock and jutting cliff. Marina was certain that if she could fly, and look down, the Isle of the

Angels would appear like one great ragged rock, tossed down by an even craggier coastline.

Sometimes, when the tide was low, a tall man—or a mounted man—could ford the distance from the island to the shore. But sometimes, when the winds whipped and storms came, the sea between the island and the coast became deep and wild, drowning the unwary, clutching them up and swallowing them whole. Ships were sometimes fooled, and captains were caught on the cliff and rocks today, just as they had been since the Scotia tribes had first come from Ireland to settle this coastline, giving the country its name.

Looking up at the solid rock wall of the island, Marina shivered. The Isle of the Angels had become home to well over five thousand men, women, and children. They raised their surefooted sheep here. They kept fields of wheat and corn in the expanses of land made safe from the sea by the great stretches of rocks that rose to the sky. It was her home. They were her people.

But she hadn't wanted to return.

"You must come and reside in the palace," her cousin Kevin had written. "Uncle Fraser is dead in the war with the German, and all here is dependent on you. I am still in control of our forces, and of our family, but as you are the MacCannan in truth, you must now come home. God bless, us, Marina, but they've taken the best of the Highlands, they've cut us down and sliced off our heads. They've stripped us of our rights to our tartans and our colors, and they seek to strip us of our honor. We can hold this place. If only we've the colors to rally round. Come to the palace . . ."

He had called the family castle a palace.

Now, that stretched anyone's imagination. And, as usual, he had referred to King George as "the German." Well, that was much the way he was thought of here, for right or wrong. No matter what the religious differences, the Highlanders still looked to the Stuart line as the true kings of Scotland and England. A Stuart hadn't ruled since Queen Anne died in 1715, when the very Protestant English gov-

ernment had ignored James, the Catholic son of Anne's
father, the deposed James II, and sent across the sea to the
House of Hanover for another great-grandchild of James
I—George. The first Hanoverian king had never bothered
to speak the English language, but to a nation where the
reformation of the church had been strong and firm, the
idea of a Catholic—and a foundling!—on the throne had
been unacceptable. Those who supported the Papist James
had taken on a title for the Latin of his name. They were
Jacobites.

And continually, so it seemed to Marina, they lost.

James was no longer for the crown—it was his son,
Charles, the Young Pretender, as the English called him,
who had fought at Culloden Field. In the Highlands, they
called him Bonnie Prince Charlie. He was a charming man—
Marina knew him well—dedicated, intelligent, and handsome. But his quest had brought great grief to many, and
for that, Marina was heartily sorry.

Just as she had been sorry to leave France.

There had been no hopeless causes in Paris, no sheer rock
cliffs to rise above the sea—and no thousands of clan members to shield from the wrath of the English. Two years
ago, her Uncle Fraser had determined that she must be sent
to Paris while the battles raged here. She had been weary
of the constant tug between those supporting the Protestant
causes and those championing the handsome young prince.
She had been weary of the battle cries. Were any men more
argumentative than the Highlanders? More determined to
wage battle after battle?

But she was back. She had been ordered home by her
family, and so she was here. Watching the rising stone
appear closer and closer as her dinghy from the mainland
neared the shore, Marina bit lightly on her lower lip. She
would not let Kevin and Darrin have the best of her, she
swore it. As Kevin had written to her, she was the
MacCannan now. They were not going to press her into any
action that she did not deem fit.

She did not want to be here . . .

But even as the dinghy came closer and closer, sliding

smoothly through the shallow water at the practiced command of a Glenraven oarsman, she felt a trembling, as if a shivering had begun in her heart. It echoed throughout her limbs with a hum, and to her surprise, she felt a growing sense of excitement.

Yes, she was home.

She loved the sheer and brutal rise of rock—

She hated it!

No, rebel as she might, this was her home. She loved the fields on the spit of rock, and she loved the wind when it came. She loved the westwardly view out to the seemingly endless Irish Sea, and she loved to turn her eyes to the east, the craggy rise of the Scottish mainland.

"We're nearin' shore, me lady," Howard, the oarsman, informed her cheerily. "I kin see yer cousin, Sir Kevin, awaiting ye there. And the clan, lady, see, there! One by one, they be coming to the dockside, all to pay ye tribute!"

Indeed, they were coming. Men, women, and children, flocking down to the docks. A cheer had rung out, and people waved, from the sheepherders in their simple wool garments to the merchants and soldiers with their more fashionable wives. Yet even the women with their embroidered bodices and boned skirts were oft wearing some piece of their colors, a scarf in a plaid, a swatch of wool across a chest here or there, a band for a hat.

And then, of course, there was Kevin.

"See, lady, there be your cousin, in the midst of them."

"Aye, I see him," Marina said. And she lifted her hand, gesturing toward her tall, proud cousin. Kevin, ye knave! she thought, feeling a sinking in her heart. For more so than any man or woman there, he was dressed still in his colors, kilted in the MacCannan plaid of heavy blues and greens and cross weaves of brilliant red. He wore a white ruffled shirt as well and a handsome black frock coat. He was dressed in formal wear to greet her, she saw, but she knew him well, and knew that he would ride into battle much the same.

We press our luck with the German king! she thought.

"Marina!"

The small dinghy thrust hard against the shore. Marina prepared to step carefully from the dinghy to the dock, but Howard quickly rose and handed her over from boat to shore.

As she stepped on the wooden dock, a chill suddenly swept through her, hard and fierce. She looked up. Far up. The sun was nearly out this day, breaking through the clouds. She stared up to the tower, to the oldest section of the fortress. It was surrounded by the cliff that formed a natural barrier to the island, but the structure itself had been crafted of hardwood hundreds of years ago. The very first laird of the isle had begun its construction, holding tenaciously to his little kingdom with it.

A high, narrow window looked out from it to the sea below, to the spot where she now stood.

And someone was watching her. She was certain that someone was watching her.

She raised her hands, trying to shield her eyes from the uncanny touch of sunlight that had suddenly seemed to stream down on her.

"What is it, lady?" Howard asked her.

"Why, I think—I think someone is watching me."

"Hundreds are watching ye, lass."

She shook her head. "Nay, Howard. From up there—"

Howard shrugged, releasing her hand as he watched Kevin coming toward her. "A servant perhaps, but not likely, Lady Marina, for that be the laird's room—rather, the lady's room now, eh? Kevin will have seen that it be set for yer arrival. Perhaps the sun, playing tricks . . ."

Nay, someone was watching her . . .

She still felt the curious warmth, the heat that sailed down her spine. Did she see . . . something? Nay, nor could she give it any more thought, for cheers and waves were going up. " 'Tis the MacCannan, Lady Marina, home at last!" came a cry.

Then there was a shrieking sound, one she hadn't heard in a long time, one that truly wrapped around her heart.

The pipers were playing. Playing a tune to welcome the MacCannan back to her home.

Marina smiled and waved broadly to the players. Jesu! she thought. For those men, too, were proudly dressed in their kilts, and if she had heard right, the pipes had been outlawed along with the colors.

Ah, but the Highlanders had never felt themselves bound to other men's rules. They had reigned supreme in their rugged hills and cliffs too long. The war that they really understood was the battle waged between clans.

But we must take care, for this is a different world, and this German king a hard man! she thought. And she raised her chin, for she must lead them to fight, if the English thought that they could take a single man from the MacCannan clan a prisoner. Yet if peace could be met by lip service, then she would agree that the colors must be banned.

The men would wear them when they chose, the moment the English threat was gone.

"Marina!"

Even as Howard released her and she waved gaily to her people, Marina was lifted from her feet, swept into her cousin's arms.

"You've come!" he announced with pleasure.

"You summoned me," she reminded him.

He smiled, shaking his head, a man with hazel eyes when hers were green, with dark blond hair when her own was a startling, sun-drenched blond. He reached down, grabbing a handful of sandy shoreline and rock. Then he took her delicate hand and transfered the earth to it.

"This summoned you. Our home. Our land."

"This is cold sand," she said lightly. But the warmth had begun to sweep through her again, the excitement. Yes, this was home. She did love it, and she would fight for it. Like every fool man here, she would risk her head on a block to salvage it—and their right to their own way of life.

Kevin waved a hand in the air, dismissing her words. He grinned broadly at her, then lifted her high and spun her around again. "Ah, Marina,'tis glad I am to have ye home once again! And home safe through the lines. Walk with me to the fortress. We have the closest lads coming to dinner

in yer honor, cousin, but ye'll have a minute to wash and
change, if ye so wish.'' His whisper moved nearer her ear.
''Look around ye, Marina. Feel them! They've been waitin'.
Waitin' fer the true MacCannan to lead them onward! Feel
the love they bear ye!''

She felt breathless, unequal to the task. She had come
home from France where the people had looked upon the
plight of the Jacobites with some fair distance, though many
French soldiers had risen to fight with the displaced prince.
The French and the Scots had often been careful allies
against the English.

But they could see, as the Highlanders could not, that
the English were completely and determinedly set on their
German king. There would be no mighty revolution within
the English kingdom itself.

George was there to stay. Marina was certainly sorry for
Charles, but the Bonnie Prince was doomed to wander his
days away from foreign court to foreign court.

''My lady!'' Cries went up. Kevin smiled to her and
offered her his arm. She took it while servants scrambled
behind her to bring her bags.

They walked through the crowds. Children rushed forward to touch her skirts. The men jockeyed to offer her the
deepest bows; the ladies strove to touch her hand. Aye, it
was home, Marina thought. She spoke to Conar, the blacksmith who had always cared for her ponies, and she laughed,
hugging the baker's fat wife, the woman who had sneaked
her marzipan candies when she was a child. There was
Gunther—named for a distant, Viking relative—aging now,
but once the head of her father's guard. There were Elizabeth
and Joan, her closest childhood friends, and Dame Mar-
garet, her tutor. She hugged them and swirled around again
to wave to the others. Exhilaration filled her. The wind
suddenly picked up, wild and cold against her cheeks. Yes,
she was home!

She came at last through the crowd to the entrance to
Fortress Glenraven. Built of brick, continually mended and
altered through the centuries, it now had a gothic appeal,
with tall slender spires and gargoyles, some handsome,

some hideous, to stare down at her. Men-at-arms awaited at the entrance, all bowing to her as she came through the large doorways. She saluted in return and paused on the last steps to turn around. She addressed the people with a strong voice that carried well to all of them.

"My dear friends, relatives, and all who live beneath the banner of the clan MacCannan, thank you for this welcome. Thank you for your loyalty to our island, and for your faith in me. We will survive this storm, as we have survived those storms that came in years past!"

A vast cheering went up. It was wonderful. The sun touched her face, her people believed in her.

She had not wanted to come . . .

Because she had known. Known that she belonged here. Known that she was the MacCannan now, and that she was letting herself in for danger and tempest. But she could not shirk the duty. It was hers.

Suddenly, again, she had the curious sensation that she was being watched.

How very strange. Of course she was being watched. People were standing before her, cheering her on, in the hundreds.

Nay . . .

Someone was watching her from afar. She could almost feel the heartbeat, almost feel the danger . . .

"Marina, come in now. I'll see ye to the lady's chamber, and Peg will see to yer needs, and then ye'll come down to dinner and a meeting with the chieftains."

And so he escorted her in.

As Kevin had promised, Peg was there to greet her, bobbing a quick curtsy and, to Marina's dismay, catching up Marina's hem to kiss it almost reverently. "Ye're home, m'lady, home!" Peg told her.

"Indeed, yes," Marina said, lifting Peg up by the shoulders. She was a thin, pretty woman, with salt-and-pepper hair and bright, light blue eyes. Peg had been with her since Marina had been a little girl, and Marina hugged her gently. "I've missed you, Peg," she said sweetly. "Please, quit acting as if I'm royalty."

"Ah, but ye are the MacCannan now, lass," Peg whispered. "Near enough to royalty here."

Marina refrained from mentioning that true royalty might soon be seeking the heads of their finest young men. "Come up with me, Peg, tell me about your family. I must wash off some of the dust from travel and gather my wits about me for this evening." She grinned engagingly at her cousin and continued, "Kevin will have the lesser chieftains chewing my ears off with their proposals and complaints, and I must be ready for them."

"That you must," Kevin agreed.

Peg nodded, "Aye, lass, 'twill be a long night."

Peg had already seen to it that she would be ready for the night. The big wooden hip tub that sat between the wardrobes in the great tower master room had been filled with steaming water. Sweet-smelling salts—French salts—had been left for her. The bath was the first thing that Marina saw when she entered the chamber. After she expressed her appreciation, she paused to look around.

The master's chamber, the room for the MacCannan. Until her uncle's death at Culloden, he had resided here.

Marina's father, the second eldest of the previous generation, had been killed in a minor skirmish with the troops of George I. As their Uncle Fraser had left behind no children, Marina came next in line for the inheritance, for Kevin's father had been the third and last of the sons of the generation. He had died in a border feud. Their grandfather had been killed at the uprising of 1715.

It was a pity that Kevin had not been next in line, Marina thought, for he was a fine young man and would have done well as Laird Glenraven. But the people here were incredibly strict about tradition, and since the days of Mary, queen of Scots—no matter how it might be seen that she had failed as queen—the MacCannans had followed the direct lineage for their leader, be the new MacCannan a laird or a lady.

So it was her chamber now. "And perhaps it is for the best," she murmured softly. She would not face any of the British commanders in battle. When it came time to negotiate, she might stand in better stead.

She gazed around the huge room. When the first laird had claimed this land, his men had often gathered here to plan their battle strategies. There had been nothing but a rope bed against the far wall, and mats for all the lesser chieftains. And there had been the windows. The circular chamber was surrounded by windows, so that the laird might see every angle of attack.

The windows remained. The mats were gone. A handsome Tudor-style bed, big and comfortable with massive posts and a high flat canopy, was positioned between two of the windows. The dressing section was set on a dais. A large full-length mirror stood to the left of the stairway, and numerous trunks and a very handsome dressing table accompanied the wardrobes. It was a beautiful chamber, no matter how old—and drafty upon occasion!—it might be. It was beautiful because, at those rare times when the MacCannans were not embroiled in some war or another, the windows looked upon scenes of startling, wild magnificence, the sea in all its splendor, and the rugged, wave-slashed cliffs of the mainland far beyond.

"Indeed, I am home," she said softly.

"What, lass?"

She shook her head. "Ah, for that bath!"

Peg helped her with her fashionable French skirts and bodice, corset and petticoat. Down to her silk stockings and soft chemise, Marina sat on a small chair to peel the stockings from her calves. A curious sensation stirred within her once again, that sensation of being watched. She looked around uneasily, wondering if things were not even worse than she had imagined, if some nearby clan had not chosen the English side of the issue and come to spy on her.

Here, in her own chamber!

Outraged, Marina rose and looked around the room. Peg, carefully laying out a fresh gown from the traveling trunks that had been delivered, looked over to her, startled.

"What is it?"

Pressing a finger to her lips, she threw open the door to one of the wardrobes. Nothing greeted her but rows and rows of the family plaid, white ruffled shirts that had been her uncle's, and a fine array of gentlemen's frock coats and boots.

"There is someone—watching me!" she whispered.

"Nay, lady!" Peg protested. "Ah, Marina, do ye think yer cousin Kevin would allow fer ye to come to danger? Nay, lass, the wolfhounds were brought here; I set the flowers on the stand meself. There is none to harm ye here!"

Marina had to agree with her. Ruefully, she smiled. "It must be the travel."

"It must be the king's reckoning," Peg muttered. " 'Tis said he's sworn to behead the whole of Scotland if he don't have what he wants from it."

Maybe that was it, Marina thought. Indeed, the days that loomed before her were threatening ones.

She cast aside her chemise and stepped into the tub. The heat of the water seemed to sink deliciously into her body. She had not realized just how chilled she had been from the boat trip across the water. Maybe it was the cold that had given her the shivers.

"Ah, I could die here in delight," she said softly.

"Nay, Marina, don't say such things!"

"You've just assured me that there are no king's men awaiting me in the wardrobe!" Marina said, laughing. "It is wonderful, Peg, the water. I could lie here forever, that is all I meant."

Peg sighed softly. "I'll bring you tea here, then, lass? Some hot, sweet tea, laden with cream and sugar. That will warm ye more."

"I'd love it," Marina assured her.

Peg left her. She leaned her head back against the wooden rim of the tub, her hair creating a pillow for her. She closed her eyes. The steam rose all around her like a gentle, encompassing blanket.

It was a wonderful, comfortable feeling. She tried to luxuriate in it. She tried to forget that Lord William Widager was still in the Highlands, seeking out the troops who had fled Culloden, seeking to cut them down, slay them all, or bring them to London to rot in the Tower and die at the whim of the headsman's axe.

"Tea, lass, is at your side."

She dimly heard the words. "Thank you," she told Peg softly.

What could she do?

They would have to fight again. If not, as Kevin had written her so urgently, she would be forced to turn over Kevin as well as the lesser chieftains. Oh, God . . .

If they could not hold the island . . .

But we will hold the island . . .

She almost started, for it seemed that she had been answered in the softest whisper. It wasn't Peg, she knew.

It was in her own mind.

She sighed softly, leaning forward, burying her face in her warm, wet hands. Her hair cascaded damp around her shoulders. Then she felt it lifted.

Felt a touch on her flesh, a gentle but firm touch on her shoulders, kneading against them. Ah, the touch was both strong and tender, easing away the little aches. She kept her eyes closed. Peg was so good. So quiet and kind a servant. So talented! Ah . . . it was good.

Lean back . . .

It was a whisper. A whisper in her mind. Peg hadn't spoken.

Nay, this whisper was . . .

Husky. Masculine. Seductive.

I am losing my mind! she thought briefly.

Lean back, it said, yet she felt as if she were floating. Ah, it was the mist, and the comfort, in a world of tumult.

Illora . . .

She could have sworn that she heard the whisper then again, in a curious gathering of syllables. She hadn't the strength to raise her head, though. The feel of her massage was too compelling. Too sweet to her weary heart and soul. Too . . .

Tender. Seductive. The fingers moving over her flesh with such expertise. Like a masculine touch, not Peg's at all. Sensitive, sensual, sweeping over her nakedness . . .

It was suddenly gone. She felt bereft, cold.

And startled.

"Peg?"

Her door opened and closed. "Ah, sorry it is, m'lady, but I went down fer a brick to be warmed by the fire fer yer bed tonight, lass. I didna mean to be gone so long."

Marina started violently. "You haven't been here?"

Poor Peg seemed very concerned. "Nay, I'm sorry, I didna mean to distress—"

"Someone was here!"

Peg shook her head. "Marina, by the cross, I swear to ye, lass, none has come here. I left young Thomas at the door, knowin' how ye were worried. Now, young Thomas be a scamp of a boy, but a lad more loyal to the MacCannan clan, I cannot imagine."

Marina took one look at Peg's pale but passionate eyes.

No one had disturbed her here.

Then . . .

Had she dreamed it all? Had she been far more exhausted than she thought?

The water suddenly seemed to go cold. Icy cold. A shivering set into her.

"Ah, lass, I'll bring yer bath sheet," Peg cried, and she hurried to Marina, ready to wrap the large linen sheet around her. Her teeth nearly chattering, Marina gladly stepped from the tub, thanked Peg, and hurried over by the fire, kneeling down beside it.

"M'lady, are ye all right?"

She nodded slowly. Nay, she was not all right. She was weary, she was worried . . .

She was losing her mind.

Ah! This was home.

"I am the MacCannan," she whispered softly to herself.

"Lady—"

"Peg, I am still Marina. Just Marina. Please, call me by my name."

"Aye, then, lass, if that's what ye wish."

"It's what I wish," she said. She turned and smiled at Peg. "And I'm really all right. I need some privacy, though, if you don't mind. A little time for myself."

Peg nodded, but she still seemed worried, as if Marina had gone to France and become quite daft.

Well, maybe she had.

"Young Thomas will stay just beyond the door, should ye need him."

"Thank you," Marina said.

Peg left her. She laid her head down on one of the needlepoint chairs that faced the fire. "I am the MacCannan. I, in truth, alone."

She closed her eyes. She was weary. She felt she was ready to doze even as she closed her eyes.

She did sleep, she thought. Yet if she slept, could she still think?

But she must have slept. Long, powerful fingers touched her hair. Cradled her head.

Nay, not alone, lass. Never alone. Illora . . .

She could see him, coming toward her. He was tall. Taller than the sun in the sky. He was like the sun, for his hair seemed to be a blaze of golden fire, and likewise his beard. And his eyes . . . they were brilliant blue, a startling blue, the deepest shade of blue that she had ever seen. He walked with long, arrogant strides, as well he might, for his shoulders were broader than those of any warrior she knew, his limbs were longer, muscled like oak. He came toward her, walking through fog and mist . . .

A log cracked in the fire.

With a violent start, Marina awakened.

There was no one with her. No one striding toward her. She leaped to her feet and swirled around.

And still, she spoke aloud to calm her own fears.

"I am the MacCannan. I—alone!"

Her only answer now was the lonely wailing of the wind beyond the fortress walls.

She was, indeed, alone.

2

THEY were all arrayed before her at the grand dining table in the great hall.

Like the tower bedchamber, the great hall had been there since the first crude earthworks of a castle had begun. Then the flooring had been dirt, the table had been rough-hewn oak, and the surrounding chairs had been stiff and graceless.

And no matter how the English—and perhaps even some of the city dwellers of Scotland—liked to mock the Highlanders, they had come far from those days. The laird's table in the great hall now was a masterpiece of polished mahogany. The twenty-two chairs that surrounded it were made of the same wood, yet all seated and backed with hunting scenes in a fine needlepoint. Great, plush chairs, covered in deep purple velvet, were arrayed before the fire, and the buffets and cabinets that held the family plate and silver were polished to a high and beautiful shine. Hospitality was prized here as greatly as it was across the sea in Ireland, perhaps because the people had been emigrating over the centuries from Ireland to these outward isles, bringing the name Scotia along with them very early in Scotland's recorded history.

As she looked at the lesser chieftains seated down the length of the table, she was reminded of the many peoples who had come here to form the devoted and loyal natives of the Isle of the Angels. There were Lairds Cunard, Gunnar, and Ericson—proof of the Viking sweep of the island. Lairds deMontfort, Montpasse, and Trieste gave credence to the fact that some Normans had decided to travel forth from England, and brave the rugged mountains and coast-

24

line. There were seven men at the table carrying the family name, seven fine Sirs MacCannan, her cousin Kevin among them, then her second and third cousins, Jamie, Ian, Geoffrey, Gavin, Angus, and Magnus. The six other chieftains at the table were still members of clan MacCannan, though they bore other family names, for the island was their home, their forefathers having come to settle here by choice. Each gave his sworn loyalty to the MacCannan, and sitting at the table as all the great warlords had done before her, Marina felt overwhelmed.

Uncle Fraser had had no right to go and get himself killed, she thought wearily. Then a deep-seated pain seemed to sweep through her, for she had loved Fraser MacCannan. He had been a father to her since her own had died, she had been bounced on his knee, and he had even told her wonderful fairy tales many a night to get her to sleep.

But maybe he hadn't planned on dying himself. He had prepared her to manage a household, and he had seen to it that she spoke French and Latin and Spanish as well as English and Gaelic, the last well enough to deal with any Scottish or Irish dialect. He had seen to it that she could play the piano, the harp, and the violin, and that she could sing like a lark. He had taught her to dance with the wildest of the Highlanders, and with the most gracious gentlemen of Europe.

He hadn't prepared her for this—this line of men staring down at her, awaiting her words for their own salvation.

Kevin would have been the better leader, she thought.

But even as dinner was served, Angus, second in command now, beneath Kevin, stood and addressed her. "As ye are well aware, Marina, we of clan MacCannan chose to fight for the Bonnie Prince, our Laird Charles, now a-running in sad and bitter defeat. The English gave no quarter then, chasing after the men who left the battlefield, weary and wounded and sore of heart. They still seek us out for vengeance's sake, and their orders are no quarter, no mercy. But we've a stronghold here at Fortress Glenraven. And though they seek the blood of the chieftains who led our

men against them, no MacCannan can turn over his men to
the likes of the English horde.''

''We'll fight, of course,'' Marina said. ''But are we
strong enough to do so?''

Angus was much older than Kevin, silver-haired, gray-
eyed, dignified—a survivor. He had fought during the uprising of 1715 and lived to tell of it.

''We're strong,'' he said. He gazed down at Kevin, who
shrugged. ''We've a few marriage offers on the table to
make us stronger.''

''What?'' Marina said, pausing with her wineglass halfway to her lips.

Angus cleared his throat. ''Marriage offers, my lady.''
He rushed on. ''The MacNamara of Castle Cleough has
asked for ye. He's a mighty host of forces beneath him,
and he'd then be honor-bound to fight fer our cause.''

Marina sat there in silence. The MacNamara of Castle
Cleough was also nearing sixty if he was a day.

''Go on,'' she said.

''Aye. Then there's Geoffrey Cameron, laird of Hun-
tington. He's made it known that he's willing to battle the
MacNamara fer yer hand.''

''For the island,'' Marina corrected sharply. Lord! Geoffrey was not old. Some even said that he was handsome
with his fire-red hair and dark eyes. Perhaps he was handsome. He also had a reputation for cruelty that had spread
far abroad. Even in France, the young women had heard
that his first wife had died mysteriously, yet it was suspected
that the mysterious cause had been Geoffrey himself.

''Why not the English lord general, my fine counselors?''
she demanded lightly, her bitterness barely touching her
words. ''That might give the English host pause before
decimating the island.''

She had spoken in ironic jest, of course. She was astounded to see that Angus seemed to give her words grave
concern.

''Nay, ne'er an Englishman! 'Twould not do!'' he responded, after pondering the question.

She gazed down the table at Kevin. Her wine seemed to

have formed a knot in her stomach. He wouldn't look at her.

Well, then, they might have been just as glad to rule the clan themselves. She wasn't so important for who she was. She was important for who she could be married to.

She hadn't protested; she knew where duty lay. Yet they obviously knew what they were doing to her, for Angus suddenly spoke passionately, and from his heart. "Lass, lass! None of us would ever do ye ill, ye must know that! But how many men can we lose before the hangman or on the block? How many women must weep and wail?"

And why hadn't they thought of that before rushing out to do battle for a fool prince? she wondered, feeling a pounding in her head. Not a one of them, she was certain. They were Highlanders, impetuous, and passionate to a fault.

She rose, her meal untouched. "Do I have time to think about this?" she asked.

"Aye, Marina!" Kevin said, rising, finding his tongue at last. "Surely we've several days, I think."

"Days," she murmured. She stiffened her shoulders. "All right. Then I will think. My lairds . . ." She inclined her head. The men at the table stood quickly to a man, bowing in return. She swept from the dining hall, shaking.

She hurried from the hall to the stairway and swept fleetly up the steps. But when she reached the second level, she paused before going the next set of steps to her tower room. She wandered into the gallery that sat above the dining hall. Once, guests had been received here. When she had been a child, entertainments had often taken place here. Numerous narrow windows looked down on the rocky cliffs below. A minstrel's gallery was at the far rear, and a set of large regal chairs stood at the opposite end—one for the laird, one for his lady.

There were paintings here, too. Paintings that traced the history of Fortress Glenraven, from the first laird to travel over with the Scotia to the uprising of 1715, and all the wild and reckless border wars and feuds in between.

Candles burned in sconces along the wall. Marina walked

slowly along. There were the portraits with which she was very familiar. Her Uncle Fraser on horseback, the proud Scot, kilted in his colors. There was the portrait that had been done of her parents together, down in the great hall below. There was the one of herself that Fraser had ordered the summer before she left home. She was different now, she thought. Perhaps she had changed just today. The girl in the painting was young, with clear, passionate green eyes that seemed to believe in love and life and magic.

Marina kept walking, pausing before a painting of a great battle that had taken place during the time of Mary, queen of Scots. Those had been treacherous times indeed, for it was said that the young queen's husband had one of her favorites murdered, and that Mary was involved in the plot when Lord Darnley was murdered in turn. Soon after, Mary married Bothwell and fled to England, but the Scots fought one another then, too, some wanting to bring back their queen, some wondering why it took so long for Elizabeth Tudor to sever her cousin's head.

The battle painting, though, was intriguing. Marina moved closer to it. There they were, the clan MacCannan, riding forth. They were dressed in their colors, many in half armor, some just in their kilts and shirts, their legs bare against the flanks of their horses. At their head was a blond man with a red-gold beard. Like the others, he was kilted, standing high in his stirrups as his sword swung above his head. He was young, he was indeed passionate—a strikingly handsome man. And his battle cry could almost be heard on his lips. He could nearly leap down from the painting, Marina thought, he was so very real. A tribute to the artist.

She kept walking, smiling as the paintings and artworks took on a far more medieval flair. She paused before a grave etching of Angus James MacCannan, laird in the early 1300s. He wore armor and held his sword stiffly at his side. His eyes closed, he seemed at peace—even if his jaw and body were just a bit disproportionate.

There was a beautiful gold leaf drawing of the hall with the Latin descriptions beneath it from the twelfth century.

Then there was a painting of a blond woman at one of the tower windows up above.

And then there was . . .

Him.

Marina paused, forgetting that her own life was in awful turmoil. This painting was by far the most intriguing of the many in the room. She couldn't tell the time, or the place, for he stood against the blue sky, one foot planted on a rock. He looked to the sea, and the wind swept by him, catching the gold of his hair. Face forward, he met the wind. His features were handsome, strongly crafted; a hard, determined jawline met with high, wide cheekbones. He stood as if he defied the world and would meet any threat with that same arrogance and defiance.

He was dressed in some sort of short tunic. His arms and most of his legs were bare, the taut, hard muscle of his calves crisscrossed with sandal straps. Whatever laird he was, Marina determined, he had ruled here long, long ago.

"Ulhric, the Viking," Marina heard. She didn't need to turn to know that Kevin had come to find her here.

"Ulhric, yes," she murmured vaguely. She'd heard the name before. He'd been born on the Scottish mainland, but his father had been one of the Norse invaders to settle the area, so they had called him the Viking. He'd been fierce and heroic, so she had heard. All manner of legends surrounded him. He had stormed the fortress and taken it for himself, and then saved it from a more hostile clan.

"I'm sorry, Marina," Kevin said.

She turned to him, forgetting the portrait for a moment. "Kevin, is there no other way to turn?"

He opened his mouth, shut it again. "I think not, Marina." He paused again as she stared blankly at the pictures before her. "With such men as those you have chosen, the MacCannan name will die out on the isle."

"And worse," Kevin agreed glumly. He set his arms around her like a brother. "Ye should have married that French marquis when he asked, Marina. Ye'd not be in this position now."

Aye, she should have married Jacques St. Amand, and

she would have been a marquise now, residing in his fine palace outside Paris. He had been charming, with his dark eyes and flashing smile, and he had loved her. And she should have said yes, and heaven help her, she had certainly flirted enough with the young man, but in the end . . .

Had she known that she wanted to come home? As barren and wild as the rock might have been, as backward as their society was compared with that of the elegant French, had she been unwilling to spend a lifetime away from it all?

Or had it been Jacques himself? Had she liked him tremendously, but not loved him well enough? Something had been lacking. She didn't know what right now.

But she had made a mistake. Jacques would have been decidedly preferable to either of the men set before her now! And if she had been married already . . .

"The one doesn't have any teeth, and the other comes laden with fangs," she said sorrowfully.

"Now, ye don't have to marry either of them, Marina—"

"Right. We can lose even the fortress itself, and the English can carry away half of my clan, and slice off their heads on Tower Hill. Aye, Kevin, I will live with that easily enough!"

"Perhaps . . ." Kevin began.

"Perhaps what?" She was ready and willing to leap on any form of hope.

"I shouldn't have spoken."

"Well, you did, so continue."

"Perhaps, before they come against us here on the isle, seeking the king's vengeance, some other form of rescue will arrive."

Her heart seemed to fall. What other form of rescue could there be? Only another Highlander would so recklessly place himself in battle against men who already—and with proof of their triumph behind them!—claimed victory.

"What we need is a hero."

"Indeed," Marina murmured. She was exhausted. She wanted to hold her shoulders square and her chin high. Both were drooping.

"Stranger things have happened here, for clan Mac-

Cannan,'' he said. He was staring at the battle painting that had so caught her attention earlier. The scene in which it seemed the horses' hooves moved in truth. The scene with the kilted blond chieftain waving his sword high in the air.

Kevin seemed caught up in the painting. Marina stared at him.

''Eric MacCannan,'' he said, pointing to the blond giant on the horse. ''They were coming once before to decimate the island when he came riding in with four score horsemen. They fought off an army of near to five hundred alone, pushing them back to the sea.''

Marina stepped forward, staring up at the blond man. '' 'Tis a pity we've no long-lost cousins to come our way now,'' she said with a sigh. Then she frowned. ''Look Kevin! Look at the resemblance! See, there, Ulhric the Viking, Eric the chieftain. They are incredibly alike!''

Kevin studied the paintings, then smiled in agreement. ''Perhaps the artist of the later painting borrowed from the artist of the first. This battlescape was surely done after the fact.''

''Aye, I suppose,'' Marina murmured.

''Speaking of likenesses, little cousin, come here,'' he said. She frowned and followed him down the gallery. They came upon a scene of a far earlier time in which a woman sat before a fire, her hair hanging in long plaits behind her, her fingers held lightly over the strings of a small instrument that resembled a lute. Rich lashes fringed her eyes, but their green color was still apparent, as was a curious twist of sadness in them.

''She could be ye,'' Kevin said.

Marina did not see the striking resemblance here as Kevin did, but she shrugged. ''I suppose they are our ancestors.''

''Ah, but so far removed!'' Kevin said. ''Generations upon generations!''

Marina shrugged. ''Why do you suppose she looks so sad?'' She shook her head. ''Perhaps she was given a choice similar to mine for a marriage partner—one with no teeth at all, and one who has fangs as long as a wolf's!''

''Nay, lassie!'' came a voice from the entryway. Marina

spun around. It was Angus, and the sorrow in his eyes as he studied her was so deep that she promised she would never let him see how dismayed and horrified she was over her own future.

"That fair damsel, so they always told me, was the Lady Illora. And the sorrow in her eyes was for her laird, the Viking Ulhric."

Marina tried to smile for Angus. "But he was a great warrior. He fought for the island, and for Illora, and saved it from the upstart nobles who would have kidnapped her and flattened the fortress."

"Aye, but those very barbarians came back. Illora was threatened once again, and Ulhric was forced to ride against them. Dying, he was placed up in his saddle, and there he commanded his men. Even as he died, he carried with him any number of the enemy. He had been betrayed, so it was said, by those within his own house." Angus walked closer to the picture. "He was cast out to sea in his funeral bier, as was the Viking way. The bier was set afire, yet as it drifted into the sea, it did not burn. Legend has it that Valkyries, Viking goddesses, appeared at either side of the bier. And some say that they came to the Lady Illora at night and swore that he would come again, in times of darkest need."

Well, the way that Marina saw it, they were in the midst of darkest need now. If a dead Viking was going to rise from his funeral bier, now was the time for him to do it.

"'Tis a wonderful legend, Angus," she said lightly. She kissed him on the cheek, for he was still studying the painting, that haunting sadness in his eyes. "I am exhausted. Perhaps I shall better be able to choose between the two lairds by morning!" She tried so hard to speak lightly.

"Perhaps we should all turn ourselves in to the English authority," Angus said.

"Never, Angus, never!" she told him passionately. "Don't you fear. No man shall ever have the best of me, I promise you." Brave words, she thought. But no man would do so, she decided. Fortress Glenraven was her birthright—that was why she was now condemned to defend it and her people.

"Good night to you both," she said, determined that she would still be cheerful. She waved to Kevin and left the gallery behind her, then climbed the remaining steps up to the tower room that had now become her own.

A fire was blazing comfortably. Peg had fallen asleep before it, awaiting her. Marina patted her lightly on the shoulder. "Peg, I'm for bed now. You must go and get some sleep yourself."

Peg's eyes only half opened. "Let me aid ye, lass—"

"Nay, I've no need of any aid. And you just as weary as you might. Go on now, for I will need you in the morning."

"Aye, lass, I'll bring ye yer tea early. With a big pitcher of cream and big lumps of sugar and the very best of me scones!" Peg assured her a bit sleepily before she left.

Marina began to disrobe. Peg had unpacked her belongings. Her dresses were hung, her dainty French underthings had been neatly placed in drawers and trunks. She had to look about for a nightgown, and as she did so, she discovered that the room had been well stocked with the Mac-Cannan colors in various forms for her to wear: a floor-length skirt, a sweeping sheath for a banner across her chest, and several scarves. A tam sat high atop the wardrobe, cockaded back with a MacCannan pin bearing the coat of arms and a parcel of the wool plaid.

She sighed. These were proud people. And she was their leader. She needed the courage for the task, and she suddenly and fiercely prayed that she had it.

Despite the fire, the room seemed cold to her. She found a long white flannel gown and slipped it over her naked shoulders, then plunged into the laird's large bed.

She had never felt so alone, so tired, so uncertain.

She swallowed hard, moving her hands over the expanse of the bed beside her. Who would come here? She shuddered fiercely. The MacNamara? God spare her! No teeth, no hair—

No way to judge a man, she warned herself fiercely. But

he was old and shrewd and cunning, his tanned face like leather, his old eyes frightening when they fell upon her.

He was a deadly old warrior. That was why the clan would be wanting him.

Then there was Geoffrey . . .

She shuddered again. Aye, now there was a deadly man, too. He looked like a wolf. He had beaten Mary MacGregor, his first young bride, Marina was positive. And she had heard worse. She had heard that he practiced what were whispered to be "perversions of the harshest kind."

Oh, God. She inhaled sharply. Her clan members would let no harm come to her. She was sure of it. But once she had been married to the man . . .

She twisted over in the bed, slamming her fist into her pillow. Sleep. She just had to have some sleep.

But for the longest time, sleep seemed to elude her.

And when she did sleep, she dreamed.

It was so very strange, for she was not sure when wakefulness and restlessness gave off, when she entered into the dream.

She was suddenly in a field of mist. And she saw him.

He was coming toward her. Riding hard, but in a slow, slow motion. She could see each rise and fall of his horse's hooves; she could see the mud and the earth torn up and flying beneath the great beast.

She could see him. Study him, long and hard.

Blue eyes blazed into hers. Keen, sharp. The wind caught his hair. Sun-gold hair, brilliantly blond. He rode the horse bareback, and he was nearly naked himself, clad only in some form of short pants or leggings. A silver bracelet curled around his forearm in the image of a snake. An amulet hung around his neck.

His bare chest was bronzed so deeply it was near to brown in color. He did not seem to feel the cold. The closer he came, the more she could see the sheer ripple of the muscles in his chest and arms and shoulders. The sun played down on his chest, hard corded, riddled with short, coarse, red-gold hairs.

And as he came . . .

She felt a thrill rising within her, an unprecedented excitement.

She wanted to fight with him . . .

She wanted to touch him.

The horse came closer. Came close to running her down where she stood, waiting. But she would not falter, she swore it. She would stand before him, she would best him.

The hooves continued to thunder, closer and closer.

She could almost feel the stallion's breath. She could feel the blue fire of the man's eyes, searing into her, warming her from head to toe, lighting some secret fire deep, deep within her.

In seconds, the mighty hooves would fell her.

She could feel the quaking of the earth.

Feel the hooves rising, parting the air . . .

He reined in, the horse reared, and the forelegs fell, just inches from where she stood.

"Surrender to me now! Spare the isle from battle!"

"Surrender? To you?" Her voice was imperious. She was riddled with the sweet fire that he had brought. "To you, a heathen? Never!"

The great hooves of the war-horse pounded beside her. She stood her ground. Then she heard the thunder of his laughter, and before she knew it, she was swept up into his arms, and she was flying through the mist.

"But you will surrender, because I will have you."

The words were bold, determined. The huskiness of his voice rang with laughter.

The mist swallowed them up.

She tossed in her sleep. She dreamed, and she knew that she dreamed.

But then she saw him again.

Out of the mist, he walked to her like a stalking beast. More than his chest was uncovered then. He came to her naked as a panther, his long strides equally as sure as those of a great cat intent upon its pursuit. And like a great cat, he was completely, supremely confident in his nakedness, in the agility of his movement, in the ultimate victory of his quest. He came out of the silver of the mist, to the place where she lay . . .

In her own bed.

It was not real. It was a dream.

She should scream. This was her bedchamber. He could not be here. No man had a right here. She was the . . .

She was . . .

She could not remember her name, nor could she remember quite why men would leap to her defense, why they would fight for her, why they would die for her.

She only knew that he was coming closer and closer, her golden panther in the night. And his eyes were on her, raking over her, ravaging her even as they traveled her length, creating fire.

A scream rose to her lips. She closed her eyes. She dreamed . . .

Dreamed . . . erotic, fantastic dreams.

He crawled atop her, sleek, blatantly masculine. "Bastard!" she cried, and tried to fight him.

But his lips touched hers. The softness of the mist swept around her, and she was sinking, sinking into the mist, into the downy softness of the bed.

His mouth . . .

It was not tender, but neither was it cruel. It demanded, it ravaged. It formed over hers, parted her lips to his. Hot and thirsting, it brought wildfire to her. Her temper soared with indignation and fury . . .

Her body burned.

His kiss went on, his tongue tempting, teasing. Breaking the barrier of her teeth. Thrusting evocatively into the very deep recesses of her mouth.

His lips parted from hers. The fever of his kiss moved against her, discovering the pulse at her throat. She found some strength, and slammed her hands against his chest. He caught her wrists. She opened her eyes and saw him again.

Saw the eternal, sky-blue blaze of his eyes. The handsome curve of his taunting smile.

His fingers entwined with hers, bringing her hands flush back against the bed.

And his kiss moved downward against her throat. Found the thundering pulse that beat there. Moved downward again, his mouth forming over fabric, over her collarbone, over . . .

Her breast. His mouth was so hot, so wet, just against the hardening peak of her nipple. She arched back, ready to scream, yet his kiss was suddenly on her lips once again, swallowing the sound of her cry.

She was looking at him again. Meeting those eyes.

Eyes she knew.

"Tonight, lady . . ."

Was it a whisper? Was it the wind? Had she gone mad? Did she dream?

His rakish grin deepened. "Tonight!"

With one swift movement, he caught hold of the edges of her gown, and with a rending sound, they were ripped asunder. Shocked, she sprang to action, trying to rise, trying in all earnestness to strike him.

She was no match for him. No matter how she flailed, he caught her wrists again. She swore savagely and did not understand her own words. She did not sway him. Once again, his lips moved over her, flesh now naked and bared to him. His kiss traveled the long column of her throat. He breathed hot fire against the rise of her breasts.

His mouth closed around the nipple; his tongue slowly traced erotic circles around it.

Somewhere in the mist, she ceased to struggle. Somewhere in that same mist, she felt the soft, exotic movement of the clouds, of time, of night. She felt him, sweet and tender and savage.

A kiss that would not be denied. A body fierce, hard-muscled, proud. Sliding against hers. Causing her to lose her breath.

A kiss, a touch, that wandered places she'd never dared imagine.

That brought sensations she'd never dared dream . . .

Ah, but they were there. The feel of molten lava streaking

through her body. The rippling fire dancing along her spine, centering in her middle, arousing, wicked, fantastic . . .

Then his eyes were on her again. Bold, blunt, demanding. And she cried out sharply as he knelt before her, sweeping up her knees, parting her thighs to his pleasure and scrutiny.

She gasped, stunned, shocked . . . protesting, as his kiss so boldly seared flesh so intimate. But her protest fell to a series of gasps as the sensations burst into a miraculous climax that swept her breath away.

She struggled against it. It was a dream! A dream, no one felt this from a dream . . .

But even as she fought the feelings, a new one descended on her. A quick moment of startling pain. And she realized that he had become one with her. That her dream lover had entered her. That she was filled with the startling size and heat of the man, that bold strokes were seeming to tear her in two . . .

She bit his shoulder. She tasted salt and blood. He whispered to her. She did not hear the words. The pain ebbed. Slowly. To her shock and embarrassment, the fire began to wind within her again. Brilliant, wicked, wild, rising and rising . . .

Bursting in a shattering of stars, sweeping through her, filling her again with a touch of sheer mystery and magic and wonder . . .

She drifted down in amazement. Slowly, sensually. The mist crowded in around her. It billowed and deepened and darkened, despite the whisper of the wind.

Mist . . .

And then darkness.

It had been a dream.

She slept peacefully.

When she awoke in the morning, she didn't remember the dream at first. She felt so very groggy.

She was worn, nearly as tired as she had been when she had gone to bed after the wearying days of travel.

Perhaps it took a day or two to recover, she told herself.

But light was suddenly streaming, and Peg was in the

room with her. Peg had drawn back the tapestries over the eastern windows, and sunlight now touched her with its brilliance and warmth.

"Tea's here, Marina," Peg said. "Angus and the others will await ye in the great hall this morning. Ye must ride and see the ranks of the MacCannans."

"Are they ready for me yet?"

"I don't know, but ye must take yer time, luv."

"Nay, I'll hurry!" Marina said. She started to throw her covers back and stopped, her eyes widening in horrified amazement.

She was naked.

She quickly drew the covers around her. A misted remembrance of her dream rushed back to her, and she frowned with growing panic and confusion.

"Marina—"

"I—I'm fine, Peg," she said quickly. She jerked the covers back around her and tried to smile at Peg.

Nay, she was not fine! She was losing her mind, and doing so damn decadently.

"Peg, there's no way for anyone to reach this chamber in the night, is there?"

"Indeed not, m'lady! At night, why, the hounds guard the door with one of the lads, and the men of the household sleep just down the next level!"

Marina moistened her lips, fighting for a sense of sanity. It could not be. She had tossed and turned. She had imagined a hero, a man young and bold and beautiful because she was so very afraid of what was to come. That was it, surely.

"Peg, see for me, please, if the chieftains are in the hall yet. Quickly now, I beg you."

"But, m'lady—"

"Now, Peg, please?"

"But I told ye—"

"Now!"

Peg sighed, shaking her head. "Aye, m'lady."

The second that Peg was gone, Marina leaped up to dress. She dug into a trunk quickly and slipped into a long cotton chemise, determined to be decent at the very least before Peg could return.

She looked at her hands. They were ceasing to shake. She breathed deeply.

Was she losing her mind?

She ran her hands under the sheets, looking for her discarded gown. Her fingers curled around it. She sank down on the foot of the bed.

Well, she hadn't lost her mind completely. She had gone to bed dressed.

But as she lifted the garment to fold it, she started to shake all over again.

The garment was torn, wrenched cleanly in half from the bodice downward.

3

S HE had scarcely dressed and come downstairs before she heard the sudden clamoring of the church bells, bells that pealed out an alarm. Rushing straight into the great hall, she discovered everyone scrambling to his feet and heading from the fortress, as stunned as she that they seemed to be under attack at that very moment.

One of the tower guards burst into the room even as Angus swore and Kevin leaped to his feet, buckling on his sword.

"Be it the English?" Angus demanded swiftly.

"Nay, it's Geoffrey's Camerons!" the young guard told them swiftly. "He's riding hard, demanding surrender, swearing that he will take Marina MacCannan and hold this fortress by nightfall!"

"Why, the bloody wretched bastard!" Angus exclaimed.

"He couldna wait to negotiate; he would come and blast us all down when what we seek is strength?"

"I think, cousins," Marina said calmly, "that Geoffrey Cameron does not want negotiations. He believes he can have the fortress unconditionally, and then perhaps better negotiate with the British himself."

"By the Lord Jesu!" Kevin breathed to Angus. "She is right! Best us quickly, and he shall have everything! And he can use MacCannans as his own blood sacrifices in atonement to the German king!"

"Then we had best fight him, and swiftly," Angus said, striding for the door. He paused, a gallant old warrior, before Marina. He took her hand in his and bowed low over it. "Fear not, Marina, for every man here would die ere letting this upstart come near ye by force!"

She smiled and tenderly touched his graying beard.

It was fine for the upstart to have her—if she had agreed. But they were under attack, and the Highlanders here would fight.

The men were swiftly gone from the hall. Marina paused, watching from the entry as they mounted. Peg stood behind her with a silver tray and cup on it. "Fer Angus, luv; he be leading," she whispered to Marina.

Aye! She had forgotten the proper way to see her men to battle. She smiled her gratitude to Peg and hurried out. Angus was mounted, at the front of the troops. She hurried to him with a smooth and dignified pace, offering up the cup as he sat his horse. "Godspeed, Angus MacCannan!" she called out. He raised the silver cup in a salute to her. "Aye, Godspeed! Hail the MacCannan."

A cry went up, half cheer, half battle cry. Then Marina could hear the sound of the invaders. It was coming louder and louder, a sure pounding of horses' hooves.

The tide was low, and Geoffrey Cameron knew it. He was riding across the shallow sea to take them.

"We ride!" Angus called out. His sword flew into the air, and Marina stepped back as his huge war-horse reared into action. Behind him, Kevin, jaunty in his kilt and feathered and cockaded bonnet, saluted her with a promising smile. His horse followed Angus's, and then hundreds of men were racing on by her while the people waited behind, cheering on their warriors.

Marina hesitated, then hurried to the stables. She found a young groom there. "I need a horse, and quickly. A mount who will not panic at the sounds of battle."

"And what do ye think ye're doing?" came a voice behind her. She swung around. Peg was standing there with her hands on her hips, her eyes worried.

"I'm riding behind the troops. I'll stay clear of the danger, Peg, I swear it, but I'll be there to support them as they ride."

"Marina, ye cannot—"

"Peg, I am the MacCannan!"

That she was. The groom did not intend to insist otherwise, and even as she argued with Peg, he brought her the mount she desired.

Perhaps she had never really prepared for war, but she had learned to ride. Any child of clan MacCannan knew how to ride the wild Highland ponies as soon as he or she could walk.

She leaped onto her mount, and as she looked down at Peg and the young groom, she was every bit the vision of both a fine lady and the MacCannan of Fortress Glenraven. She wore a fine white ruffled blouse beneath a deep blue jacket, and one of the long skirts in the family plaid made from fine wool. Her small black bonnet was adorned with a brooch bearing the MacCannan motto—"God and courage shall lead." A jaunty feather danced above the pin, and both were held in place by a thin band of the plaid.

Beneath the bonnet, her hair was free, a golden banner streaming down her back. Her chin was high, and the emerald of her eyes sizzled beneath the rising sun.

"I am the MacCannan!" she said to Peg. Waving, she set her heels to her bay horse and followed behind the racing trail of men.

Perhaps it had been a fool thing to do. Angus would have told her so. But she was determined that she should be seen.

If men were to die for her, then it seemed only fair that she should, at the very least, ride with them.

Yet as they plowed down the fields from the fortress, she saw that the forces were already engaged in the shallows. Marina led her horse back upward along the slope, looking for a vantage point from which to watch the proceedings. Her heart seemed to fall into her stomach and there burn, for seeing the battle was a horror. Gunfire roared, and men fell into the water, men in the green and blue and red of the MacCannan, and men in the Cameron colors. Together, they fell within the shallows. Swords were drawn, swords were slashed. Battle cries ripped the air.

It was then that she saw their enemy, and saw him splitting his troops.

Looking far across the shallows, she saw Geoffrey Cameron. He was far from the battle, as she was herself. He sat his large black horse and viewed the carnage. Dark and deadly, he lifted his arm, splitting his forces so that they would ride around the MacCannans and take them from the back.

"Nay!" Marina cried out. Without thought, she rode down from her slope, crying out the warning. Her mount raced far across the fields and toward the shallows. Moments later, the salt water ripped up and flew around her as she began to pound through, seeking the attention of the chieftains.

"They come around. Form ranks! Take heed!" she screamed.

"Marina! Get ye far from here!"

It was Kevin, racing up beside her. A sword flew—too close to her! Kevin slashed and fought, his horse dancing beneath him, the sea water foaming and flying. "Ride, lass, we see the bastard's cunning now!"

He slapped her horse's haunches with the flat of his sword. The animal leaped, bearing her from the twisted melee of fighting men.

Yet even as she came free of it, she looked up to see that a horseman was riding down on her.

Geoffrey. Geoffrey Cameron.

She spun her mount about. She could not head back toward the island. She was cut off by the bulk of the Camerons. She could strive for the cliffs of the mainland to the south.

Her horse reared, and she gripped her reins tightly, holding dear to the mount with her thighs. Her heart sank as she caught a brief sight of the battle.

Camerons were surrounding them.

Yet, unarmed, here in the midst of her men, she endangered all of them. She had come, she had given them warning. She had done all she could do.

Now she had to ride south, out of their way.

Even as they were slaughtered there . . .

Her mount's forefeet landed hard into the shallows. She urged her horse toward the south. Leaning low, she raced from the pursuit she knew was coming.

She was startled as the sound of a new chilling and savage cry suddenly rang out on the air. Ducking low against her horse, she turned.

The wind whipped her hair around her face, nearly blinding her. Her eyes stung. Yet, coming from the mainland now, bringing with him that awful, bloodcurdling cry, was a new combatant.

Marina could see little of him, for she rode so fast and the spray of the sea cast up by the horse's hooves was all around her.

But he was dressed in the MacCannan colors.

Indeed, he was dressed very much as she was at the moment, in a frill-ruffled shirt, dark jacket, and kilt, his long limbs encased in tawny leggings, a cockaded hat on his head with a band of the colors, a brooch, and a dark flying feather. A sporan lay against his waist beneath his scabbard, and a swatch of the colors was looped over one shoulder and held in place beneath that scabbard, too.

Beneath his plumed bonnet, his hair was gold, a fierce, reddish-gold, a color that caught the sun like a banner.

And his face . . .

He was a clean-shaven man, striking. His features were

rugged, as threatening now as a storm, wild, challenging, proud, and ever defiant.

The enemy seemed to fall back, even as he rode. The stranger's cry itself seemed to promise death.

Much as the sword that he swung above his head in a mighty arc as he rode into the battle.

She did not know if he rode alone or with others, but somehow he was bringing about a turn in the tide of the battle. He entered into the melee with that awful cry still on his lips.

She cried out herself, nearly unseated as her mount bore her out of the water and onto the rugged shoreline. Here, dangerous cliffs and rocks jutted out to catch the unwary. She reined in on her panicked horse and fought for her seat while the animal danced.

She heard the sound of hooves crashing behind her and turned quickly.

Geoffrey Cameron was behind her. Dark; a slow, evil smile curling his thin lips, he watched her. "So ye'd ride into battle, me pet!" He laughed. And his voice deepened. "And into me hands, lass!"

There was nowhere for her to go on horseback with the cliffs before her.

She knew them well. She had climbed them often enough as a child.

She leaped down quickly, not bothering to give him an answer, and raced along the rock-strewn beach to the first slim trail that led upward into the cliffs and caves.

"I'll have ye yet, Marina MacCannan! And at me mercy, it will be!" he shouted furiously.

Panting, she ran. He would be fleet behind her, she knew. He was familiar with these cliffs and caves, too.

She had to be fleeter. She had to know the terrain better.

She ran nimbly, swiftly. She knew a place where the rock seemed to jut as one piece, but where there was a narrow space that led into a cave. If she could but reach it . . .

She could hear his sword, clattering over the rock. She moved even more swiftly, gasping, inhaling desperately for breath. Her path grew harder and harder; the ground became more treacherous. Her heart pounded fiercely, and she scarcely heard anything else for the sound of her breath rushing from her lungs and the sea pounding against the rock.

She found the opening and slipped within it, then leaned back against the rock, gasping. She held still for a moment, regaining her breath, then started forward.

"So there ye be, Marina! Did ye think that I'd not know the fool's gap here as well as ye?"

She spun around. Geoffrey was there, standing before her, legs spread apart, hands arrogantly on his hips.

"What in the Lord's name is wrong with you, Geoffrey Cameron?" she demanded haughtily, tossing back the mane of her hair. "Your offer was on the table; it was being considered—"

"Ah, but I knew ye, lass, and I knew ye'd choose that stooped-o'er old fox of a MacNamara long before ye'd choose me. And I've coveted the island, girl, just as I've coveted ye!"

"Well, you'll not have me, or the isle, Geoffrey Cameron," she vowed bravely and indignantly. But who was there to stop him?

He knew the thought that ran through her mind, for he stepped forward. "The MacCannans, bah! Always with their noses in the air, and now ye've come home with yer Frenchie ways about ye, lass. Well, I'll have them tamed out of ye, I will."

"I'll never marry you, Geoffrey Cameron. The clan will not have it now."

He started to laugh. "We need no blessing from the clan, lass. We've the rock we stand on, and when I've had ye beneath me, bearing a Cameron heir perhaps, the clan will be quick enough to agree to a wedding."

She tried not to show the least fear to him, yet she felt the color flee from her face, and the thunder of her heart began to roar once again. By God, he meant to rape her, and she had little help to stop him. If only she had remembered to strap her little dirk to her calf, but she had dressed so quickly this morning, and with no thought of danger.

The laughter left his face. Dark eyes narrowed as he strode forward with sudden urgency. "I'll have ye now, me great and fine lady!" His hands landed on her shoulders, wrenching her toward him. She was quick and furious and desperate, and she lashed out at him with her nails. She caught his cheek with them and drew thin lines of blood across his cheek, bringing a howl from him.

"Bitch! Wretched, arrogant bitch!" he exclaimed in amazement, losing his grip on her in his astonishment as he touched his face. She turned instantly to flee, determined to escape now through the rock.

His hand landed like a vise on her shoulder, throwing her back. She stumbled, then tripped and fell backward to the ground. Her head struck rock. Stunned, she lay motionless for several seconds.

For a moment, he didn't move. Did he think her dead?

Nay! Nor did he seem to care if she was dead or alive. His feet straddled her waist, and he started to lower himself down to her. "Bloody bitch, Lady MacCannan, ye'll pay now, and dearly."

"Nay!" she shrieked, flailing at him. But he caught her wrists. He stared down at her with dark malice and evil intent, coming ever closer. Then, even as the blood seemed to freeze and curl and congeal within her, he suddenly yelled out.

As if picked up by a giant's hand sent down from heaven, he was plucked off her and cast hard against the wall of rock to his right. Marina was able to see the incredulity and fury that touched his eyes.

"Lay a hand on her again, Laird Cameron, and forfeit said hand! Threaten her with any other piece of your anatomy, and said anatomy will likewise be forfeit, sir!"

Marina struggled to rise on her elbows, staring at the deep-voiced savior who had come to her aid. At first she saw only his back, the deep blue jacket, the wild head of sun-gold hair, the massive breadth of his shoulders. Then he turned, and the most awful and curious rush of fire seemed to rip into her and through her.

Blue eyes, bluer than the sky, deeper than the sea, piercing, endless, stared into her own. His was a clean-shaven face, harsh and rugged, yet handsome, strikingly handsome in its cleanly defined planes and angles, the high-set cheek-bones, the firm, unyielding jaw, the generous mouth, the high-arced honey-deep brows. She knew him . . .

Nay, nay, she'd never seen him before.

Not before this day.

He was the warrior who had ridden across the shallows, come to their aid when the house of MacCannan was near to a fall.

"Who the bloody hell are ye!" Geoffrey Cameron demanded, pushing off from the wall. Careful now, he circled the stranger. He stared at Marina, still on the ground. "Who is this impostor wearing yer colors, girl?"

The stranger bowed in a mocking, courtly gesture to Geoffrey. "No impostor, sir. The colors are mine to wear, for I am a MacCannan; a cousin, if a very distant one at that."

"And ye'd refuse me!" Geoffrey swore, staring down at Marina. "This man would have yer place, yer fortress, yer island. He's probably come from the king, come to steal into yer place and have at the brave MacCannan lads who fought against him fer the Bonnie Prince!"

But the stranger was offering a hand, a hand with long, strong fingers. They touched hers and entwined with them as he drew her to her feet.

"Nay, I've not come for her fortress or her title, Laird Cameron. Only for her defense." His ice-blue gaze shot to Geoffrey Cameron again. "And I say again, sir, touch her once more, and your life might well be forfeit."

"Why, ye bloody rogue!" Geoffrey swore. "Ye'll not speak so cocky, man, once I've sliced the tongue from yer mouth!" And so saying, he drew his sword, already bloodied from his day's work.

Yet there was no contest. Even as Marina gasped, stepping back, the stranger drew his own weapon, a heavy broadsword that he swung as lightly as if it were a thin rapier. Steel clanked against steel, sparks lit the air. But ere the swords could clash again, the stranger whipped his up with a strength that sent Geoffrey's weapon flying into the air and clanking down harmlessly on the rocks.

"Why, ye bastard—" Geoffrey began again.

But the stranger was angry, and angry in a way that brought a shiver even to Marina's spine, though he was supposedly on her side.

His voice did rise; it deepened. It seemed to shake the earth, it came forth with such fury and such command.

"Have done with it, my Laird Cameron, have done with it! I've let you live, you callous swine, for the sheer fact that you, too, need fear the German king, and 'tis likely you'll need to fight beside us for your own salvation when the English seriously come against us. So for now, Laird Cameron, I'll not kill you. Not if you can get from my sight within the next few seconds!"

"I'll kill ye yet, I will!" Geoffrey swore in a rage. But he took no step toward the stranger. "By my word, ye rogue bastard, I'll find ye, and I'll kill ye yet! Take heed. And ye—lady!" He swung suddenly and fiercely on Marina. "Ye will suffer fer the both of yer sins!"

Then Geoffrey was swiftly gone, pausing only for his sword. He gave no backward stare and left as quickly as he might.

Yet when he was gone, Marina felt no greater comfort. She found the stranger far more frightening than Geoffrey, for she didn't know at all what she felt in his presence.

"My lady—" he began, extending his hand to her once again.

She stepped back warily. "Aye, my laird rogue! I'll have the answer that you failed to give Geoffrey Cameron. Who are you?"

He hesitated, shrugged, and dropped the hand that he had offered to her.

"Does it matter?" Brilliant blue eyes rose to hers, eyes filled with laughter now. "I came when I was needed. I fought well."

"Are you a MacCannan?"

"Oh, aye, a distant relative, surely."

"I've never seen you before," she snapped out quickly.

But she had seen him. Where? "Are you from the island?"

"Nay, lass, not from the isle, but from this very mainland."

"But—"

"I have been away a long, long time," he stated softly.

That was it, she knew. The end of it. She could question him until winter came and the snow fell, but he was done with giving her answers now.

"All right, sir, so you've no intention of telling me the truth about yourself—"

"I have told you the truth, my lady!"

She waved a hand in the air. "But you haven't—"

"My lady! I had somewhat expected a thank you rather than this barrage!"

She felt as if the tiny gold hairs at her nape rose, and she gritted her teeth. "It is not that I am unappreciative, it's just that I am surprised to learn of the existence of a distant relative, and I'm even more surprised to find myself rescued by him. How did you know I was in danger?"

His handsome mouth quirked upward in a grin. "I simply knew you needed me."

"But how—"

Taking her arm, he interrupted, "Come, my lady, let us join your men on the beach."

Marina's eyes blazed at him, but she said no more as he led her down the cliff. Just before they reached the rocky beach where the MacCannan clansmen were gathering, staring curiously up at them the blond stranger turned to her. "Allow me to introduce myself, my lady. My name is Eric. It's an old MacCannan family name."

E RIC.
     He was another Eric MacCannan, like the bold High-
lander in the picture above the stairs in the gallery. His
name—she knew that at least, for though he managed to
avoid any of her determined questions, he had been quick
enough to answer Kevin and Angus and the others.

But then, they were treating him like a conquering hero.

It was difficult sitting in the main hall that night, for
naturally all the men who had not been injured in the battle
were gathered around the table, intent on getting to know
the man who had come to their rescue.

Eric.

At the swift rise of her brows when he had mentioned
his name, he had smiled serenely and informed her it was
a very old family name; that if she were to delve, she would
discover any number of Eric MacCannans in their history.

Somehow, she didn't doubt him.

His explanations to her clan were no more satisfactory
than any words he had given her, but not a man among
them seemed to care.

He had changed the tide of battle. He had ridden out,
and the Camerons had been bested. That was enough. And
he seemed to have proven that he was an extraordinary man
in battle, for in the midst of the meal, Kevin and Angus
and the others were forming maps of the area, pointing out
their weaknesses and their strengths, and planning ways to
fight off a larger army indefinitely. And they hung on his
words as he explained why both the Camerons and the
MacNamaras would fight with the MacCannans when the

51

British came, for in their numbers they would find a strength that they had never found before.

It had been one thing for the English horde to defeat them at the site of the previous battle. Now the Highlanders would be in a position to weary the Englishmen, for the enemy would have to come after a sheer wall of stone, time and time again, taking great losses for very little gain. Once they had done this, a negotiated settlement could be achieved, and that was all the Scots sought at the moment.

The prince was still in the Highlands, but he was not at Fortress Glenraven, and his cause was lost, truly lost, in the bloody field at Culloden.

Marina maintained her place at the table, listening to the man and watching the faces of the others around them.

She was at the head of the table. She was the MacCannan. And despite the fact that he seemed to know very well what he was doing, she was determined to question him sharply at every turn.

Angus and Kevin, it seemed, had been ready to hand the fortress over to him the moment they saw him climb from the cliffs with her safely in his company. But then, they had already fought with him. And they were men. Show them a good warrior, and they would ask no other questions, just gladly accept him.

Marina was not so certain. She sat out the meal, and she was careful to keep her tone level and her words civil as she spoke with the blond intruder. But there was something about him . . .

Something that both angered and excited her. Something that made her want to lash out at him . . .

And something that made her want to touch the handsome, clean-shaven lines of his cheek. The mere sound of his voice still created a slow-burning fire within her. The flash of his eyes on her could make her feel a simmering in her blood, a fire deep within her center.

And each time he looked at her, it was as if he knew her so well. As if he could read her mind. As if he saw into her soul, and even into the secret, intimate places where she burned and wondered. And he was amused, so it seemed.

With the meal barely over, she rose in a sudden and swift determination to be away from him. She stared straight at him while she excused herself, explaining that she was bone weary.

As she left the room, she could hear Angus complaining that she had entered into the battle herself and must not do so again.

She could also hear the stranger answering Angus.

"Oh, aye, she'll not do anything so foolish again, Angus, I shall see to it, I promise."

He promised, did he? Well, he had best learn to take grave care regarding his promises!

She had thought that she was exhausted, but when she reached the second level, she did not proceed up the steps to the laird's—or lady's—bedchamber. Rather, she found herself in the upper gallery again, striding along the length of the room, idly gazing at the pictures.

Aye, he might well be a distant MacCannan, an Eric MacCannan at that. With his eyes so fierce a blue and his hair so bright a reddened gold, he might well fit in with many a MacCannan male.

She had walked down half the length of the hallway when a curious feeling crept over her.

She knew that she was being watched.

And she knew by whom.

She spun around. Just as she had suspected, he was there in the doorway, arms crossed idly over his chest as he watched her.

"Aye, what is it?" she demanded sharply, staring at him.

He strode into the room, gazing over the portraits and paintings.

" 'Tis a long and restless history we've made, eh, Lady MacCannan?"

"The 'we' of it I most certainly still question," she told him coolly. The closer he came, the faster the blood seemed to race through her body. She must not allow him to see his effect on her.

She backed away from him.

Poorly done! she warned herself. She mustn't let him see the weakness in her movement.

But he smiled and seemed to sense her unease. Her temper soared quickly. "MacCannan or nay, sir, you are unknown to me, and you are a guest in this house, and I do not remember inviting you here. I do, in fact, specifically remember saying that I was weary, and that I was going up to bed."

"But you're not in bed, are you, my lady?" he queried softly.

"Where I choose to be is none of your concern!"

Despite her words, he walked toward her. She backed away again, her eyes widening. "I am the MacCannan!" she began indignantly.

But he had come before her then, directly before her. And she was backed against a wall, and his hands were on either side of her face, and the muscled length of his body was like the wall of a dungeon about her. "My lady—"

"How dare you!" she breathed furiously. "Leave me this instant!"

He was not about to leave her. She saw the wild challenge and defiance in his eyes, and she knew she had merely piqued his interest in their battle.

"I dare anything, lady," he assured her.

She slammed her fists hard against his chest, trying to pass by him. She might as well have chosen to push by the wall of stone that formed the fortress.

"I shall have you thrown out—" she began imperiously, her green eyes flashing.

"I think not," he advised her softly. The blue of his eyes burned into her. Burned like a swift and secret fire, igniting her anger, igniting a raw and reckless stream of excitement. How could he know what she felt?

She lifted her chin again. "I am the MacCannan, and you mistake the gratitude of my menfolk if you dare to harm me in any way—"

"Had I thought to harm you in any way, my lady, I had the opportunity in the cave and on the rocks earlier today.

And not to disillusion you, for your menfolk do love you, lady, but those same menfolk have already and eagerly offered you in marriage to me for the strength of my sword.''

Marina gasped, amazed. They couldn't have done such a thing! They hadn't even mentioned such an arrangement to her!

''I don't believe you!''

He shrugged. ''As you wish.''

Her eyes narrowed sharply. ''If that is the truth, Eric— if that is really your name!—why aren't you down below now, completing those arrangements? You are intending to be laird here, are you not?''

''Oh, aye!''

She hit his chest furiously again. ''Arrogant oaf!'' she gasped. ''Then—''

She didn't complete her words. Before she knew it, her fingers were entwined with his, and his head was lowering to hers. And even as she cried out, trying to twist aside, his lips found hers. Found and seized them, his mouth parting hers beneath it in a wild, reckless onslaught of heat and searing fire. For a dazed moment, she remained there, awed by the masculine command of his lips and mouth and tongue, knowing the feel of him, the taste of him, and the wonder of the sensations that burst and shivered and grew within her.

Then she realized that she was but a pawn in his expert hands. She was the MacCannan. He was a stranger with much more to prove.

She twisted from his kiss at last, shoved against him, and tore free, spinning around. ''Ah! So you are better than Geoffrey Cameron, eh? You'd choose a gallery instead of a cave of rocks!''

He moved toward her, his eyes narrowing sharply. ''I haven't that much time, my lady, else I would take greater care. But, aye, lady, I am better than Cameron. I am better than any man you have known.''

''And more humble, too!'' she exclaimed.

''Nay, I am better, lady, because I love you. And I've

no intention of forcing you. I seek only to make you remember.''

''Remember what?'' she exclaimed in exasperation. She was free of him now. She could run if she chose.

But she was trembling, watching him. Waiting . . .

He bowed deeply to her. ''I'll bid you good night, Lady MacCannan. I am here to obey your every command.''

''Indeed!'' she said incredulously.

''Aye,'' he said, stepping by her and heading out. He paused, looking back. ''You shall command me to love you, and that, as you know, I do.''

He was gone then. She wasn't even sure that she really saw him leave the room. She only knew that he was gone.

She let out a long oath of extreme aggravation, slammed a fist against the wall, and started out herself.

But there was something wrong, she thought as she left the gallery. She had seen something that wasn't quite right . . .

She turned around and studied the pictures. She could almost see it, almost touch it . . .

But it eluded her.

She hurried on, determined to sleep.

That night, she dreamed again.

He was there once more, the man who had come before, the tall, striking blond.

And she was expecting him.

Nay, she was glad of him. She heard her own voice, welcoming him, the soft sound of her laughter as he came around to her. Her arms stretched out to greet him, she was so glad of him.

She heard his voice, husky, tender. Heard her own.

She felt the hot rippling of the muscles beneath his shoulders as she touched him. Felt the ripple of sheerest, softest fabric as the gown she wore slipped from her shoulders, caressing her flesh as it fell.

She felt him . . .

Felt his arms, felt his kiss. Felt the fabulous eroticism as he touched and stroked her. Caressed the length of her body.

Covered it with the powerful strength of his own.

The movement began. The slow, seductive movement. His eyes touched hers. Their fingers entwined. The slick warm feel of his body sliding against hers, stroking in and out, the wondrous sensations building and building.

His fingers, tightening around hers . . .

His facial muscles constricting . . .

The tempest coming faster and faster, and the call to ecstasy building. It burst on her suddenly. A cry tore from her throat and was swallowed up in the sweet fever of his lips as they tenderly caressed hers once again. Falling by her side, he swept her into his arms.

Arms that were so powerful, so warm, so strong, so real.

It was a dream . . .

A dream with strange shadows. She heard laughter then, and the laughter was hers. And there was comfort, and wonderful security. There was being with him.

Loving him, being loved by him. There could be no greater glory, no sweeter happiness.

But the darkness was still there. Waves of it, washing over them, leaving only glimpses of the happiness between rushes of black. Then she realized that the darkness was a shadow, the shadow of a man, reaching over them. She could see the shadow then, see it plain. His hand was raised, and a dagger was in it.

The dagger was falling down toward her.

She screamed, she raged—and she waited for the blade to pierce her flesh.

But no pain touched her, for he was there. Within seconds, she was swept beneath him.

She heard the fall of the dagger, heard the awful crunch as it connected with flesh.

His flesh.

He did not cry out; he fought the assailant as the blood poured over them both. He leaped from the bed, and she screamed again, calling for help.

It didn't matter. Even stabbed and bleeding, he could wage a one-man battle. The assailant lay on the floor, and her love was over him, demanding to know the truth of the attack.

She was up herself, staring down at the man who would have killed her. She gasped in horror. "We are betrayed!"

The guards were there, dragging away the offender. And her love was up, shouting to her, clutching his side where the crimson tide of his life's blood came through the barrier of his fingers.

He was rushing out to do battle.

It was a dream . . .

She rose and walked to the tower window, and she watched as he mounted, and his men mounted with him. His sword swung high in the air. She heard cries, and the riders thundered out to the mainland.

It looked as if they rode on water, phantom warriors able to fly, waging their fantastic battle, the sounds on the night air bloodcurdling.

"Nay!" she whispered and touched her cheeks. His blood on her fingers now mingled with her tears. "Come back!" she whispered. "Bring him back to me. Bring him back. Let me staunch the flow of his blood!"

Indeed, they brought him back to her.

He had fought bravely, and he had fought well. But the wound in the side was deep. No dressing held back the blood. He winced, helped by two others, as he returned to her by the morning's light.

"I will heal you."

"Nay, I cannot be healed. And . . ." He paused. "I have to go out again. Their forces are stronger. The men will only rally if they see me."

Tears streamed down her face. "You cannot go out there! You cannot lead an army! You bleed like a stream. My laird, my love, you must stay with me!"

She gazed down at her hand. Where she had touched him, her palm was now covered in blood again. She stared at him, newly, horribly alarmed.

She had tried so very hard to deny what had happened.

But then she realized the truth. He was dying, and he knew that he was dying. And he knew, too, that he must lead their forces, or they would falter and fall.

"My love . . ." she breathed. Her words choked off. "Nay, you cannot leave me . . ."

He found the strength to set his hands on her. His fingers curled around her shoulders, and then he paused, lifting her chin so that she met his eyes. She could scarcely see him, she was so blinded by her tears.

"Nay, you mustn't fear for me, you mustn't weep for me. It will be well, my wife, for I will love you forever."

For I will love you forever . . .

She looked up. Into the blaze of his eyes. Into his heart. "Forget me not," he bade her. Then his lips closed over hers, and the taste of tears and blood mingled in that kiss. "You must remember me, love," he whispered.

But then he was gone. And when she tore from the tower, she discovered that he was tied into his saddle so that it could not be seen that he slumped.

"Come back to me!" she shrieked to him. And as the horses pounded away, she fell to her knees, defying the Christian god and all the gods. "Bring him back to me! Please, bring him back, for we were betrayed! It should not have been, we deserved life, bring him back!"

And he came back again. Still tied upon his horse.

But the fierce blue eyes were never to open again. The handsome face was ever still in repose.

With his body laid before her, she shrieked and covered it with her own, weeping.

They could not take the body from her, or her from the body.

Nor did she even care that the isle had been saved from the attempt to overtake it.

She closed her eyes, and darkness descended.

She stood on the shore. The distant shore. She was still at last.

The body was laid out at last.

Dressed in his finest, clad in linen and leather and fur, his sword stretched out above his head, his belongings around him, he was ready for his bier to be set out to sea and set afire.

The smoke would carry him to Valhalla.

She stood, cold and alone, for ice now seemed to weigh down her heart.

One last time, she kissed his lips. She tried to breathe life into him again.

But his lips were silent, his body cold.

Then his eyes flew open. Blue as the sea. His lips moved. One word touched her.

Remember.

"Wait!" she cried, but the bier had been set free, the torches had been lit. The bier was set adrift, and the flames should have risen in seconds.

They did not. As the people lined the shores and watched in wonder, it seemed that two white-clad figures formed on the bier.

They were clouds, they were fog . . .

Whatever, the fires ceased to burn.

The bier drifted into the clouds of eternity.

Her tears fell. "I will love you forever," she whispered. "Forever."

Marina awoke, shaken. She touched her cheeks. They were soaked with tears.

She was shivering, and she leaped up and found a warm robe at the foot of her bed. She wrapped it around her, breathing deeply as the details of the dream began to fade.

"I am losing my mind!" she said aloud.

Perhaps she was.

She needed a drink.

With her robe around her, she hurried downstairs to the great hall. A fire still burned there. The fortress wolfhounds lay about the hearth, one big nose laid on another as even the hounds sought companionship. Marina patted a dog and made her way past the table to the buffet and the bottles of liquor there. She didn't read any labels, but selected one and poured herself a long drink.

She had barely taken a swallow before she heard a crackle in the fire and knew that she was not alone. "Oh, nay," she moaned and spun around.

And indeed, he was there.

"What is it, sir? Must you plague me every waking moment?" she demanded.

He smiled and shook his head. "I did not mean to plague you, my lady. Only to guard you. I heard that you were up and about and came only to see to your safety."

"Well, I am quite all right."

"Just thirsty, eh?"

"Aye, just thirsty." Defiantly, she cast back her head and gulped the glass of whiskey she had poured. It was too much. She coughed and choked and started coughing again, and before she knew it, he was behind her, laughing, patting her on the back.

"You're shaking," he said. "You're cold."

She wanted to protest. The searing blue of his eyes was on her, and no words would come. He lifted her up, fur-lined robe and all. Cradling her in his arms, he carried her to one of the deep chairs before the fire and held her there, gently.

Firelight touched his eyes. They were the most extraordinary blue. Really, she couldn't deny the family resemblance, no matter how he infuriated or disturbed her.

She reached up and touched his chin. "Who are you?" she demanded softly.

"Does it matter so much?"

At the moment, it did not. She didn't understand him, nor did she understand her dreams.

But somehow, he was the lover in them. The tall blond giant who came to her, haunting her sleep.

"I keep dreaming . . ." she whispered.

"We all dream."

"But you know what I'm talking about, don't you?"

He didn't reply at first. His eyes were on the fire. "You needed help. I was here. Why must you question these things?"

"You came back—from where you will not tell me—just in time to save us in battle. How is that?"

He smiled. "My lady—we are always at battle, so it

seems. It is not hard to come upon a battle here at the Fortress Glenraven.''

"You know the family history then," she murmured, studying him.

"Aye."

"Tell me about the Viking."

"The Viking?"

"The Viking Ulhric."

He shrugged, but his arms were warm. The blue steel of his gaze traveled from the fire to her eyes, and then back to the fire once again. "He wasn't a true Viking, you know. He was born on the mainland—his father was a Viking jarl. He had known Illora all his life, watched her from afar as she grew. As she watched him. Those were tempestuous times indeed. The Danes raided, the Norwegians raided, and the host of Picts and Scots and Gaels had waged constant war on one another.''

"And what happened?"

"Well, he went to war for her, and for the isle," he said softly. "Radwald, a mainland chieftain, planned to take the isle, and Illora. She hadn't enough men to fight off an invasion herself, so it was a matter of the two fighting over her, and the island. To the victor went the fortress—and the princess.''

"Then he was a cruel and brutal conqueror, no more!" Marina exclaimed.

His gaze claimed hers once again. The fire was reflected in the sheer blue color of his eyes as he spoke. "Oh, nay! He had watched her for years, he had loved her for years. And she did love him, you see. No matter what words she said at first, she loved him. Women are like that, so it seems, my lady. They fear a man; not his strength, but the weakness that he may bring out within the lass herself. So they fight. They say nay when they truly want nothing more than they want him.''

She suddenly felt the pressure of his arms and the intimacy of their time together.

And looking into his eyes, she saw the eyes of a dream lover. Of a man who had come to her . . . somehow. She saw the tattered remnants of her gown on the bed, and she felt the salt tears of her terror and anguish on her cheeks.

She pushed away from him, leaping to her feet. "Nay, sir! When I say nay, indeed I mean the word. If you'll excuse me, I will retire once again."

He did not try to stop her. She did not hear a sound from him. When she was halfway up the stairs, she had to pause to look back.

He was standing by the chair by the fire, noble, striking, handsome. He was still clad in his battle regalia, his frock coat over his kilt, ruffled white shirt, and cockaded bonnet with his feather. He seemed eight feet high there, golden as the sun, regal and glorious.

And her heart began to pound, so fiercely. Her mouth felt dry. Dear Lord, she wanted him. Not a dream. She wanted to touch this man, in the flesh. She wanted to give in, surrender to desire.

Nay . . .

"Marina!" he said suddenly, striding to the base of the stairway, looking up at her.

"Aye?" She tried to keep her tone imperious, regal.

"Just . . . remember," he said softly, watching her with a sudden, dark passion. "Remember . . . love."

A tension suddenly seized her. "What happened to the princess?" she asked.

"What?"

"The princess. Illora. In your fine family tale. What happened to the princess? I understand that he died. What of her?"

"Ah, well," he said with a shrug. "It was hundreds of years ago. She died, of course."

"But how, when? You know, don't you?"

"Aye. All right. She died nearly nine months later. She gave birth to the son and heir of the fortress, and passed from this life. Crying out her lover's name."

"You do embellish, I am certain. Good night," she said determinedly.

She was certain she heard his laughter as she hurried up the stairs.

When she would have turned to her bedchamber, she paused once again, wondering why the hall and the pictures and portraits had so disturbed her before.

She walked in among them. She looked from painting to painting.

Then she halted.

She went back to the battle scene. The one in which another blond Eric MacCannan had led his forces into war, his sword flying, his passion so great that it could almost be felt from the canvas.

Only . . . no more.

It was just a painting now. The man leading the charge was scarcely visible.

The life had gone out of the painting, so it seemed. She walked backward, questioning her sanity in truth. Then she looked at the painting of Ulhric the Viking.

And she started to shiver.

It, too, seemed to have changed.

A handsome man was still portrayed, but he was different. He no longer seemed to look on her with burning blue eyes.

Again, the passion, the very life force, seemed to be gone. ''Nay!'' she cried out softly.

Illora. She needed to see the painting of Illora.

Nay, nay, not this night! No more dreams, she could not bear the dreams!

She turned to flee the gallery. She took the steps two at a time to her room and slammed the door behind her. She bolted it.

Then she began to laugh and cry, and sank down beside it. A bolt meant nothing to a man, to a lover, who came in a dream.

''Nay, no more dreams!'' she cried aloud.

And then she realized that, merciful God, she would have no more dreams that night.

The sun was rising in the eastern sky.

5

MARINA was in the upper hall by midmorning, having spent the early morning hours trying to make up for her lack of sleep in the night by finding some rest in the daylight, but it was difficult even then to sleep when she was so very determined not to dream.

By ten, though, Peg had come to warn her that a number of the MacCannan men were waiting to see her in the upper hall. She attended some of them there. It was the chieftains that the British wanted, she knew, but few of the men who stood sorrowfully before her then were chieftains. They were farmers who had sprung up with the excitement to do battle at Culloden, and now they were sorely afraid. They were anxious to take their chances in the New World, having heard that there was a ship leaving the countryside soon, and that the captain was asking few questions of the men who were ready to sign on. She listened to them all, reminded them that the English were not anxious to hang farmers, but gave them her blessing when they seemed determined to go.

Angus was with her then, and as the men filed out, she found his eyes on her, heavy and sad.

"What would you have me do? Command them to stay?"

He shook his head. "Nay, lass. But ye must do something, and soon. It seems as though ye wish no more to do with the Cameron, and as he saw fit to attack us, demanding an answer, I'd not be inclined to give him the time of day, much less the hand of the MacCannan in marriage. That leaves the MacNamara, or . . ."

"I've heard. This Eric MacCannan."

Angus shrugged. "Well, lass, ye did ask fer a fellow with a full set of teeth, ye know."

Was she doomed to pay forever for her foolish comments? She sighed softly.

"What are our losses, Angus, from the battle waged with the Camerons?"

"Thirteen wounded, and all have survived the first night, though young Neall was bashed severely in the head and faces a grievous fever now."

Still . . . no losses. Yet thirteen men who could not fight when the English came against them.

"Ye must decide, Marina," Angus warned her.

She nodded. "By tonight, Angus," she promised him. "This morning, I think that I will ride."

Angus must have told Kevin her intent, for her cousin was awaiting her down by the stables. "I'll accompany ye, Marina."

"Nay, Kevin, I've a wish to ride alone today." She smiled. "To survey my domain."

His frown assured her that he worried for her safety. "I'll not leave the isle," she promised.

She didn't know if he was relieved or not, but she didn't care. She simply wanted to be alone.

The groom brought her the same small bay that she had ridden into battle, and Marina was glad of it; she was coming to know the mare. She left the ancient tower behind her and started to race across the open fields that faced the mainland straits, then turned westward and finally began to climb the cliffs and jags that faced toward the Irish Sea.

She had slowed her frantic pace, of course, for she could not run the bay here lest she break the horse's slim legs. But the bay was from local stock, she was surefooted and accustomed to the rugged landscape, and so they quickly climbed the rock until they were on a precipice, looking far down to the sea.

It was beautiful here. Wild, barren, with heather growing in sparse clumps from cracks in the rocks. The wind seemed stronger here, it seemed to whistle, and the sea today was dark and deadly and dangerous, and as tempestuous as her mood.

The urge to walk the beach struck her, and she lifted her reins, prodding her small mare to take her down the rock to the cliffs and the stretch of beach beneath. When she had arrived on the narrow border of sand, she dismounted and left the mare to chew on the weeds that grew by the rock. She started to strip off her shoes and stockings when she noticed an old woman in a long black dress and a black shawl wandering the sands nearby. She finished with her task, feeling the sand beneath her toes, then rose and wandered to the water line.

The woman came closer and closer.

She seemed ancient, with flesh like wrinkled leather. Her black shawl covered incredibly thin strands of gray and pure white hair, and she stooped as she walked, as if weighed down by the years. All that seemed young in her were her eyes. They were gold eyes, not brown or green but gold, and they were sharp as a blade as they studied Marina.

"So ye're the MacCannan come home, all growed up."

"I am Marina MacCannan," she told the woman.

The woman smiled, a toothless smile. She clutched Marina's arm. "And ye'll stay, and it'll be all right. This time. The fields will grow rich, fer ye'll know now, ye'll take heed, ye'll take care."

Marina shook her head, growing alarmed at the woman's desperation. "I've come home, aye. I'll not be going anywhere—"

"Ye'll marry him! But that canna be all, ye must listen to me!" For a stooped old thing, she had tremendous strength. She swirled Marina around, and her fingers seemed to dig into her arms. "Treachery come from within, Illora; when will ye learn?"

Marina freed herself, her teeth chattering. This was an old crazy woman, she told herself. She had to be kind but firm.

"Listen to me, please," she said and clutched the old woman's wrists lest she try to take hold of her again. "I am Marina MacCannan. My name is Marina. But I will stay here. Things will be well. You mustn't worry. The English will not hurt you.''

The woman looked at her as if she were the crazy one. Then she broke away.

Heedless of the cold waves against her feet and ankles, she walked out into the water. '' 'Twas from here that they set sail to the bier. But it would not burn. For it was said on that very day that he would return. Why, 'tis on Illora's tombstone. 'He will come again, this lion among men, and stay when love meet him, not die if love will greet him.' ''

''That's, er, lovely,'' Marina said. Could she leave this daft old woman here alone? Would she drown herself if Marina did so?

The woman spun around. It seemed that she moved in slow motion. That her black cape took flight around her like the wings of a giant raven. Water flew from the long hems of her sleeves and shawls, catching the sunlight in magical droplets.

''Nay, listen to me, lady, heed the warning this time! Fer he has come afore, yet the treachery made mockery of love. Ye must take the blow, lady, ye must take the blow. Know that it is coming, and do not let him perish again! 'Tis up to ye, Illora, 'tis up to ye!''

''I am not Illora—''

''*Cuimhnich!*'' the old woman shouted. For a moment, Marina did not understand her. Then she recognized the word. *Cuimhnich*. It was Gaelic for ''remember.''

Then the old woman turned away and started running toward the cliffs that curved inward from the horizon.

''Wait!'' Marina called to her.

But for a hunched-over old woman, she moved extremely well. It seemed that she raised her black shawl, and, almost like the giant raven she resembled, took flight across the sea and land. Marina ran to catch up with her, but she could not.

Exasperated, weary, panting, she wandered back across the sands. She looked up at one of the dunes. A man there sat on a horse. A huge black horse, a war-horse with thighs and flanks as muscled as those of the warrior who sat his back.

Eric. Even at a distance, she could feel the blue of his eyes. Feel their touch on her.

His thighs nudged against the great black horse. The animal walked her way until man and beast were right before her, dwarfing her.

She stared up at him, suddenly very tired and very confused. He had appeared from nowhere. Had he stepped down from a painting? Or had he returned from the dead, as a prophecy had promised?

Had he come before, riding in his clan colors at the head of an army when the forces turned against Queen Mary and came here to battle MacCannans then?

She was losing her mind. And to think of it, she could have remained safely back in France rather than coming here where the clans fought one another just as swiftly as they fought any alien foe.

Back in France . . .

His eyes touched hers. The warmth spread through her. Nay, she could not be back in France. She knew why she had not married the marquis. She had liked him, aye. But she had never felt this. Never known this fever, this excitement, just because a man's eyes fell on her. She had never wanted to touch a man as she wanted to touch this one. She had never felt the passion, the fever . . . the need to be wildly, wickedly loved; to be held and treasured and caressed.

Taken, as a ghost lover touched her in her dreams.

Nay, nay, this cannot be, she assured herself quickly. He is not the Viking laird returned, for I am assuredly not his Illora!

Nor had he come to speak to her of love. "The British have gathered on the mainland, in some few miles. They'll take their stand against us this day," he said.

She gasped, coming nearer, taking hold of his saddle as she looked up at him in dismay.

"So soon? I thought there was time—"

"You need no time, Marina. I've come to tell you, I will

lead your army. And I've come to demand you, too. Marry me, Marina.''

Command, indeed! ''But the battle—''

He pulled back on the reins, and his great black war-horse moved away from her touch. ''Be it then as you wish, Marina MacCannan. I'll fight the battle again. And I'll take the prize as I see fit.''

Fury instantly rose within her, but with it, a rich flood of excitement. Aye, let him win, let him have what he would. She did not know what she was fighting.

''My dear sir—''

''My dear lady! I could be tender, I could be coercive. I could demand that you marry me because you do love me, but perhaps I cannot convince you yet that it is so. I can command that you marry me, for I will be the victor; I will prevail. Then, too, I can suggest that you wed me because I have all my teeth, and all my hair, and my limbs are sound and strong. It will not matter. I will return tonight. The threat to you, and to the isle, will be done with, and this night, lady, you will lie with me!''

''How dare you—'' she began, hands on her hips, her temper flying. But he meant to have none of it. The great black reared and turned, and soon the sand was flying beneath its feet.

And he was gone.

The battle, the big battle, was nearly joined. They would make their stand. They would find peace, or the clan would be decimated.

And he would lead . . .

She moistened her lips, fearful of the longing, the shivering that began within her. He seemed determined that he would have her that night . . .

A slow smile touched her lips.

He did have all his teeth, and all his hair.

And, indeed, he was sound in limb and body!

Marina turned, forgetting her shoes and stockings, and raced along the shore to her bay. She leaped astride the mare and gave the horse free rein to hurry her back to the fortress with all speed.

She returned to the courtyard just as the men were preparing to march out again. She rode into the middle of them, her hand raised high in salute, a cry on her lips. She rode to the very entrance of the fortress, knowing that she would find Peg there with the stirrup cup of wine to be offered to the leader of the forces.

Marina leaped down and took the tray from Peg with a nod of silent thanks, then made her way through the horses with their riders to the very front of the ranks. She passed by Kevin, and by Angus, and proceeded onward. "Laird Eric!" she cried.

His eyes fell on hers, yet betrayed no emotion. He was a warrior, prepared for his battle now.

She offered up the cup. "Godspeed, sir!"

He took the wine. She thought that a small smile played on his lips. He drank the wine, then raised himself up in his saddle, his great sword swinging.

"*Cuimhnich!*" he cried out.

And en masse, the great horses began to move, and in seconds, there was a thunder that seemed to split apart the land as they galloped onward.

Marina stood alone where so very many had been. *Cuimhnich* . . .

Gentle hands touched her shoulders. Peg was there. "Come in, lady, now, come in. Ye're wanderin' round with no shoes upon yer feet, and ye'll catch yer death."

Marina didn't move. She stared after the riders.

"There's naught we can do here, lass. Naught at all. Messengers will come. The guards will keep sight on the horizon, and keep shelter on the fortress itself. Come in."

Marina went with her. She climbed to her chamber high up in the fortress, and she put on new stockings and shoes. Restlessly, she wandered back down to the main hall, but it was so empty. She went back up to the second-story hall and wandered along the paintings and portraits.

Today they told her nothing. They were just as they had been the night before. Paintings. Color on canvas.

She stared at the Eric MacCannan who had come in the time of Mary. Take away the beard, and . . .

She felt a presence behind her. Peg, come after her to see that she was all right, she was certain. "What happened to him, I wonder?" she said aloud. "Did he rule wisely and long? Did he die an old man, with a full score of grandchildren about his feet?"

"Eric MacCannan?" Peg said softly. "Nay, lass, he did not. Why, he was stabbed in his bedchamber in the middle of the night, and died in the morn. 'Twas said that the blow was intended for his lady, for she was the heiress in truth, if legend serves. But he couldna let her die, ye see."

Cold—severe, eerie, icy—swept down her spine. "Like Ulhric the Viking," she said. And her voice grew bitter with the fear that raced through her. "And I'm sure that he rode against his enemy, bleeding though he was. And that he bested his enemy. But he died. And his wife bore a single child. And she died, too. And perhaps he was Ulhric come back."

"Ah, legend. Stuff and legend." Peg sniffed. She was quiet then. Marina did not turn. She swallowed hard. She walked down the gallery to the painting of Illora.

Surely it had been done at a later date. The artist must have guessed at the way Illora had looked.

But she had been a woman with emerald-green eyes, with long blond hair flowing down her back. And her head was bowed in the greatest sorrow . . .

Go to the tomb, Marina. Go to the tomb.

"The men are at war!" Marina protested. "I must await every word. And there is good reason to expect that I may be called to meet with the English general, if all goes well and peace is to be made. I cannot go running around believing in legends and tales—"

She broke off, for she was alone in the room. Peg was not with her.

The chills that assailed her then were awful. She couldn't bear being in the gallery a second longer. With a startled cry, she tore down the length of it.

She did not pause until she had run down the stairs, and come to the great hall beneath.

"Peg!" she called, her hands gripped by her sides.

From the pathway to the kitchens, Peg ran out.

"Where is it?" Marina demanded.

"Where is what?" Peg asked, mystified.

"The tomb. Illora's tomb."

Peg frowned, wiping her hands on her apron. "Why,'tis in the cliffs by the sea. Down by the strip of beach that looks outward toward Eire."

Marina swung around. She was going riding again. Peg followed after her quickly. "Where are ye goin', lass? Ye must stay now, ye must listen fer the messengers, ye must be ready to meet with the Englishmen."

"That's exactly what I just told you," Marina snapped, and ignoring Peg, she hurried out.

Behind her, Peg frowned more deeply, terribly concerned. "Ye didna tell me a thing, lass, not a thing," she said, but she spoke to herself.

Marina made it back to the cliffs, climbed the rocks and shale on her bay mare, and trekked down toward seaside once again. She dismounted and led the bay until she came to the connecting maze of cliffs and caves. She had come here often enough as a child. She and Kevin had played here. She should have remembered the tomb. Someone in the family had always cared for it. The ancient rock had been protected. The inscription had been rechiseled time and time again.

She'd never even glanced at it. She'd had little time for the past then. Fraser had led the clan—she'd had no call to worry about it.

The crypt had been dug high against the wall of the cave, protecting it against any encroachment of the water. A massive stone had been set before it, and marble had been brought and a massive cross created of it.

Then there were the words. They were in Gaelic, and despite her knowledge of her native language, the spellings were very old and difficult to read. She touched the words "Our fair princess here shall sleep. One day with destiny, her tryst she'll keep. For he will come again, this lion among men, and stay when love meet him, not die if love will greet him."

Marina stepped back, biting her lower lip. It was madness. All madness.

"I am not Illora!" she cried out. She said it again, loudly, letting her words echo in the caves. "If that tomb were opened, her bones would be there, her flesh would have rotted, but her bones remain! I know that they do!"

She closed her eyes, clenching her teeth. She was so afraid.

And then she was not afraid. It was as if tender, gentle arms had embraced her. He was there. In some presence. He was there, holding her, caressing, assuring her. It was going to be all right. He loved her.

Cuimhnich . . .

Remember . . .

"Nay!"

She swung around, suddenly as desperate to leave the cave as she had been to leave the gallery. He was not with her, he could not be with her. He was flesh and blood, and he was out on the battlefield.

She tore through the caves and found the mare. She was so frightened that she fumbled trying to remount the horse, and had to try again and again.

Finally, though, she was mounted, and, once again, she gave the mare free rein, anxious to return to the fortress with all possible speed.

She came back just as a messenger in her colors raced in from the opposite direction. The tide was rising, and he was soaked from the waist down, and his horse gave a mighty shake, throwing off a rain of sea water. Marina did not care. She urged the bay toward him.

"What news? What has happened?"

"My lady! Battle was quickly engaged! The English meant to have us by surprise, but my Laird Eric was the one to surprise them. And by heavens, my lady! They all rose as one! When the force of Laird Eric's troops was seen, the MacNamara came into the battle, too, with his own. As did Geoffrey, of clan Cameron."

"Go on, go on! Quickly!" Marina urged him.

"The fighting was fierce and furious, lady. The English

wanted to have no quarter with us mountain heathens, as they call us. But as they began to fall like slaughtered sheep before our onslaught, their general sent a messenger to Laird Eric, and a halt has been called. I've a parchment now for your approval as the MacCannan of the Isle of the Angels. A truce will be signed. The MacCannan men will be granted their freedom and their lives, all who fought at Culloden pardoned. We will abide by the rules set down for the Scots, forsake our colors for the time, and live in peace. 'Tis all there, lady. It needs but your signature.''

Marina read over the long parchment she had unfolded carefully. It had all been laid out, step by step, in neat and legible script. Everything that they wanted would be granted them. Once this was signed, she had managed all that could have been hoped for after the dreadful defeat at Culloden. Her clan would survive. They would be left in peace on the Isle of the Angels.

She had not managed it. Nay, he had done so . . .

Did it matter who had done what? she asked herself furiously. Angus would live, Kevin would live. Her kinsmen had bravely and heroically found their way.

"Come into the hall. I will set my hand to it," she told the young messenger.

Thirty minutes later, the deed was done.

And as darkness fell, the triumphant warriors began to return.

Marina had prepared for them. There would be a feast in the fortress that night, one the likes of which the Isle of the Angels had yet to see. Lambs and sheep and cows were slaughtered; fowls lost their heads by the dozens and were stuffed with breadcrumbs and seasonings and prepared with fine sauces. Barrels of ale were brought up, along with the best wines in the fortress.

And when the men returned, Marina was ready to greet them. She had chosen to wear a rich taffeta gown in the family colors, with a fine black velvet jacket over a soft chemise in white silk. She was very calm, greeting the lesser chieftains with handshakes and kisses on their cheeks. Angus she hugged fiercely, and Kevin she was loath to let go.

Yet all the while, she knew that he watched her. And that he waited.

And she felt his eyes. Felt the searing blue send fire into her.

She would not fall to him. Nay, she must take care, must keep her distance. Indeed, he had been triumphant. But this was the eighteenth century. Their courtship would be slow.

She had to know him. She had to understand.

"My lady," he greeted her, when it was his turn at last. And he offered her the deepest, most civilized bow.

"Eric MacCannan. Laird MacCannan. 'Tis a title that you deserve in truth, sir, and one I readily hand to you," she told him regally. "The table is set, gentlemen. A celebration is in order, and so it will be!"

"Oh, it will be more," he told her. "Much more. Where is the Reverend Sean Hamilton? Come forward, sir, and let the wedding come now." His steely gaze set upon her. "Then we may celebrate in truth!"

A great cry went up from the chieftains all around them. Marina gritted her teeth, trying to keep her smile. "My dear laird, I am not ready for this!"

"I am the victor, I have won the prize. The prize is mine. Not a man here would deny me."

"But I am a woman, sir. And I deny you."

"This wedding will take place. I will be laird in truth tonight."

"But—"

"I fought, my lady. I gave you all that you desired. Would you have so little honor that you would deny your own word now?"

Marina gasped, furious. He was whispering, but the chieftains—her chieftains!—were all beginning to look at them. "Fine!" she snapped. "Have the wedding then. But my dear laird—almost husband!—remember that I deny you still!"

"I am the victor," he repeated softly. Then his voice rose again. "Sirs, the wedding shall commence, and then the wedding feast!"

Again there were roars of approval. And the reverend

stepped forward, and before Marina knew it, Angus was at her side, and everyone was looking on, and Sean Hamilton was reading from his prayer book. Eric gave his vows in a loud, strong voice. He had to squeeze her fingers to get her to give hers at all.

When it was over, when she was pronounced truly his bride, he kept his grip on her fingers. And they sat at the great table together while everyone ate and raved about the battle and celebrated in good stead.

As soon as she could, Marina escaped the table. She hurried upstairs, leaning against the door to her chamber.

Then she was half thrown and half leaping away from the door as it suddenly slammed inward. Her heart beat furiously as she spun around, staring at him as he came in, shutting the door behind him.

"How dare you! How dare you come here like this. You know that I am not ready for—for—you!" she stammered.

He smiled, slowly, wickedly. "Lady, were I to wait for you to bid me ready, I might well lose all my teeth, just like the MacNamara."

"Oh! Joke then, sir, if you will. I still don't know who you are, or where you've come from. Or why so many seem to ride to battle with you when you are alone. I don't know anything about you. I don't—" She left off with a short cry as he started toward her. The pillow was on the bed. She threw it at him. "Stop now! I mean it, my laird, I swear that I do!"

He had nearly caught her on one side of the bed. She tried to leap over it. His fingers wound tight around her upper arm, and rather than flying away, she was being lifted up, and then thrown flat, and before she knew it, her conquering warrior was straddled over her.

She tried wildly to strike him. He simply caught her wrists. "Mine the prize," he whispered softly.

"Bastard—" she began.

But his lips found hers. Found them, caressed them, parted them. Brought sweet magic to them. Her heart began to pound. The rampant thunder of longing began to weave throughout her. A cascade of rich, ardent crystals of fire danced throughout the length of her as she tasted the rogue's demand of his tongue.

She ceased to struggle. She had wanted him. Wanted him so.

"I am not a prize!" she whispered as his lips rose just above hers.

"You are a prize. Cherished, beloved," he whispered in turn.

His hands were on her. And her clothing was leaving her. A rustle of taffeta. A whisper of silk. The fire of his lips touched her bare flesh.

"A man in truth, tonight, my lady. Flesh and blood. No longer a creature of dreams . . ."

She did not dwell on his words. His lips lowered against her flesh. Her fingers played on the heat and ripple of his muscled shoulders.

"A man in truth. Flesh and blood . . ." she repeated.

"Tell me to love you, my lady," he commanded her.

"Love me," she whispered.

"Aye, I will love you." Again his lips seared hers. Traveled down the length of her throat. Brushed and burned and fed on the hardened peak of her breast. Cries left her lips, soft cries of longing, of desire.

He rose above her, naked, determined. A golden warrior of any age.

"I will love you," he vowed softly. "Forever . . ."

6

THE waves rushed out into the sea with the pull of the
tide, and Marina laughed, running out with them, then
running in again before the cold water could wash over her
bare feet. She turned and saw that Eric was stretched out
on the linen sheet she had laid on the sand. Leaning on an
elbow, he watched her, a slight smile curving his lip as he
idly gnawed on a blade of grass.

Marina left the waves behind, compelled to be at his side
again. She lay down on her stomach, propped on her elbows,
too, her chin held up by her knuckles as she met his gaze.

Why had she ever, ever thought to deny this man? she
wondered. In the days after their wedding, she had come
to know him so much better. They had laughed, they had
talked, they had spun dreams for themselves and dreams
for the clan. She had learned that he was hard, but fair. She
had seen that men followed him instinctively.

She had discovered that she was sensual and passionate
herself, just as she had discovered the fire and passion in
him. Dreams faded away as reality eclipsed all else. He was
a demanding lover, a demanding man. But he had his quirks
of humor, too, and he could make her laugh. And when
she was weary, the strength of his broad chest was marvelous. No man could be more tender, she thought. No man
could hold her quite so gently, sleep with his arms curled
around her quite so protectively.

And still . . .

"Where did you come from?" she asked him.

His eyes met hers with their startling, deep blue color.
He rose up, walking out to watch the waves. "I was born

on the mainland, not far from here," he said.

"Then where have you been?" she pressed.

He turned to her, a smile curving his lips. Then he walked back to her and sat at her side, smiling. "Ah, my love. I know what you're hinting at. That I rose up from the sea. That I came here first as the Viking Ulhric, and perished on this shore. That the gods were merciful and kind and sent me back last century. And that now, while the isle and my princess lay threatened again, I returned."

She flushed. "That's absurd, of course."

"Aye."

"But is it true?" she appealed.

He didn't answer for several long moments. Then he turned to her, and she felt a chill snake along her back. "Would it matter if it were true? Would it be so horrible to discover that you were Illora?"

"I am not Illora," she said flatly. "And . . ."

"And what?"

She stood suddenly. "Aye, it would be horrible if it were true. For if it were true, it would mean—" She broke off abruptly.

He stood, too. "It would mean what?"

"It would mean tragedy," she said. "Ulhric died, that Eric died, their wives died," she added quickly. "And I can't begin to understand—"

"Understand what?" he demanded, waiting, watching her.

She was suddenly cold. She hugged her arms about herself. "I don't know."

"Marina—" he said softly.

He was going to come to her. He was going to put his arms around her and hold her, and she wouldn't care anymore.

She had to care. She had never been so desperately happy, or so desperately afraid that she was going to lose the happiness that she grasped.

"Nay! Come no nearer!" she implored him. And backing away, circling, she let the words spill from her. "I knew from the moment I came back that I was being watched.

Someone was in my room with me. Someone came at night.''

"Dreams," he said, meeting her eyes.

"You're lying!"

He threw up his arms. "Marina, let it be—"

"I can't! There was more. The paintings in the gallery. They are part of this, too. First the Viking was so real. Just as the portrayal of Eric at battle. And now you can scarce see the color of the eyes in the pictures.''

"Marina—"

"Then there was the old woman."

"The old woman?" His voice hardened, his eyes sharpened narrowly on her.

"I met her here. I came to Illora's tomb, to read it. You were supposedly in the midst of battle. But I felt, I felt as if you were behind me—'' She broke off, closing her eyes, now so very, very chilled. "Are you real?"

She opened her eyes. He was still standing there. And standing there so silently.

Cry out! she wanted to command him. Tell me that I am mad, that of course you are real!

"I ask you again, Marina, does it matter? Not because of the past, but because of the present. If you love me, truly love me, what difference does it make?''

She did love him. She loved him with all her heart.

Not because of any legend.

She loved him because he had swept her off her feet. Because he had stormed across the sand on a giant black war-horse and saved her kinfolk and her world. Because he had kissed her and stolen her soul. She loved him because he could make her laugh, and she loved him because she never felt as wonderful as she felt in his arms.

"I am not Illora!" she whispered fiercely. "So you tell me, my laird. Do you love me?"

He moved at last, striding for her. And though a protest formed on her lips, he would not allow her to speak it. He caught her arms, drawing her close against him. "I love you. I love you, Marina. Before God, I love you. For now, for this life, for always.''

She started trembling, and could feel the chattering of her teeth. "She said that I must take the blow."

"What are you talking about?" he demanded harshly.

Marina shook her head. Now she was losing her mind in truth! She couldn't tell him the words of a madwoman. He would think someone in her household meant to betray her. He was just, but he could also be merciless, she was certain.

"Marina! What—"

"Nay! Let go of me! Perhaps you are laird of this fortress, of this isle now, but I am lady here still!"

"You're my wife," he declared, his jaw locking. "Tell me what is troubling you now."

"I'm afraid."

"Nay, nay, don't be afraid, my love," he told her softly. "Marina, think on it. If I were this ghost you claim me, then perhaps the promise is that of happiness. Twice he has come, twice he has awaited his love. Now, this time, perhaps he is to be given life."

"You said—"

"Marina! I'm trying to make you happy, nothing more. Give us a chance."

Give us a chance . . .

Nay, she could not think of it so simply. The old woman had warned her. She must take the blow.

But that, too, would separate them. She would be the one to die this time.

Dear Lord! She was losing her mind.

"Marina, my love." He tried to pull her close, tried to set his arms around her. But she was so torn now that she could not bear it, and wrenched away from him hard. Startled by her force, he let her go. Barefoot, she raced across the sand for her horse and leaped on it.

"I am going to have her disinterred!" she called to him.

"What!" Hands on his hips, he stood watching her in amazement.

"Illora. I am going to have the rock moved away, I am going to have her dug up. I will know whether she truly rests in her tomb or not."

"You'll not do such a thing," he protested, eyes flashing.

"Illora's story is legend here, and I'll not have it."

"I am the MacCannan!"

His eyes narrowed. "You were the MacCannan."

"Oh!" she exclaimed in fury. He was coming quickly toward her, ready to stop her, she knew. She waited until he was nearly before her, then shoved her heels against her mare's flanks. Sand spewed behind her as her horse gave flight.

Men! she decided.

Yet he could catch her. Catch her so easily, if he desired . . .

But when she reached the cliffs and looked back, he was still standing on the sand. His hands remained on his hips. His chin was high; his golden hair shimmered beneath the sun like a banner.

If he had wanted to, he could have caught her. He had chosen to let her go.

She returned to the fortress, her heart in a whirl. In the great hall, she peeled off her gloves and stood before the fire.

Peg hurried in. "Lady Marina! Why, I thought that ye and yer laird were out fer the day. What can I bring ye, lass?"

Marina spun around. "Nothing, Peg. Wait, no. I'll take tea upstairs. In my room. And a steamy hot bath, please. Set the lads to it, if you will."

Peg nodded, as if she had decided herself that the best thing for her mistress's tempestuous condition might be a soothing cup of tea and the even more soothing feel of a long hot bath.

Within minutes it was done, and Marina was upstairs, her body warmed by the water, her eyes closed, her head resting on the rim.

Once, she had heard whispers when she rested so.

Whispers. As if he called her name . . .

She heard no more whispers. Because he was a ghost no longer? Because she now held him in the flesh?

But he had called her Illora.

I am not Illora! she persisted to herself. I cannot be Illora.

Because the old woman said that I must take the blow.

The battles are over. We are at peace with the British. Things have gone as things should have gone. Who would seek to harm me?

No one. No one at all.

And so she was dreaming, after all.

"Marina!"

Again she heard a whisper. Soft. Sensual. She turned. And she smiled slowly. He was with her again.

He walked across the room to her. He knelt by the tub. He kissed her elbow, licking away a drop of water. He kissed her throat. He took her into his arms.

"I love you," he said.

"I love you, too, and it is all that matters," she said.

And for a spell, she might have dreamed again. As darkness came, they dallied as lovers, nothing more and nothing less. A flesh and blood woman, a flesh and blood man, with no darkness near to haunt them. Again and again he made love to her. Again and again she returned his kiss, and made love to him in kind.

Night fell. Peg tapped on the door to see if they needed anything.

Nothing, Marina told her.

Nothing, for they had all they needed in each other, Eric added.

Peg's footsteps discreetly faded away.

In time, Marina fell asleep. She was deliciously tired, and there was no way better, or sweeter, to sleep than on his chest, her fingers curled into the crisp red-gold hairs on his chest.

But even as she slept, certain that any dreams that could plague her must certainly be good, she felt as if the darkness of a raven's wing was moving over her.

She felt as if she were on the beach again, walking along the sand.

And the raven came toward her. It made its unearthly cawing sound, sweeping down from above.

Then, suddenly, it landed. The wings adjusted, the head

rose. It was a bird no longer. It was the old woman she had met on the beach.

"Now, Illora, now!"

"I am not Illora!"

"He will die!" the old crone warned, her arm snaking out to point toward the heavens, the black draping all around it. "With the morning's light, he will die!"

"Nay, he will not die. I will not let him die. I read the tombstone. I do love him. I love him with all my heart."

"Then hurry. Challenge him no more. Stop the blade that would pierce his heart. He has so little time . . . Look! Look at your hands! Already the blood flows."

She stared down at her hands. The old woman was right. Blood was beginning to stain her palms.

"Nay!" She shrieked the word, then screamed it out again and again, bolting up.

She no longer slept. The dream was done.

She was awake, and in her own room. Dreams were gone—

But shadows were not.

There in the darkness before her, she saw the shadow of a man. A man with his hand raised. Across the room, she could see his silhouette on the wall.

And she could see the dagger raised above her.

"Nay!" she shrieked again. And then she knew that Eric was up beside her, and that he was trying to cast himself over her, before the blade could fall against her flesh.

"Nay, not again, not again!" she cried. And she did not care if she died; oh, so much better that she should perish than him! In those awful seconds she heard him cry her name.

And she knew that it was her name.

Illora . . .

And twice she had lost him. Twice she had lived without him.

She could not do so again.

"Nay!"

With all the force in her, she thrust him aside and leaped

to her feet. The blade, already begun its motion, continued to fall.

There was an awful tearing sound in the darkness. She screamed.

"Marina, my love!" Then he was up, leaping to his feet, seeking out their assailant. "Bastard, henchman! Coward in the darkness!"

Eric! Eric was crying out the words. He was all right.

And she was all right . . .

The door was pounded on and thrust open. Light flooded the room as Angus was followed in by Peg and a number of the chieftains, wearing their nightdresses but armed for battle with dirks and guns and swords and daggers.

And in the sudden flood of light, Marina saw where the blade had fallen.

And she knew what had ripped.

Not flesh this time. She looked at her hands. There was no blood on them.

She looked across the room to where Eric now had dragged their assailant to his feet, his arms wrenched behind him.

"Kevin!" She gasped, astounded. And she stared at the cousin she had loved all her life.

Eric thrust Kevin toward Angus. He was one of their own. Angus and the chieftains would be left to deal with him. Marina ran to Eric, quickly finding shelter in his arms. She stared at Kevin again.

"Why?" she asked in amazement.

"Ah, Marina, why?" he replied bitterly. "I fought for the fortress, I bear the family name! I am a man, and I deserved to be laird of this isle. I did not seek to see ye suffer, lass. 'Twas not personal, fer I have cared fer ye, and deep. But I would be laird, ye see. And he"—he inclined his head toward Eric—"well, he is laird by virture that he is yer husband. If ye were dead with no issue, then the isle would fall to me."

"Get him out of here!" Angus cried with fury. "We dinna turn on our own! Betray our name!" he said with disgust. "Bah, blood of my blood!" he thundered. "My laird,'' he said to Eric, ''what will ye have with him?''

Eric was watching Marina, staring down into her eyes. ''We will have it as my lady wishes,'' he said.

''Banishment!'' Marina cried. ''I will have him banished. We'll not have the blood of a kinsman on our hands.''

''He meant to murder you,'' Eric reminded her.

''Banishment, please!'' she implored.

Angus nodded to Eric. Kevin, his head lowered, was taken from the room.

And then, suddenly, there was silence.

''You shiver. You are cold,'' Eric said to her.

Aye, she was shivering. She was shaking. She wanted to tell him about the dream.

''I saw the danger coming, Eric,'' she said swiftly. ''I was dreaming. The old woman was in the dream.''

''Was she now, lass?'' he said softly. Blue eyes caressed her with the greatest tenderness. He picked her up gently into his arms and brought her before the fire.

''Eric—''

''Hush now, the danger is over.''

''But, Eric—''

''Hush, love. I am with you.''

She wanted to talk; she needed to talk. But the words wouldn't come. And in his arms, she felt the greatest peace, and the greatest exhaustion.

She should have been wide awake. She shouldn't have been able to sleep for all of the night.

But she did sleep. She closed her eyes, and she slept. Deeply.

With no dreams to plague her.

When she awoke in the morning, Eric was gone. She leaped up, feeling faint twinges of fear. She wasn't sure why she was so afraid—she remembered the night, but she knew that Kevin had been stopped. She still felt ill—she had loved Kevin, loved him deeply, and his betrayal was painful. It was incredible to think that he could have found the coldness in his own heart to murder her.

But though she had loved Kevin, she did not love him

as she loved her new husband. With the morning, she remembered that she had been dreaming of some danger when he had come, and that the dream had made her awaken, the dream had warned her of the danger. But try as she might, she could not remember the dream. It had something to do with a raven, and something to do with the warning, and something to do with the words, the legend, on Illora's tomb. But now it all escaped her.

She was desperate only to assure herself that Eric was all right, and that he was near.

She dressed quickly and started to run from the room, so very anxious to find him. She raced down the stairs, but he wasn't in the great hall, and Peg hadn't seen him. She ran back upstairs and searched the gallery, but he wasn't there, either.

At last she hurried to the stables, and found out from the groom that he had taken his great black war-horse and ridden out early that morning, and the groom had not seen him since.

Growing more desperate by the moment, she asked for her bay to be brought out. She didn't even wait for the mare to be saddled but leaped on her, urging her into a canter the moment she was mounted.

She knew where she was going. To the cliffs before the Irish Sea, and to the beach there. She closed her eyes, terrified that she would come to the beach . . .

. . . And would see him leaving. A Viking warrior again, laid out on a bier, riding the waves into eternity.

It could not be . . .

He was flesh and blood. She had touched him, loved him, lain with him. She had been tortured by dreams, nothing more. Even last night, the dreams had tormented her. Somehow saved her, but tormented her, too. And now the dreams were lost, and she could not remember them, but no matter how foolish she told herself she was being, she was afraid still.

She came to the cliffs at last. She gave the bay free rein, and rode haphazardly over the steep and treacherous footing.

But then she came to the other side. And a burst of gladness seemed to fill her heart like the startling gold of the rise of the sun.

She blinked against the fierce light. Aye, he was there, a man. For the briefest moment, she was certain that he stood tall in leather leggings and the short tunic of an ancient Viking warrior.

He stood tall, a ghostly figure of mist and legend.

A Viking, looking to the sea . . .

Nay!

It was a trick of the sunlight, nothing more. A trick within her own mind.

He was there.

Not a ghost disappearing on an ancient Viking ship, veiled in the mist of the isles. He was there, in the flesh. By agreement with the English, he had forsworn his colors, and so he stood in hose and breeches and shirt and frock coat, his tam cockaded but unadorned. His hands clasped behind his back, he looked out to the sea.

Aye, he was there.

Returned to her from the mists of legend? Or a man, nothing more, nothing less, come upon the isle just at the time of her distress.

Could she be a princess, risen for a chance once again to taste the sweetness of life, and of love?

Nay . . .

She did not know.

And it did not matter.

All that mattered was that they did have each other, and that they did have love, and now, life. Sweet, sweet life. Together.

"Eric!"

She shouted his name, leading the bay over the last of the rocks. He turned to her and smiled slowly.

In seconds she had the bay racing across the sands. The mare pounded the surf until she arrived before him. There, she leaped down and into his arms.

Strong and sure, they folded around her.

"I was afraid! So afraid!" she whispered.

"Why, love?" he asked, holding her from him. "The danger was gone with the night."

His eyes searched hers, puzzled, so very blue.

"I—I don't know," she whispered. "You weren't there. I was afraid."

"I'll never leave you now, you know. Never," he told her.

She smiled slowly. "You were willing to die for me," she said.

"And you were willing to die for me." He stretched out a hand, staring at it against the golden sunlight. "Flesh and blood," he murmured softly. He gazed down at her. "Are you going to ask me again where I came from, Marina?"

She smiled and shook her head slowly. "I don't care where you came from. Only that you are here to stay."

He wrapped her in his arms once again, and then they started down the beach together, arm in arm. His great black war-horse and her bay followed slowly behind.

Soon they neared the cliffs. Eric turned and lifted Marina, setting her back atop the bay. He leaped up easily on the black, then paused, frowning, as he watched her stare at the caves within the cliff.

Toward Illora's gravesite.

She smiled slowly and looked at her husband. "I think that I shall let her rest in peace, my laird. What do you think?"

He smiled in turn. "Aye, lady, I think that that would be best. Let them both rest in peace. Let the Viking Ulhric and his Illora go down in legend." He brought his mount closer to hers. "And as for us, my lady, I say, let us live this life, and savor each moment, for life is precious, and love even more so."

She cast back her head, feeling the sun on her face. "Indeed, my laird, aye!" She nudged her horse's flanks, and the mare pranced gracefully forward, ready to climb the cliffs again. Marina turned back, a light, a fire of mischief in her eyes. "Come then, Laird Eric, ride with me, live with me, savor the sunlight with me. For I—"

"I will love you forever!" he interrupted with a gallant cry.

And she laughed, and his laughter mingled with hers, and echoed throughout the cliffs, even as they rode off hard together.

Lovers, in love, forever.

The mist rolled out to sea, and the sun rose high above the Isle of the Angels.

Shannon Drake

Spooky things and things that go bump in the night!

"I love the entire concept of a lover who's just a little bit different. Truly from the moment I first laid eyes on Patrick Swayze's "Ghost," I knew there could be love after death. But I'm a believer in happy endings and so in my story I leave the question open—When emotions are involved and they are strong enough, can there be a second chance at love and life?"

SHANNON DRAKE is the author of eight historical romances, including *Damsel in Distress*, which Avon Books will publish in early 1992. She has received numerous awards from Waldenbooks, *Romantic Times*, and *Affaire de Coeur*. She also writes under the names "Heather Graham" and "Heather Graham Pozzessere." The mother of five children, she lives in Coral Gables, Florida.

A Certain Magic

Betina Krahn

1

Devonshire, England
October 1887

DARKNESS crept into the room at the top of the ancient stone tower, dragging with it the chill of night. In the deepening gloom, three old women sat huddled before a red-glowing hearth. Their aged countenances did not catch the firelight; it fled past their circle to dance around the shadows they cast on the cluttered walls, shelves, and workbenches behind them.

"For seven years she has been ours," one said in a voice like leather brushing leather.

"Bright as sunshine, fresh as dew," came a second voice.

"Sweet as buttercups, fragrant as rue," supplied the third.

An age-thinned hand reached for the fire iron and prodded the log. The fire flared golden and wheezed in the lengthening silence.

"Season upon season, she unfolded before us," murmured the first.

"Warm as a meadow, soft as a sigh," said the second.

"True as an arrow, earnest as a cry," added the third.

The log popped loudly and spit a shower of red-gold sparks out onto the worn stone of the hearth. One after another, three long sighs issued forth.

"The promised tomorrows have all been spent," the first declared.

"Nineteen now and a woman full grown."

"Time to find her a life of her own."

A life of her own. The three old women glanced dolefully at one another and shifted in their heavy, claw-footed chairs. A pall of silence settled over them as each sank into her private store of memories.

Moments later, there was a scraping noise from the shadowy region near the door. The spell of the moment was broken as a tall, dark-skinned manservant clad in bloused silk breeches, an English tailcoat, and a turban emerged from the darkness carrying a tea tray.

"Here, Shaddar," ordered tall, rail-thin Miss Caroline Asher in her wizened voice, waving him into their circle before the hearth. "Place it here, so that we don't have to move away from the fire."

The manservant shifted a small table into their midst and deposited the tray before them. As he bowed and withdrew, short, rotund Miss Phoebe Asher took immediate charge of the pouring and of their council.

"We shall have to find her a husband, of course."

"A husband?" Caroline looked down her hooked nose.

"Well, I believe you have to have one if you're to be married," Phoebe asserted, looking to the third member of the trio for verification. Miss Flora Asher nodded solemnly.

"Well, who says she has to be married?" Caroline demanded. "We've never married, and we've gotten on quite well."

"*We* are a different story," Phoebe insisted, "and you very well know it. Miranda is a lovely young woman . . . with hopes and dreams of her own. And needs."

"Needs?" Caroline's wiry eyebrows shot up.

"Tell her, Flora," Phoebe insisted.

Flora nodded rueful agreement as she stirred her tea. "Phoebe is right, Caroline," she said in a thin, reedy voice. "Of late I've seen Miranda walking the old tower ramparts in the evening, staring off into the distance . . . with such a look of longing. And more than once, as I've worked late in my laboratory, she has risen from her bed, unable to sleep, and come to sit with me while I work.''

"See there," Phoebe crowed, plunking the teapot down on the tray with a flourish. "Longing looks . . . sleepless nights." She leaned forward with a determined squint. "*Needs*, Caroline."

"I think it would be lovely for Miranda to have a daughter of her own someday," Flora mused wistfully. "Remember how we always wanted one? And I understand marriage is absolutely essential for having children, in society."

"Besides," Phoebe added in somber tones, "we won't be around forever. She'll need someone else."

The force of Phoebe's and Flora's doleful looks and the weight of their arguments overwhelmed Caroline's resistance. At length, she sighed and nodded.

"We're agreed, then," Phoebe declared in a satisfied tone. "Miranda is to have a husband."

As they sipped their tea, Caroline brightened and announced firmly, "Well, if she must have a man, I know exactly the one she should have."

"You do?" Phoebe paused, mid-sip. "Who?"

"That Mister Bruno, in the village. He's industrious, well-fixed financially, and"—she fairly glowed as she announced his most important qualification—"he has the most astonishing way with metals."

"Metals?" Phoebe harrumphed. "He ought to, he's a blacksmith."

Flora shuddered. "Imagine our little Miranda with that great, grimy-fingered brute . . ."

"He's not a brute. I've spoken with him . . . he's perfectly capable of speech," Caroline declared, pushing to the edge of her chair, her mouth a thin line of resolve. "And he has a positively splendid animal magnetism about him . . . the strongest I've ever witnessed."

"You and your animal magnetism." Phoebe's nose curled with distaste. "I knew it was a mistake, letting you run off with those Mesmer fanatics back in the teens. Them with their coils and electrical thingumabobs and trances—

you've had a few tiles loose on the roof ever since, Caroline!''

''Mesmerism and the enhancement of the body's natural animal magnetism are the answer to all mankind's difficulties.'' Caroline lifted a gnarled finger into the air as her voice rose stridently. ''Constitutional weaknesses, mental deficiencies, and the moral ills of humankind could be utterly eradicated by the proper magnetic and electrical applications—''

''Not again.'' Phoebe rolled her eyes, and Caroline twitched as if spurred.

''Well, there's a word or two to be said about your humiliating little stint with that Franz Joseph Gall and his lunatic cohorts in Paris!'' Caroline retaliated furiously. ''Running higgledy-piggledy up and down the continent . . . feeling every old lump and bump on every available head—''

''Phrenology is a recognized science, Caroline Asher, and you know it!'' Phoebe rose to the challenge as she wriggled to the edge of her chair. ''The contours of a person's head tell the whole of his character . . . his capacity for 'construction,' his 'ideality' . . . 'ambition,' 'suavity,' 'amativeness,' 'benevolence'—''

''Pure bunkum!'' Caroline announced with a snort of derision.

''I'll have you know—''

''Sisters!'' Flora interrupted Phoebe's hot rebuttal, reeling forward and depositing her cup on the tray. ''This argument is decades old and not at all helpful in deciding what sort of husband to get for our little Mimi. I think we should consider what sort of man would complement her nature . . . what sort of man would make her happy.''

Both Caroline and Phoebe colored and huddled back in their chairs. Happy? What sort of man would make their beloved Miranda *happy*? They hadn't thought of that. They exchanged looks of consternation as Flora hurried on.

''Our Mimi is a gentle and refined young girl. She should have a gentleman of some sort.'' Her habitually dreamy look was replaced by a serious, contemplative frown. ''A

gentleman who could appreciate her sweet fragrance . . . the
natural purity of her virgin essence. Someone who knows
heliotrope from verbena . . . someone who appreciates the
perfect accord of the scents of sunflower, vanilla, and orange
blossom." She brightened and gestured with a lilting hand.
"A perfumer would be ideal . . . or a florist . . . or even a
chemist . . ."

Phoebe leveled a dubious look on her sister. "And where,
pray, do you propose we get this gentleman perfumer-florist-
chemist?"

Flora thought deeply about that for a moment. "Perhaps
an advertisement in the *Times*?"

Phoebe wrested about on her chair with a hiss of disgust.
"I very much doubt that an advertisement in the *Times* will
yield up a gentleman whose cranial capacity and protuberances of the head——"

"*Bumps*," Caroline corrected darkly.

"Yes, *bumps*, to the vulgar and uninitiated," Phoebe
declared, her plump cheeks flushing like fierce pomegran-
ates. "Someone whose cranial bumps will be compatible
with our Mimi's. Make no mistake about it . . . I shall give
no consent to any marriage unless I have personally felt the
fellow's head and determined his suitability."

A footfall across the door sill and a bloom of light against
the aged stone walls startled them, and they twisted about
in their chairs. Coming through the doorway, dispelling the
darkness with a double candlestand and her own sunny
presence, was their Miranda. Her cheeks were rosy from
her trip up the long flight of stairs to the tower room, and
her golden-hazel eyes fairly sparkled as she paused just
inside the door.

"I thought I'd find you here. Whatever are you doing,
sitting here in the dark?" she chided good-naturedly, turning
to search one of the cluttered workbenches behind her.

"You've said we should conserve candlewax," Caroline
answered for the threesome as they watched her locate a
candlestand among the old pipes, crocks, and contraptions
on the workbench, and light the stubby tapers.

She moved like flowing water, effortless, graceful, unstudied, their Miranda. Her hair was dark and lustrous, auburn kissed with a hint of gold and pulled up in a mass of unruly ringlets that cascaded from the crown of her head to past her shoulders. She was softly curved, marble-skinned, and delicately boned, but there was nothing fragile in her frame, her countenance, or her spirit. She set both candelabra on the mantel and turned to them. Wrapped head to toe in the rosy glow of hearth and taper, she was at that moment the very essence of warmth and life.

"Conserving candlewax does not mean sitting in the darkness." Miranda broke into a winsome smile. "Our household accounts will certainly stand for a few tapers here and there." She scrutinized the three old ladies and frowned at their pensive mood. After a light supper, they had retreated to the ancient tower room as they always did when they had weighty matters to discuss. "Ah, you've been in council. And what is it that furrows your brows and clouds your countenances so?"

Aunt Phoebe shifted a bit straighter in her chair, glancing at her sisters and smoothing her black bombazine over her rotund knees. "Mimi, dear," she said experimentally, as if testing an idea in her mind. "Suppose—now just suppose—that you were to marry. What sort of man would you wish to have for a husband?"

Aunt Flora and Aunt Caroline came bolt upright in their chairs, their attention riveted on the surprised heat flooding her face. "By all means," Aunt Caroline took it up. "Do you have any particular preferences?"

"Tall or short? Merchant . . . professional man . . . or gentleman?" Flora asked.

"Someone strongly magnetic, perhaps," Caroline proposed.

"Or with particular cranial protuberances," Phoebe suggested helpfully.

The notion astounded Mimi. Preferences for certain characteristics in a husband? That's what the old dears had been up here discussing in grave and heated council? A husband for her? She bit her bottom lip to squelch a laugh—and to contain her reaction to the unexpected twinge in her chest that followed it.

"I have known very few men besides my father. And I've formed no particular preferences . . ." She squared her lovely shoulders and donned a very authoritative expression. "But whether I have or have not is quite irrelevant, since I have no intention of marrying and leaving you."

"B-but, M-Mimi, dear—" Aunt Phoebe sputtered, casting a glance at the others. "It's time to think of your future."

Miranda gave them a blithely determined smile. "Whatever is there to think about? I'm reasonably certain I shall have some sort of future. And if I don't have a future, then thinking about it would be perfectly useless. Either way, the time and effort spent on such stuff is probably better used elsewhere." She finished with an irresistibly impish shrug, her own unique gesture of stubbornness. "Now, if you'll excuse me, I have some work to do on the accounts before I retire. Good night, Aunt Phoebe . . . Aunt Flora . . . Aunt Caroline." She kissed each of the old aunts' weathered cheeks, picked up her candlestand, and was halfway to the door before she felt the crinkle of vellum in the pocket of her apron.

"Oh, I nearly forgot. A messenger brought a letter for you late this afternoon." She hurried back and held out the envelope to them. "It's all the way from London," she offered brightly, hoping to generate a spark of interest in their downcast faces. When none of them showed the least bit of curiosity about it, she sighed quietly and placed it on the edge of the tea tray.

On the way out, she paused at the door and glanced back at them, finding them sagged in their chairs. She knew she had disappointed them just now, and the thought settled a hard lump in her stomach. She hated disappointing the old dears in anything. She turned reluctantly and started down the long, steep set of stone steps that were built into the walls of the ancient stone tower.

Her three great aunts, spinster sisters of her long-deceased grandmother, had taken her in when her father died several years ago. She had arrived at their rambling old mansion a somber and earnest child, her spirit weighted by the serious business of life and death. Aunt Caroline had read to her by the hour, Aunt Phoebe knitted her outrageous purple stockings, and Aunt Flora taught her to make daisy chains. Slowly, they peeled away the layers of hurt and the silent, respectable despair that imprisoned her girlish heart. And for that—for the way they released her from her sober, stifling shell—she would always be devoted to them.

But in the matter of her future, she knew she had to be firm with them. Imagine them trying to find her a husband . . . marry her off!

She slowed and paused before the great, iron-bound door at the bottom of the stairs. Her future. She had spent several sleepless nights of late, imagining that very thing—a future, a marriage—and had finally set such pointless thoughts aside. How could she even think of taking up a life outside the walls of Asher House when her old aunts needed her so?

She tugged hard on the heavy door and stepped through it into the upper hallway of the little-used west wing of the house. The sight of faded furnishings, laden with the dust of genteel neglect, was all she needed to bolster her determination. If she weren't diligent, the center hall and the east wing of the house would probably look the same as these forlorn chambers.

Her aunts were precious old dears, but their minds were rarely fixed on practical, or sometimes even *earthly*, considerations. Tall, imperial Aunt Caroline, a devotee of Anton Mesmer's theories of animal magnetism, was constantly in her workroom, tinkering with her magnets, electrical coils, and static generating devices. Plump, impulsive Aunt Phoebe was obsessed with creating the first instrument for objectively measuring the potential in a human head—her "cranial mapper." She spent her days rummaging about the house; cannibalizing old clocks, parlor stools, and piano strings for parts; and giving the occasional "phrenological reading" to moonstruck young girls from the nearby village. And sweet, soft-spoken Aunt Florabunda, whose sense of smell would put bloodhounds to shame, was usually closeted in her glass-domed conservatory or her "perfumery," where she pored over botanical journals for word of newly discovered "aromatics" and produced wonderfully exotic perfumes and pomanders.

None of them gave a serious bit of thought to the tasks of cleaning, laundering, cooking, dealing with tradesmen, or repairing leaks in the roof. Thus, in recent years, the role of ordering and maintaining the aging household had fallen more and more on Miranda and on their eminently capable manservant, Shaddar. And it never occurred to Miranda that it should be otherwise. The old aunts were her family; she owed them her very heart. And she was determined not to abandon them to their decaying house and eccentricities, even if it did cost her a "future."

"Oh!" A movement nearby startled her. Poised at the top of the center hall stairs, she looked up to find their bronzed Indian manservant looming before her.

"Shaddar. You gave me a start." She melted with relief and smiled into his dark features. "I think my aunts are finished with their tea. Once it's cleared, I think that will be all for the night."

The manservant bowed and moved off as silently as he had come. Miranda smiled, watching his rolling, effortless stride. Whatever would she do without Shaddar?

With an unsettled sigh, she gazed out over the dimly lit center hall, toward the drawing room and the cramped study which lay beyond. The ledgers and stacks of "payment due" notices that awaited her there suddenly seemed too much to face, just now. She tucked her arms around her waist and chewed the corner of her lip as she considered the alternatives. Perhaps a warm shawl and a brisk walk in Aunt Flora's garden instead, she decided. A bit of fresh air might help her sleep better tonight.

Far above, in the ancient tower room, the old ladies stirred in their chairs and stared balefully at one another.

"Who would have guessed she'd be so dead-set against having a man?" Phoebe said, bewildered. "I know it's been a while, but I don't recall men being *that* bad."

"They're not bad," Flora said emphatically. "In fact, they can be quite delightful. Unfortunately, our little Mimi doesn't know that."

"Well, what shall we do about it?" Caroline said in her no-nonsense tone. Then she straightened, her face alight with inspiration. "Suppose we invite that marvelously magnetic Mr. Bruno to come for dinner . . ."

"He smells like horse sweat, Caroline." Flora sniffed. "I'll not take dinner in the same room with a man who reeks of animal effluvia. I'd positively suffocate!"

"Here, here," Phoebe put in.

"Well, we could always ask him to bathe," Caroline insisted stubbornly.

"Caroline—" Flora's face filled with uncharacteristic choler.

"Sisters, please!" Phoebe insisted. "We're all at sixes and sevens here. Perhaps we'd better wait until we're better rested and clearer-headed."

As Caroline muttered mutinously and settled back in her chair, her gaze fell on the envelope Miranda had left for them. She snatched it up and squinted at it, trying to make out the engraved lettering of the return address.

"It's that snooty, interfering bunch of solicitors again . . . probably more nonsense about Mimi's inheritance," she announced, dropping the letter onto the tray as if it scorched her fingers.

Phoebe and Flora recoiled visibly, and all three heaved and swayed to their feet, avoiding all contact with the tray. None of them was of a mood to confront legal demands just now.

Shaddar suddenly appeared in their midst to clear away the tea. A rustling, scratching noise came from a darkened corner as he lifted the tray, and it tilted in his hands, setting the cups sliding and clattering. His countenance darkened as he stiffened and looked to see where the sounds were coming from. Phoebe caught his look of concern.

"Probably just mice," she observed, patting the manservant on the arm. "See to it, will you, Shaddar?"

His turbaned head bobbed gravely. As he turned to go,

the London letter dropped from the tray unnoticed, and with his first step, he knocked it into the edge of the coals in the hearth. One corner of the letter nudged the glowing heat, and soon the expensive rag stock paper burst into flames.

As the old ladies exited with the guttering candles and darkness descended on the venerable chamber, a small, rosy glow bloomed on the stone hearth . . . unnoticed and unheeded.

A fortnight later, a fierce late October gale ran aground on the south Devonshire coast. Torrents of wind-driven rain pelted the dark countryside with an elemental fury that bore down from seemingly every direction at once. In that dark, disorienting swirl of wind and water, a lone horse and rider struggled to make progress along the Old London Road.

"Come on, boy—don't quit on me now!" Graham Hamilton shouted above the storm's roar, grappling to stay aboard his frantic, lurching mount. "The cursed place can't be that much farther!" But even as he said it, a tendril of panic coiled through him. In the howling blackness, he might have already passed wretched Asher House . . . He could be lost . . . He could be riding straight off a bloody cliff for all he knew . . . He wrestled staunchly with his fears, and reason soon seized control again.

"Get hold of yourself, Hamilton," he commanded.

Suddenly a massive bolt of lightning streaked to ground close by, setting the hair prickling all over his body as it illuminated the entire landscape for one sizzling, breathless instant. Then he saw it. Half a mile ahead, the craggy old mansion sat huddled on a barren, storm-lashed hill, glowing an eerie silver against the unrelenting black of storm and night.

The deafening explosion of thunder which followed knocked him half out of the saddle, and the horse reacted with a spurt of fear-spawned might, pulling free of the mud and rearing. Hamilton flailed wildly, then pitched into the muck, landing hard on his shoulder.

By the time the rumble of pain in his head and shoulder subsided and he could draw breath again, he was alone on the road, with only the mocking sound of the rain splashing on the puddles around him. Struggling to his feet, he groaned and winced, testing his shoulder and reaching for his handkerchief to wipe the grime from his face. Afoot now, wet to the bone, befouled with mud, and humiliated to the core, he realized there was nothing for it but to walk the rest of the way.

With his boots weighted with mud, his damaged top hat sagging, his ears still ringing from the thunder, and his shoulder throbbing, he slogged his way along the road toward Asher House. Each step fired both his resentment and his determination against the cunning and contriving mistresses of Asher House. The larcenous old crows hadn't complied with his demands, or even deigned to answer his inquiries! Well, they had pushed his tolerance too far. He was going to have justice . . . or die trying!

2

ASHER House, as revealed by the stark flashes of lightning, was a large gray-stone manor built around the remnants of an ancient castle which had once guarded that forlorn, windswept bit of coastline. In the background, rising above the craggy and uneven roof, was a circular stone tower, complete with battlements and crenellations. As Hamilton drew closer, he saw that the shutters on the upper windows of the main house hung askew and that dead vines and overgrown shrubs clung to its aged walls. The wrought-iron gates by the road hung at a neglected angle. The place had a brooding, twice-faded glory about it that perfectly matched Hamilton's dismal expectations of its owners.

He trudged through the weedy, rain-scoured front court and assaulted the iron-bound doors with the side of his fist.

On the third volley of blows, just as his hand was beginning to throb, the massive doors swung open, and he literally blew through the opening in a gust of wind and rain.

"Damn well about time," he muttered irritably, lowering the shoulder cape of his greatcoat and shaking the water from his sleeves. He found himself in a faded and dimly lit center hall and wheeled to address whoever had admitted him. He stopped abruptly at the sight of a huge, swarthy manservant in a turban and tailcoat looming over him, scrutinizing him with sullen green-gold eyes. Ripping the remnants of his hat from his head, he squared his shoulders beneath his dripping garments.

"I've come all the way from London to see the Misses Asher and Miss Miranda Edgethorn." He summoned his frazzled air of authority and insisted, "And by heaven, I'll see them . . . now!"

"And who are you, sir, to be making such demands?" an age-brittled female voice came from behind him.

He whirled.

Lord, Hamilton thought, there they were: two of the old crows themselves. They were standing in a huge, arched doorway to the left of the entry hall. Gray-haired and black-clad, withered and wizened, they looked as tough as pine knots and as imperious as Caesar. And they had to be eighty if they were a day. He stalked forward, heedless of the trail of water and muddy footprints he left across the aged marble floor.

"I am Graham Hamilton of Farnsworth, Farrow, Hamilton, and Benchley, Solicitors, executors of the late Sir Peter Edgethorn's estate." He fished around in the breast pocket of his coat and produced a sodden, crumpled card.

The taller, thinner of the two old women blanched and stiffened as she accepted and examined it, then exchanged a look with the shorter, rounder one. "In that case . . . I am Miss Caroline Asher, and this is my sister, Miss Phoebe. I suppose you'd better come in. Shaddar, take Mister Hamilton's coat." She glanced disapprovingly at his ruined footgear. "And boots. Then ask Miss Flora and Miranda to join us in the drawing room."

Yielding up his water-logged coat and muddy boots to the huge manservant, Hamilton followed the two old ladies into a large, drafty chamber with a ceiling so high it was lost in shadows. Dark, massive antique furnishings, suits of armor, stuffed trophy animals, and old iron candlestands loomed around the ill-lit edges of the room. The walls were hung with faded tapestries, ancient-looking portraits of dour-faced forebears, and a number of battered shields emblazoned with what he presumed must be the Asher family crest.

His first impression was that he'd stepped into a museum of some sort, and his second was that the old crows hadn't used their ill-gotten gains to feather their nest. The latter was little comfort, however, when he realized that a vulnerable young girl had been sent to live in these faded, gloomy surroundings. Perhaps it would have been better if they *had* spent some of the money fixing up the place, making it a suitable home for the child. He planted himself before the roaring fire, legs spread and hands clasped behind his back, while the old ladies seated themselves in chairs before him.

"You know why I am here, of course," he declared testily.

"Of course," and "Indeed not," they said together, the tall one jerking a nod while the plump one shook her head vigorously. He expelled an impatient breath through his teeth as they exchanged looks of annoyance.

"I am here," he intoned in his best Etonian English, "because you have disdained all my efforts to communicate with you regarding your role as Miss Edgethorn's guardians. I have written to you decently, civilly, asking for assurances and accounting. And you refused to so much as acknowledge my letters."

"We have always dealt favorably with that amicable Mister Benchley," Miss Caroline Asher charged defensively.

"Mister Benchley is no longer amicable—he is deceased," Hamilton said, his eyes narrowing as he saw the old ladies' dismay. "I am now senior partner of the firm, having succeeded my uncle Throckmorton Hamilton in that capacity more than a year ago.'' He allowed a moment for that impressive accomplishment to register. It was rare indeed for a man of just thirty years to achieve such recognition in the legal world. ''It appears that old Benchley had been on the decline for some time—he'd let a number of matters slip. And while his files were being cleared out and reassigned to other partners, the shameful matter of Miss Edgethorn's trust was uncovered.''

''Sh-shameful?'' Miss Phoebe Asher paled.

''Disgraceful,'' he pronounced ominously, leaning toward them. ''Perhaps even *criminal*. It appears that you have made a number of large and frequent withdrawals from Miss Edgethorn's trust—so large and so frequent that the principle has been dangerously eroded.'' Anger seeped into his voice, and his hands curled into fists behind his back.

''What on earth could be so—'' An aged woman clad in dark violet bustled into the drawing room and stopped short at the sight of him. ''Oh.'' Her gaze flew to the others, and she slowly made her way toward them.

''Florabunda, this is Mister Hamilton . . . the solicitor . . . from London,'' Caroline said, her voice laden with undercurrents of meaning as she rose from her chair.

''He's here about Mimi's inheritance,'' Phoebe added with a dark look, shoving to her feet.

''Thousands of pounds are missing from the trust accounts,'' Hamilton announced, annoyed by the covert glances among them. ''It was nothing short of plundering . . . unconscionable pilferage. And I intend to hold you responsible for it. If necessary, I shall not hesitate to make use of the civil and *criminal* proceedings of the courts—''

''Pilferage? Courts?'' came a feminine voice from the doorway. He flicked an irritable glance in that direction . . . then looked a second time and froze. In the opening stood a stunning young woman with dark, burnished hair, fair skin, and a rather extravagant set of feminine curves, which were cloaked in a simple, unbustled dress of gold wool challis trimmed with touches of velvet. As she came forward, Hamilton's gaze fixed first on her large, thickly lashed eyes, which were astonishingly close to the color of her dress, then on her prominent cheekbones, straight nose, and finally her lush, cupid's bow mouth. He realized she had spoken and scrambled to recall what she had said while he had been staring at her.

"What has been pilfered? And what could my aunts possibly have to do with a theft of any sort?" She stopped nearby, frowning expectantly at the old ladies.

"This is Mister Graham Hamilton, Miranda dear. He's from the firm of solicitors which administers your father's estate . . . come all the way from London," Phoebe informed her. "He seems to think we've been *imprudent* in drawing from your inheritance."

Hamilton felt himself swaying and braced his long legs a bit further apart. *Miranda?* He blinked to clear his vision. This was Miranda Edgethorn? The same Miranda who had written the girlish notes he discovered in sentimental old Benchley's files? He had known the undated notes were old, but, even allowing for a few years, they'd somehow formed a picture in his mind of a fledgling young girl, not of a gorgeous young woman in the full bloom of—he caught a fleeting scent of something flowery and tantalizing, and sucked a long, intense breath, trying to recapture it—in the full bloom of lush, delectable womanhood.

". . . dare to suggest that my aunts have pilfered my inheritance?" he heard when he managed to focus again on the words those rosy lips were forming. He reddened all the way to his ears at being caught speechless and staring, and—Lord!—*sniffing*. He pulled his chin back and glowered his fiercest.

"Miss Edgethorn, the trust your father created for your security has been drastically reduced over the past several years. And your aunts have stubbornly refused to give an accounting of the thousands upon thousands of pounds—"

"My aunts—stealing from me? Such an accusation would be ludicrous, sir, if it weren't so perfectly vile!" Miranda advanced angrily on him, determined to defend the dotty old dears with everything in her.

Color bloomed in her face as she suddenly found herself so close to him that she could feel the heat radiating from his body. Too close, she realized too late. She braced, wishing she could back up a few steps as he filled her vision and overwhelmed the rest of her senses. He was tall, nearly as tall as Shaddar, and dressed in a wet, rumpled charcoal-gray suit, which at the moment exuded a distinctive blend of male-seeming smells: wet wool, mud, sandalwood, and a hint of pipe smoke. His starched collar had long-since dissolved into a limp rag, and his royal-blue silk tie was shriveled and lying askew. He was shoeless, mud-spattered, and had a huge streak of dried mud across his right cheek-bone.

Her attention fastened stubbornly on the dark hair that framed his strong, angular face and the lock which drooped willfully over his forehead, then slid to those light gray eyes which were topped by dark, feathery brows and rimmed by indecently long lashes. When he spoke, at such close range, his voice penetrated her skin and rumbled along her nerves like echoes of distant thunder, setting her quivering and tingling in all sorts of odd and interesting places.

"Whatever money my aunts may have claimed, Mister Hamilton, was certainly their due," she protested through a constricted throat. What was happening to her? "And it is absolutely none of your concern."

"It is intensely my concern, Miss Edgethorn, when a member of my firm permits the wanton thievery of an estate entrusted to us to provide for the security of a defenseless child," he said, edging closer, looming over her.

"Thievery?" Miranda raised her chin in defiance of his forbidding male glare and found herself face to face and nearly nose to nose with him. Then her eyes fastened on his lips, little more than an inch away, and her knees weakened strangely. "The boldest and blackest of lies, sir," she said hoarsely. "How dare you stand in my aunts' house and slander their good and honorable names?"

The eruption of her anger gave her an excuse to jerk back one, then two, reason-restoring steps. She flung a trembling finger toward the door. "Please be so good as to remove yourself from this house immediately!"

Her order lay burning on the air, while she and her old

aunts held their breaths. He seemed to grow before their very eyes as his broad shoulders squared and his face took on the semblance of granite. He took one step, then another . . . but neither in the direction of the door. Instead, he closed the distance between himself and Miranda, and now stood shockingly toe to toe and button to button with her.

The silence sizzled and crackled around them as his flint-gray eyes struck sparks against the burnished gold of hers.

He was so heated, so male, so foreign to anything she'd ever experienced . . .

She was so warm, so womanly, so utterly unexpected . . .

"I would remind you, Miss Edgethorn, that I am here on your behalf," he said with a noticeable thickness to his voice. His hands clenched and unclenched at his sides.

"Then"—she swallowed hard—"on my behalf, remove yourself back to London." The surge of anger in his arrogantly carved features was somehow satisfying. And disturbing. His head lowered half an inch toward hers before it snapped up with a jerk, and he stumbled back a step.

"I've spent the last three days and nights, Miss Edgethorn, hazarding life and limb to reach this godforsaken place. I've been squashed witless by fat matrons in rail cars, bounced mercilessly on top of a crowded mail coach, and robbed of three nights' sleep by portly merchants who snore like ailing rhinoceroses. I've been caught in a fiend of a storm, drenched to the bone, thrown from a horse, and damn near struck by lightning. I've lost a horse, a raft of crucial legal documents, and half my blessed hearing!"

His eyes narrowed, and his voice dropped to a harried rasp. "I am not leaving this house until I discover what happened to every last penny of those purloined funds." With that, he strode straight to the hearth and slammed his long frame into the closest chair, looking for all the world as if he were burrowing in for the winter.

Mimi sputtered and gasped, turning to her old aunts, who stood watching the unthinkable encounter with shock-widened eyes and drooping jaws. A half-stifled noise of outrage issued from deep in her throat, and she whirled toward the door. "I'll call Shaddar to remove—"

"No!" Aunt Caroline jolted forward to catch her arm and hold her back. "I mean . . . we certainly cannot send Mister Hamilton packing before we've had a chance to clear our good names. And we could never send him off in such a hideous storm. Why, Mimi, dear, we don't even put the cat out on a night like this."

"Caroline?" Phoebe started to protest but was quickly overridden.

"I fear we're partly to blame for the unfortunate misunderstandings that brought Mister Hamilton all this way." Caroline turned an intense, speaking look on Phoebe and Flora.

"Oh . . . oh! Ohhh, absolutely!" Flora took it up with sudden enthusiasm. "The very least we can do is provide a bit of hospitality while we redeem ourselves in his legal opinion. Why, he must be exhausted," she said with a look of concern. "And those wet clothes—he could be taking a dread chill even as we speak."

"B-but—" Mimi sputtered.

"Then it's all settled," Caroline announced, looking quite pleased as she went for the bell pull to summon Shaddar. "You shall be our guest, Mister Hamilton. And we shall open both our coffers and our estate books to you, first thing in the morning."

Aunt Flora seized his sleeve and gave a ladylike tug that succeeded in peeling him from the chair. "We'll have Shaddar bring you a good hot bath and a tasty bit of supper . . . and a good strong toddy."

"This makes no sense at all, Aunt Flora . . . Caroline . . . Phoebe," Miranda protested, appalled by their gracious attitude toward a man whose expressed intent was to prove them a trio of unprincipled thieves. Didn't the bighearted old dears realize they were clasping an adder to their breasts?

"But it makes perfect sense, my dear," Caroline intoned loftily. "How else will Mister Hamilton learn the truth about us, except by staying with us and coming to know us?" Her smile was so well-intentioned and guileless that Mimi ground her teeth in frustration.

"This is most . . . accommodating . . . of you." Hamilton scowled.

"Make no mistake, sir." Caroline drew herself up regally, reading his suspicion and responding with disarming candor. "Our purpose is to change your mind about us. When you come to know us better, you'll see that our Mimi's welfare is always uppermost in our hearts and minds."

He shifted back on one long, sinewy leg, scrutinizing the three old women. They were up to something. He could just feel it.

Caroline nodded, dismissing him as if she were the veriest of doyens. "The room at the end of the hall, Mimi, dear."

Miranda stiffened her spine, lifted her skirts, and sailed from the chamber, leaving Hamilton to stride after her in his stocking feet. She stomped up the center hall steps, and when she reached the first landing, well out of her old aunts' hearing, she turned on the solicitor with her chest heaving and her eyes flashing angrily.

"My aunts are lovable, distractible old ladies, whose hearts are often bigger than their heads, sir. And I give you fair warning: if you do anything—*anything*—to hurt them, I'll . . . I'll . . ."

"If they've done nothing wrong, then they've nothing to fear from me, Miss Edgethorn," he said crossly, struggling to keep his gaze from fastening on her lips in the inviting darkness of the stairs. For some reason he felt he had to add: "I'm no beast."

By the time he trailed the very grown-up Miss Edgethorn down the hallway to the guest room, he was thinking that he was no gentleman, either. He watched her light the tapers on the table in the center of the large, paneled chamber, then check the freshness of the linen of the large tester bed— all while keeping a wary, accusing eye on him. And why shouldn't she resent and mistrust him, he groaned silently; he was behaving like a surly, rampaging Hun! Not at all like his eminently reasonable and logical self. What in heaven's name was the matter with him?

He felt all out of kilter somehow, out of control. Whatever

had possessed him to leave his orderly office with its dutiful clerks and obedient clients, its neat stacks of clipped papers and tidy sheaves of documents, all with their binding ribbons tied just so? That was where he belonged, in that comprehensible world of law and precedent, making sense of other people's muddles and bringing order to the chaos that afflicted his clients' affairs. That was his role, his calling in life; he was an ordained *order bringer*. Always had been . . . always would be.

He sank down on the side of the bed, scowling into the faded carpeting, scarcely aware of the huge manservant's arrival with steaming buckets of water and tinder to lay a fire. His thoughts went back to that day when his clerk brought him old Benchley's files on the Edgethorn estate and to the frustration that had gripped him as he plowed through the mess. He had come across one of little Miranda's notes to old Benchley . . . a child's hand, a child's earnest assurances that she was studying her geography and progressing at her watercolors, which the old fellow had apparently sent her.

Then he had found the note in which she wrote of some newborn kittens that inhabited a box by the kitchen hearth and included, somewhat apologetically, a small poem that she had written about them. He read that little verse with stinging eyes and an unexplainably tight throat, and flew into a veritable fury at the thought of the child's mismanaged inheritance and diminished prospects for a future.

When his two strongly worded letters to her old guardians went unanswered, he had thundered out from London, determined to rescue little Miranda from their calculating clutches. Only she wasn't "little Miranda," and she didn't seem to want rescuing of any sort. And he was sitting on a bed in the old ladies' gloomy old house, feeling as if he'd been tilting at windmills and his armor was showing signs of rust.

Rousing from thought, he took a fortifying breath and forcefully dismissed Miss Edgethorn's prickly and ungrateful attitude. She was regrettably loyal to her wily old aunts and obviously didn't understand the full implications of her reduced circumstances. Well, he had come to help her, and he was going to do so, he vowed hotly, whether she wanted his help or not!

Out in the hallway, Miranda stood staring at the paneled door to their little-used guest room. She couldn't recall having yelled at anyone like that in her life. But honestly— if there was anyone on earth who deserved to be yelled at, it was that insulting . . . arrogant . . . interfering . . . *lawyer!* Imagine, accusing her old aunts of something as low and unscrupulous as overspending—stealing—her inheritance. Why, the old dears scarcely even knew what currency was in circulation! *She* was the one who paid their accounts and kept the ledgers and—

Her eyes widened. That meant *she* would have to be the one to explain where their funds had gone. The prospect sent a heated shiver through her, and she backed another giant step from the guest room door. She thought of that huge, intimidating frame, those penetrating gray eyes, and that voice like rumbling thunder, and imagined confronting that intense and overwhelmingly masculine presence at close range. Her knees began to feel weak again, and her cheeks began to heat.

A moment later, she blushed at the shockingly personal tone of her dread. Whatever was the matter with her? She should be concentrating on finding a way to convince him that her aunts were good-hearted, if somewhat impractical, old ladies—and that if something had happened to her inheritance, it was no fault of theirs. Her mind flew down the stairs to the small study where the ledgers and records were kept, and she frowned, thinking of all the sorting and organizing she'd put off doing in the last few weeks. She had a good bit of work to do tonight, before facing his arrogant suspicions across the books tomorrow morning.

Downstairs, in the drawing room, Caroline and Flora had broken into cackles of glee and now whirled around and around in a tottering dance of unrestrained joy.

"Did you see them?" Caroline's face glowed with excitement as she stumbled to a breathless halt. "Couldn't you just feel that electricity?" She shuddered with pure ecstasy. "Magnificent. The most astonishing example of interactive magnetism I've ever witnessed!"

"Magnetism?" Flora wheezed, clutching her chest and scowling. "He caught her scent—that's what happened. He positively breathed her in—I saw him! What olfactory acuity he must have," she marveled, spiraling off into private realms of awe, "to be able to detect and savor her delicate virgin essence so . . ."

Phoebe pulled in her double chins and stared at the pair of them in horror. "Minerva's knickers—you've both gone mad as hatters."

"Not a bit of it." Caroline straightened with a canny glint in her ageless eyes. "We've just found our little Mimi a husband!"

"A husband?" Phoebe's face puckered, and she folded her arms over her ample chest. She sputtered, glowered, and fidgeted first one way, then the other. Faced with their united opinion, she began to reconsider, then to relent. "Well, he did seem to be rather well developed in the region of 'perceptives,' " she admitted, fingering her own eyebrow as she recalled the shape of his. "And his faculty of 'comparison' was clearly superior . . ." Her voice faded as she ran her fingers up the middle of her forehead and tried to remember more of his cranial anatomy.

Caroline snagged both Flora and Phoebe by the sleeves and dragged them closer to the fire. "I'm afraid they won't have much time to work it out," she mused in hushed tones which the others had to huddle closer to hear. The wrinkles above her eyes drew into a web of concentration. "Perhaps we should give them . . . a little nudge."

"A nudge . . ." Flora considered it for a moment, then a demure hint of mischief stole over her face. "Oh, by all means . . . let's do." Together, she and Caroline turned on Phoebe, who knotted into a skeptical ball of resistance.

"I'm telling you right now, I won't agree to any of this until I've had a good, thorough feel of his head"—she shook a pudgy finger at them—"and that's my final word!"

* * *

Late that night, as Graham Hamilton lay in the great tester bed in the guest chamber of Asher House, something brushed his sleep-shrouded mind. Pale and moving, it drew him toward the edge of consciousness, and he stirred, rolling onto his side with a heavy sigh. But before he could return completely to the land of Nod, it came again, touching his cheek, moving up his temple. He fastened on it as it moved over his forehead, creeping, pausing, then rubbing back and forth. When he moved his head groggily, it ceased. He rolled onto his back, and his arm brushed something as it flopped at his side.

He struggled toward wakefulness, dimly aware that it required a great deal of effort for some reason. There was a light blur, something pale near the bed, when his eyes fluttered open, then slammed shut. Hearing took less energy than seeing; he caught a *shoosh* on the rug nearby and the distinctive creak of a floorboard underfoot, from near the door. He managed to push up onto his arms and focus his gaze just as a hint of light disappeared from around the door, and he heard the latch click softly.

The perceptions fitted together slowly: someone had been in his room. Like a warm, fragrant mist, Miranda Edgethorn rose in his mind, and he threw back the covers. His legs seemed weighted with lead, and his head felt as if it were encased in spongy cotton. As he slid from the bed, he banged into the night table, and set the cup and saucer he'd used earlier skittering and clattering.

Lumbering to the door, he leaned heavily against the frame and rolled around it into the inky hallway, just in time to catch a brief glint of light from far down the passage. Compelled by a sixth sense, he followed it. Walking was a bit awkward at first, but the process seemed to smooth out after a few steps. He shook his head repeatedly, trying to clear the persistent fuzziness from his senses.

When he came to a place where the wall became railing on one side, he deduced that he'd come to the center stairs. The light had come from farther down the hall, in the other wing of the house. And suddenly he understood why he was following it: somebody could be up to something. The memory of sweet, curvy little Miranda teased his thoughts, replaced quickly by a vision of three wizened faces with canny, knowing expressions. What if the old crows were plotting against him, or destroying evidence, or doctoring the books?

A scrap of moonlight from a window at the far end of the hall provided enough light for him to make his way down the far hall, where he came to a great, iron-bound door set in rough stone. He ran his fingers over it, judging that it was about where the light had disappeared and wishing he could be rid of the strange mushiness at the edges of his perceptions.

The massive door swung open with only the tiniest scrape of a hinge. Beyond, he could make out a set of worn stone steps, spiraling gradually upward. As he mounted the steps, feeling his way along the stone wall, a dim shaft of light from above pierced the gloom, and he could make out a strange buzzing sound and the low rumble of what might have been voices. As he neared an ancient door left ajar at the top of the steps, he instinctively flattened against the wall.

Edging to the sizable crack in the hinge side of the door, he put his eye to it. Inside the large, shadowy chamber, framed in blood-red firelight, stood three, hoary, age-bent figures clad in stark black robes. They muttered and bobbed as they stood beside a long table, their heads huddled together over something in a small copper pot, under which a fire set in a stone lamp burned. Propped and mounted around them were coils of copper piping, all manner of vials and jars, stacks of books, and bizarre-looking metal wheels attached to wires and cables.

He blinked and swallowed hard, feeling his gut tighten and his mouth go dry. As he watched, transfixed, a shimmering vapor began to rise from the caldron and hang over the frizzled white heads; iridescent gold, turning to shimmering blue, then to a pulsing ruby-magenta. There were cackles of approval and mutters and ahs.

Suddenly an upright metal wheel nearby began to spin,

whir, and hum. Tiny blue-white veins, like miniature lightning, wriggled and danced from one wheel to another nearby. There were odd clicking sounds, and the wheel began to rise as the figures jiggled and gyrated in frantic delight. Then—*wham!*—there was a loud bang, a wild explosion of blue-white sparks filled the chamber, and the old crows threw their bony arms around one another and began to dance in a circle, chanting in low, droning tones. He strained frantically to make out part of what they were saying.

"... perfect to furnish her delight," the tallest of the three crooned.

"... sweet and curvy," the short, wide one added.

"... senses topsy-turvy!" the third finished with a shrieking flourish.

He shook his head, trying desperately to clear it of this fantastical vision. His heart pounded wildly, and he grew icy with dread as they continued to dance and laugh in eerie, cackling tones. They gradually turned into his line of sight, and he froze.

It was the old Asher sisters! But—dearest Lord!—their faces! Withered and sunken, noses drooping, chins protruding, mouths puckered, and all but toothless! Their hair, now shock-white, hung in frowsy strings, their eyes burned with strange bright fires, and their hands were gnarled and enlarged. The horror of it fixed him to the spot while his mind reeled from one chilling detail to the next.

Crones ... black-clad and hideous ... chanting and dancing ... stirring and mumbling ... raising vapors and summoning the elemental powers of lightning ... *The old Asher sisters practiced black arts.* He felt the strength drain from his legs as the inescapable conclusion burst on his beleaguered brain. They were *witches*!

"Aggh—" He strangled the cry that filled his throat, so that only a whisper escaped. One of the old crones shushed the others, and they all stopped to listen. He ripped his eyes from the crack, closed them, and held his breath until he heard them speak.

"Probably just mice."

"I thought Shaddar got rid of them," came a response.

"Oh, I'm sure he did," said a third voice. "Must be a new batch. I'll have to remember to mention it to him."

The sound of ordinary human speech poured over him like warm water, thawing his frozen joints. With his heart pounding wildly, he stumbled down one step and then another, feeling his way down the stairs to the hall below.

Witches. It rolled about in his head, refusing to lodge in one place so he could examine and cross-examine it, subject it to the test of logic and rational scrutiny. *Witches.* The possibility went against everything he believed, every standard he held—against the very foundation of science, reason, and inquiry. But in the dark, with his wits oddly soft and permeable, the word had a powerful, haunting impact. *Witches.*

Suffocating alarm sent him banging through the iron-bound door at the bottom of the tower and running down the darkened hallway toward his room. He had to get out of here! Then his jerky stride slowed and faltered as his eyes flew wide. *Miranda*—he had to find Miranda!

3

MIRANDA paused on the stair landing, shifted the single candlestick to her left hand, and rubbed the back of her aching neck. She had just spent half the night in the study, preparing evidence and organizing the case she would present the next morning. And with each receipt she filed and every entry she made into the estate books, her spirits had sunk a bit lower. Asher House was a rather unusual household. Some of their expenses would probably seem odd, even to the most open-minded of individuals. She could just imagine what straitlaced, skeptical, penny-pinching Mr. Hamilton would have to say about them.

She lifted her skirts and climbed the steps, thinking longingly of her soft bed and trying not to think about the coming confrontation with the executor of her father's estate. As she neared the top of the stairs, a series of muffled thuds from the upstairs hall stopped her in her tracks. Definitely *not* mice, she judged. Then came the distinctive creak of a door being opened, and she heard her name being called in hoarse and urgent tones.

"Miranda . . . wh-where are you?"

It wasn't Aunt Flora, Aunt Phoebe, or Aunt Caroline, she thought, hurrying up the last three steps. And Shaddar never spoke. That left only . . . Her fatigued senses came to attention as the realization and the sight of him struck her in the same instant. The imperious solicitor was bent over, lurking along the hallway, calling her name in a frantic whisper as he opened first one bedroom door, then another.

"Mister Hamilton?" she exclaimed softly, her eyes widening as he started and whirled to face her in a defensive crouch. His face bore a shock-blanked expression, his hair was rumpled, and he was clad only in his borrowed nightshirt. The sight of her seemed to jar him back toward reality, and he snapped upright with a wilting look of relief.

"Miranda! Thank God—"

"Mister Hamilton, whatever are you doing?" she asked, trying not to look at his bare feet and the long, muscular legs his nightshirt didn't quite cover.

"Looking for you!" he declared in a hoarse whisper as he hurried toward her. "I have to . . . Wait—" He froze and visually scoured the hallway around them, as if afraid they might be overheard. Spotting the window nook at the far end of the passage, he seized her wrist and headed for it, pulling her along. "Down here, where they can't see us!"

She was dragged halfway down the hall before she recovered from the surprise and balked at his ungentlemanly treatment of her. "Really, Mister Hamilton, this is most improper!"

"Miranda—Mizz Edgethorn—please, come with me—"

"Have you taken leave of your senses?" She braced and huddled back, but her slippers slid over the worn hall runner, betraying her straight into his hands. He snagged her other wrist, and in the ensuing tussle, she dropped the candlestick, and they were plunged into darkness. The shock of losing the light created just enough of a pause in her resistance for him to clamp an arm about her waist and haul her against his side, lifting her toes off the floor. He carried her, wriggling and gasping, down the hall and into the curtained window well.

Once in the secluded darkness, behind the heavy drapes, he set her on her feet and clasped both of his arms around her waist to pull her tight against him. As they faced each other, the air around them filled with the intimate sound of heavy, uneven breathing, both his and hers. They would have been button to button . . . if he'd been wearing any buttons.

"Mizz Edgethorn, you have to listen," he said in an agony of earnestness. "I came to protect you—"

Her eyes slowly adjusted to the thin moonlight streaming in through the window, then grew wide and expectant as they searched him. The feel of his lean strength pressed so forcefully, so provocatively against her body seemed strangely more tantalizing than threatening, and the slightest wriggle of resistance on her part only emphasized it. So she stood very still in the hard circle of his arms, growing ever more aware of her own body as she felt his heat seeping into her and watched the play of shadows over his finely chiseled features. Where his body pressed against her, she was beginning to feel quivers and tingles again, and where her palms were braced against his lower ribs, she could feel the hard, naked contours of his belly through his thin nightshirt. She'd never been this close to a man before—much less one in nightclothes. For some reason, she couldn't bring herself to struggle and break free, even though she felt his hold on her easing.

His hand came up to touch her face, and she was unable to speak for the tightening in her throat. She stared up at him, examining the sweet, almost haphazard stroke of his fingers over her cheek and down the side of her face. What was it about him that seized her senses and made her aware of every peak and valley of her woman's flesh? Then a sound rumbled up between them, generated deep within him and made resonant by the receptive hollow within her. It was a moment before she realized it was his voice . . . and another moment before she managed to decipher what he'd said.

"Sp-sparks—I saw sparks . . ."

Yes, well . . . she was close to seeing sparks, too, just now. And if his head would only bend a bit more and his lips would only come a little closer, she might learn just what the poets meant about the splendor of . . .

". . . vapor . . . rich colors, shimmering and glowing . . ." His voice sounded thick and urgent.

Ah, yes . . . colors. Rich and penetrating. She was beginning to see them, to feel them cascading over and through her, swirling . . .

". . . like lightning . . ."

Ummm, lightning . . . His broad, sensual mouth was so close now that she could feel his breath bathing her sensitive lips. The searing impact of his male presence was rather like lightning, liquid and powerful as it surged along her nerves and coiled through her very sinews . . .

". . . witches! They were *witches*!"

Oh, yes, definitely wit— witches? Her head snapped upright, and her eyes refocused. She found him clutching her shoulders and staring at her with a wild-eyed expression. "Witches?" she echoed. She had thought he was talking about . . . while he was rambling on about *witches*? Her face flamed with chagrin as she realized just how drastically she had misinterpreted his words and behavior. "Whatever are you talking about?" she choked out.

"Up the stairs, in the dark! I saw them, I swear—dancing and chanting and conjuring—st-stirring some sort of brew in a caldron. They called up vapors and lightning, and there was an explosion and sp-sparks flew everywhere!" He flung

his hands wide in demonstration, then grabbed her shoulders
again.

"I'm afraid *you're* the one conjuring things, Mister Hamilton," she said, shrinking back, her mind racing under the
lash of her stinging pride. She might have no experience
with men, but she had a wealth of experience with eccentric
behavior. And he certainly was behaving oddly . . . She suddenly recognized the symptoms; the occasional slur of a
word, the odd luminosity of his eyes, the uncharacteristic
emotion in his manner. He was behaving like someone
who'd imbibed too much after-dinner port. Or—it dawned
on her—one of her old aunts' powerful toddies! "I think
you'd better take yourself straight back to bed."

"No! I swear to you," he said with a rasp of panic in
his voice. "Something woke me, and I followed a light.
And there they were! They're witches, I tell you, and I have
to warn you—"

"Witches," she repeated, with as much restraint as she
could muster. "You saw witches upstairs, minutes ago."
He nodded and glanced feverishly around them again.

"It was your old aunts—*they're witches!*"

Her aunts? That was what this was all about—accusing
her old aunts of more wrongdoing . . . of *witchcraft*? Her
face flushed with humiliated anger, and she shoved his hands
from her shoulders. "First they're thieves, then they're
witches. Really, Mister Hamilton, that is the limit!"

He caught her as she turned to go. "No—wait—let me
tell you—"

"No." She whirled in his grasp, glaring at him as if he
belonged under a rock. "Let me tell *you*! My aunts always
put a few herbals in their toddies, to help ward off colds
and influenza and to help a body get a decent night's sleep.
You're obviously under the influence and not seeing or
thinking straight. You may have seen my old aunts in the
tower room, and you may have seen some odd and unusual
things"—*lightning, sparks, vapors, and caldrons; it sounded just like the old dears*— "but I can assure you, none of
it was witchcraft. My aunts are wonderful, sweet old ladies,
and tomorrow I shall prove to you that they are neither

thieves nor witches!'' She jerked away and stalked to the edge of the curtains.

"Be so good as to go back to bed, Mister Hamilton,'' she ordered curtly, "and sleep it off.''

Graham Hamilton stood motionless for several minutes after she left, and he slowly began to feel the chilled air from the drafty window swirling around his bare legs and the cold floor beneath his feet. He looked down, blinked at the sight of his bare feet, then straightened and looked around him with a bewildered expression. He was standing in a cold hallway in the dead of night, clad only in a night-shirt, proclaiming he'd just seen a witches' dance. His eyes closed, and his whole body flushed crimson. Had he lost every scrap of sanity he possessed? Miranda Edgethorn certainly seemed to think so.

But he *did* see witches, damn it! Didn't he?

He felt his stomach, then his head. Was he indeed drunk? Drugged? That droning chant, that unholy laughter recurred in his head again, and he shuddered. Could he only have imagined those hideous sounds?

Part of him prayed Miranda was right, that it was just the effects of a doctored toddy he had consumed. And part of him, the same pragmatic, analytical side of him that an hour earlier would have argued that there were no such things as magic and witches, now refused to dismiss the powerful evidence of his own senses as an herb-induced delusion. It was too vivid, too real—the mere thought of it brought the whole experience back in a chilling wave of total, nerve-tingling recall.

But even as the cold air and his returning reason sobered him, he could not escape the feeling that he had seen the old ladies up to something strange and unearthly in that room at the top of the stairs. His recollections were too strong, too unexpected, too compelling. Now there was nothing for it but to stay and to prove it to the prickly Miss Edgethorn. He scoured the darkness around him, then crept with exaggerated stealth back to his borrowed room, vowing to get to the bottom of it.

* * *

The next morning dawned cool and gloriously sunny. When Phoebe, Caroline, and Flora collected in the family dining room for breakfast, Flora could scarcely contain her news.

"I finished it . . . the perfume," she announced with hushed excitement. "And I put it in her favorite decanter, the one she always uses, on her dressing table."

"Perfume?" Phoebe snorted irritably, wriggling about in her chair to give Flora a narrow look. "You mean love potion."

"Most certainly *not* a love potion," Flora declared huffily, lifting her chin. "I prefer to think of it as a sort of *human catnip*."

Phoebe harrumphed and folded her arms over her chest.

"Well, I say we have to enhance the natural electricity between them—make the sparks really fly!" Caroline insisted, making small explosions with her hands. "By tomorrow my new coils and electrical enhancers will be ready. A few in his collar and belt and boots . . ." Her calculating gaze drifted toward the sun-filled window as she worked at some mental computation. "To get a proper circuit, I'll have to put a few in Mimi's corset stays as well." She paused, then came back to the present with a crafty smile. "We can have them matched and mated in a matter of days."

"Coils and catnip," Phoebe grumbled disparagingly. "And what if his bumps aren't compatible with hers?"

"You had a chance to feel his head last night," Caroline hissed.

"He woke up before I even got past his regions of 'causality' and 'eventuality,'" Phoebe declared petulantly. "Flora didn't put enough herbs in his toddy. Heaven knows if the fellow has any 'agreeability' or 'suavity' in him at all."

Just at that moment, Miranda came into the dining room and greeted them with a thoughtful look, which melted to an affectionate smile. As she dropped a kiss on each of their upturned cheeks, they exchanged expectant looks. She was wearing Flora's "human catnip."

Mimi felt their eyes on her as she settled in her chair across the table from Aunt Flora, but she didn't give it much thought. The unthinkable events of the previous night were still tumbling about in her head . . . a lunatic solicitor raving about dancing witches. She had fully intended to tell her old aunts about Mister Hamilton's disgraceful behavior and accusations to counter their misguided generosity toward him. But she discarded the idea the minute she set foot in the dining room. Aunt Caroline, rail-straight and dignified; Aunt Phoebe, apple-cheeked and energetic; and Aunt Flora, soft-eyed and ladylike . . . she simply couldn't bring herself to worry them or to hurt their feelings by repeating his outrageous charges against them. She would just have to take care of Mister Hamilton and his wretched accusations by herself.

"Mimi, dear." Aunt Caroline's voice called her back to the present. She looked up to find her old aunts studying her over their teacups. "We've been thinking that perhaps with Mister Hamilton here we should observe a few of the amenities. Dress for dinner . . . that sort of thing. He's probably used to London ways and doing things quite up to snuff. Perhaps it will help if he sees that we've brought you up to proper standards."

Mimi sighed, thinking that a few formalities and dressing for dinner would hardly change Mister Hamilton's unreasonable prejudice against them. But she didn't want to upset the old dears. "I suppose that means I'll have to wear my blue velvet. And a corset." She winced as she refilled her cup from the large silver teapot in the middle of the table. "And you know how I dislike corsets."

Above her head, Aunt Caroline sent the others a supremely satisfied smile.

Moments later, Graham Hamilton appeared in the dining room doorway, looking collected and determined as he surveyed the sunlit room, his recalcitrant client, and her three larcenous—and perhaps sorcerous—old aunts. He had somehow managed to fall asleep after his bizarre midnight encounters and had awakened to find his clothing—cleaned, starched, and pressed to perfection—laid out meticulously on the side of his bed. He had risen and dressed, feeling fortified by each piece of clothing he donned. There was nothing like a good stiff collar, he mused, to give a fellow a reassuring sense of orderliness and self-control.

His first order of business, he had decided, was to find that wretched witches' lair—to verify what he'd seen. He stepped out of his room and followed his recollections down the hallway toward the other wing of the house. He was just past the stairs, looking for that iron-bound door, when the hulking manservant stepped directly into his path. Hamilton recoiled and reddened under the fellow's unblinking glare.

"I was just looking for . . ." He drew himself up straighter. "If you will just direct me to your mistresses . . ." But the formidable servant simply crossed his arms over his chest and stared. Hamilton could do nothing but back away and plan to continue his search another time.

"There you are," he now addressed the foursome with a brush of his once more immaculate cuffs. "I hope I'm not late. I asked your man where to find you"—he motioned to Shaddar, who stood near the kitchen doors wearing his customary air of inscrutability—"but he declined to answer."

"Shaddar . . . doesn't speak," Mimi declared in clipped, accusing tones.

"Oh." He reddened slightly, then raised his square chin and resumed his air of superiority.

Mimi expelled an irritable breath and set her fork down hard, as if to declare that his presence had put her off her appetite. How dared the man show up at their table with such a lofty and disagreeable attitude, after his absurd behavior last night?

At the old aunts' invitation, Hamilton joined them at the linen-draped table and was soon savoring a cup of strong, flavorful tea and spooning mounds of fluffy eggs, smoky kippers, and sweet clotted cream onto his plate. Avoiding Mimi's resentful looks, he quietly scrutinized the old ladies in the bright sunlight for traces of deception or disguise—and found none. They were the same wizened countenances he had seen in the ill-lit drawing room the previous night. When they inquired after his health, he assured them that he had rested well, that his appetite was undiminished, and that the food was quite tasty. A moment later, Shaddar circled the table with a plate of fresh scones, stirring the air in the sun-warmed room . . . and Hamilton stopped dead, a forkful of egg suspended halfway between his plate and his mouth.

Something curled tantalizingly through his sense of smell—something both sweet and spicy, something delicious and yet not quite edible. He quietly sniffed the eggs, then lifted a buttery scone to his nose, then the jam pot, his teacup, and finally even one of the smoked kippers. Frowning, he looked around the table and saw no flowers, no fruit bowl, nothing that he could identify as the source of that faint whiff of paradise. His face darkened. *Paradise?* He sat straighter in his chair and dismissed it with an irritable breath . . . which brought him another teasing waft of that intriguing scent.

He sucked in a deep draft of air, and the smell filled his head, his lungs . . . faint but entire and compelling. What in heaven's name *was* it? His nostrils flared, and he sniffed in first one direction, then in another, so absorbed in the pursuit that he didn't even notice the way the old ladies were staring at him. It was something like flowers . . . but with an irresistible undertone of spice that made his mouth water. It expanded in his sense of smell and began to spill over into his other senses. Velvety . . . it was richly textured and velvety. And golden . . . the color of goldenrod and buttercups . . .

Jaw set and eyes glowing, he inhaled over and over, growing light-headed from taking in too much air. All he could think about was locating the source of that marvelous smell, and he concentrated so fiercely on it, he didn't even hear the old ladies' questions.

But Mimi had heard. And she'd watched his face growing darker and his eyes growing hotter as he deigned not to respond to their polite inquiries about his family. She'd watched the indignant flaring of his nostrils and the rapid rise and fall of his chest. The way his eyes darted about the table and the room, he seemed to be tallying the silver and linen, the elegant old walnut sideboard, and the crystal chandelier on some mental ledger, as evidence of her aunts' larceny. It was more than she could endure. She threw her wadded napkin on the table and pushed up from her chair.

"I'll be in the study, whenever Mister Hamilton is ready to begin," she informed her aunts. Then she turned and sailed out, carrying the source of Hamilton's distraction with her.

Suddenly that entrancing scent was gone, and Hamilton found himself sitting with his knuckles white and his heart pounding as if he'd just finished a footrace. When he looked up, he found the three old ladies gazing at him with curious frowns, and he reddened to the roots of his hair. *Ye gods— get hold of yourself, Hamilton.* By the end of a second calming breath, he had seized control of his own senses once again—just in time to hear Miss Phoebe say, "Our Mimi keeps all the estate books and records, Mister Hamilton. She will show you everything you need, after breakfast."

At Miss Caroline's request, the great, sinewy manservant led him through the house to a small study located just off the drawing room which he had seen the previous night. He paused outside the door to glance around the large, high-ceilinged room that had seemed so outlandish to him the night before. Heavy brocade drapes had been opened at the far end of the room, revealing massive leaded windows which admitted sunlight in abundance. In the brightness, everything looked a bit worn and faded, but surprisingly ordinary; the stone carvings that held up the huge mantel-piece looked more like cherubs than gargoyles, and the portraits on the walls looked more dignified than sinister. He tugged at his stiff, fortifying collar and entered the study.

It was a small room, lined with shelves which were filled with books and stacks of paper and an occasional stuffed bird and antique wooden globe. A great, battered rolltop desk stuffed with papers dominated one wall, and two faded red parlor chairs and a heavy oak table occupied much of the rest of the floor space. And in the center of it all, standing with her chin tucked and her expressive lips forming a succulent pout, was Miranda Edgethorn.

The sunlight coming from the window behind her sent rivulets of fire through her auburn curls and transformed her skin into luminous pearl. She wore a fitted, sage-green challis dress with a white silk collar and cuffs, and a supple, draped skirt and demi-bustle. She was an impossibly appealing combination of business and pleasure, vulnerability and threat. And suddenly he caught a whiff of that scent again . . .

Mimi felt as well as saw his entrance into the room; his forceful presence seemed to push all the air out of her lungs. Bracing against the desk behind her, she waved him to a seat in one of the stuffed parlor chairs. When he shook his head, the room got noticeably smaller.

She hadn't anticipated how unsettling it would be, closeted with him in these confined quarters. Her cheeks began to flush, and her heartbeat quickened as she carried a stack of ledgers to the table and opened the drawers of the desk and an adjoining cabinet to reveal boxes stuffed with due bills and receipts, all done up in bundles with ribbons tied just so.

"First, I suppose I should explain how I keep records. You see, I record everything in columns . . . all of our income here." She opened the top book and dragged a slender finger down the sparsely inked columns on one side of the page and the densely filled rows on the other. "And our expenditures over here. Then I sort and categorize all due bills and list them on a separate sheet for each month—a sort of summary." She held up a sheet of paper on which categories and amounts had been listed in feminine script. His eyes had widened as she spoke, and now his jaw flexed and his hands curled into fists at his sides.

"You do all this yourself . . . with a homemade system of accounting?" he demanded hoarsely, his eyes glowing and nostrils flaring as they had at breakfast.

Something in the way he said "homemade" rankled her pride. "If you will just allow me to finish," she said irritably, retreating to the desk and pulling out a bundle of receipts. "I apportion the monies for each expenditure . . . and write a draft or put the pound notes for each in an envelope for the tradesmen who come each month to settle accounts." She felt her hands growing icy and her heart beating faster as he advanced on her, his face dusky, his chest heaving. "Then I mark the bills with a number which corresponds to . . . and file them . . . in boxes . . ." He was so close, so big. His dark hair looked so soft and his lips looked so . . . Her knees were going weak again, and she turned and slid shakily into the straight chair that faced the desk. "So you can see, everything is quite orderly."

Graham had barely heard one word in three. The minute he stepped through the door, he had caught that scent again, and his senses had cast off all rational control to go racing after it. By the time he reached the center of the room, that bedeviling smell filled his head, his lungs, and was seeping into his heart, his blood, even his blessed bones! *More*, he moaned silently. He had to have *more*. His pulse was pounding, his mouth was watering, his skin was beginning to ache. He rubbed one hand over the other to relieve it.

The urge to sniff overwhelmed him, and he began to track the source like a cat on the prowl. Step . . . sniff, sniff. Closer, *sniff, sniff*. The trail led straight to Miranda Edgethorn.

Cinnamon and vanilla . . . hibiscus and hyacinth . . . peppermint drops . . . rose petals warmed by sunshine . . . all a part of it and yet only the tiniest component of it. The scent concentrated until it tickled his nose and curled through his blood, a powerful sneeze that would not come, a desperate itch that couldn't be localized enough to scratch. It was all around her . . . It radiated from her . . .

Lord—it *was* her!

When she sat down at the desk, her back to him, he closed his eyes and swayed. His skin ached and burned for some sort of contact. He pressed closer, wanting to rub against her, desperate to feel his skin against hers. He rubbed his palm over the knobs at the top of the chair . . . *ohhh* . . . and then ground his ribs and waist against the spokes on the back of it . . . gently . . . biting his lip to keep from making a sound. An ache roared through his skin, a burning need to rub his bare chest against her, to nuzzle the nape of her neck and bury his nose in that mass of silky burnished curls.

He couldn't help himself. He wanted to roll and rub and slither and arch against her—to have her stroke and pet him, ruffle his hair. He sniffed hungrily as his head lowered toward her shoulder and his burning lips neared the cool, satiny skin of her neck.

Mimi sat at her desk, frozen with expectation, feeling his heated presence at her back and coming nearer . . . nearer. His breathing was a hard, exciting rasp that pulled her own into the same erratic rhythm.

"Do you understand . . . my system?" she whispered. He didn't answer, but she sensed his movement, felt his rising heat. She closed her eyes, and her head swayed to one side. Something warm and soft brushed the side of her neck, and a sound vibrated her ear, low and liquid, like a purr.

"Mimi, dear . . . Mister Hamilton. You're hard at work, we see." Aunt Caroline's strident voice pierced the air like a gunshot.

With their faces crimson and their eyes dark and luminous, both Mimi and Graham jolted and whirled to face the old aunts. He lurched back two steps; she sprang to her feet like an untied coil. He stiffened and glowered; she clutched her throat and stammered.

"I . . . we . . . were just . . . getting started."

"So we see, dear," Aunt Flora said sweetly. "Well, I shall be in my garden most of the day, putting it to bed for the winter," she informed the red-faced pair, "in case you should need me."

"And I have to take the horse into the village to have a loose shoe repaired," Caroline put in. "I'll be gone awhile."

"And I've promised to give the rector's wife a reading and consultation for her eldest boy," Phoebe announced. "Won't be back until time for tea, Mimi, dear."

The old ladies smiled and nodded as they ambled away, each to her own devices.

Graham seized a ledger from the table and dragged a

chair to the door, depositing himself as far from Miranda as he could get and still be in the same room. He was dumbstruck, mortified at having been caught sniffing and panting and rubbing, like some deranged animal! He could only hope the old ladies hadn't seen his unthinkable behavior. Lord, he groaned, what was happening to him?

He looked up to find Mimi staring at him with her delicate face flushed and her golden eyes wide and hauntingly beautiful. For a moment, he was spellbound. The gold reminded him of the color of the downy buttons at the centers of daisies. A slash of heat cut across his belly, and he tightened his grip on the ledger, using every ounce of his self-control to fight the seductive pull of her scent.

"Perhaps I should explain some of the expenditures," she said, starting toward him.

"No!" he barked hoarsely, throwing up one hand to stop her while his other hugged the book to him as though it contained his sanity. "I mean . . . I'd prefer to look the ledgers over myself." Anything to keep her away from him! he thought.

She blushed violently and stepped back. Horrid, unpredictable man, she thought irritably. One minute he was hot, the next he was cold. One minute he couldn't seem to get close enough, the next he couldn't get far enough away! She couldn't wait to be rid of him!

For the next several minutes, he pored over that ledger, scowling, fidgeting in his chair, and occasionally rubbing his hands over his face or pulling at his collar as if it were a bit too tight. She sat on the edge of her chair with her hands clasped tightly in her lap, waiting, preparing herself. And finally it came.

"And just what the devil is this supposed to be? Five hundred bloody pounds to some Spaniard!" he exclaimed, looking exasperated beyond all bearing.

"A South American, actually." She sprang up defensively and took a step toward him before his forbidding look stopped her.

"South . . . American," he echoed with a nasty bit of patience.

"Señor Aloquina is an import broker. He arranged the purchase of two very rare South American aromatics for Aunt Flora," she said tautly.

"What the hell is an aromatic? And what does Aunt Flora need two of them for . . . at two hundred and fifty pounds apiece?" he demanded.

"They're plants," she declared tautly, taking offense at his crude language. "And you can't have just one and expect it to live. They live and breed in pairs."

"Plants?" He choked on the word. "Five hundred pounds for two bloody plants?"

"Aunt Florabunda is a highly skilled horticulturist. Her collection of exotic specimens is unparalleled in England."

"Dashed well ought to be—at five hundred pounds a crack. Where the devil is this South American wonder? I have to see this for myself!"

"Fine! Come with me!"

He stalked along at a safe distance behind her, through the center hall, then along a faded corridor in the little-used west wing. She led him through a large set of brass-bound doors and into a soaring glass-domed conservatory filled with lush greenery and bright bowers of blossoms. The air was humid and crowded with the heavy fragrances of exotic flowers. She led him along one of the brick paths that circled the terraced beds and paused before a pair of glossy, thick-leafed plants bearing huge, intricate pink and purple blossoms.

"Here they are . . . the Xinqotec passionflowers from the Amazon River basin. They're very rare and very potent."

He scrutinized the pair, then stepped back from the penetrating sweetness, wrinkling his nose. He glanced around with a look of broadening horror and pointed to a pair of elegant, lace-leafed trees nearby. "And those?"

"Those are rare Carpathian spice trees . . . from the East. My aunts traveled the Orient in their younger days, and Aunt Flora learned all about the eastern aromatics."

"Then—good Lord—there must be thousands and thousands of pounds' worth." He groaned, waving his arm at the rest. "She's beggared your inheritance just to have something fancy to smell?"

"Hardly," she managed through the frustration squeezing into her throat. "She uses them to make scents and perfumes. I suppose you'll want to see her laboratory with your own eyes, too." Without waiting for a response, she lifted her skirts and sailed toward another set of doors at the far end of the conservatory, leaving him to follow.

A double set of doors separated the conservatory from a large sunlit room lined with shelves which were filled with pots, crocks, and vials. Several tall tables occupied the center of the floor, cluttered with mazes of suspended coils, bubblelike spheres of glass, caldrons, and mortars and pestles such as chemists used to make up pharmaceuticals. As he stared at those tables, the vivid memory of what he'd seen the withered old sisters working on—caldrons and conjuring and vapors—flooded his mind.

"This is it! This is what I saw last night!" He stalked feverishly back and forth, looking at the walls and the apparatus on the tables from several angles. "The room's not quite the same . . . but these caldrons and all these coils hanging everywhere . . ." He gave Mimi a look that said he'd been vindicated as he prowled around the tables, craning his neck to peer into crocks and crucibles, and poking at things with his finger. "You see, I wasn't dreaming or drunk. I did see your old aunts brewing and conjuring!"

"What you saw, Mister Hamilton, and what you see here, is Aunt Flora's distilling apparatus for concentrating the essences of flowers and making extracts from her aromatic plants," she announced, watching the look on his face as her words sank in. "Aunt Flora is a master perfumer . . . who believes strongly in the power of smells and scents. Mister Hamilton, you saw my aunt working on some sort of perfume—not some sort of witch's brew!"

Perfume, he thought, how utterly ridicu— He stopped dead, and some of the high color drained from his face. A *perfume*? He thought of his behavior that morning, of the scent that had bewitched and bedeviled him and nearly caused him to disgrace himself. Could something that com-

pelling, that enthralling, actually be just a perfume? His
sane, orderly, supremely rational self rebelled against that
possibility. A scent—the smell of bananas, mildew, wood
smoke, even the bouquet of good brandy—was just a scent.
It didn't take over a body, affect his sight and hearing . . .
didn't make him rub and writhe and pant like a damn animal
in rut!

"It was most certainly not just a perfume," he said to
himself, not realizing that she would think the words were
meant for her and take them as a personal challenge. "It
was more powerful than any bit of rosewater."

"Smells can indeed be very powerful things, Mister Hamilton," she declared, her eyes flashing. "They can evoke
strong memories and feelings, change a person's mood or
his whole outlook on life. But they have nothing to do with
witchcraft or magic. And I'll prove it to you!"

She hurried to a cabinet on the far wall and returned a
moment later with a wooden box containing several crystal
vials. Selecting one, she held it out to him with a tilt of
defiance to her chin. "Most people don't understand just
how potent a scent can be. Try this, Mister Hamilton."

Warily, he came around the end of the table and accepted
the little bottle full of amber liquid. He lifted the crystal
stopper, raised the vial to his nose, and sniffed suspiciously.
Cool essences of pine and rich earth and the musk of damp,
decaying leaves invaded his senses . . . each recognizable
separately, but blended into an intriguing whole that was
easily identifiable as the essence of a forest. A second,
deeper breath and he could actually see green—new green
like the first delicate leaves of spring. And in the midst of
that earthy swirl of color he could see Mimi, clothed like
a wood nymph, her shoulders bare, her hair down and tousled about her, and her smile an alluring combination of
innocence and invitation. He started and blinked, then thrust
the vial back into her hands and fell back a step. When he
opened his mouth, only one hoarse word came out.

"Unbelievable."

Her eyes twinkled as she handed him a second vial. For
a moment, he could only stare at her, letting the woodlands

fade in his sight and realizing that his precious nymph remained. His hand trembled as he brought the second bottle to his nose.

He smelled warm sand, a hint of dust, then cinnamon bark, allspice, and oil of cloves. He gave a short laugh of astonishment. A second whiff, and he heard the ping of finger cymbals and the drone of a zither and beheld a rainbow of shimmering, multicolored veils . . . swirling about Mimi's soft, undulating body. Twining in her gloriously disheveled hair were small carnations, verbena, and orange blossoms. A coral-red hibiscus was tucked behind her ear. All around her were dried strings of vanilla beans and heaps of nutmegs, their sweet scents permeating her, making her the choicest treat in that exotic spice market of sensation. With his gaze fixed on the shimmer of her eyes, he threw caution to the wind and inhaled deeply. He could actually feel it spreading from his lungs into his blood, taking him over, seizing his whole being. He swayed dizzily, grinning, growing intoxicated by the scent . . . by her . . . by the wild and wonderful possibilities she embodied.

When she removed the vial from his tightly clenched fingers, he was a reeling, inarticulate mass of sensation. It took a long minute and several repetitions of his name to bring him back to reality. "Mister Hamilton . . . Mister Hamilton, are you all right?" When his vision righted, she was still the glorious center of it.

"It's Graham, sweet Mimi. Call me Graham." He raised his hand and feathered his fingertips across her cheek. She looked and felt like cool satin. "Let me hear you say it."

"Graham." Her voice was soft and breathy as she looked up at him, her eyes wide and glowing. She bit her lower lip, and he ran a finger over it, entreating her to release it. "Do you want to try one more?" she asked quietly. He could only nod. He would try anything . . . as long as he could be with her like this.

He lifted that third vial to his nose, and his senses exploded. Sunshine—everywhere—seeping through every pore, drenching his soul, setting him free! Suddenly he was barefoot in soft, thick grass, so green and lush, littered with daisies, buttercups, and primroses. Birds were singing, and a cool breeze brushed his face again. And there she was, wearing a coronet of daisies on her sun-kissed curls and a gauze-thin smock that hung adorably askew, baring one shoulder. She was a meadow sprite, a child of nature, a goddess with soft, beguiling eyes and warm, touchable curves.

"Mimi!" he cried, seizing her hands, feeling as if he were soaring on sunlight with her . . . laughing . . . giddy with release. He paused and put the vial to his nose once more, then it was somehow gone from his hand. And all he could see was Mimi, sweet Mimi smiling at him, laughing with him. Suddenly her scent engulfed him again, sending him into a state of pure euphoria.

She had pried the vial from his fingers and set it aside. His wide, often hard-set mouth drew up into an irresistibly boyish grin, and he pulled her body full against his and wrapped her in his arms, whirling around and around with her until they were both dizzy. They stumbled and stopped, steadying each other. And he began to fill her heart as he filled her arms.

For the first time in her life, she was held in a man's embrace. Tingles collected all along her front, wherever her body pressed tightly against his. His head lowered, even as hers tilted up to meet it. And she experienced the softness, the firm possession of a man's mouth on hers for the first time. It was heavenly . . . sweet and silky . . . intimate beyond her wildest dreams. His tongue stroked her lips, coaxing, exploring, then slid between them to caress their sleek inner borders. She yielded, opening to him, wanting more, and catching her breath when his body began to rub against hers, his chest against her breasts, his hardened loins against her belly. She shivered and sent her fingers up his neck, tracing his square jaw line, ruffling through his hair. It was soft, so silky that her fingers tingled. As he picked up handfuls of her hair and buried his face it, she began to rub her cheek against his shirt and the soft wool of his coat front.

He kissed her temple, her cheek, her ear, and slid his

mouth down the side of her neck, breathing her in like a greedy child, craving sweets. More . . . She expanded in his head, in his lungs, and still he wanted more. His senses were swollen with the taste, the sight, the smell, and the feel of her, and yet he couldn't seem to get enough. "Mimi, my love . . . sweet, beautiful Mimi . . ."

He twirled her around and around, then released her to dance on his tiptoes, prancing to some melody only he could hear, while spiraling ever higher, to dizzy, rapturous heights. He spread his arms, rising on updrafts of rarest pleasure, whirling, gliding, soaring . . .

Suddenly he lurched and swayed around and around, muttering, "Ohhh, Mimi." And he keeled straight over, landing flat on the floor with a horrendous thud.

"Graham!" Mimi staggered with shock, then rushed to his side, calling his name. "Graham, are you all right? Please—oh, Graham, wake up!" But he just lay there, out cold, with a blissful grin on his face.

She ran to fetch Shaddar, and the big manservant knelt and ran his hands over Graham's head and pried open his eyes one at a time. He nodded gravely, indicating that Graham would be all right, and Mimi sighed her relief and stroked his hair. Apparently, he wasn't used to happiness in such large doses.

Shaddar lifted him gently and carried him back through the conservatory and the west wing, headed for the stairs and Graham's borrowed room. When they reached the center hall, they met the old aunts returning early from their errands. The old ladies' eyes widened on Graham's limp form, then flew to Mimi's flushed cheeks and lowered lashes.

"Whatever happened to Mister Hamilton?" Aunt Caroline inquired, craning her neck to get a better view of the grin on his face. She and Flora exchanged looks.

"Please don't be angry," Mimi said, blushing hotter. "Mister Hamilton seemed to think we paid an excessive amount for Aunt Flora's Xinqotec passionflowers, and I just thought I'd convince him that Aunt Flora's collection and her perfumes were . . . not to be taken lightly."

Aunt Flora stepped forward, her wrists folded over each other as she gave Graham a long, searching look. Then she turned a chiding expression on Mimi. ''You gave him some of my special stock to smell, didn't you?''

''I'm sorry, Aunt Flora.'' Mimi's cheeks flamed. ''But he was being so disagreeable about it all . . .''

''I understand, Mimi, dear. But in future you really ought to be more careful.'' Aunt Flora sighed and gazed at Graham, shaking her head. ''Some men just can't hold their perfumes.''

But when Shaddar and Mimi were well up the stairs and out of earshot, Caroline and Flora joined hands and tottered around, giggling like schoolgirls and chanting: ''He kissed her . . . he kissed her!''

4

LATER that evening Graham came downstairs for dinner, walking as if he was afraid his head might topple from his shoulders at any minute. His eyes were tight with suppressed pain, and his expression was stern and forbidding. He would scarcely look at Mimi, and her inexperience with the vagaries of male pride made her see disgust and blame in his avoidance of her. But in truth, it was his own behavior that placed the grim lines at the corners of his mouth and stiffened his spine and his verbal responses.

Never in his life—well, not since he was seven years old—had he abandoned all restraint, as he had that afternoon with Mimi. With his tutors, in his Uncle Throckmorton's staid household, at his public school, and certainly in his university days, he had always comported himself with the utmost gravity and restraint. Even in the occasional lapses of youth—his first drinking rout and his first experience with a woman—he managed to retain both his consciousness and something of his dignity. He had never completely lost control—until he smelled Mimi Edgethorn's irresistible scent and saw her standing there with her eyes and lips so soft, just begging to be kissed.

The worst of it was: he wanted to do it again, this minute! He had the most appalling urge to vault across the damn dinner table, pull her into his arms, and kiss her breathless . . . right under the eyes of her three conniving old aunts. That compelling desire for her and all the pleasure she represented shocked him to the very bottom of his logical and orderly soul. She was his client; he was supposed to be protecting her and her interests, not making mad, passionate love to her! He clamped a ruthless hand on his undignified stirrings and scowled a bit more fiercely.

Mimi sat across the dinner table, wearing her blue velvet gown with the scooped neck and fashionable demi-bustle, looking quite ladylike and feeling quite confused. She was scarcely able to take her eyes from him. Her lips were burning, remembering the heat of his against them, and as she reached for her goblet, her fingers grew sensitive, recalling the slide of his hair through them. She had meant to teach him a lesson that afternoon, to defy that smug male certainty that he carried about him like a cloak. Instead, she'd gotten a lesson of her own, in the pleasures of men and passion and her vulnerability to them. She was supposed to be protecting her old aunts from his wretched accusations, not relishing his every look and longing for his kisses. She felt her aunts' eyes on her and lowered her own eyes to her untouched plate of food. Nothing would come of such longings anyway. He was obviously mortified by what had happened between them. The most she could hope for now was that he would pack up his groundless suspicions and carry them straight back to London with him. But increasingly, that particular prospect filled her with an even greater sense of dread.

"How is your head, Mister Hamilton?" Caroline asked solicitously, after an embarrassing lull in the stilted conversation.

Graham's hand went to the knot on the back of his head before he realized it. "Fine, really." He stiffened. "No cause for concern."

"How careless of me to leave things out in my laboratory so that others trip on them." Flora graciously offered him an excuse, which he accepted with a pained look and a nod.

"Perhaps I'd better have a look at that lump on your head . . . just to make sure you're all right," Phoebe declared with a determined squint. She was on her feet in an instant and had her fingers on the back of his head before he could react.

"Thank you, no!" He jerked back and glowered at her. "I shall be fine."

Phoebe could do nothing but resume her seat with a red face and an air of injury. Within minutes, Graham excused himself for a walk in the evening air, and Mimi excused herself to the study, to tidy her record books a bit more. Caroline and Flora turned to Phoebe.

"Well, you tried," Caroline said with a taunting smile.

"He landed smack on the back of his head," Phoebe said, coming out of her huddled posture to announce her discovery. "And he's all swelled up in his 'amativeness.'"

After a long, restless night, Graham awakened to discover his clothing once more freshened and pressed and laid out neatly on the end of his bed. He donned them, thinking that if he caught the slightest whiff of a flower or a hint of sweet spice at breakfast, he wasn't setting foot anywhere near Mimi Edgethorn for the rest of the day. Fortified by determination and a good stiff collar, he made his way down to the family dining room.

The old ladies were there, heads nodding, eyes closed, basking like aged salamanders in the strong morning sun. When they roused and greeted him with genuine pleasure, he felt a momentary twinge and amended his thought: very hospitable and accommodating old salamanders. He sniffed covertly, all the way to his chair, and detected nothing out of the ordinary. Then, halfway through his griddlecakes and sausages, Mimi arrived, and he swallowed with a gulp and pushed to his feet, bracing for an olfactory assault.

None came. He did feel an odd, momentary tingle race across his shoulders and plunge down his arms as she swept by him on her way around the table. But the sensation was so fleeting and he was so relieved that she seemed not to be wearing that perfume that had sent his rational faculties into total decline yesterday, that he dismissed it altogether. When Shaddar seated her she looked up, and he was caught staring at her as if she were a honey-glazed bun.

He tucked his chin and stuffed a huge slice of griddlecake into his mouth, chewing doggedly. It was a moment before he realized that one of the old ladies had spoken to him and looked up. "Pardon? I don't mean to be rude . . . it's just that these cakes are perfectly beautiful." He colored at his choice of words. "Delicious, they're delicious."

"Why, thank you," Aunt Flora said sweetly. "Shaddar always does such a fine job on our cook's day off." She nodded at the capable manservant, and he nodded back. "But tell us, Mister Hamilton, about your family. Where do they live?"

Graham stayed his next bite of food and shifted restively in his chair. "I . . . have no family, to speak of. My parents died when I was quite young, and I was raised by my uncle, Throckmorton Hamilton. He died just more than a year ago."

"No family." Flora smiled sympathetically. "What a coincidence. It appears that both you and our Mimi were orphaned young."

"Undoubtedly that was what prompted you to take such a keen interest in our Mimi's welfare," Caroline observed sagely.

"The similarity of your circumstance," Phoebe clarified.

The old ladies looked at one another and nodded, then returned to their teacups and scones and marmalade, while he sat in complete bewilderment. They had easily put into words what he hadn't managed to admit, even to himself: from the first he had felt some sort of link to Mimi because of their similar loss and the subsequent circumstances of their lives. Both had been orphaned while they were young, and both were sent to live with elderly relations. But there, he thought sternly, all similarity ended.

The table was plunged into awkward silence as they all watched the troubling of his features. Mimi had the most compelling urge to touch him just then, to reassure him somehow. But a moment later her compassionate impulse mystified her. If there was anyone in the whole world who didn't need concern and understanding, it was the solicitor who had come to prove her aunts were frauds and thieves . . . and probably witches as well. But all the same, she wanted to reach for his hand, to invade that grave and somber countenance, to coax a smile from him, to hear his deep, rolling laughter again. Feeling more than a little disturbed by her thoughts, she pushed her chair back and rose, excusing herself to the study.

Graham dawdled over a second, then a third cup of tea, dreading being closeted in that small room with Mimi after the perfect fool he'd made of himself yesterday. But when his old hostesses left the table, he had no choice but to leave as well and make his way to the study.

"Let's get started straightaway," he declared as he forged into the room. She was seated at the desk, wearing a most fashionable coral-colored challis—and a corset that enhanced her elegant curves. Her auburn curls were bathed in sunbeams, and when she looked up, her face ringed by a halo of red-gold light, he completely lost his train of thought. "I . . . we . . . the . . ." He swallowed desperately. "The records I had with me were lost when that wretched horse bolted and left me stranded," he said, recovering. "But I believe I can recall most of the dates of the withdrawals. They were usually made at the start of a quarter. If you will locate such entries in the ledgers, Miss Edgethorn, it will speed the process enormously."

She rose, and as she approached he felt the most unnerving tingling sensations radiating from his neck out along his shoulders and down his arms. The sensations intensified with each step she took toward him, and by the time she reached the table in the center of the room, even his fingers were tingling wildly. He stood bolted to the floor, his face rigid with horror. What the devil was happening to him?

She selected a ledger, opened and perused it. Then as she rounded the table to hand it to him, the skin of his belly began to hum. Another step closer, and it was positively rippling with an excitement that was spreading all the way down into his . . . Oh, Lord!

He flamed and jolted back a few steps, and it faded to a light, ticklish sensation . . . which he grew progressively more desperate to scratch. Her frown of confusion halted his retreat, and he lurched forward just long enough to snatch the ledger from her hands, then withdrew hastily to the same chair where he'd taken refuge yesterday.

"Do have a seat, Miss Edgethorn," he said gruffly, holding the ledger stiffly before him and trying to maintain a semblance of dignity as he sent his hand beneath his coat to give his belly a frantic scratching. Then he flung a tingling finger toward the chair by the desk, insisting, "Over there, if you please." She stood for one defiant moment, staring at him, then complied. And in that short time he felt those shocking excitations trickling down the backs of his legs and collecting in his toes. When she turned away, he curled his toes inside his boots and writhed in silent agony as he collapsed onto the chair. His whole body was aquiver with the impact of her presence, and it took every ounce of his self-control to keep from either pouncing on her or running from the room in sheer panic.

"I feel I really must protest," Mimi said from her perch on the edge of the desk chair. She felt like a child who was being scolded and set in a chair for correction, and she hadn't the faintest idea what she'd done to deserve such treatment. She was "Miss Edgethorn" again, and that thought produced a spreading emptiness in her chest. "I really don't care how much money my aunts have withdrawn from my trust. In fact, I would give it all to them, if I could."

The slight waver in her voice made him look at her. She was sitting with her hand clasped over her heart. Her golden-hazel eyes were large and luminous, so warm and sincere and generous. *She was a woman who would give everything she had, everything she was, to those she really loved.* That realization sent an ache searing through him, from his crowded chest all the way to his restive loins. In a pure panic, he sat straighter in his chair.

"Fortunately, your sentimental feelings have little to do with it," he said thickly. "Right is right, Miss Edgethorn."

He tore his gaze from her and buried it in the ledger again, squinting and scowling as he struggled to make sense of the writing on the page. It was hopeless. He scrutinized the same column of figures five times, seeing none of it. He kept getting lost in the orderliness of the columns, the neatness of her feminine script, and the round prettiness of her numbers. Sighing heavily, he flicked a glance at the bundles of receipts on the table, all neatly stacked, their ribbons tied just so. Astonishing, he thought, that she'd been able to organize it all without even a clerk of some sort to guide her. He ran a square fingertip around and around over her numbers, admiring them, wishing he could tell her how much he admired her. For he truly did admire her . . .

When his eyes refocused, he realized he was staring at an astronomical number on the page before him. He choked, blinked, and shot to his feet.

"What in the devil is this?" He pounded a finger into the open ledger. "Two thousand bloody pounds for 'custom metallurgy'? What in creation do you need with *metallurgy* in the first place . . . much less the custom variety?" he blustered.

She sprang to her feet with a surprised and irritable look. "My aunts have rather unusual interests, Mister Hamilton," she started to explain.

"So I've gathered," he responded through clenched teeth. That unholy tingling and tickling was suddenly back . . . and this time there was an alarming prickling running up the back of his neck and racing up the insides of his thighs, headed straight for his . . . Oh, God! He clamped his legs together, but it did no good. His eyes widened in horror.

"Aunt Caroline was a student of Franz Anton Mesmer, and she conducts scientific research into the medical and hygienic uses of electricity and—" She halted, aghast at the way his eyes crossed and he shuddered visibly. How dare he make fun of Aunt Caroline like this, in front of her! "Very well then," she declared angrily, jerking the ledger from his hands and slamming it down on the table. "Come and see for yourself!" She seized him by the sleeve and pulled his balky frame out the door.

Somewhere in the center hall, he managed to disengage her hands from his sleeve and retrieved some measure of sanity, amid the burning in his fingertips and the unbearable itch that was twiddling beneath every square inch of his skin. He sucked a deep breath and stalked along after her, trying to understand what was happening to him. It had to do with her, he reasoned desperately. Whenever she came near, his nerves went haywire!

He tried to put more distance between them, but she grabbed his sleeve again and hauled him into a large chamber filled with wheels of all shapes and sizes, huge coils of wire and cable, workbenches littered with tools and drawings, and shelves stuffed with all manner of lamp globes, stones, and odd pieces of metal. She led him to the center of the room and turned on him with her fists jammed firmly at her waist.

"This is Aunt Caroline's workroom. This is all electrical and magnetic apparatus, much of it custom built to her specifications. That"—she pointed to a series of upright metal wheels attached to a wooden crank—"is a static electricity generator. And those are Aunt Caroline's 'voltaic piles.'" She pointed to a series of huge glass cylinders that contained metal plates. "They produce currents of electricity to power her experiments. That's where part of the money for custom metallurgy went. The other parts were her magnetizing table and her static cloud machine."

Graham staggered back against a bench, staring at the series of metal wheels and pointing a trembling finger at them. "Th-those . . . I saw those that night! Making lightning!"

"They were making *electricity*. That's a static generator," she declared firmly, stepping to the machine and seizing the handle to give it several energetic cranks. The wheels started to move, and a low hum filled the chamber . . . then a bright blue vein of miniature lightning jumped from the main wheel to a metal rod with a great pop. "You see?" she said with a bit of vengeful triumph in her smile. "No black magic, no witches. Just pure science, Mister Hamilton. But perhaps you need a bit more proof."

His tongue was stuck to the roof of his mouth, and his skin was contracting, and his body hair was prickling wildly. Anxiety paralyzed him as she reached for his hand. His heart all but stopped as her fingers closed around his. Miraculously, the humming, the prickling, the agonizing itch subsided, dispelled by the touch of her hand. Surcease . . . sweet release! He stared at their joined hands, dumbfounded, as he lurched along behind her. That was all it took to end his peculiar, unearthly misery? Just the touch of Mimi's hand?

When he looked up, he found himself staring at a large metallic mushroom sort of contraption, which gave him a very bad feeling in the pit of his stomach. "This is a special sort of static generator, Aunt Caroline's own experimental design. Put your hand here," she said, laying his hand on the top of the rounded metal dome and removing hers from it. Instantly the tingling began to creep back under his skin, distracting him so that he could barely make out the words: "And whatever happens . . . *don't* take your hand away."

"No—wait—don't leave—" He managed a dry whisper that was lost in the sound of her movement.

She threw a small iron bar across some metal pegs, and he began to feel a strange hum, an exaggerated prickle all through his body. The hair on his head stood straight up on end, and he began to vibrate at a low frequency. His eyes were huge and terrified. It was exactly what he'd been feeling before—only more so! Then she smiled, swayed closer, and placed her hand on the contraption, too. Her curls began to rise from her shoulders, and her eyes sparkled with unmistakable mischief as his chin dropped. She giggled.

"How does it feel?"

His mouth worked, but no sound came out. After a moment she slid her hand over his on the machine . . . and the tingling was replaced by a warm, saturating glow all over his body. He stared into her eyes, into the warmth of her impish smile, and saw salvation in it . . . and not just of the electrical variety. He was still staring, entranced, when she moved the lever back and ended the demonstration. Then she stepped away, and that bothersome buzz and tickle returned.

"Mimi!" He grabbed her wrist, and she turned to face him. He let go for an instant, testing it, and the hum and prickle returned. "Mimi, I'm still tingling." His eyes were dark and compelling. His voice dropped to a rough, velvety rasp. "Touch me, Mimi. It won't stop unless you touch me."

She looked at the luminous entreaty in his gray eyes, felt the seductive pull of his need for her, and was at a loss for how to respond.

"One minute I'm Miss Edgethorn, the next I'm Mimi. One minute you kiss me, the next you glower at me. I don't know what to expect of you . . . or what you expect of me."

The muscles in his jaw worked visibly as he struggled to master the riot of sensation in his body. "God—I don't know what to expect of me either, Mimi. Please," he said with a groan, "just come and touch me."

No one had ever said such a thing to Mimi in her life. *Touch me.* And she knew that once Graham Hamilton left Asher House, she would probably never hear it again. She stared at the dark, half-pained desire in his eyes, and her whole body was swept with the same longing she had felt earlier . . . to touch him, to comfort him, to experience him as a man and herself as a woman. She walked straight into him, with her arms, her senses, and her heart wide open. He pulled her against his body and banded her with his arms, holding her tightly against him for a long, breathless moment. Then she felt him relax, and his deep sigh sent a quiver of pleasure through her heart.

"Is that better?" she asked quietly.

"Much." His voice rumbled above her head. "Though I think it could probably be even better."

He lifted her chin and gazed at her with a look of wonder that caused her throat to tighten. Then his head dipped, and their lips met with the intensity of a striking spark. She gasped silently as a glowing streak of sensation traced a path through her cheeks and down her throat, to tumble about in the tips of her breasts. His tongue darted between her parted lips and raised a tantalizing, liquid charge along the sleek inner surfaces of her mouth with its silky strokes.

Her entire body was electrically alive against his. The tingle in her breasts grew to a delicious burn that could only be soothed by rubbing them against his ribs, and that erotic friction built a wild static in her blood . . . hot, crackling, irresistible. Prickles danced over her shoulders, and her fingers burned as if sparks clung to their very tips.

Freed somehow by her responsiveness, he clasped her feverishly to him, claiming her with deep, penetrating kisses. He slid his hands down her narrow waist and the sides of her bottom, savoring her soft, elegant curves, then pressing her tightly against his swollen, aching loins. He undulated gently against her, imagining, anticipating . . .

"Lord, Mimi, you make me feel so . . . You're so sweet, so warm, so . . ." He couldn't find a word to describe the effect she was having on him. She supplied one.

"Magnetic?" Her kiss-swollen lips curled into an innocently seductive bow. Her prompting helped him find the perfect word.

"Electrifying." His eyes flickered with newly freed feelings. "I'm positively on fire."

"Burning?" she asked, pushing back in his embrace with alarm.

"Aching," he declared. "And throbbing . . . and gnawing . . ." He groaned and closed his eyes as if in extreme discomfort.

"Oh, no!" she exclaimed, grabbing his hands and pulling him along. "I have just the cure."

They soon stood beside a long, upholstered table, which was ringed with hinged wooden arms bearing pieces of metal wrapped with loops of copper wire. She looked up at him with a bit of mischief in her smile. "Aunt Caroline's mag-

netizing table. She conducts research to show that magnetizing the body can alleviate any number of discomforts.''
She sent him an earnest, through-the-lashes look. ''Lie
down. And we'll soon have you feeling better.''

He sat and slid back on the edge of the table, then swung
his legs around, avoiding the wooden arms. The tingling
that had plagued him earlier returned, but in such a mild
form that it was rather pleasant among the other excitations
he was experiencing. Mimi swung the arms over the table,
positioning the electrical coils around his body, then moved
away to pull a few levers. He braced and waited. At first,
nothing seemed to be happening.

''The coils become magnets when the electricity is turned
on,'' she informed him. ''By moving the coils over your
body, I can align your magnetic poles. And when your poles
are properly aligned, your body will be at perfect rest.''

''Exactly what I need,'' he said in a strained voice. ''Having you align my poles.'' He raised his head to watch her
as she directed a large coil along the arch of his foot and
up his ankle, without quite touching him. ''Am I supposed
to feel something?''

''Not necessarily. Magnetism can't be seen or felt. Only
its effects.''

He watched her slender hands manipulating that coil,
pushing it higher on his body, skimming just above the
fabric of his clothing. His blood began to rise, following
the coil, then anticipating its movement and racing ahead
to collect in his tightening loins. Higher and higher she
moved with that peculiar nontouching touch; to his knees,
up the sensitive insides of his thighs, to his throbbing male
parts.

''Do you feel anything now?'' she asked, sensing the
growing tension in his body and puzzled by it. Magnetizing
was generally known for its sedative effect.

He was feeling quite a bit—none of which he wanted to
admit to her just then. So he bit the inside of his lip and
shook his head.

''Perhaps I need to increase the magnetic strength.'' She
stepped away and turned up the voltage. When she returned,

she moved back down to his feet. "We'll start over. Sometimes in difficult cases—people with stubborn poles—Aunt Caroline actually touches the body with the magnet."

She touched his foot, and he twitched. She looked up to find him red-faced and grinning, and she continued to direct the coil around his foot, then up the inside of his ankle and calf. By the time she reached his knee, he was squirming and his body was jerking oddly. "I'm not hurting you, am I?" She halted on the inside of his knee. And he burst into full laughter.

"Oh, God, Mimi—it tickles!"

"It does?" She scowled at the apparatus. "But it's not supposed to tickle."

"Well, it tickles," he said, twitching as he fought for control. "Ohhh, Mimi—it really—" Then he suddenly lost the fight and broke out in abandoned gasps and gulps of laughter.

It felt as if his feet were being attacked by feathers, relentlessly poking, twiddling, and stroking. And no matter how he jerked his feet to avoid it, the tickling continued— right inside his boots! The tickling sensation worked its way up his legs just as she had, and soon the sensitive backs of his knees and inner surface of his thighs were involved! He squirmed and raked one foot against the other, trying to scratch, and he almost succeeded. But another surge of agonized laughter rolled over him, and while he was trying to conquer that wave, invisible fingers attacked his waist and began wriggling and brushing up his ticklish sides to his armpits. He jerked and twisted and laughed that much harder.

"Oh, Mimi—" he gasped. "*Ple-e-ease*—"

"Where does it tickle?" she demanded, wringing her hands.

"Everywhere!" he roared, then was off in another peal of laughter.

She ran to shut off the magnetizer and hurried back to help him up. He was lying limp against the table, letting the eruptions of laughter wash through him and die away.

When he finally drew a breath and turned his head to look at her, his eyes were moist.

"Lord, I haven't laughed like this in years," he said, swallowing back a chuckle. "Your dotty old aunt paid a thousand pounds for a customized tickling machine!" And he erupted into spasms of laughter again.

There was something so contagious and liberating about his laughter that she began to laugh, too. It was as if years of bottled glee were rolling from him, and they caught her up in their long suppressed tide.

"It's not supposed to tickle," she protested, red-faced and gasping. "I don't know what could have gone wrong."

"It's all right," he assured her, struggling up to a sitting position. He wiped his eyes and managed a deep, shuddering breath. "I won't hold it against your Aunt Caroline. This seems to be my week for odd things to happ—" He stopped dead, staring at his boots. They were smoking.

"Agghhh!" He began kicking his feet. "My boots are on fire!" He finally managed to pull one off, and Mimi somehow wrenched the other from his thrashing foot and tossed it onto the floor. They stared in mutual horror at the tiny wisps of smoke curling up from the toes of his immaculate boots.

Graham began to laugh again, this time in huge, bone-jarring convulsions of laughter that he couldn't seem to stop. Mimi tried calling his name, then shaking him. He just stared at her and went off on another, breathless round of mirth, holding his sides. She ran for help.

Halfway down the hall, she met Shaddar, hurrying toward the laboratory; close behind him were her aunts, bustling along with frowns of concern on their faces. They had apparently heard the ruckus in the laboratory and were coming to investigate.

The old ladies found poor Mister Hamilton in desperate straits, doubled over, breathless, weak with convulsive laughter. He slid off the table to greet them, and his legs were so weak they would scarcely support him. Before their anxious eyes, he made a last valiant effort to achieve sobriety by holding his breath. His cheeks puffed, his eyes bulged . . . and he slowly turned purple and passed straight out of consciousness.

Mimi and Shaddar caught him before his head hit the floor again. And for the second time in as many days, the manservant hauled Graham's unconscious form up onto his shoulders and carried him back to the guest room.

"Miranda," Aunt Caroline said, her hands folded and her mouth pursed with displeasure, "you have a bit of explaining to do."

"I just brought him here to tell him about the cost of the custom metallurgy for your experiments, Aunt Caroline. I was demonstrating your magnetizing table, and he said he couldn't feel anything, so I turned up the power. Then he claimed it tickled, and before I knew it he couldn't stop laughing. Then he saw his boots smoking . . ." She pointed to Graham's discarded footgear, and Aunt Caroline's eyes widened in horror.

"His boots caught fire?" Caroline croaked.

Mimi winced and nodded. "I'm sorry, Aunt Caroline, but something must have gone wrong with the apparatus."

"I'm sure it's nothing to worry about, Mimi dear." Phoebe patted Mimi's tightly clasped hands. "Now go . . . see to poor Mister Hamilton."

When Mimi was gone, Phoebe picked up one of Graham's scorched boots and waggled it in Caroline's crimson face with a taunting chortle. "Well, Caroline, I don't know about his *passions,* but you and your electrical enhancers managed to set the fellow's boots on fire!"

The next day dawned unseasonably balmy for the end of October. Even it had been a howling blizzard outside, Graham Hamilton would still have risen, dressed, and set off on foot for the local village, before breakfast. He had to get out of that house for a while, away from the scene of his humiliations, away from his own incomprehensible behavior, and most of all, away from the distracting and desirable Mimi Edgethorn.

He shoved his hands into his coat pockets and stalked along the road toward the village, letting the crisp autumn air curl through his lungs and savoring the steady warmth of the sun on his face. The ordinariness of it was a balm for his harried soul. His entire life had been turned upside down and inside out in the last three days.

Three days? he thought. It seemed like a bloody lifetime since he'd come roaring off to Devon, a self-styled knight errant, determined to do battle with the old dragons who watched over Miranda Edgethorn.

He paused on the dusty road to stare out over the cliffs, across the sparkling white-capped bay. He had taken an unthinkably personal interest in Miranda Edgethorn's situation, right from the start. And he had convinced himself it was his pride in the reputation of his law firm that made him so determined to set things straight. But, he admitted now, he had felt an oddly personal link with the little orphan girl who had been sent to live with a trio of crusty old maiden aunts. Too well, he remembered being carted off to an elderly uncle's house as a child.

He had arrived at Asher House to find not a child, but a very determined young woman, who wanted neither his help nor his interference. And then he'd stumbled across her old aunts engaged in God knows what that first night, and had the misfortune to run smack into her immediately afterward. He closed his eyes and clenched his teeth, shuddering through another potent dose of humiliation at the memory of their encounter on the stairs: him in his nightshirt, grappling and tussling bodily with her while babbling that her old aunts were witches. She had politely told him to go sleep it off.

Perhaps he had been a bit cup-shot, but that didn't explain what he'd seen or why the memory of it still had a strangely powerful effect on him. At the slightest nudge of recall, it took substance once more in his mind and senses, full-blown and hauntingly real—the bloodred firelight; the withered faces and gnarled hands; the pulsing, colored vapors; the spinning wheels and sparks . . .

His heart was racing and his hands were clenched into fists even now, as he stood at the side of a public road in broad daylight. He shook off that disturbing memory and began to walk again, with longer, more determined strides.

Perfume, Mimi said. He had seen her old Aunt Flora distilling and blending fragrances to produce some exotic perfume. And she'd shown him the proof of Aunt Flora's expensive and eccentric, but otherwise innocuous, avocation. But her demonstration of Flora's creations, meant to allay his suspicions, had raised more questions than it answered. What the hell kind of perfume sent a man into giddy, spiraling raptures and caused him to see and feel and taste, as well as smell things? It had partly explained his bizarre compulsion to sniff and rub against Mimi—it was undoubtedly her perfume. But a few boiled flowers and a dollop of ambergris did *not* render a man bloody well unconscious! There had to be something besides a bit of toilet water involved.

And there was Mimi's explanation of the wheels and lightning and sparks: he'd seen some of Aunt Caroline's electrical apparatus in operation, she said. Perfectly reasonable—except for the things it didn't explain, like the strange sensations that had plagued him in Mimi's presence and why he'd been damn near tickled to death by a table and a few coils of wire! He slid his hand beneath his coat to massage his ribs, which were still sore from his laughing binge. There had to be something besides a bit of electricity and magnetism involved.

But what?

He stopped dead on a rise overlooking the village. What else?

Magic. The old ladies had been working a bit of magic on him—trying to get rid of him so they could have Mimi all to themselves again!

But no sooner had he completed the thought than the logical rational side of him rebelled at being forced to defend such a wild and fanciful conclusion. There wasn't supposed to be any such thing as magic or witches; he didn't believe in such stuff! But if it wasn't *magic*, the debate raged in his head, just what in the hell *was* it that had taken over his senses and reactions and made him act against his very nature?

Shoving aside his troubling questions about Asher House, he strode into the sleepy village and made his way to the local smithy to inquire whether they might know something about his missing horse. They did. The beast had been found wandering around by a local farmer and brought to the local livery stable, to await claiming by its owner. Greatly relieved, he retrieved his bags and paid the smith for his trouble. Then, with his mud-stained document pouches slung over his shoulder, he inquired of the local postmaster, who ran both the local dry goods shop and the tavern, if there had been word from his firm or his clerk. There was none. Graham sighed and sat down in the pump room for a bit of breakfast and a hot, bracing mug of tea. As he sipped, he chatted with the postmaster-cum-tavernkeeper, who seemed impressed to hear he was all the way out from London and staying at Asher House.

"Odd old things, them Asher sisters," the fellow mused. "But always hospitable and willin' to help. And their niece . . ." He sighed. "Pretty as a picture."

Graham's interest piqued, and he would have asked the fellow a few questions, but a matron trailed by a string of freshly scrubbed children bustled in, demanding to know if the crackers and party favors she ordered had come in. The tavernkeeper introduced her as the local rector's wife. When she learned Graham was a guest at Asher House, her manner warmed considerably.

"Why, Miss Phoebe Asher was at our house just a day or so ago," she said. "She does readings of the head, you know." She pulled her plump chin back to counter her glow of pride as she pulled her eldest boy in front of her and patted his head. "She says Bertrand here has a great deal of development in his regions of 'dignity,' 'veneration,' 'firmness,' and 'faith.' True *bishop* material if ever she's seen it." She turned to the tavernkeeper. "Now about my crackers and favors . . ."

When the rector's wife moved away, the tavern man explained: "Her and the rector, they're havin' a bit of a social on All Hallows' Eve. Determined to keep the young'uns out of mischief"—he glanced around warily—

"and outta the woods." He delivered a verdict on their efforts: "Fuss an' bother, if you ask me. Nobody goes into the woods on Halloween around here, anyway."

Prickles ran up the back of Graham's neck. "And why is that?" he asked, as casually as he could. The tavernkeeper scowled and leaned closer with a confidential air.

"The dance, of course." At Graham's frown, he elaborated. "The witches' dance. Everybody in the county knows that on Halloween, witches gather to dance in the woods, out north of the village." His voice dropped to a whisper. "There's a meadow where nothin' but starflowers grows. I seen it myself. And they say"—his eyes widened— "that if a body gets caught out in the woods that night, he's forced to join in their unholy dance . . . or _die_." He drew back, his manner secretive and certain.

"They truly believe such stuff?" Graham asked thickly, his toes curling inside his fire-damaged boots.

"We lost two fellers out in th' woods a few years back. They didn't believe it and sat out in the woods to see for 'emselves. Nobody's seen or heard from 'em since." He nodded smartly to punctuate the truth of his tale. Just then another customer came into the tavern, and he was pulled away to wait on him.

But Graham had heard quite enough. Witches. The whole village believed the woods were haunted by _witches_. In his mind, an inescapable linkage was made: the witches who danced—and his vision of the old Asher sisters, chanting and dancing. It was too much of a coincidence to ignore. He had just made up his mind to ask the tavern man what he knew about the supposed witches when the rector's wife reappeared with her hands full of parcels and a broad, ingratiating smile.

"I didn't think to ask," she said apologetically, "since the Asher sisters socialize so seldom. But we'd love to have you and Miss Miranda attend our party on All Hallows' Eve."

Graham stared at her in surprise, then mumbled something about having other plans for that night. He stood watching her depart with her future bishop and his brothers and sisters, and wondered at her attitude. The parson's wife and the tavernkeeper—and probably the rest of the village— not only failed to connect the Ashers with their "witchy" superstitions, they seemed to actually respect, even revere, the old ladies. Was he the only one around who suspected— or knew—the truth about them?

5

THAT same morning, Mimi came down to breakfast determined to banish Graham Hamilton's fears regarding her aunts—and failing that, to declare that she would use what was left of her inheritance to fight him in court. But when she entered the breakfast room, she found her old aunts sunk into the doldrums.

"Such glum faces," she chided as she took her seat at the table. "You'll scare Mister Hamilton away."

"He's already gone," Aunt Phoebe announced, with a miserable sigh. "Shaddar went to wake him this morning, and he was already up and gone."

"Left," Aunt Caroline confirmed, "without so much as a word of farewell."

"Having his boots catch fire was probably too much for him," Aunt Flora surmised, wagging her head. "A pity. He had such a marvelously keen nose on him."

Mimi heard only part of what they said. Graham gone? He had just risen and dressed and left the house without so much as a "good riddance" or an "I'll see you in the courts"? It felt to her as if the bottom had just dropped out of her stomach. *Gone.* He had washed his hands of them and charted a course straight back to his fashionable London offices. And she would probably never see him again. She declared she wasn't hungry and excused herself from the table.

As the old aunts watched her go, Phoebe sniffled and dabbed at a tear. "I was afraid of this. I should have checked his region of conscientiousness, first thing. There's nothing worse than being in love with a man who is deficient in his 'conscientiousness.'"

Mimi went straight to the study and stood in the midst of it, staring at the ledgers and receipts, then at the stuffed chair by the door, where he had sat. She thought of his handsome gray eyes, in all their moods and guises of his lips, firm one minute, soft the next. The sound of his laughter echoed in her ears, the feel of his embrace lingered in her skin, the excitement of his presence still burned in her heart. She realized that against her own best judgment, she had begun to nourish a bit of hope regarding Graham Hamilton.

It was a silly thing, really, daydreaming about him. He was her adversary. And even if they weren't at odds over her aunts, they would still be an unthinkable match. He was a handsome, wealthy solicitor, the head of a prestigious old firm who probably had ladies swooning all over London. And she was only a country girl, the product of an admittedly unconventional household and upbringing, without well-placed family or social connections, and without even a proper inheritance to recommend her in marriage. It was a pure waste of time, thinking about the soft way he said her name and the tenderness with which he touched her face.

She sank into the chair by the desk and wrapped her arms about her waist. Her future was here with her old aunts; she had always known that. But somehow that prospect had been a lot easier to bear before she had glimpsed an impossibly sweet "might have been" with Graham Hamilton.

She roused some time later and began to gather up the ledgers and to stuff the packets of receipts back into their boxes. Her fingers trembled over the bits of binding ribbon she had seen him stroke while deep in thought. She swallowed hard and squared her shoulders and turned to place the books on their shelf—and stopped in her tracks.

Coming through the drawing room, growing louder, was the sound of heavy footsteps—boots with char marks on the toes and heels? Her heart lurched in her chest. When she turned, Graham was looming in the doorway, his hair wind-ruffled and his cheeks cold-reddened. Across his shoulder was a mud-stained leather document pouch, and in his eye was a light of purpose. They stared at each other for a long, decisive moment.

"Now, Mimi Edgethorn," he declared, laying the bags on the table and working the buckles free, "we'll finally get to the facts and figures. I walked into the village this morning and learned someone had found my horse and taken him to the livery. I was able to retrieve the documents which contain incontrovertible proof that your aunts initiated the massive and ruinous withdrawals that violated the terms of your trust."

His smile should have seemed wicked and vengeful to Mimi; it anticipated her aunts' entanglement in legal and perhaps criminal proceedings. But for some reason, she thought it was the most beautiful thing she'd ever seen.

The pleasure that bloomed in her face dazzled him. She was so incredibly lovely. He pulled his eyes away and glanced down at the table where a few packets of receipts still lay. And she was so marvelously organized. He'd never met a woman who understood the basics of a good accounting system, much less actually organized one. He prayed she would also understand the implications of the numbers he was about to put before her.

"Here are letters and the charge drafts." He opened the pouch, and his jaw dropped as he stared in disbelief at the disorganized, mud-caked mess inside. His papers, his proof . . . they looked as if they had been taken out and ground underfoot in a mud puddle, then returned to the pouch to molder. In horror, he pried first one, then another ruined document from the stack. The ones that didn't tear apart were unreadable, smeared beyond recognition. And some were actually beginning to disintegrate. He looked at Mimi in disbelief.

"B-but . . . it was all here . . . and now look at it!"

"I'm sorry, Graham." She couldn't quite contain her pleasure at seeing the mess, and couldn't quite express it, either. She looked up at him with perfect sincerity. "But perhaps it's for the best."

"How can you possibly believe it's for the best, Mimi?" he said, running an exasperated hand through his hair as he stared at the quiet determination in her face. "You started out with more than eighty-three thousand pounds, enough to provide you income for a lifetime, or a fine dowry. And now you're down to just more than fourteen thousand." He could see that the numbers surprised her, but after a moment, she dismissed it with a bittersweet smile.

"Money is just . . . money."

"Don't you understand what they've done to you, Mimi? To your future?"

"Perhaps not. But I do understand what they've done *for* me, Graham. And that's just as important." When he settled a dark look on her, she screwed up her courage and prayed that the man who kissed her so tenderly and insisted on protecting her so earnestly would also listen to her. "Will you walk with me, in Aunt Flora's garden? Will you let me try to explain?"

He looked down at her slender hand on his sleeve and felt himself going soft inside. He nodded, and she led him through the center hall and past the breakfast room to a side door, where she snatched a thick shawl from a peg. Once outside, they passed through an old stone portico and emerged in a huge, impeccably kept garden. He paused to survey the brick paths, bushes trimmed in fanciful topiary, small delicate trees, and vast beds of late-blooming chrysanthemums. Beyond was the glass dome of Aunt Flora's conservatory, and he could clearly see both wings of the house and the old stone tower.

Mimi led him along the tranquil paths, pointing out Aunt Flora's favorite flowers and aromatic shrubs, with frequent mention of having helped to plant and prune them. He watched the glow of her cheeks and the unconscious sway of her body, and began bracing for the disaster that always accompanied a close encounter with her. But she paused by a bench set under an arbor and looked at him with a soft, feminine radiance in her eyes, and he simply had to know what she wanted to say to him. When she sat down and patted the bench, he sat down, too.

"I love this garden." She looked around with a sigh, then turned to him. "I don't know if I can make you understand. When I came here to live with my old aunts, my father had just died and I felt as if my whole world had been ripped from me. We had only each other, my father and I. He was a physician, a very sober and diligent man, devoted to his profession and to me. And I adored him and did my best, in my ten-year-old way, to take care of him after my mother died. But he became ill . . . and died. And when they packed me up and sent me off to live with three old aunts I never even knew I had . . . well, I just didn't want to go on.

"I arrived here a frightened and desperately unhappy child. And little by little, my dear old aunts stuffed the life and the spirit back into me."

The scowl on his face worried her, and she threw caution to the wind and reached out boldly to take his hands in hers. "Do you know . . . the first month I was here, I had chocolate cake morning, noon, and night . . . at every single meal."

"A terrible indulgence," he declared with parental outrage. "Why, it could have ruined your teeth, stunted your growth—"

"I suppose it might have . . . if I had eaten it. You see, I never even touched it. Not for a whole month. I had lost my love of sweets . . . and just about everything else. I couldn't bring myself to enjoy anything." Her eyes grew luminous and haunting as the vulnerable little girl in her was revealed. She held him spellbound. "I had forgotten how to have fun.

"Aunt Caroline read me books, all sorts of books, by the hour. Books about faraway lands and famous people, stories about animals and adventures, princesses and dragons. She painted pictures so vividly in my mind that I couldn't help but be delighted. Then Aunt Phoebe made me a bright yellow smock to wear over my dresses, trimmed it in the wildest shade of purple she could find, and sewed big, red pockets on it. And she knitted me matching purple stockings. They let me wear the brightest, silliest clothes imaginable . . . just for fun. And slowly, I learned to smile again.'' She willed the gratitude she felt to flow through their joined hands, carrying its warmth to his heart. His stern-set features softened, and his pale eyes darkened to a gentle dove-gray.

''And Aunt Flora brought me into her precious garden and taught me to plant flowers and prune and weed them . . . to care for living things. She said that anytime I started to feel sad, thinking about my father's death, I should come and plant a flower here in his memory.'' She laughed with a wistful lilt. ''By that autumn, she had a whole garden full of marigolds named Peter. And she didn't seem to mind a bit.''

With poignant clarity, he could suddenly see her on her knees in her yellow smock and purple stockings, planting both tears and flowers, with a smudge of dirt on her cheek. That lonely, hurt little girl had grown up to be a woman of warmth and spirit and integrity. The old crows had to have done something right.

''They're odd and eccentric old things, I know that. And they're impractical and forgetful sometimes . . . and they don't always make sense. But I owe them my very heart.''

He felt her hands squeezing his, and there was a painful tightness in his throat and a hollow burning at the backs of his eyes. His smile bore traces of pain.

''I'm glad they knitted you purple socks.'' He freed one of his hands and ran his fingertips down the warm curve of her cheek. ''I wish someone had knitted them for me.''

It was in that moment, hearing that precious admission of longing, that Mimi realized she was falling in love with Graham Hamilton. She knew because she wanted desperately to have been the one to knit those socks . . . wished with all her heart she could have been there when his parents died and he had been sent to live with an Uncle Throckmorton.

She would have asked him about his own childhood, but he leaned closer, and the sweet heat of anticipation filled her lips. Then he took her face between his hands and tilted it down to plant a soft kiss in the middle of her forehead. When she looked at him again, his eyes were shining, and she felt as if she'd just been kissed on her very soul.

That evening, after a sumptuous and surprisingly genial dinner, Mimi and Graham retired to the drawing room with the old aunts for "civilized amusements." Flora played spirited Spanish numbers on a guitar, Caroline recited selections from a translated Norwegian epic, and Mimi played the pianoforte with enchanting skill.

Graham had watched Mimi's aunts closely through dinner, and what he saw confused him. He had come straight back to Asher House that morning with the intention of confronting Mimi with what he'd learned in the village, the talk of witches in the immediate area. But then he'd seen her standing in the study with her hands full of ledgers and her face glowing at the sight of him, and he'd decided to simply let the more rational evidence—the financial records he had recovered—speak for him. They would be enough, he had thought, to indict the old ladies. Then he'd found his proof destroyed and himself immersed in Mimi's story . . . then in Mimi herself. And his intentions had been turned upside down and inside out, once again.

Now, as he watched the old ladies, he detected the genuine warmth in their manner toward Mimi and their maternal pride in her accomplishment. For the first time, he noticed the arthritic hitch in the old ladies' gait, the dry crackle in their voices, and the tremble in their hands as they gestured. Their skin was age-thinned and fragile, and despite an irascible twinkle, their eyes were faded. He began to see them as eccentric old ladies, stubborn and impractical—and even nonsensical at times. And he realized he was seeing them through Mimi's eyes.

The softening in his thoughts disturbed him, and he countered it by conjuring up another mental picture of them— with grotesquely aged faces, frizzled hair, and gnarled hands. But neither picture quite satisfied him. Were they dotty old aunts . . . or canny old witches? Were they unintentionally reckless . . . or calculating and manipulative? He was desperate for some way to get at the truth about them.

"How about a hand or two of cards?" Aunt Caroline was saying, when he roused from his musings. In a twinkling, she had produced a deck of cards from a drawer in a nearby table.

"But," Graham protested, trying to think of a way out of it, "we can't play with five."

"Oh, we won't," Aunt Caroline said, shuffling the cards. "We never play with Phoebe. She always cheats."

Phoebe snorted and glared at Caroline. "You mean, I always *win*. As it happens, I have a bit of knitting to do, anyway," she declared heatedly. "I've started Mister Hamilton a nightcap." She reached in the tapestried knitting bag by her chair and pulled out a small ring of yarn that had been worked onto needles. Caroline and Flora exchanged dread-filled looks as Phoebe advanced on Graham's chair and he shrank back in it.

"No, no, really . . . I have no need of—"

"That guest room is drafty as a barn, and I won't have you catching your death!" Phoebe declared, trying desperately to thrust the ring of knitting over the moving target of his head.

"Miss Asher—please!" He feinted and dodged, trying to escape her groping.

"For goodness' sake, Phoebe." Caroline finally yanked her sister away by the arm. "If the man doesn't *want* a nightcap—"

"Well—where has the time gone?" Flora hurried over to insert herself bodily between her tussling sisters. "I think we've had a very full day," she declared irritably, wrenching their hands apart with a disgusted look and hauling them toward the door. "We should retire . . . and leave Mimi and Mister Hamilton to secure the fire and snuff out the lights."

Mimi bit her lip as she watched them go, then she turned to Graham and found him scowling.

"Your Aunt Phoebe," he declared indignantly, "has designs on my head."

"I'm afraid you're right." She laughed. "Please don't be offended. She's—"

"—a phrenologist," he supplied. "I heard about her head readings in the village this morning."

Mimi smiled at his transparent suspicions. "There's nothing occult or unnatural about it. Phrenology is a well-recognized practice."

"It's hokum."

"And Aunt Phoebe is a gifted reader."

"She's a loony."

"First a thief, then a witch, now a loony. Are we making progress or not?" A mischievous twinkle appeared in her eye. "Did I mention that she's an inventor, too?"

"No." Graham's eyes widened at the look on her face. "Ohhh, no—"

"Oh, yes." She took his hands and pulled him to his feet, but he planted his heels and stiffened. She tossed him a challenge she knew he couldn't resist. "Don't you want to investigate three thousand pounds' worth of imported Swiss clock gears and machinery?"

"Three thous—!" He grabbed the candles, and they were out the door in a flash. They soon stood in another large chamber, lined with tables and shelves and the debris of invention. As Mimi lighted a second set of candles, Graham edged forward to scrutinize a large, sheet-draped shape in the middle of the room. Together, they rolled back the cover and revealed a large, cabinetlike box, fitted with levers and knobs . . . and something that looked like a cross between a hat and a bushel basket, filled with wires and flat-headed nails, which was suspended over a stool. Just looking at it gave Graham a dry mouth and sweaty palms. It appeared to be another perfect opportunity for abject humiliation.

"This is Aunt Phoebe's cranial mapper," Mimi said proudly. "It may be the very first machine ever to make accurate, detailed maps of the potential in a human head. This cabinet"—she dragged him to the bank of dials and levers—"is filled with precision works, capable of measuring and recording the dimensions of the head to a hundredth of an inch. Want to try it?''

''Absolutely not,'' he said grimly, eyeing the machinery, thinking it looked positively diabolical.

''I'll show you, then.'' She hurried over to set the dials and levers, turned on the electrical power, and settled on the stool. Graham had to be coaxed into closing the final switch, but soon the machine was whirring and clunking merrily. When the sounds ended, Mimi ducked out of the mapper with a smile and retrieved a silhouette drawing of a human head, with numbers printed randomly over it, from the machine. ''Come on . . . your turn. It doesn't hurt a bit.''

''That's what you said about the magnetizing table,'' he grumbled. ''I've made quite enough of a fool of myself. Passing out from sniffing perfume, laughing myself into oblivion . . . You probably already think I'm the most peculiar man who ever walked.''

''No, I don't. I'm rather used to eccentric behavior, even a bit fond of it. And I think you're—''

His whole body suddenly came to attention. ''You think I'm what?''

''Wonderful.''

It came out on a breath, before she had a chance to think whether it was wise or not. It must have been the right thing to say, for it produced a boyish, lopsided smile on his face. With a deep breath, he ducked under the mapper to seat himself on the stool. When the machine started to work, Mimi could see his hands blanching as they gripped his knees. Her smile broadened. He really was the most adorable man.

When the noise stopped, Mimi released him from the contraption and held up the paper containing the numerical map of his head. ''Well, here you are—your character, your talents, your destiny.''

''So . . . what does it say about me?'' He gave his still-tingling head a good rubbing.

''I haven't the faintest idea.'' She shrugged with an impish smile and set his cranial map aside with hers. ''Only Aunt Phoebe can interpret the numbers. The rest of us have to do it the old-fashioned way, feeling a person's bumps.'' Her cheeks warmed under his intensely personal look.

Lord, there was nothing he wanted more at that moment than Mimi Edgethorn feeling his bumps—every last one of them! "Show me," he said, his voice thickening as he lifted her hand and gave her slender fingers a sultry glance and a coaxing caress.

She led him to a straight-backed chair and stood before him. Her skin glowed warmly in the candlelight as she nudged forward and her knees made contact with his. She wet her lips and swallowed hard, then set her fingertips to his eyebrows, feathering a touch over them, pausing to rub here and there along that ridge around his eye.

"Doctor Gall determined that human intelligence and character are located in thirty-six well-defined regions of the brain, which correspond to the shape of the outer skull. This one"—her thumbs stroked the outer edges of his eyes and arched over his brows—"is your area of 'perceptives.' It indicates how observant you are. This is your sense of 'time and tune.''' She massaged his temples and ran her fingers up into his silky hair. "Ummm . . . I can feel you have a very nice sense of rhythm," she observed breathlessly. The throb in his temples migrated through her fingertips and began to drum in her blood.

"And you seem to be quite developed in your regions of 'ideality' and 'acquisitiveness.' But that's balanced nicely by your 'conscientiousness' and 'veneration.''' She could feel the intense heat of his gaze on her lips, and she licked them. He was so close . . . so solid . . . so male . . . Tingles were rippling up and down her front, beneath her properly laced corset. "And it's quite obvious," she said, rubbing the top of his head, "that you possess a great deal of 'firmness.'''

"Firm . . . ohhh yes . . . I can be very firm." The low rumble from deep in his throat drew her gaze to his. His features were bronzed, his eyes were molten silver rings around dark wells of simmering heat. She felt herself melting into those eyes, turning hot and liquid inside.

"And here . . ." Her hands slid to the back of his head,

curling in his hair, caressing, exploring as she sank deeper
and deeper into the fluid heat he was generating around her.
"Here is your area of 'friendship.'" His hands were hot
as they closed on her waist and he drew her between his
thighs. "And below that is . . ."

"Is what?" he demanded, nuzzling and nibbling the lace
that trickled coyly down the front of her dress, over her
breasts. The sight of his sensual lips, moving, caressing
her lace as a proxy for what lay beneath it, set the tips of
her breasts on fire.

"Your 'amativeness.'" She held her breath as his arms
closed slowly, relentlessly around her, reeling her to his
broad chest, clasping her against his hardened male frame
so that she felt the swelling of his passion. "You seem to
have a lump . . . on your region of amativeness."

"Oh, Mimi, I have more than a lump." He groaned and
writhed on his seat as he pressed hard against her and
threaded his fingers into her hair. In a heartbeat, he joined
their mouths in a searing kiss that melted all the barriers
between them. His mouth was so hot and soft and caressing
. . . Then he was rising, rubbing against her as he gained
his feet.

"Aunt Phoebe says a man and woman should have compatible . . . bumps," she murmured into the corner of his
mouth. His wicked chuckle rumbled through her lips and
trickled down the back of her throat.

"Then by all means . . . we should see if our bumps are
compatible." He lifted her and carried her to an old armless
settee he had spotted in the shadows. Soon he was seated
with her on his lap, his hands sliding up her sides and
spreading over her breasts. The rigid boning of her corset
and the soft bulge of her breasts above it made a starkly
erotic contrast against his burning palms. "Oh, Mimi . . .
such lovely—" Her mouth on his cut off his next words,
and a moment later her hands left his neck to slide the draped
silk of her dress down her shoulders. He groaned as her
tongue darted softly over his, and he accepted her invitation.
His fingers pried the tightly budded tips of her breasts above
the restrictive edge of her boning and ran his hands over

them again and again . . . soft, sinuous abrasions that made her gasp and squirm delectably.

He pulled back to look at her sitting on his lap, her eyes heavy with desire, her dress peeled down around her shoulders, her full, silky breasts and taut velvety nipples bared to him. She was perfection, sensuality and innocence, rare clarity of heart, cloaked in feminine mystery. And a moment later, she was working the buttons of his shirt. "What are you . . . ?"

"Seeing if we're compatible . . . my bumps and yours," she whispered, tugging his shirt open and pushing it aside. Breath stopped in his throat as she shifted on his lap and pressed her nipples against his bare chest, slowly, instinctively rubbing against him. It was his dream come true . . . his bare chest, her sleek breasts . . .

"Oh, Mimi, sweet Mimi—" He clasped her tightly against him and shuddered through the shattering eruption of need that rocked him. "I have other lumps—" he said in a rasp. And he slid her onto the settee beside him and lowered her onto her back, pressing his length against her, letting her feel his heat, his maleness . . . finding the rounded parts of her, molding his hands to her woman's heat . . . and letting her find him. Her touch was gentle, exploratory, then her fingers wrapped him, claiming him, and he stilled, unable to absorb one more drop of pleasure without exploding.

In the dim light, his eyes found hers . . . liquid and shimmering, receptive. "Your other lumps . . . should we see if we're compatible there, too?" For a long, precious moment the possibility stretched between them, hot, breathtaking, perfect. Almost.

"We're compatible, sweet Mimi," he whispered with all the urgency in his blood compressed into each syllable. "Can't you feel it . . . in your skin, in your blood, in your very bones? Lord—I'd never even imagined a wanting like this. I'm half afraid I'll burst into flame every time you touch me."

She cradled his face in her hands, and he turned it to kiss each of her palms. "I'm not sure what's happening to me,

Mimi. I don't know if I'm dreaming or losing my sanity. Everything I wanted, everything I was, it's all turned upside down since I came here. I've tried to think how long it had been since I smelled a flower, or a pretty woman's perfume, and I couldn't remember a single time, a single event. Lord, Mimi, did I never smell anything wonderful before now . . . before you? And laughter—I can't remember a hale, hearty laugh in years, no expression of joy, no delight deep enough to actually penetrate my body. Suffocating years without the release of laughter . . . Can it possibly be true?''

He paused and showered savoring kisses on her glowing cheeks, her eyelids, her temples, and her nose. "You made me smell and laugh and think and feel . . . You're a feast for the senses, Mimi, a banquet of life." His voice poured over her like heated cream. "And I want every morsel of you."

She closed her eyes, gathering those precious words into her heart. Then she arched, offering him the laces at her back. "My corset," she whispered.

"My tie . . . my collar," he countered.

Suddenly, all was a sweet flurry of heated yearning, fumbling fingers, and shifting limbs. Her laces snarled, his tie knotted, and the button on his collar seemed to shrink. She twisted to give him access, and he slid to give her room, and rolled straight off the old settee, landing with a thud.

She sat up, her eyes wide and glowing. "Perhaps it would be easier for you to reach my laces if I just stood up."

But the short fall had jolted more than just his frame; it had jarred his deeply ingrained sense of honor. When he helped her to her feet he paused, holding her hands and gazing at the sweetly disheveled picture she made . . . with her curls tumbling onto her shoulders, her bodice and corset cover peeled aside, and her rosy nipples peeping above the edge of her boning. She seemed so girlish, so open and vulnerable. Every protective instinct he'd ever harbored toward little Miranda Edgethorn suddenly roared to life in him again to do battle with his own desire. After a long moment he kissed her fingertips, then tenderly began to restore her clothes.

"Graham?" she breathed, a tremor of uncertainty in her voice. In the shadows, her eyes were great, burnished disks of wonder.

"I'm here to protect you, Mimi, and I will." His smile grew wistful. "Even if it's from myself. I want it to be right for you. No . . . I want it to be *perfect*." He caressed her cheek and ran his fingertips across her shoulder.

She shivered, feeling that touch on her very heart. "Perfect," she murmured. "I'd like that. But I'd also like it to be *soon*."

He laughed.

Somewhere in the hallway, as he walked Mimi back to her room, Graham realized he was in love with her. *Love*. The divine madness. The ultimate mystery. The conqueror of kings. He was passionately, feverishly, distractedly in love with sweet, mystical, quixotic Mimi. And he was solidly, sensibly, understandably in love with orderly, logical, and compassionate Mimi. She was a woman who fitted every part of him: his hands, his habits, his very soul. And she had breathed joy and passion back into the arid order and stultifying predictability of his life.

He stood in the dark hallway for a long moment after she said good night and slipped through her door, carrying the candles with her. The heady impact of it washed over him again and again, like joyous, foaming waves. He understood now: it wasn't just the prospect of saving Miranda Edgethorn that had sent him charging out of London. He'd been fleeing the suffocating limitations of his overplanned existence—searching, seeking, but unsure of what it was he wanted or needed. He'd come to the rescue, not realizing he was in equal need of saving. And he'd run straight to Mimi and her crazy old aunts . . .

At the thought of them, his smile faded. Mimi's aunts. They were a threat to his love, the one point of contention that still stood between him and Mimi. There had to be a way to learn the truth! He looked around the gloomy hallway, realizing that it looked much the way it had that first night. The notion seized him; he had to find that tower room again, had to see it for himself.

As his eyes adjusted to the dark, he retraced his steps down the east hallway, past the center stairs, and into the unfamiliar territory of the west wing. The wall became rough stone once more, and he found that iron-bound door. It was so similar to his recollections that he had to fight back a wave of remembered panic. He entered the tower and began to climb through the blackness, keeping to the side of the wall, feeling his way along.

The doorway at the top loomed before he realized it, and the door stood ajar as it had that first night. Dim, silvery light spilled over the landing, beckoning, lighting the way into the unknown. With a thudding heart and a dry mouth, he stepped through the door . . . into the moon-drenched silence.

The chamber had an odd, undisturbed air about it; the atmosphere seemed heavy and stale. He located a candlestand on the mantel and managed to light the stubby candles. By that dim golden glow, he surveyed the odd bits of wire and metal, the crocks and coils and piping that littered the tables, and found them to be very like what he'd seen in the old ladies' workshops and laboratory. There was one difference; these were covered with a notable layer of dust. He tested it with his fingers . . . and felt a part of his anxiety slide. No one had used this stuff in a very long time.

He drew a heavy breath, and a flush of chagrin spread from underneath his collar. The chamber was as he recalled it . . . *almost*. And those small but significant differences made him doubt his own perceptions. How much of it was real and how much had been manufactured by his herb-tainted wits? He had to know. For Mimi's sake, for the sake of the future he wanted to make with her, for his own sanity . . .

There was only one sure way to learn the truth. If they were witches, they would dance by moonlight . . . on Halloween . . . in the meadow where only starflowers grew.

6

P HOEBE barreled into the breakfast room the next morning, her eyes alight and her plump face crimson from
her run through the hallways. She lurched to her chair and
braced herself on it as she waved two pieces of paper at her
sisters. "I got it," she declared triumphantly. "The map
of his head. Mimi must have taken him to my workroom
last night after we retired." She held up one cranial map.
"This is Mimi's head. I've done her a hundred times, I'd
know her numbers anywhere." Then she brandished the
second paper. "And *this* is his!"

"Well?" Caroline demanded. "What did you learn?"

"He is well developed over all," Phoebe informed them,
savoring her pronouncement, "except in his 'parental love'
area. And wherever she's a bit shy of something, he's got
an abundance. Wherever he's deficient, she's got a plentiful
supply. Extraordinary, how complementary they are." She
scowled, pursing one corner of her mouth. "All except in
one area. You wouldn't happen to know if Mimi hit her
head on something recently? She's all swelled up in her
'amatives,' too—"

Just then Graham started through the doorway, and
Phoebe frantically stuffed the pages on the seat of her chair
and plopped her ample frame on top of them.

"Good morning, Mister Hamilton," the old ladies cho-
rused together.

"Good morning, ladies." He nodded, seeming a bit
preoccupied. But when Mimi entered the dining room, he
shot to his feet and looked at her as if she were made of
bonbons and peppermint drops. The boyish admiration that

warmed his countenance also warmed the cockles of the old ladies' hearts. They smiled and nodded secretively to one another.

"And what have you planned for today, Mister Hamilton?" Caroline inquired. "More poring through our books? Do give a care . . . we wouldn't want you taking an eyestrain or getting that disagreeable accountant's hump."

"I've finished with the books," he said without taking his eyes from Mimi. "And it's such a marvelous autumn day, I had hoped I could persuade Miss Edgethorn to take a walk with me."

"Oh, just excellent . . ." "Wonderful idea . . ." and "Do see the view of the bay from the cliffs!" the old ladies answered all at once. When he turned to them, they smiled so sweetly at him that he actually blushed.

Midmorning, he helped Mimi don her cloak, and together they strolled the paths along the cliffs overlooking the bay. When they reached a crumbling round wall and a pile of stone rubble that had once been a castle watchtower, he scrambled up onto the stones and took in the view. He called to Mimi and pulled her up to stand beside him. Wrapping his arms around her to steady her, he nuzzled her temples and the warm skin of her neck with his cold nose, and she laughed. From that vantage point, standing with their arms around each other, they gazed over the white-capped bay toward the ocean. Slowly they turned their attentions inland, to the village and the woods just north of it, along the road toward Asher House.

Graham asked her to walk through those autumn woods with him, and soon they were strolling hand in hand through fallen leaves, marveling at the colors and stopping occasionally to kiss. Mimi coaxed him into talking about his family, his childhood with crusty, irascible old Uncle Throckmorton, his partners, and his London house.

"Electrical lights and marble mantels—it sounds perfectly lovely," she said softly.

"I think it sounds lonely," he said, pausing and gazing intently at her. "Come with me to my big house, Mimi."

Her smile faded, and her heart beat faster. "Don't be silly. What would I do there?"

"I'm not being silly. I've never been more serious in my life. You'd do all the things women do—rearrange everything; spend money; organize people, places, and events . . . and generally make the world a more decent and enjoyable place." He strode through the leaves to take her hands in his. She was so adorably wide-eyed. "And, of course, you'd have to sleep with me," he said with a roguish twinkle in his eyes. It was wicked of him to shock her like this, but he just couldn't help himself—it sounded so deliciously indecent. And he'd never made an indecent proposal to a woman in his life.

"Sl-sleep with you?" she said, forcing the words past the tightening in her throat.

"Wives do that, I'm told." He countered her resistance and pulled her into his arms. "They sleep with their husbands. Marry me, Mimi, and come to live with me in London."

The longing his words generated in her was awful to behold. "But I can't be a wife, Graham. I don't have a proper dowry or family or social connections. I don't know anybody in London." He laid a finger against her lips and countered her objections point by point.

"I don't care about your money, Mimi. I'd want you if you had only the clothes on your back. And as for not knowing people in London, I know hordes of them and I'll arrange to introduce you, to as many or as few as you like. Knowing you, you'll soon have lots of friends and admirers."

It sounded so wonderful . . . Graham, London, a whole new life of her own! Her winging hopes were pierced by a sharp thought and plummeted back to earth. "But, Graham, my aunts. What about my aunts?"

What indeed. He'd been wondering that very thing for the last several days. What would the old things do without her? "I have a notion they'll survive." He took her face between his hands and delved deeply into her daisy-button-gold eyes. "They got along before you came, Mimi. They'll find a way to get along after you're gone.'' He brushed her lips with his and took a deep, steadying breath. "I love you, Mimi. And if they love you at all, they'll want you to have a life of your own."

They did love her and want her to have a life of her own! They'd spoken to her of marriage . . . "Wh-what?" She grasped the sides of his coat to keep from staggering. "What did you say?"

"I said, they have to let you have a life—"

"No, the other part—" She yanked urgently on his coat. "Say that other part again!"

His frown smoothed as he realized what she wanted. "I love you, sweet Mimi, and I want you to marry me."

"Oh, Graham!" She threw her arms around his neck and pulled him down to smother his face with kisses. "I love you, too!"

He lifted her and swung her around and around, laughing. When they staggered to a halt, she just had to expend the energy bubbling up in her or burst. She seized his hand and pulled him into a run. They began to chase each other like joyful children, darting around trees and stumps and half-bare bushes, teasing each other with threats of kisses and tickles. He caught up with her in a clearing and swept her into his arms, his eyes hot, his laughter booming free and clear. When they settled back to earth together, toe to toe and button to button, their breathless kisses deepened and softened, becoming achingly sweet.

It was some time before Graham lifted his head and re-focused his eyes enough to realize they were in a small clearing. He relaxed his hold on her and brushed wisps of her hair back from her rosy face. "Do you have the foggiest idea where we are?" he asked, taking a calming breath and clamping a stern hand on his escalating passions. "Not that I'd mind being lost with you . . ."

In the midst of tidying her wind-teased hair, she paused and shaded her eyes to look around. "Oh, I know this meadow. We're not lost." She smiled up at him. "Aunt Flora used to bring me here sometimes to pick flowers, when I was younger."

"Flowers?" He was staring past the toes of his boots to a trailing green plant that covered the ground everywhere in the clearing. He felt his muscles contracting, one by one. "What sort of flowers?"

"These," she said, raking her foot over the weedy growth beneath her feet, "among others. They're starflowers . . . tiny white blossoms with five points like stars, only they're not blooming just now. There used to be a big stand of sweet William over there." She pointed toward the far end of the meadow. "And we always found fragrant Devon violets in profusion around the edges of the meadow." She looked up to find his expression darkening as he stared at the starflowers under his feet. "What is it, Graham?" When he lifted his eyes to her, they were dark and guarded.

"You know what this place is, don't you?"

"Well, I thought I just said. It's where Aunt Flora and I used to—"

"It's the meadow where nothing but starflowers grow." They had found it, as he had both hoped and dreaded they would when he had asked her to come for a walk with him. He searched her, realizing that she didn't understand. "It's where the witches gather to dance on All Hallows' Eve. I heard about it in the village the other day. They come and dance among the starflowers."

The implication of his words struck Mimi like a blow in the stomach. She sucked in a shocked breath. "And you think . . . my old aunts . . ."

"It is suspiciously close to Asher House, Mimi. And after what I saw, I believe they're the ones everyone in the village talks about."

She gathered fistfuls of her cloak in her hands, staring at him. Hurt dulled the brilliant gold of her eyes. "You've lived with them . . . you've seen how generous and loving they are. And still you accuse them?" Already knowing the answer, she whirled and started for the house.

He jolted after her and caught her by the arm. "Please, Mimi . . . I don't mean to hurt you. I know why you love them. I can almost love them myself, for all they've given you. But I can't deny my own senses. I have to know whether it's true or not.'' He gritted his teeth, wishing he could take back his words and his wretched suspicions, lock them away in his own heart and mind forever. ''Don't you see, I have to know for my own sanity, for my peace of mind. I have to know because . . . I love you. And I don't want this between us any more. There's one way to settle it, once and for all time.''

He hesitated, then made himself say it. ''Tomorrow night is All Hallows' Eve. Come here with me and watch. If they don't come, then we'll know it was all just the herbs and the odd hour and their crazy inventions. And I'll never doubt them again.'' The plea in his face and words was filled with love and regret, and with a tiny spark of hope. ''Please, Mimi.''

She stared at him, wondering, hoping. Would it really be enough to satisfy him? If she came with him and her aunts didn't appear, would that really be the end of it? She prayed that it would, for she could never marry a man who believed such a terrible thing about her dear, dotty old aunts, her only family. There were tears in her eyes when she raised them to him.

''I'll come with you, Graham.''

The following night, All Hallows' Eve, the moon rose before sunset and waited patiently for its chance to shine. When darkness fell, the old aunts tottered off to bed, leaving Mimi and Graham alone by the fire in the old drawing room. They were oddly silent with each other, exchanging wistful looks and trying not to show how the waiting depressed them. Graham refused to think about what would happen if he were right—he wanted so desperately to be wrong. When he slid his hand over hers and she squeezed it, some of the tension constricting his chest eased.

The fire burned low and as they had agreed, they set the screens and made their way upstairs, as if to retire. After a while there was no sound except the occasional creak of the aged house settling. Mimi heard the pecking at her door, squared her shoulders, and snatched up her cloak. They tiptoed down a set of servants' stairs and paused in the deepest shadows of the hall to don their outer garments. When they slipped through the little-used side door, there was scarcely a whisper of noise.

The light of the half moon seemed bright as midday to their dark-adjusted eyes. Mimi took his hand and led him through the chilled quiet toward the path to the woods . . . and the meadow beyond.

They walked, close and silent, clutching each other's hands. The half-naked trees cast odd shadows around them, and the dry leaves rustled both above their heads and underfoot, heralding their presence and their passage in the night. A quarter of an hour later, they stood at the edge of the trees, gazing over a moonlit expanse of meadow. They looked at each other, and their hands tightened.

"Over here," Graham whispered, propelling her toward a fallen log, just barely visible in the dense shadows beneath some heavy-limbed old trees. When she was seated, he squeezed down beside her and gathered her against him.

"Graham?" she whispered.

"Hmmm?" He rested his cheek on top of her head.

"They won't come."

In the moonlight and silence, they waited. The night seemed to stretch out endlessly around them—the owl hoots, the quiet *shoosh* of leaves overhead, the crisp night air, and the dark, endless sky above. Their eyes grew heavy, and they snuggled closer. After a while, she sagged against him, and his own eyelids began to droop. How much time passed, neither could know. But sometime in the deepest hour of night, he stirred and came wide awake, his blood humming, his senses clear and sharp.

"Mimi," he whispered softly into her ear. Soon she was sitting up, looking at him with a similar keenness of perception, with the same sense of wondrous expectation. They looked up to find the moon sinking and the sky sparkling with points of light . . . dazzling, brilliant, blue-white sparks and fainter, glowing yellow flames. Suddenly a shooting star streaked overhead, burning a glowing arc across the sky as it fell to earth. And it seemed to them both that it had landed in their meadow. They looked at each other and smiled. There was a certain magic about the moment, being there together, being at one with each other in the cradle of the night. Both felt as if that shooting star had written their love and their destiny across the sky for all creation to see.

He touched her face and brushed her lips with his. When she opened her eyes, moonglow had collected in them, turning them into pools of wonder. Her heart soared on the moment, believing . . . then knowing. "They're not coming, Graham. It's just us. No one else."

He gazed at her with eyes littered with starlight. "I know, sweet Mimi. Just us."

They sat looking into each other's faces, bathed in silver splendor, wrapped in love's transcendent warmth. Their smiles grew to broad grins of delight, then became sparkling laughter that bubbled like fine champagne onto the still night air. He thrust to his feet and pulled her up with him, his face radiant.

"They aren't coming . . . there is no dance!" He caught her up in a crushing, exuberant embrace that made her squeal with pleasure. Around and around they whirled, and when they stopped, the entire world was set spinning around them. "Oh, Mimi—it's so beautiful—the night, the moonlight— It's a shame to waste a minute of it!" His eyes shone; his face glowed with sensual excitement as he squeezed her hands. "Dance with me, Mimi . . . here, now."

She stared at him with glistening eyes, dimly aware that he was removing his coat and her cloak and tossing them aside. Could this be the same man who had come to Asher House with anger and accusation in his heart and cold authority in his manner? No, this man had outgrown that shell of duty and denial; this was the dreamer inside that tightly dignified man of law and letters, a secret prince of starlight, a dancer in moonbeams.

One of his hands slid to her waist; the other lifted her hand. And they began to move, with small steps at first, discovering, adjusting to each other. Their movements slowly melted together, and they waltzed around the meadow in graceful, ever-widening circles, sinuously beautiful swirls of skirts and boots and tautly held bodies and passions. The night invaded them with its own impulsive rhythm, guiding their steps over a blossoming carpet of snowy-white starflowers. Around them swirled warm caressing breezes, stirring melody across their heartstrings, creating resonance within their souls.

They danced as the world turned, and the night slid gently through and around them. They danced for joy and for love . . . and for the magic of finding the one created just for them. And as they danced, he realized it wasn't some arcane sorcery that had claimed his senses and taken over his responses and made him into a different man . . . It was love. Love, and the very human enchantment of Mimi's awakening sensuality.

They slowed and swayed to a stop in the middle of the meadow, seeing into each other's hearts, feeling the warming rise of passion.

"Love me, Graham. Now. Here." Desire flickered in the opened core of her, flamelike, entrancing. She led his hands to her breasts and undulated with response when his lean fingers closed around them. He lifted her and carried her to the shadow of that old tree, spreading her cloak and his coat on a bed of leaves. And when he pressed her back into that softness, the very earth itself sighed contentedly through her lips.

Enveloped in a cocoon of their own warmth, they shed clothes and inhibitions, neither thinking it odd to feel so warm and sheltered in the midst of a chilled forest. They touched and caressed, kissing endlessly and reveling in the feel of their bodies molding pleasurably together. She was by turns a silken nymph, and a love-warmed woman whose body cradled and welcomed his, whose heat became his exquisite torment and his sweet release. And he was by turns a teasing satyr, and a roused and passionate man, who sheltered her with his body and invaded her woman's heat as he had invaded her woman's heart.

Under the stars, in a bed of nature, they were joined. All creation seemed to shiver as they found exultant release in that first loving. And the stars winked at each other, and the wind sighed softly.

She lay in his arms, savoring each inch of his body against her . . . and within her. But after a while, the chill of the air curled through her senses, and she shivered.

"You're cold," he murmured, pulling her cloak up and around her. "We'd better get you dressed. I wouldn't want to have to explain to your Aunt Caroline how you happened to take a dread chill." Her laughter was pure music.

"In a minute. Just hold me for a minute longer."

He kissed her nose, her closed eyes, and her lips. "I'll do better than that. I'll hold you for a lifetime . . . if you'll marry me."

She stirred beneath him, wriggling sinuously, luxuriating in the rich new sensuality of loving. "Ummm . . . just name the day. And make it *soon*."

And he laughed.

They awakened in the first gray wisps of predawn light, to find themselves lying on their bed of leaves, wrapped snugly together in his coat and her cloak. Dew covered their clothes and dampened their hair, and the chill had nipped their noses and ears red. In the distance, they could hear a voice and a rustle through the woods; someone was approaching. It took a moment to register, but Graham untangled her arms from his waist and sat up . . . just as the voice and its owner arrived.

"Mimi? Mister Hamilton? Where are you?" Caroline's strident tones floated out over the hushed morning air. Mimi sat up and looked at Graham in horror.

"Aunt Caroline!" she gasped. "They must have found us gone!"

The old lady, clad in an oversized coat and leaning heavily on a walking stick, emerged from the trees not far away. She stood panting from exertion, her gaze scouring the clearing in the dim light. When Graham scrambled to his feet, she saw him, and her whole body reacted with a start, then melted with obvious relief. "Phoebe—Flora—I found them!'' she shouted hoarsely. ''They're over here . . . in the meadow!''

She worked her way through the dewy leaves and chilled starflowers, to where Graham was helping Mimi to her feet. Before her aged eyes, they had to untangle his coat and her cloak, and they fumbled and blushed and stammered.

''Mimi—we've been looking everywhere for you! Flora stopped by your room to see if you were awake yet and wanted to help her, but she found you missing—your bed not even mussed! She roused us, and we began to look and discovered Mister Hamilton missing as well . . .''

''Thank heaven you found them!'' Phoebe arrived just then, red-faced and huffing and puffing, and Flora wasn't far behind. The two teetered to a halt near their sister, and their eyes widened in amazement on the truant pair. Mimi's hair was a charming tangle, her cheeks were stained with embarrassment, and through her gaping cloak, they could see that her dress was badly mis-buttoned. Graham's hair was ruffled, his clothes were littered with leaves and dried grass, and his impeccable starched collar dangled from the side pocket of his coat. The old ladies murmured and peered around the pair to the thick pallet of leaves, which still bore the telling imprint of their bodies.

''Ohhh, Mimi!'' Aunt Flora exclaimed softly, clasping her hand to her throat.

''You were out here . . . with Mister Hamilton . . . all night?'' Aunt Phoebe's chins drew back in dismay. The old sisters shuffled closer together, looking bereft and reaching for each other's hands.

''Please . . . it's not what you think!'' Mimi cringed to see them so. The shock and disappointment in their faces were difficult to bear. Yes, it was what they thought . . . but it was so much more! ''If you'll just listen, let me explain . . .'' They looked at one another, deciding, then nodded, agreeing to hear her out. She drew a relieved breath and hurried to them. ''Graham . . . Mister Hamilton heard some talk in the village—stuff and nonsense, really—about a witches' dance in the meadow on Halloween.''

"Witches?" The old ladies' eyes widened, and they looked at one another in consternation.

"And Graham wanted to see it for himself . . . to see . . . ." As her explanation faltered, he came to her side and put his arm protectively around her shoulders.

"I wanted to know . . ." He hesitated for a moment, deciding what to say. ". . . who the witches were."

"Merciful goodness!" Phoebe exclaimed, leaning closer with avid curiosity. "Who are they?"

"Well," Graham said, shifting his feet and glancing down at Mimi's expectant face, "we didn't see any. None at all. We were here all night and nobody danced in the moonlight."

Mimi looked up at his handsome profile with glistening eyes and corrected softly, "Except us." At that moment, she didn't know if her heart could hold one more drop of love without bursting. He hadn't told them of his suspicions. He didn't want to hurt their feelings! It was glorious proof that his doubts had truly been laid to rest.

"Well, that's the way it is with superstitions." Phoebe sighed. "You get all excited, and nothing comes of it."

"Witches." Caroline turned it over in her mind. "Mister Hamilton, I'm surprised to find you so superstitious. Science teaches us better these days. Years ago, they were always denouncing some old woman or other . . . dragging her out and stuffing her in a pond somewhere to see if she'd float." Her voice and her pointer finger rose as she climbed on a favorite soapbox. "Any time a woman did something a man couldn't understand, he declared her a witch. And men being what they were, there was always plenty they didn't understand about women . . ."

"Caroline—not now!" Flora dragged Caroline's hand down and glared at her. Then she turned that dark look on Graham. "There is still the little matter of our Mimi alone with a man for a whole night in the woods." A somber air settled over the three at that reminder. "Think of the disgrace if anyone should—"

"It's no disgrace, Miss Flora," Graham insisted, albeit with a reddened face. "I love your Mimi with all my heart.

And, with your blessing, she has agreed to become my wife. We want to be married as quickly as it can be arranged.''

The old ladies started and looked to Mimi's glowing face for confirmation. "Mimi, dear," Aunt Caroline choked out past the catch in her throat, "is this true?"

She nodded, and lowered her lashes. "It's true, Aunt Caroline. I love Graham and want to marry him and go to London with him. Please don't be angry.''

"Mimi and Mister Hamilton?" Phoebe clamped a pudgy hand over her heart as if steadying it against the shock. "But, Mimi, dear, we didn't think you even liked Mister Hamilton. Why . . . this is splendid!" She began shaking Caroline and Flora by the arms. "Our Mimi's in love!"

"In love!" Joyful tumult broke out among the old dears. "Our Mimi's going to be married!" They cackled and whooped and clapped their arms around each other and began to bob and hop about. Then as Graham laughed and hugged Mimi, the old ladies engulfed them, hugging them both and jiggling, so giddy with delight that Graham and Mimi were caught up in their irresistible joy and were drawn along, whirling and soaring and dancing for the sheer excitement of being alive, of being together. Clasping hands, they spread into a rowdy ring, which split into a line that wound higgledy-piggledy through the meadow, until all of them were dizzy and breathless, and until the first rays of sunlight broke over the horizon and All Hallows' Eve was over.

The wedding was a lovely affair, held exactly one month later in the small church in the village, with the rector's wife playing the organ and the Ladies' Aid Society providing a lovely wedding dinner afterward. Mimi was radiant in a bridal gown of cream and eggshell-white shot silk, and a pert little high-crowned hat with a veil of silk illusion. And Graham, who had only just returned from London, looked quite handsome in a gray cutaway with a shot silk vest cut of the same cloth as Mimi's gown. Wedding clothes cut of the same cloth were good luck, Aunt Phoebe had insisted. Graham had offered to have the old aunts come to live with him and Mimi in London, but his generosity was graciously refused. They had lived in Asher House for many years, the old ladies said, and they didn't think they'd take to London—or that London would take to them. They even declined Graham's kind offer to hire a staff to look after them at Asher House. The very capable Shaddar and their occasional help from the village were all they needed.

As the carriage arrived to carry Mimi and Graham away to their wedding trip and their new life together, the old aunts hugged her tightly and brushed away her tears, assuring her they would be all right and reminding her of her promise to write and to visit. Graham lifted her into the elegant carriage, and, with tears rolling down her cheeks, she waved until the carriage was out of sight.

Graham held Mimi close and felt the trace of sadness that mingled with the joy in her heart. So when darkness overtook their carriage on the London Road, Graham had the driver pull to the side and stop. And he carried her out into a starlit field and danced with her there in the moonlight.

The old aunts gathered in the tower room when they returned to Asher House. The fire blazed a hot, vivid red as they shed some of their wedding finery and sank with sighs of relief into their claw-footed chairs.

"It was a perfect wedding," Caroline declared with a huge, satisfied smile. "Our Mimi was so pretty with her hair done up like that . . . in those little curls." She pulled the pins from her own hair, and as she ran her fingers through it, it grew progressively whiter and frowsier.

"And Graham was so handsome," Flora said, shucking her shoes and watching her feet and toes double in size. "My, this feels good. It's been eons since my feet had a breather."

"Well, I for one can't wait to get out of this contraption," Phoebe declared, drawing a deep breath and holding it while her corset strings popped one after another and the noise ricocheted about the chamber like rifle shots. "Ahhh." She sank back, looking greatly relieved. "I don't know why women put up with those things."

"I wonder where they are now," Flora said wistfully, rubbing her face with her hands. As she rubbed, her skin withered and her nose grew long and pointed.

"Somewhere along the London Road," Phoebe supplied, holding her hands out to the fire . . . and watching them enlarge with an air of satisfaction. "They'll soon be stopping at an inn for the night. I trow they can scarcely wait."

"Phoebe!" Caroline glowered at her sister, her eyebrows thickening to veritable bushes as her eyes burned with fiery red sparks. "You promise me this instant that you won't use your crystals to peek!"

"Don't be a toadwart, Caroline," Phoebe snorted irritably. "I wouldn't do that." She hitched about in her chair. "Anyway, I'm too old for such stuff."

Flora sighed as she conjured up a memory. "Remember how lovely they looked, dancing around in the meadow that night . . . and after." Before their eyes, a shimmering mist appeared, and in the mist Mimi and Graham materialized, dancing, whirling on a carpet of stars. The old ladies' withered faces broke into toothy smiles. And as the two beautiful, naked lovers sank onto their bed of leaves together, the mist evaporated and they issued three long sighs, one after another.

"I'm going to miss her something terrible," Phoebe declared, dabbing at her eyes.

"Me, too," Flora said, propping her bony chin on one gnarled, blue-veined hand. "I never imagined it would be so much fun, having a real live daughter. Maybe we should think about finding another wealthy orphan to adopt."

"Tsk, tsk," Caroline clucked. "Having a child is so very wearing . . . you have to do everything so conventionally. Have you forgotten all the times we couldn't practice spells or travel astrally or collect exotic specimens? And just think . . . we barely got our dance in before sunrise this year."

"That Hamilton fellow was a sharp one," Phoebe observed thoughtfully. "Fortunately for us, Mimi pulled the love over his eyes."

"And look at us . . ." Caroline waved a gnarled hand at their frizzled white hair and bulbous feet. "We've just barely got our freedom back. Do you really want to have to stuff yourself back into shoes and corsets?'' She harrumphed. ''I agree . . . having a daughter was lovely. But I do believe *one* was quite enough.''

''Well, when you put it that way . . .'' Flora sighed. A moment later she brightened. ''Mimi will have a daughter someday. We'll be grandmas! And we can invite the little thing to visit and spend summers . . .'' She turned on Phoebe. ''You're sure she'll have girls?''

Phoebe smiled wickedly. ''That Hamilton fellow's got pink in his loins, all right. A regular ladymaker. Trust me.'' The old ladies threw their heads back and chortled.

Just then a huge, exotic cat with a tawny coat and black-tipped ears and tail padded into the tower room. He headed straight for Phoebe, crouched and sprang onto her lap, stretching flagrantly and flicking his tail. He gazed at the three old sisters with sultry green-gold eyes, then began to rub his body luxuriantly against Phoebe's plump frame.

''Oh, Shaddar,'' Phoebe crooned, ruffling his fur affectionately. ''You handsome boy—I've missed you!'' She gave his ears a good scratching and as he started to purr, she glanced at her sisters with a wicked glint in her eye. ''You know, having a daughter around did have compensations. I sort of enjoyed inventing and using all my old phrenology stuff. Flora collected a whole raft of fancy plants, and Caroline learned all sorts of new ways to use her electrical thingumabobs.'' She gazed down at the lolling cat. ''And we learned a whole new side of Shaddar here.''

The old ladies' cackles drifted through the silent halls of Asher House.

Betina Krahn

BETINA KRAHN, who lives in Eagan, Minnesota, with her husband and two sons, grew up hearing ghost stories told by her older sister at slumber parties. Despite a lingering habit of turning on lights before entering rooms, she has developed an irrepressible irreverence for things spooky, supernatural, or occult. Thus she can only create witches who have hearts of gold.

As part of the research for the story, she located a real phrenology parlor, operated with antique "psychograph" machinery in a set of specialty shops in Minneapolis, and skeptically submitted to having the bumps on her head "read." The results were astonishing. On a scale of one to five (one being pathetically deficient; five being a step away from sainthood) she scored *five* in twenty-five out of thirty measurements! The readings indicate that she is *very superior* in "agreeability," "perceptives," "ideality," "individuality," "dignity," "wit," and "suavity"—in all the real important qualities of human character. The experience has caused her to completely reevaluate her previously unenlightened and regretfully derogatory opinion about the science of phrenology. Any system of analysis that accurate, she now believes, deserves real respect.

That Other Katherine

Linda Lael Miller

*For yet another Kathy, Kathy Miller.
Thanks for planting rose bushes,
cooking turkey dinners, and
being a first-class stepmother to Wendy.*

*Seattle, Washington
1991*

KATHERINE Hollis. Her name was Katherine Hollis.
    She thought.

Katherine listened to the steady beeping of the hospital machines, the low murmur of the nurses' voices as they attended her. *Poor creature . . . terrible accident . . . coma . . .*

She became aware of the pain suddenly, the crushing, ceaseless pain, and at the same time, she realized it had been there all along. She seemed to be climbing some kind of inner stairway, with each step bringing her closer to full consciousness.

Katherine tried to remember the accident, but not even a flicker of memory lighted her way. She had no idea who would be standing there if she peeked behind the name she'd recalled.

The pain was agonizing, and Katherine wanted to cry out, but she couldn't. For all its suffering, her body felt lifeless and cold, as rigid as a statue, while her spirit seemed to be gaining strength with every passing moment, a flame burning brighter and brighter. An explosive sensation of joy flared within her, completely separate from the misery of traumatized bone and muscle.

She felt a tear pool along the lashes of her right eye.

197

The voice Katherine heard then was masculine and hoarse with emotion. "Look—she's crying. She could be waking up, couldn't she?"

Katherine felt a strong hand close around one of her own while the voice caressed her soul. Jeremy. A few ragtag memories trickled back. That was her brother up there in that other dimension, that place of wakefulness and reason, trying to hold on to her.

Her heart constricted. She would have given practically anything for the chance to say goodbye, but her lips might as well have been made of marble. She couldn't even manage a flutter of her eyelids.

I want to live, Katherine thought desperately, with the last strength left to her. There are so many things I didn't get a chance to do!

The machines began to make strange noises, and then there was a burst of activity all around her.

"I'll get the doctor . . ."

". . . crash cart . . ."

"Please, Mr. Hollis . . . no time . . . waiting room . . ."

"No! Kathy . . ." That was Jeremy's voice, frantic and young. Jeremy, whom she'd pulled behind her in a red wagon when they were both children, over a bumpy sidewalk with weeds growing between the cracks . . .

In the next instant Katherine was enveloped in light more brilliant than the dazzle of a thousand spring suns. It was a moment more before she realized that a subtle change had taken place in the form and substance of her body.

She was the same and yet different, standing on an arched bridge that seemed to be fashioned of multifaceted crystal.

"I don't want to die," she said firmly, knowing there was someone in the light to hear her argument and weigh it. "I never fell in love, or made a wreath of spring flowers for my hair, or wore a long dancing dress, or had a baby . . ." She paused, then finished plaintively, "Oh, please."

That was when Katherine heard the other voice calling, pleading, storming the very gates of heaven. It was a lusty feminine shriek.

"No more . . . please . . . oh, God, help me . . . let me die . . ."

There was an interval then of fathomless peace, followed by a wordless answer from the glorious, unutterably beautiful light. *I have heard*.

Immediately after that, Katherine was caught up in a spinning storm of iridescent fire. She tumbled end over end through a crystal tunnel and then landed with a sudden, solid thump.

Joy filled her. She was back inside her body; she could feel her heartbeat, the moist tension of her skin, the movement of her fingers. Even better, she was fully conscious, and she could see.

A frown creased her sweat-dampened forehead. She wasn't in the hospital; this room had high ceilings with plaster molding and pale pink wallpaper striped in silver, and instead of the standard railings on the sides and foot of the bed, there were huge bedposts with carved pineapples on top.

Her stomach was bare, and it resembled an overripe watermelon with skin stretched over it. Her bare knees were drawn up, her legs apart, and there was an old man standing in the V, looking ponderous.

She decided she was having some kind of crazy dream, fraught with Freudian meanings.

She didn't recognize the body or the room. None of what she was seeing could possibly be real . . .

She screamed. Except the pain. That was totally authentic.

"What the hell is going on here?" she cried when she got her breath back.

The white-haired man looked up from whatever medical intimacy he'd been performing, his florid face a study in Puritan disapproval. "Now, Katherine, there is no need to use profanity. I should think you would be trying to redeem yourself, rather than make things worse."

"This hurts," she babbled, panting. "This whole situation was sprung on me with no warning . . . no preparation

. . . I never got to go through Lamaze training . . . I want morphine!''

"Mrs. Winslow," the doctor replied with testy patience, "during the war, I treated men who'd had their legs and arms shot off. Not one of them carried on the way you have today."

"They weren't having babies!" Katherine blurted, and then she screamed again. It seemed that the whole lower half of her body had become one giant muscle, about as much under her control as a runaway train would have been. "Oh, God . . . nobody told me it would feel like this!"

"Kindly stop bothering the Almighty," said the man. "It would have behooved you to consult Him a little earlier, it seems to me."

Katherine recalled the voice she'd heard from the crystal bridge, calling out to heaven for mercy.

Her body . . . this body she didn't recognize . . . tensed again, violently. Her cotton nightgown clung to her skin, transparent with perspiration.

"Push," the doctor instructed crisply, his face taut with concentration. "Mary!" He barked the name over one shoulder, and the door popped open, revealing a pale young woman in long skirts.

"Yes, Dr. Franz?" The girl's eyes were the size of soccer balls, and she was wringing her hands nervously.

"Fetch Gavin," ordered the physician. "Immediately. Tell him his child is about to be born, just in case he's interested!"

The fitful maid rushed off to obey.

Katherine was braced on her elbows, tears streaming down her face. "Why are you people in costume?" she managed to gasp out, after her next contraction. "Who's Gavin?"

Dr. Franz arched one bushy eyebrow. "There is no need to add insult to injury, Mrs. Winslow, by pretending you don't know your own husband."

"I don't have a husband." Katherine panted, clutching the bedclothes as another pain began to gain steam on the inside of her pelvis. "And my name isn't Winslow. It's Hollis. Katherine Hollis."

"Nonsense," said the doctor briskly. "You're Katherine Simmons Winslow. I've known you since you came to Seattle—heaven help the hapless place."

The thrusting sensation in Katherine's abdomen was building to another crescendo, and yet the tears on her face were ones of happiness. She was alive! She didn't know where she was, or how she'd gotten there, but *she was alive!*

An impatient knock sounded at the door, but Katherine was too busy with the current contraction to pay much attention. When a dark-haired man appeared beside the bed, however, she was thunderstruck by his good looks and by her own sense of shattering recognition. She'd seen his face in her dreams a thousand times—she recalled that if little else.

"Nice of you to make an appearance, Gavin," grumbled Dr. Franz. "There now, Katherine, one more good push."

Reluctantly, it seemed, Gavin reached down and took her hand between both his own. Even in that state of great confusion and greater pain, she felt a jolt at his touch.

Her torso arched high off the mattress, taking no command from her mind. She clung to Gavin's hands, and her primitive cry, half groan and half scream, echoed against the walls of the strange, old-fashioned room. The anguish of childbirth peaked, and then there was relief, a sensation of something slipping from her. Soon after that she heard the angry squall of an infant.

She saw Gavin's steel-gray eyes dart toward the newborn, then shift away. He looked down at her with what seemed to be a mingling of contempt and furious hurt.

"You have a son, Gavin," Dr. Franz announced, as though Katherine had had nothing to do with the process.

Gavin's strong jawline flexed, relaxed again. His gaze scored her face. "Kathy has a son," he corrected, and then he let her hand fall to the mattress, turned abruptly, and left the room.

"Let me see the baby," she pleaded hoarsely. Later, she

would try to reason things out. For now, she just wanted to see this child she'd given birth to but never conceived.

He was tiny and red and messy, and she couldn't imagine even a Christmas angel being more beautiful.

"Hello, handsome," she said, feeling joyous exhaustion as an infinitesimal hand closed around her finger. The far side of the crystal bridge already seemed more dream than reality now, something imagined. "I hope we can be friends. In case you haven't noticed, I'm not very popular around here."

Dr. Franz was doing painful things, things it seemed better not to think about. An Indian girl in a drab calico dress, long like the maid's, took the baby and left the room. Katherine was suddenly too drowsy to protest.

Several women came in, all looking like fugitives from an episode of "Little House on the Prairie," with their hair upswept and the hems of their dresses brushing the floor, and helped Katherine from the bed. Brisk hands washed her and pulled a clean nightgown over her head, and the sheets were crisp and fresh when she lay back down on them.

"You're to take this," one of the women said, pouring liquid from a brown bottle into a spoon. "Dr. Franz left it for you."

Katherine obediently opened her mouth and accepted the medicine, which tasted like lawnmower fuel smelled. Then she settled back against the fluffy pillows, barely able to keep her eyes open. "Gavin hates me," she said, sighing and yawning at the same time.

There was only one woman in the room then; she had gray-streaked brown hair and pale green eyes, and although her expression was stern, there was a softness about her mouth. "It isn't as though you haven't given him cause," was the answer. "But you've also given him a son. A man will forgive a great deal for such a gift."

Katherine closed her eyes, too weary to go on, and was soon dreaming. Although she caught glimpses of the light and the crystal bridge, she didn't wander close, and when she awakened it was to see her son sleeping in an ornate antique cradle next to her bed. Her heart caught when she noticed Gavin crouching on the hearth, lighting an early evening fire.

"Gavin?"

His broad shoulders tensed beneath the fine white fabric of his shirt, and he did not turn to look at her. He rose to his full height, well over six feet, and gripped the mantelpiece with strong, sun-browned hands. The light from the gas-fed fixtures on the walls flickered in his dark hair and on the shining black leather of his riding boots.

Katherine phrased her question carefully. "What will you name the child?"

Slowly he turned to meet her gaze, his pewter eyes cold and wary. He couldn't entirely hide his surprise at the inquiry, though Katherine could see he was trying. "Name him?"

"He is your son, after all." How she wished that she too could lay just claim to that beautiful infant boy. She remembered little of her old life . . . if indeed it really had been a life and not just an illusion . . . but she knew she'd longed for a baby from the day she was given her first doll.

Gavin's answer was a quietly brutal chuckle. "Is he?" he countered, turning back to the fire.

Katherine felt tears well up behind her eyes, but she refused to shed them. Somehow, through an instinct that seemed oddly like memory, she knew this man would not respond well if she wept. "Your wife was unfaithful to you," she said.

Another chuckle, sardonic and wicked. "Yes," he replied, turning to face her, his arms folded. "You were. Are."

"Then why haven't you divorced me?"

Gavin smiled cordially. "Believe me, darling, I would love to, but even in the grand and gloriously modern year of 1895, such things simply aren't done."

Katherine sat bolt upright as a series of mental puzzle pieces dropped into place. The primitive birth, the gas lamps on the walls, Gavin's oddly formal clothes, the long dresses the women had worn. "In 1895?" she echoed, awed.

"Please," Gavin said skeptically. "None of your little dramas. You know exactly who you are, where you are, and what you did. And if I have anything to say about it, you're never going to forget."

K ATHERINE was unaccountably wounded by Gavin's dislike and troubled by memories that could not have been memories. Her emotional reactions to him during their first encounter had been ones of recognition, not discovery.

She averted her gaze for a moment, fingers plucking at the elaborate lace trim of the top sheet. "Suppose I told you I'm not the Katherine you knew," she ventured hoarsely. "Suppose I said I'm really another woman, from another time?"

Gavin clasped his hands together behind his back and rocked slightly on his heels. "I would respond that pretending to have lost your grip on sanity won't save you from my revenge," he said, and the tone of his voice made the otherwise cozy room turn chilly. "Instead it might just land you in an asylum."

"Revenge?" Katherine swallowed. Just the *suggestion* of a nineteenth-century mental hospital brought on instant wariness.

His smile was callous. "I loved you on our wedding day, Kathy," he said. "Perhaps if I still cherished tender feelings toward you, I would simply send you away somewhere, with an allowance and a maid, and get on with my life. Alas, my fatal flaw is that I want you to know the same humiliation, the same sense of betrayal, that I did." He came to stand at Katherine's feet, his knuckles white where he gripped the bedpost. His gray eyes glinted like frost over steel as he looked at her. "This time, Kathy, you'll be the one people pity and hold in contempt."

Katherine's throat constricted. She didn't love this man, didn't even *know* this man, and yet his words were like hard-flung stones, bruising her soul. "Gavin . . ."

He gave a low, mocking laugh. "How tenderly you speak my name," he said, going to stand beside the cradle. His expression grew softer as he looked down at the sleeping baby. "Were you as sweet to your lover as you are to me?"

Katherine fell back against her pillows and put both hands to her face for a moment, struggling to gain some composure. "I don't know," she said, in all honesty.

When she looked again, she caught Gavin watching her with naked sorrow in his stormy eyes. The expression was so quickly sublimated, however, that she wondered if she'd imagined it.

"Good night," Gavin said without emotion, and then he turned and strode from the room, closing the door briskly behind him.

Katherine lay shaking in that other woman's childbed for a very long time, watching the shadows gather in the corners of the room and the fire die to embers on the hearth. Finally, when she felt strong enough, she rose and went to kneel carefully by the baby's cradle.

Her son slept, his thick dark hair like ebony against the white blankets, and she touched him ever so gently, marveling that so beautiful a creature could exist in such an uncertain world. He was a miniature Gavin Winslow, this tiny soul, and Katherine already loved him, already thought of him as her own.

"You look just like your dad," she said in a whisper. "One of these days, he'll notice that. Might take a while, though, because as you can see, he's a very hardheaded man. We'll have to be patient, you and I."

For a long time she lingered beside the cradle, admiring the child, marveling. Then, when she began to feel the strain in her weary body, she stood awkwardly and made her way to the bureau.

There was a mirror above the dresser, framed in dark, heavy wood, and Katherine's first glimpse of herself had all the shocking impact of a body slam by a major league quarterback.

Her knees weakened, and she raised one hand to her chest in an unconscious effort to modify the pounding of her heart. She did not remember who she had been before the accident, before crossing the crystal bridge and finding herself in 1895, but she knew she hadn't looked at all like the woman reflected in the glass.

In fact, she could almost see her previous self, standing beside this stranger she had become.

In that other life, she'd been small and slight. The woman looking back at her was tall, with a lush hourglass figure.

Before, Katherine had had short brown hair, worn in a smooth, bouncy cut. Now, dark auburn tresses tumbled, thick and wavy, around the bodice of her nightgown. Her eyes were green, her cheekbones high and well defined, her lips full, her skin flawless and very creamy, like fine ivory.

Katherine stared at herself for a long time. Then, when the weakness grew too great, she turned and made her way back to the bed.

She had barely settled beneath the covers when a woman entered the room carrying a tray. It was the same girl Dr. Franz had sent to bring Gavin when it was clear that the baby's birth was imminent.

"Supper, missus," she said without meeting Katherine's gaze.

Given that this was 1895 and that the mistress of the house had obviously had an affair, Katherine supposed the maid saw her as a scarlet woman and preferred not to associate. The thought only made Katherine feel more isolated, confused, and afraid.

"It certainly smells good," she said in an attempt to make conversation.

"Yes, ma'am," the maid answered. "Cook does have a way with biscuits and gravy. The doctor likes that dish more than anything."

"Dr. Franz?" Katherine asked. She was so grateful for

the sound of a civil human voice that she tried to keep the chat going.

"Dr. Winslow," the maid corrected, turning startled blue eyes to Katherine's face. "Your husband, ma'am."

So Gavin was a doctor, too. "Oh," Katherine said quickly, brightly. "Yes, of course. He's had a lengthy practice here in . . ."

"Seattle," the maid said, frowning.

Katherine was ravenously hungry, and the food on her tray was fragrant and appealing. "Seattle," she confirmed. That was a relief. Maybe she'd changed centuries, but at least she was still in the same city. "Your name would be?"

The young girl took another step toward the door, as though she expected Katherine to lunge at her, wild-eyed and foaming at the mouth.

"Jemima," she whispered. With that, Jemima turned and bolted from the room.

Katherine ate, trying to figure out what was happening to her.

Maybe it was the food that restored her. She seemed to recall that her blood sugar tended to fall when she got too hungry . . .

She remembered lying in a faraway hospital bed, remembered the nurses talking and the grasp of her brother's hand and the earnest way she'd begged the light surrounding the crystal bridge to let her live. Evidently, she concluded as the pleas of another woman echoed in her mind—*oh, God, help me . . . let me die*—she and Gavin's real wife had somehow exchanged places.

That was too much to credit, Katherine thought, setting her tray on the bedside table and leaning back against her pillows, and yet here she was, in another woman's body. A body she liked far better than her old one, for all the problems inherent in the situation.

Presently the Indian girl came in to take away her tray, and that made Katherine smile. Jemima must have been afraid to venture near her again after that little encounter earlier.

"What's your name?" she asked pleasantly when the

young woman had set the tray in the hall and returned. The baby awakened and gave a small, fitful cry.

"Maria," the visitor replied, unruffled, bending to lift the infant from his cradle before Katherine had managed to swing her legs over the side of the bed. Maria sat down in the rocking chair near the dying fire and opened the bodice of her plain dress to nurse the baby.

Again, Katherine felt envy. She didn't like the idea of sharing this child, or his father, with any other woman.

Maria was conscious only of the baby, humming a soft, rhythmic tune as she held him to her breast and stroked his downy head with a light finger. The firelight flickered over the pair, gilding them in crimson and shadow.

A deep loneliness overtook Katherine; she felt as though she'd been abandoned in some unknown galaxy. She remembered only the merest details about her other life, and in this one everyone seemed to dislike her.

Presently Maria finished feeding the child and brought him to the bed for changing. She handed him to Katherine, who gently raised him to her shoulder to be burped.

"Thank you," Katherine said, mesmerized by the bundled miracle in her arms.

"What will you call the little one?" Maria asked, regarding Katherine with placid dark eyes that revealed nothing of her inner thoughts.

Katherine ached with love as the child squirmed against her shoulder, and she longed to be able to feed him herself. "I don't know," she answered. "Perhaps we'll name him for his father."

The silence that followed felt awkward to Katherine. Remembering the accusation her husband had thrown in her face, she blushed and blurted out, "Gavin. He'll be called Gavin, of course."

Maria did not react, and her manner was neither friendly nor unfriendly. "Is there anything you'd like, Mrs. Winslow?" She went to the hearth without waiting for Katherine to reply and added a log to the fire. "The kitchen kettle is still on. I could brew you some tea."

Katherine shook her head. "No. No, thank you. But if you'd please put the baby to bed . . ."

The Indian girl assessed Katherine with narrowed eyes for a moment, then collected the infant and carefully put him into the cradle to sleep. "Good night, Mrs. Winslow," she said after turning off the gas that fed the lights.

Only the glow of the fire and the strained silver shimmer of the moon lit the room after Maria closed the door behind her.

Cautiously, Katherine lay down flat on the feather mattress. This body she had borrowed was very sore, and she felt like weeping with exhaustion and confusion, but beneath all these things ran an undercurrent of sheer exultation. She had been given another chance at life, and she meant to make the most of it.

Watching the firelight waver against the dark ceiling, she wondered if Gavin had ever laughed in this room or made love to his wife here. Surely he hadn't always been so grim and solemn!

It seemed to her that as she as just dropping off to sleep, the first solid memory of the other life came to her. She was driving along the Seattle freeway in her red convertible, her dark hair tossing in the wind, on the way to her brother Jeremy's downtown office. They were planning to have lunch together.

In the space of a moment, everything changed. A truck jackknifed just ahead of her, and before she could slow down, her car struck the trailer with a deafening impact. Metal shrieked, pain racked her body, and then darkness exploded around her like a bomb.

"Kathy!" Strong hands gripped Katherine's shoulders, and a firm masculine voice came to her through the smothering fog of fear that surrounded her. "Katherine, wake up!"

Gavin was sitting on the side of the bed, and her longing to have him take her into his arms and hold her was a bleak and fathomless thing. The baby, frightened by the noise, was fretting in his cradle.

Katherine started to get out of bed, but Gavin wouldn't allow her to rise.

"Never mind," he said abruptly. "I'll get him."

At once a stranger and a husband, Gavin lifted the child deftly from the cradle and handed him to Katherine.

"I'm sorry," she crooned, her lips against the infant's cheek. "I'm so sorry I woke you up, sweetheart . . ."

Something made her lift her eyes to Gavin then, and she saw that he was looking at her strangely again, as though he didn't quite recognize her.

She drew a deep breath and made herself smile at the man who so clearly despised her. "Our son will need a name, you know," she said with a little sniffle. "We can't go on referring to this child as 'he' and 'him' for the rest of his life."

Even in the firelight, she saw Gavin's powerful body go rigid. The brief, tenuous peace that had existed between them was obviously over.

"Why not name him Jeffrey?" Gavin asked in a tone that was no less brutal for its softness. "For his father."

3

"**G**ET out," Katherine breathed, glaring at Gavin. She was trembling inside, but she was as strong and agile as a lioness when she sprang from the bed to return the baby to his cradle.

Gavin stood his ground, arms folded. "May I remind you that this is *my* house?"

"I don't care," she spat. "You're nothing but an arrogant bully, and if you're any example of nineteenth-century manhood, it's no wonder there was a women's movement!"

"If we're going to call each other names—"

"Don't you dare!" Katherine clasped her hands over her ears and at the same time maneuvered herself back into bed. "I know perfectly well what you think of me, Gavin Winslow, but I've been through a lot today, and I would appreciate it if you would leave me alone."

To her surprise, Gavin's countenance grew a little less stern. He approached the bed and tucked the covers in around her with a certain brisk tenderness.

"You're right," he said, in a husky voice. "I'm sorry." With that, unbelievably, he bent and kissed her lightly on the forehead, and at that simple contact something deep inside Katherine was changed forever.

Gavin didn't come to her room the next day, or the day after that. Katherine spent her time caring for the baby, whom she could nurse now that her milk had come in, reading the books and magazines Maria brought her, and remembering.

It was that other life that kept unfolding in her mind; she still knew very little about the woman she had become.

As Katherine Hollis, she'd lived in a world of convenience and noise, working for a market research firm in Seattle and slowly paying off a one-bedroom condo overlooking Lake Washington. She'd been on the verge of getting married once, but in the end she'd realized Phillip Hughes was all wrong for her, and she was all wrong for him, and she'd given back his ring.

She recalled that she'd grown up in a modest home on Seattle's Queen Anne Hill, and that her divorced mother, Julia, had taught piano lessons in the dining room to supplement meager child-support payments. Julia had died of ovarian cancer when her daughter was twenty, and after that, there had been only Jeremy . . .

Now, Katherine marveled, she found herself in another world. Here there were no speeding convertibles, no market research companies, no semi-trucks to jackknife in the middle of the freeway. Beyond the walls of this house, which she'd had no chance at all to explore, carriages, buggies, and wagons rattled over dirt streets and cobblestones.

The sunlight was bright, the sky so blue the sight of it twisted Katherine's heart.

She was standing at the window, looking out over the garden with its gazebo and its tangle of colorful flowers, when there was a light knock at the door. Just as she would have turned to call out an eager "Come in"—she was so lonely that even Gavin would have been a welcome caller— she saw her husband walk through a gate in the side fence.

He looked so handsome in his riding breeches, linen shirt, tailored charcoal coat, and boots that Katherine's breath caught. Just when she was about to tap impulsively on the glass and wave to him, forgetting all his insufferable qualities in the face of the breathtaking attraction she felt, a woman joined him. Her dress was yellow, like the roses that climbed the walls of the gazebo and tangled on its roof, and her hair was the color of honey.

As Katherine watched, stricken, the woman held out both hands to Gavin, and he clasped them in his own. His strong white teeth flashed in a cavalier's smile as he bent his head to kiss his companion's gloved knuckles.

"There's Caroline Raynes again," a voice beside Katherine announced, and she jumped, startled. "You'd better look out for her, because she's sweet on Gavin."

Katherine turned her head and saw a petite girl standing next to her. Her hair was dark, and her eyes were the same steely-gray as Gavin's, and from that Katherine deduced that this woman was her sister-in-law. The little golden pin affixed to the bodice of her plain but expensive dress shaped the letters of her name.

"Hello, Marianne."

Marianne's attention was fixed on the scene below; she didn't see Katherine study her, or glance at the bare ring finger of her left hand to determine her marital status.

"Look at her," she said, her breath making fog against the windowpane. "What a hussy."

Katherine looked, against her better judgment. Caroline was standing on her toes, her hands resting on Gavin's lapels while she whispered something in his ear. A feeling of such intense, primitive jealousy went through Katherine that she grasped the windowsill to keep from pounding on it with her fists.

"Not that you didn't bring a lot of this upon yourself by stirring up that scandal with Jeffrey Beecham," Marianne added matter-of-factly, taking Katherine's elbow and steering her away from the window. "Come now, it's time to dress for the christening party. You can't very well attend in your slippers and wrapper, you know."

The prospect of leaving that infernal room, even for a short interval, raised Katherine's spirits considerably. Every time she got up to walk around, it seemed, Dr. Franz or one of the maids came to chase her back to bed.

"What will I wear?" she asked, confused.

"What indeed?" Marianne answered, rolling her eyes. She opened a door to the left of the fireplace, which had always been locked when Katherine tried it, and swept through. "As if you didn't own more dresses than any woman in Seattle!"

Katherine hurried along behind her sister-in-law, casting her gaze this way and that, taking in as much of the massive room as she could. "Maybe nothing will fit," she fretted.

An enormous chandelier graced the high ceiling, and the fireplace was fronted in pale marble. The rugs were Persian, the walls were paneled in rosewood, and the bed was bigger than the living room of her apartment in that other Seattle.

She stood in the middle of the chamber, looking around her in awe, while Marianne went straight to a set of double doors, opened them, and disappeared inside.

Her voice echoed. "Nonsense. You were incredibly careful about what you ate, remember?" she called. "I think the dark blue taffeta would be exactly right, don't you? Given the state of your reputation, my dear, there's no point in even *attempting* propriety. No, the occasion calls for something that shows you won't be discounted and forgotten."

Katherine flinched when the main door of the room swung open and Gavin, entered, carrying a black medical bag and a riding crop in one hand.

His eyes swept over her rumpled wrapper and tangled

hair with a sort of charitable contempt, and Katherine was instantly furious.

"Where's Caroline?" she asked sweetly.

Gavin set his things down on a table that Katherine thought would probably bring a small fortune at a modern-day antique show. "Caroline," he responded, his tone even and cutting, "is too much of a lady to engage in the sort of illicit rendezvous you specialize in, my dear."

Color surged into Katherine's face, and she pulled her wrapper more tightly around her, as if to shield herself.

"Too much of a lady, pooh," Marianne interceded, before Katherine could think of a response. She thrust the aforementioned blue taffeta dress into her sister-in-law's arms and turned to face Gavin, her hands on her hips. "For someone who's supposed to be such a man of the world, Gavin Winslow," she said bluntly, "you are certainly naive."

Gavin looked at Katherine, even though he was speaking to Marianne, and his expression was scathing. "I can't deny that," he answered, "since I once trusted my heart to a woman who probably doesn't have one beating in her bosom."

Tears stung Katherine's eyes, and she swallowed hard to keep from giving full rein to her feelings. There was nothing she could say . . . the other Katherine probably *had* been guilty of flagrant adultery. Yet on every occasion when she encountered Gavin, no matter how rare and volatile those times were, she felt an elemental pull toward him, as though her soul had somehow been magnetized to his.

Marianne popped him in the upper arm, and the gesture was so sisterly that it almost made Katherine smile, despite everything. "Stop being so mean, Gavin, and get dressed for your son's christening. That is, unless you plan on going in your riding clothes."

The look that passed from Gavin to Katherine was a private one, since Marianne was by that time bustling toward the door of the other room. His gaze was as mocking as a slap, and Katherine hurried after her sister-in-law, wondering if Gavin meant to attend the christening at all.

He did, as it happened.

Gavin announced to the assembly, without ever informing Katherine, let alone consulting her, that the baby's name would be Christopher Jennings Winslow, and he looked for all the world like a proud father.

He even took his place beside Katherine after the intimate ceremony held in the house's private chapel, and shook hands with the endless stream of strangers, well-wishers all, who passed by.

The guests clearly admired and respected Gavin, but the looks they gave Katherine were plainly speculative. A wonderful meal was served in the garden, and inside the house, tables were heaped with gifts.

Despite his attempts at keeping up appearances earlier, by the time Maria had taken the properly christened Christopher back inside the house, Gavin was totally absorbed in a conversation with the bouncy Caroline Raynes.

"I hate perky women," Katherine muttered, turning away only to collide with a tall, handsome man in an expensive tweed suit. He had green eyes and chestnut-brown hair, and his sensual mouth quirked into a sad little smile.

"So do I," he said, taking both of Katherine's hands in his, just as Gavin had done with Caroline earlier in the day, when Katherine had been watching from the upstairs window. "How are you?"

His words and tone were so solicitous that Katherine was caught off guard. She was still weak from giving birth to Christopher and bruised from various sparring matches with Gavin, so this man's attentions were like warm sunshine after a dip in a frigid stream.

"F-fine," she said.

"You shouldn't be on your feet." He led her to the edge of the fountain that graced the middle of the garden and gently sat her down. Then he brought her a glass of punch from the refreshment table, along with some small sweet cakes coated in sesame seeds.

Katherine wished she had an inkling of the man's identity. She sipped her punch, thinking it was unfortunate that everybody didn't own a broach made up of the letters of their name, like Marianne.

"Feel that sunshine," she said, lifting her face to the blue sky, closing her eyes, and smiling. "Isn't it wonderful?"

"Wonderful," her companion said distractedly. "Katherine, about our plans . . . Don't you think we should delay a few more weeks, until you're stronger?"

"Ummm," she answered, not really listening. A violin was playing nearby, and she began to sway happily back and forth with the tune. "I wish we could dance," she said, opening her eyes again, searching the stranger's handsome face. "Will you dance with me?"

A third voice answered, and it was only too familiar. So was the proprietary grip on her forearm.

"It's time you rested," Gavin informed his wife in a taut voice. "Come along, I'll see you to your room."

Katherine didn't try to pull away, though she heartily resented Gavin's tone and manner. She *was* tired, tired enough to faint. Dancing, of course, was out of the question, though it had seemed like a marvelous idea only moments before.

"It was nice meeting you," she said to the other man, without thinking, and then Gavin was propelling her toward the French doors leading to the main parlor.

Just over the threshold, he wrenched her angrily up into his arms. "'It was nice meeting you,'" he mimicked. "What kind of asinine remark was that?"

Katherine rested her head against a hard shoulder and yawned. "Oh," she said, in a tone of weary revelation. "I take it that was the infamous Jeffrey Beecham, with whom I was allegedly indiscreet."

Gavin took the stairs easily, as though Katherine's voluptuous weight was no strain at all to carry. "Allegedly," he scoffed under his breath. "I found the two of you in bed together, my darling. Remember?"

4

G AVIN'S footsteps slowed as he passed the double doors of the master suite—he had carried Kathy through them many times during happier days—but now he proceeded down the hall without hesitation.

Reaching the entrance of Katherine's chamber, originally meant to be a dressing room, he opened the door and crossed the threshold.

Maria, who had been minding the sleeping baby, rose from her chair and left.

Katherine yawned and stretched, lush and kittenlike, when he laid her gently on the bed. Gavin's loins tightened in response. He couldn't have made love to her, of course; only a brute would have expected such accommodation so soon after childbirth. But the knowledge didn't stop him from wanting her, God help him, and neither did the mental image of her lying naked in Jeffrey Beecham's arms that day months before.

Gavin closed his eyes, remembering. Regretting.

He'd gotten drunk, for the first and last time in his life, after finding his wife and her lover in the guest house. And while he hadn't actually raped Kathy in their bedroom that night, he'd used her roughly. The fact that his wife had mistaken his rage for passion and responded wholeheartedly did not absolve him.

Now, stretched out on the bed to which he'd banished her, Katherine looked too angelic, too innocent to betray a husband's love. She favored him with a distracted little smile, her eyelids fluttered closed, and then she was asleep.

Gavin was unable to maintain his stern expression, now

217

that she wasn't looking. He smiled as he gently removed
her satin slippers and covered her tenderly with the lightweight wool blanket he found draped over the back of a
chair.

She stirred beneath the coverlet, and Gavin felt his heart
twist painfully. Some ancient instinct whispered that she
was not the same woman he'd known, but somehow drastically changed. He was a physician, however, a man of
science, and he couldn't give credence to anything quite so
mystical.

He trusted facts, not feelings. It was a lesson he'd learned
the hard way.

He resisted an urge to brush a tendril of auburn hair back
from Katherine's forehead and turned to leave the room.
Then, unable to help himself, he paused beside the baby's
cradle, gazing down at the little boy he'd named Christopher
that very day.

Gavin could no longer deny, even to himself, that this
child was his own; the resemblance was too marked to be
discounted.

After glancing in Katherine's direction to make certain
she was truly sleeping, he crouched beside the cradle and
gently touched Christopher's tiny ear.

"My son," he said, his voice hardly more than a hoarse
whisper. Then he rose and walked from the room, closing
the door behind him.

In the face of emotional confusion, Gavin generally took
refuge in routine. He would change clothes, he decided,
then get his medical bag, call for the carriage, and make
his rounds.

His work at the hospital would take care of the rest of
the night, and tomorrow could look after itself.

The next morning Katherine awakened to a room flooded
with sunlight. By the time Maria arrived with a pitcher of
hot water, she had already changed Christopher and fed
him, and mother and child were sitting in a rocker by the
windows, admiring the view of the garden.

"You shouldn't be out of bed, Mrs. Winslow," Maria said, with her usual lack of inflection.

"Nonsense," Katherine responded. "It's not as though I've had major surgery, after all." She raised Christopher and kissed his forehead. "Giving birth is a natural thing, and the sooner I'm up and around, the better."

Maria set the pitcher on the washstand and laid out a damask washcloth, a fluffy towel, and a bar of soap so fragrant that Katherine could smell its perfume from where she sat. "Whatever you say, Mrs. Winslow," she parroted. "I'll bring up your tea while you're washing, and Miss Marianne really thinks you should have breakfast. Shall I take the baby?"

Katherine surrendered her son, but reluctantly, and Maria put him in the cradle. "Tea would be wonderful, but I'll have my breakfast in the kitchen or the dining room or wherever everyone else eats. I'm sick to death of being locked away in this room." She poured some of the water Maria had brought into the waiting crockery basin and reached for the soap and cloth. "Tell me, Maria, how is it that you speak the way you do?"

Maria paused at the door. "You mean, why don't I sound like an Indian?"

Katherine blushed. She hadn't meant her question to sound condescending, but evidently it had. "Yes," she admitted. "That's what I was wondering."

For the first time in their acquaintance, Maria smiled. "My stepmother was white, and she was a schoolteacher until she married my father. She taught me 'Boston English,' but I have not forgotten the tongue of my people. It is very precious to me."

"Unfortunately," Katherine said with a thoughtlessness she had not intended, "the Indian way of life will all but disappear in the coming years." When she glanced in the wall mirror and saw Maria's stricken expression, she knew she had erred.

Maria lowered her head for a moment, but when she looked at Katherine again there was a proud, defiant light in her eyes. "Indian ways will live forever, in the safety of our hearts."

Katherine rinsed away the soap and dried her face and hands thoroughly on the towel provided, giving herself time to think. Finally she turned and faced the hired girl. "Yes," she said. "Maybe that's the only hope any of us have for our traditions—the memories of our children."

Maria swallowed visibly, and she glanced toward Christopher and nodded. "The old ways and stories are too valuable to be forgotten. They are a part of who we are."

"Yes," Katherine answered without hesitation. "I'm going to write down every single thing I can remember." Except for giving birth to Christopher, she hadn't done anything worthwhile since she'd crash-landed in the nineteenth century. Now, at least, she could make some kind of record of her experience. Maybe someone, someday, would believe her.

There was a long silence while Maria hovered in the doorway, silent, not quite able to meet Katherine's gaze. Finally she said, "My stepmother was going to help me write out the old legends, but we always thought we had plenty of time. Two years ago she caught the cholera and died."

"I'm sorry," Katherine said. She knew what it was to lose a mother. Memories filled her mind: waxed floors of chipped linoleum, fresh-baked cookies filling the house with the wonderful aromas of chocolate and sugar and butter, a Christmas tree bedecked with homemade ornaments and shining colored lights, the sound of scales being plunked out on the piano by some earnest student.

Katherine had lost all those things, and much more, when Julia Hollis succumbed to cancer, and the grief had followed her even into another woman's life.

"I will bring your tea," Maria replied, closing the door.

Katherine began to pace the length of the hearth, feeling wildly restless. She still remembered only a few details of her other existence, but she knew she'd been an active, energetic person, committed to regular exercise.

"This Victorian bird-in-a-gilded-cage number is not

me," she confided to the baby, who gave a tiny little sigh in response.

She stopped and looked at her image in the elegant mirror above the small brick fireplace. Although she'd had some time to accept her situation, if not understand it, it still astonished her to see a stranger's face reflected back from the glass.

Deciding she needed to take some action, however small or even ill-advised, Katherine eyed the inner door that led to Gavin's room. If she was going to go out and explore her surroundings, she would certainly need clothes, and they were evidently stored in that closet Marianne had entered the day before.

Katherine tried the knob cautiously, all the while expecting a shout of angry warning from Gavin. The door was locked, as before.

A glance at the clock on the mantelpiece revealed that it was well after nine A.M. Surely a dedicated doctor like Gavin had long since left for the hospital or for an office somewhere.

Securing the belt of her robe, Katherine squared her shoulders, marched out into the hall, and boldly turned the brass handle on one of the towering oak doors leading into the master suite.

She wasn't doing anything wrong, she insisted to herself, zeroing in on the closet without so much as a glance toward the massive four-poster. Ever since she'd seen the bed the day before, she'd been entertaining some very disturbing thoughts and images. In short, she'd pictured herself lying naked on it, surrendering to Gavin, taking him inside her.

Entering the huge closet, she found an array of dresses she could not even have imagined. There were silks and organdies, chiffons and cottons, velvets and laces. The sumptuous beauty of the gowns made her breath catch, and she caught an inner glimpse, in her mind's eye, of a little girl playing dress-up, far off in another century, another universe.

Carefully, she took down a hunter-green dress with a short jacket. The fabric was a very lightweight wool, and both garments were trimmed in black silk ribbon.

She was so caught up in the spectacular magic of that closet that all the breath fled her lungs when she turned to leave and collided with a rock-hard chest.

Gavin was standing in the doorway in riding breeches and no shirt, his arms folded. Even with his dark hair rumpled and his beard growing in, he looked entirely too good to be true.

"Good morning," he drawled, and Katherine could see that her disconcertion pleased him.

Color surged into her face. Deciding that the best defense was an offense, she challenged, "What kind of doctor is still lying around in bed at this hour?"

He chuckled, and while the sound wasn't exactly mean, it grated against Katherine's already jumbled nerves. "The kind who didn't get home from the hospital until five-thirty this morning."

Katherine swallowed, wishing he would let her pass. "If you'll excuse me . . ."

Gavin caught her chin in one hand and lifted, and his eyes were somber all of a sudden as he studied her face. "Where are you planning to go?"

"Out," she responded. "If I don't get some fresh air and sunshine, I'll lose my mind."

His dark brows drew together for a moment. "Since when do you enjoy the outdoors, Kathy?" he asked. Skepticism stole into his features. "Ah. Yes. You're meeting Beecham somewhere."

The insult quivered in Katherine's spirit like a spear. "No."

His thumb caressed her cheek, and the light in his gray eyes was a dangerous one, like a night fire flickering in an enemy camp. He touched her mouth then, as if to prepare it for conquering.

A moment later, with a raw sound low in his throat, Gavin kissed her. The action sent a sensation of delicious violence tumbling through her, and when he pulled her closer it was as though she'd struck a brick wall at high speed.

She could not have imagined more powerful feelings than those, but when Gavin thrust his tongue into her mouth, she was confronted with a whole new level of excitement. Her knees went weak, her heart began to beat so rapidly that she feared it would explode, and there was an achy, melting stir in the center of her womanhood. When Gavin lifted a hand to her breast and caressed her, still consuming her mouth, she was struck with a sweet and cataclysmic seizure of a kind she'd never experienced before.

She whimpered, her body convulsing softly against his, and when Gavin suddenly ended the kiss, she stared up at him in bewilderment.

"Never again, Kathy," he said tersely. *"Never again."*

Katherine bent to pick up the dress which had dropped to the floor between them, not wanting him to see the hurt and embarrassment on her face. She might not have understood exactly what he was talking about, but she knew rejection when she encountered it.

Shakily, she left the room, her head held high. Gavin didn't need to know that it took all her pride to keep from defending herself to him, and all her courage to take the dress with her when she left.

One thing was clear. She could do nothing to change what had happened to her; she had a feeling there was no going back to that time and place beyond the crystal bridge.

That left the here and now to work with, and she meant to push up her sleeves and shape a life for herself.

With or without Dr. Gavin Winslow.

5

KATHERINE walked around the beautifully maintained yard and gardens, exhilarated by the fresh spring air and bright sunshine. When she grew tired, she sat on the edge of the marble fountain, drew a deep, delicious breath, and closed her eyes.

The light, unexpected kiss made her open them again, wide.

Jeffrey smiled down at her. "Hello, Kathy," he said in a throaty voice.

If Katherine could have wished the man into a parallel universe, she would have done it. She wasn't at all surprised to look up at the second-floor windows of the mansion and catch a glimpse of Gavin as he turned away.

Jeffrey sat down beside her and took her hand; she wrenched free, feeling miserable.

"Your timing could not have been worse!" she hissed, bolting to her feet and smoothing her skirts.

Jeffrey's gaze had followed hers to the row of windows in the master bedroom. "I suppose the good doctor is on his way down to bloody my nose even as we speak."

"I wouldn't blame him if he did," she replied, tightening the black grosgrain ribbons that held her hunter-green bonnet in place. She drew in another deep breath, this time for courage, and then launched into her announcement. "I don't know what happened between the two of us," she said, and blushed as Jeffrey arched one eyebrow and smiled slightly. "All right, I *do* know. But I want to forget it all. I—I love my husband."

Jeffrey's amused expression turned stormy. He straightened his silk cravat and rose to look down at Katherine's face. "You made a promise to me. You vowed that we would leave for San Francisco, just the two of us, as soon as you'd regained your strength."

Katherine frowned. "Just the two of us? Surely I never meant to leave the baby . . ."

A crimson flush moved up Jeffrey's neck. "We agreed that the child would be better off here, with Dr. Winslow and his sister. Katherine, what's come over you? You're not the same woman I knew!"

She sank back onto the marble seat, dazed. She liked having this ripe and womanly body, and she loved Christopher and . . . yes, heaven help her, Gavin . . . but the more she found out about the original Mrs. Winslow, the more quiet contempt she felt. Not only had the other Katherine betrayed her husband, she had actually planned to abandon her own baby.

Katherine's high spirits were deflated. Earlier she'd actually dared to believe it was possible to win Gavin's forgiveness, if not his love. Now the whole situation seemed more hopeless than ever.

"I don't want to see you again, Jeffrey," she said softly but firmly. "Not ever."

Jeffrey glared at her for a long moment, then turned and stormed away. The metal gate made a loud clatter behind him.

The next sound Katherine heard was slow, derisive applause.

She turned to see Gavin standing on the pathway leading to the French doors. He looked as handsome as ever in his tan breeches, linen shirt, and tailored tweed jacket, and every bit as stubborn.

"Stop it," she snapped. "I'm tired of your damnable mockery, Gavin Winslow."

"An excellent performance—the young matron bidding farewell to her lover. You belong in the theater."

Katherine stamped one foot. "Stop being such a jerk and give me a little credit, will you? I meant what I said to Jeffrey—Mr. Beecham. I never want to see him again!"

"What's a jerk?" Gavin asked, with wary curiosity.

Katherine laughed, but the sound was bitter and filled with despair. "Stupid and stubborn would pretty much cover it," she said.

For a long, long moment, Gavin just looked at her, his expression unreadable. There might have been tenderness in his pewter eyes, but there were anger and distrust, too. "I think you'd better go inside," he finally decreed.

She didn't bother to argue; she was suddenly too tired, and the events of the morning had left her feeling a little loosely wrapped. She started toward the house, her eyes averted, and when she passed Gavin he stopped her, catching hold of her arm.

"I won't forgive a second mistake, Katherine," he said.

She did not look at him. "You haven't forgiven the first one," she pointed out.

In her room, a fresh nightgown and wrapper awaited, and a maid had put clean sheets on the bed.

Katherine changed clothes, then sat in the rocking chair to nurse Christopher, who seemed to have a keener appetite with every passing day. When he'd gone back to sleep some minutes later, with that guileless propensity of newborns, Katherine crawled into bed, stretched out on the crisp bed linens, and dozed off herself.

When she awakened several hours later, the floors and corners of the room were shadowed with twilight, and there was a covered tray of food waiting on the bedside table. Maria was sitting in the rocking chair, nursing Christopher.

Katherine sat up with a sigh and moved the tray onto her lap. Like Christopher, she was ravenous. "Is your baby a boy or a girl?" she asked.

Maria's expression was remote. "A boy."

The dinner tray held a delectable assortment of fare, including a chicken pie and a dish of stewed pears. "I'd like to see him. What's his name?"

Maria gazed down at Christopher as she spoke. "The tribal elders will give my son a name, when the time comes." She lifted deep brown eyes to Katherine's face.

"I, too, would like to see him, but he lives with my people now."

Katherine, who had been eager to eat, lowered her fork back to the tray, her food forgotten. "You mean they took your baby away from you?"

"I gave him to them; his father is the chief's son. It is best."

Katherine forced herself to take a bite of her meal. "I couldn't bear to be away from Christopher," she said.

A glance in Maria's direction revealed that the woman was looking at her in confusion now. Perhaps she'd known that the mistress of the house planned to run away with a lover and leave her child behind for others to raise. Perhaps Maria had even hoped to fill the void in her heart by caring for the Winslow baby once Katherine was gone.

"I'll share him with you," Katherine said gently.

Maria blinked, looked away, then met Katherine's gaze again. "You've changed," she said. "And it seems there is much you don't remember."

Katherine nodded. "I have changed," she agreed. "I've changed more than anyone in the world would ever believe. And you're right—there's a lot I don't remember. Did Mrs.—did I keep diaries, Maria? Did I save the letters I received?"

Christopher had fallen asleep at Maria's breast. She laid him ever so gently in her lap, rebuttoned the front of her dress, and then raised the contented infant to her shoulder to be burped.

"There are papers," Maria said. "I will bring them after Dr. Winslow goes to the hospital for rounds."

"Thank you," Katherine replied.

As it happened, Gavin visited Katherine's room before he left the house. She would almost have preferred his scathing temper to the cool distance of his manner.

"I'm sending you to the island house for the rest of the summer," he announced.

Katherine was dismayed. She didn't know what island house Gavin was talking about, for one thing. For another,

she hated leaving him in Seattle with the likes of Caroline
Raynes. "Do I have a choice?" she asked.

The concept obviously caught Gavin by surprise. "A
choice?"

Katherine nodded. These nineteenth-century men were
something else. "Suppose I said I didn't want to go anywhere, that I preferred to stay in Seattle with you?"

Gavin gave a long-suffering sigh. "I would reply that
your preferences don't carry a great deal of weight," he
responded evenly.

Once again he'd used words to slap Katherine, and the
blow hurt as much as the back of his hand would have.

"Bastard," she said, angry not only because of the pain
he'd inflicted but because tears had sprung to her eyes, and
she hadn't wanted him to see her cry over something he'd
said or done.

He came to her bedside and bent to kiss her forehead.
"I love you, too, my cherished darling," he responded with
theatrical politeness. "Good night."

Finally Katherine noticed his formal clothing. "You're
going out!" she accused, picturing him dancing with one
beautiful woman after another in some elegant ballroom.
The next picture she had was of Gavin and the oh-so-proper
Miss Raynes, chatting while they ate an elegant dinner, then
clinking their wineglasses together in a toast that excluded
the rest of the world.

"Yes," he responded.

Katherine started to protest, then stopped herself. She
couldn't ask him not to socialize, especially with the track
record the other Katherine had chalked up. "Gavin . . ."
She ran her tongue over dry lips. "I don't suppose . . . well
. . . would it help if I told you I was sorry for all the things
that happened before?"

She sensed his withdrawal long moments before he actually drew back from her bedside. "No," he answered
flatly. "It's too late for that."

He turned to the cradle then, and Katherine wished she
could read the expression on his face as he looked down at

the baby, but the gas lamps and the fire had not been lit, and the room was dim.

"I suppose you've noticed that he looks exactly like you," she dared to say.

Gavin raised his eyes to her face then, and the coldness in them pinned Katherine to the headboard as surely as an Indian's arrow would have done. "Christopher is my son," he conceded, "but that is a happy accident. He could just as well have been sired by Beecham or the man who delivers coal. As far as you and I are concerned, the fact that I'm acknowledging this child changes nothing."

The lump aching in Katherine's throat made speech impossible for the moment, and her mind was reeling anyway. She would not have been able to think of a response scathing enough to match Gavin's words.

That night the house seemed to buzz with activity, but Katherine was still too stricken by her encounter with Gavin to wonder what was going on.

In the morning she found out.

"We're going to the island," Marianne announced, her face aglow. "I can hardly wait to walk on the beach again."

Katherine loved the beach, and the prospect of spending time in a waterfront house would have thrilled her in her other life, but now she only felt forlorn. Obviously, Gavin wanted his wife and sister out of the house so he could bring his mistress around with impunity.

Katherine and Marianne left for the wharf area at the head of a virtual caravan of carriages. They were followed by Maria and Christopher in another coach, and beyond that was a wagon loaded down with trunks.

Reaching Elliott Bay, where a small boat, part of the mosquito fleet, would take them to Vashon Island, Katherine forgot some of her heartache. There were creaking wharves and shouting sailors and clanging bells everywhere, and the scene was so different from its counterpart in modern-day Seattle that she was amazed. She wanted to remember every sight and sound.

After the passengers and their baggage had been loaded onto the boat, the captain tooted his whistle and the craft slipped bravely out into the harbor. Katherine stood at the railing, watching the land retreat.

The city was so like the one she knew, and so different.

Gavin didn't trouble himself to see them off, and Katherine wondered if he'd ever returned from his dinner party the night before. She hadn't seen him since his visit to her room, or caught the sound of his voice in the hallway.

"I brought the letters and the diaries," Maria said, standing beside her on the deck. At Katherine's immediate frown, the Indian girl smiled and added, "Don't worry. Christopher is with his aunt, being badly spoiled."

Katherine sighed. "Thank you for helping me, Maria—and for not automatically deciding that I'm crazy."

The girl's ageless brown eyes studied Katherine's face placidly. "You are not mad," she avowed. "And you are not Katherine Winslow."

6

KATHERINE looked into Maria's pensive brown eyes and recognized a friend. She was not ready to explain her helter-skelter arrival in this time and place; indeed, she didn't understand the situation herself. Still, it was a comfort to know there was one person who might be receptive to such a strange confidence.

After that both women watched the shore as the steam-powered boat chugged out into the bay, headed toward Vashon Island. White gulls as well as gray swooped and chattered alongside, and the waters looked like india ink under the relentless blue of the summer sky.

Katherine was entranced by the sight of the receding city. There was no evidence of the towering steel-and-glass skyline of her day, and wagons and carriages moved in the streets instead of automobiles.

She smiled. "It's like a movie," she said.

Maria frowned. "What?"

Katherine patted Maria's hand. "I'll explain some other time," she promised.

After an hour's journey, the boat docked at Vashon Island. There, another carriage awaited the Winslow party, along with a buckboard for hauling trunks and valises.

Katherine was just as fascinated by the island as she had been by the city. As they drove through a small cluster of buildings she spotted a mercantile, a blacksmith's shop, and a lovely lighthouse formed of natural stone. For her, the world had become one big hands-on museum.

The Winslows' summer house, which overlooked the water, turned out to be almost as impressive as the mansion in the city.

It was an enormous white frame house with lots of balconies and porches, and a few feet below the point of the highest gable, an octagon-shaped stained-glass window glowed with captured sunlight. There were rose bushes everywhere, along with arbors and benches and fountains, and two rows of graceful weeping willows towered like an honor guard on either side of the gravel driveway.

Although Katherine was not happy to be exiled to the island, she could not help being charmed by the magnificent house. Just looking at the place gave her a feeling of homecoming so profound that tears came to her eyes.

She sniffled. "It's lovely," she said.

Marianne hadn't even glanced out the carriage window. "You've been behaving so oddly of late, Katherine. You speak as though you've never seen the Haven, and you were married here!"

Katherine glanced helplessly at her sister-in-law, then bit her lip and ignored Marianne's remark. There was simply nothing she could say that wouldn't eventually land her in some grim nineteenth-century asylum.

If Marianne only knew how many things she didn't "remember," Katherine thought. What had happened to Gavin and Marianne's parents? For that matter, what had happened to her own? Had the other Katherine been raised in a happy home, with brothers and sisters, or as an only child? Why wasn't a pretty young woman like Marianne married?

The questions were practically never-ending, and Katherine hoped the letters and diaries Maria had brought along would answer at least a few of them.

As the carriage wheels rattled on the brick cobblestone driveway, Christopher stirred in Maria's arms and began to fuss. Katherine reached for him, astonished at the depth of love she felt. He was another woman's child, conceived and nurtured by the light of a stranger's soul, and yet she could not have been more devoted to him if he'd been her own.

"There now," she said softly, holding the infant against her shoulder and patting his tiny, flannel-swaddled back. "We're home."

The inside of the house was as splendid as the outside, and of the same gracious design. The rooms were all large and bright, filled with solid beautifully constructed furniture, but the pieces didn't loom oppressively over Katherine's head the way some of their counterparts at the mansion did.

There was a screened sunporch overlooking the orchard and, beyond that, the indigo water. Katherine intended to spend a great deal of her time in that quiet, sheltered place, working things through in her mind.

Her trunks were carried to the master suite, which turned out to be the chamber boasting the eight-sided stained-glass window. The suite offered both sitting and dressing rooms, and the floor was of bare wood, polished to a high shine. There was a small fireplace, fronted in gray and white marble, and the mantelpiece was fashioned of a wood so shiny and dark that it resembled ebony.

"There's been a mistake," Katherine confided anxiously to Marianne. Christopher had been fed, and Maria had taken him to the nursery across the hall, and Marianne was supervising the placement of Katherine's trunks.

"What kind of mistake?" Marianne asked as George, the

caretaker, and Walter, his helper from the stables, left the room.

Katherine went to close the door, and the color was high in her cheeks when she replied, "This is surely *Gavin's* room. You know he and I don't share quarters . . ."

"More's the pity," Marianne reflected. "It would be better for both of you."

Katherine was impatient. "I think I should move to another room at once."

"Poppycock," Marianne returned airily. "Gavin is not God, however he may protest to the contrary; he has no right to hand down decrees. Besides, we probably won't see him until we return to Seattle in September anyway."

"September?" Katherine loved the island, as little as she'd seen of it, but the idea of not having so much as a glimpse of Gavin for three long months was practically unbearable.

Marianne sighed, spread her hands for a moment, then let them fall back to her sides. "You've finally fallen in love with your husband, haven't you?" she demanded with kindly frankness. "Forgive me for asking, Katherine, but what took you so long? Couldn't you have recognized your tender feelings before you humiliated the man in front of half the city of Seattle?"

Katherine detected no hostility in Marianne's words, only honest puzzlement. "I can't explain," she said, stepping through the French doors that opened onto a balcony. "At least, not yet. But yes, heaven help me, I think I have fallen in love with Gavin. I would do practically anything to win him back."

Marianne stood beside her at the railing of the balcony, and the two of them watched the sunlight dancing on the sound and the pale gulls soaring over the tops of the apple trees in the orchard. "I would like to see that happen," she said with gentle foreboding, "for your sake, and Christopher's, and especially for Gavin's. But the way you flaunted your—flirtation—with Jeffrey Beecham, well, that kind of disgrace isn't easy for a man to live down."

Katherine swallowed, and she didn't look at Marianne

when she went on. She didn't dare. "Suppose I told you I didn't remember anything that happened to me before Christopher was born? No wedding, no adultery, no anything. Would you believe me?"

"I would be very concerned," Marianne replied gently.

Katherine met Marianne's gaze and knew she could not tell her more, not then. "You're so lovely, Marianne. Why haven't you married and started a family of your own?"

Marianne's flawless skin paled slightly, and her mouth tightened almost imperceptibly—not with anger, Katherine thought, but with pain. "You really *don't* remember," she said. "Katherine, I was engaged to Timothy Waynewright, the vice president of the Merchants' Bank. He was shot and killed in a robbery two days before our wedding."

"Dear God," Katherine whispered, sagging against the railing for a moment. "Marianne, I'm so sorry."

Marianne looked more concerned with Katherine's state of health than her own tragedy. She took her sister-in-law's arm and escorted her firmly back inside the house.

"Gavin should be told about this—this memory lapse of yours. It might make a lot of difference." As she spoke, Marianne was maneuvering Katherine onto the big bed and covering her with a creamy cashmere throw.

Katherine shook her head. "None at all," she said. "He would think I was only pretending, in an effort to escape the consequences of Kath—of my mistakes."

Marianne left then, and Katherine slept for several hours. When she awakened, a lavender hatbox had materialized on her nightstand, like something left by Santa or the Easter Bunny. Katherine sat up, smoothed her hair, and set the box on her lap.

It was filled with scented vellum letters, and there were sepia photographs and two thick leather-bound journals as well.

Katherine started with the letters, which were mostly from school friends and family members back East. From the collection of mail, she learned that the other Katherine had been raised by a wealthy maiden aunt in Maine. She'd gone to boarding school in Connecticut from the first grade through the twelfth, then attended a Boston finishing school.

The photographs showed Katherine standing with Gavin, smiling brightly, and the two of them looked so happy. How could things have gone so terribly wrong?

Katherine leaned back against the carved mahogany headboard for a long time, staring at the empty fireplace and assimilating what she'd garnered from the first dozen letters. Only after Mrs. Hawkins, the housekeeper, had brought her tea and fresh strawberries did she tackle the rest.

It was strange, examining the images of another person's life, seeing her hopes and dreams reflected back in the handwriting of an elderly aunt, an understanding friend, a cousin. Even though Katherine learned a lot about the other Katherine in those leisurely hours of reading, the questions multiplied even faster than the answers.

The journals awaited her, promising the most intimate insights of all, but Katherine's mind was already spinning with details. She would save the diaries for another day.

At dinner that night Katherine was preoccupied, pretty much letting Marianne carry the conversation. Her predecessor had been a flighty and somewhat selfish creature, and very spoiled despite her isolation from her family. She must have been a lonely child, though privileged, starved for love and attention.

The next morning Katherine rose very early. She saw to Christopher's needs, then left him with Maria and went out for a walk, carrying one of the journals with her. Following a winding path down through the orchard, she heard the low, summery murmur of the tide, and the sound stirred some long-dormant hope within her.

Katherine walked along the shoreline for a time, delighting in the sights and sounds and smells, the wet, rocky sand, the water-beaten pilings and swaying boat docks. She came upon a bed of oysters, stopping to speculate, one hand shading her eyes from the morning sun, as to whether any of the hoary shells contained a pearl.

When she began to feel tired she returned to the orchard, found a tree with a low, sturdy branch and a clear view of the water, and climbed up. Once settled, her cumbersome skirts tucked in around her, she pulled the first journal from her pocket and started to read.

The diary's author, whom Katherine now thought of as Katherine the First, had visited Seattle after sailing from San Francisco to Hong Kong and back again. She'd met Dr. Gavin Winslow at a party and deemed him "handsome, if dreadfully serious." She'd also recorded that he'd inherited a fortune from his father, who'd been among the first timber barons in the area, a fact that apparently redeemed him a little for practicing the humble profession of medicine.

As Katherine read, her legs dangling from the tree branch, one shoulder resting against its trunk, she confirmed her earlier suspicions. Gavin's young bride had not been a wicked vamp, bent on shaming her husband in the eyes of the world, but a confused, lonely child. She'd needed *everyone's* love and attention, not just her husband's. When people failed to notice her, she'd written, she felt as though she were invisible and sometimes even began to doubt her existence. Often, she'd sunk into "black melancholia" and sincerely wished she'd never been born.

Her name came tumbling toward her on the warm, salty breeze.

"Katherine! Kaaathy!"

It was Marianne.

Katherine closed the journal, tucked it back into her skirt pocket, and clambered down from the tree. Her skill at this endeavor was a holdover from the life she'd lived on the other side of the crystal bridge. There, as a child, she'd been an inveterate tomboy.

When Katherine reached the ground and turned to start toward her sister-in-law, she found the young woman staring at her, openmouthed.

"Katherine, were you up in the boughs of that tree?" she asked incredulously.

"You know I was," Katherine answered pleasantly. "You must have seen me."

"But you *never* do things like that."

Katherine smiled. "I do now."

7

KATHERINE and Marianne had lunch on the screened porch, with Maria to keep them company. Katherine was preoccupied, as she had been the night before at dinner, and the journal, hidden away in her pocket, consumed her thoughts.

When the new idea bobbed to the top of Katherine's mind, it startled her so much that she dropped her soup spoon with a clatter and even gave a little cry.

"Excuse me, please," she blurted out, shoving back her chair and bolting to her feet.

The other two women looked surprised at her behavior.

"Katherine, are you all right?" Marianne inquired.

She merely nodded hastily and dashed into the main part of the house. In a massive and very masculine study off the main entryway, she found what she was looking for: a desk, paper, a bottle of ink, and a pen.

Sinking into a cushioned chair of the finest Moroccan leather, Katherine pulled several sheets of expensively made vellum stationery from the desk drawer. After arranging the paper on the mirror-bright surface, she opened the ink bottle, dipped her pen, and began to write.

Excitement mounted within her as she penned one nonsensical sentence after another. Only when her hand became too tired to write did Katherine finally wipe the pen's nib clean and put the lid back on the ink.

Without waiting for the pages to dry, she compared them to the flamboyant script in the journals. The letters on the loose papers were narrower, neater, and much smaller.

She had retained something more of that other life than

a tangle of memories, then. She had kept her own hand-writing.

Within a moment Katherine was so breathless that she dared not rise from the chair, lest her trembling knees refuse to hold her.

She laid her head down on the desk and tried to gather her composure. The other Katherine was almost surely lying in that hospital bed in the Seattle of a hundred years hence, or perhaps she'd even died.

Katherine had sympathy for Gavin's bride, but she also wanted this body, this man, and this life, even though the last tenant had botched things up royally.

She began to shiver, feeling chilled even though the room was warm. Maybe the whole process would reverse itself. Maybe she would be wrenched away from Christopher and Gavin and the elegantly antique world she had come to love . . .

Finally Katherine drew a deep breath and made herself sit up. She would take things one day at a time and deal with trouble when she came across it. In the meanwhile she planned to somehow, some way win Gavin back.

During her first week at the Haven, Katherine read and reread all the diaries and letters, and she must have studied the tintypes and sepia photographs a million times. She tried on all the summer dresses that had arrived with her in the trunks and studied herself in the mirror.

The second week brought a letter from Gavin. Katherine was disappointed if not surprised that it was addressed to Marianne. While the message carried warm wishes for his sister and inquiries about Christopher's progress, Katherine might not have existed at all.

By the time twenty-one days had gone by, Katherine was riding all over the island on horseback. While she enjoyed her adventures, she also knew she was trying to outdistance her own doubts and injured feelings.

After a month, Marianne announced plans for a garden party. Everyone in the Winslow social circle, both on the island and in Seattle, would be invited.

Katherine went through her wardrobe, garment by garment, and prayed that Gavin would attend.

In early August, five weeks after Marianne, Maria, Katherine, and Christopher had moved to the island for the summer, the party was held.

Gavin sent word from Seattle that he was too busy to join in the festivities.

Katherine attended the social event, smiling the whole time, barely able to breathe because her heart was in her throat. She spoke with warmth and graciousness to all the guests but was careful not to behave inappropriately, for she hoped to undo some of the damage the other Katherine had done.

After the last guest had retired, Katherine locked herself in her room and wept because Gavin had stayed away.

On a hot day at the end of August, when Maria went to visit friends on the far side of the island, taking Christopher along, Marianne journeyed to Seattle to attend a wedding. Katherine looked at the roiling charcoal clouds on the horizon and felt a sweet, dangerous anticipation.

There was a storm coming, and Katherine loved storms.

As night fell, the very earth seemed to rock with the force of the thunder. The wind howled around the house, and Katherine knew the water in the sound would be churning, the waves white-capped. Lightning outlined the old lighthouse Katherine had sketched so many times, and the housekeeper and caretaker hurried from room to room, securing the windows.

Katherine's fascination with the natural panorama seemed to confound them, but they offered no comment. Despite her earlier efforts to let the old couple know that she regarded them as equals, they still saw themselves as servants.

"Would you like me to bring you a brandy, Mrs. Winslow?" the housekeeper asked anxiously. She was a sturdy but compact woman with large blue eyes and white hair wound into a coronet on top of her head. "I know you always get a little nervous when the weather gets like this."

"Nervous?" Katherine laughed. "Heavens, no—I'm not afraid of a little thunder and lightning."

But *she* had been, Katherine realized. That was why Mrs. Hawkins was looking at her as though she was turning into a werewolf before her very eyes.

Before the housekeeper could reply, the front door slammed and a voice as domineering as the thunder echoed through the house.

"Marianne! Maria!"

Gavin.

It wounded Katherine that he hadn't called her name as well, but of course she shouldn't have been surprised. From the first, Gavin had allowed her not even the skimpiest illusion that he cared for her.

At least he was consistent.

Mr. Hawkins was busy building a blaze in the parlor fireplace, so his wife went to greet her grumpy master. When Gavin entered the room, he looked through Katherine as if she were invisible and went to stand on the hearth, warming his hands.

The housekeeper and caretaker left immediately, and Katherine herself was edging toward the towering double doors when Gavin stopped her with a brusque "Where is my son?"

The very roof of the house shook with the force of two fronts colliding high in the sky, no more elemental than Gavin's formidable will meeting her own.

"*Our* son is with Maria," Katherine answered evenly, wondering how she could love Dr. Winslow so much when he invariably made her yearn to strangle him. "They went visiting this afternoon, and I'm sure they're perfectly safe."

Gavin assessed his wife with eyes as cold as a frozen steel blade. "You've been well?"

Katherine was secretly thinking how fitting it would have been if he'd snarled and shown vampire teeth, but Gavin was as stunningly attractive as ever. The reflexive pitch and roll in her stomach was proof of that. "Very well."

A blast of thunder rattled the windows, and his gaze narrowed as he stared at her. "I rather expected to find you cowering under the bed in fear, my dear," he said. "You were always terrified of storms."

"You don't know me as well as you think you do," she responded crisply. For all her light words, she had a dizzying fancy that some dangerous enchantment had settled over the big house with Gavin's arrival.

"I know you all too well," Gavin corrected her, shedding his long coat and tossing it aside, then crossing to a teak-wood cabinet near the doors and pouring himself a brandy.

Katherine decided to ignore the statement. "What brings you here, Dr. Winslow?" she asked, moving close to the fire because he had abandoned the space. "Did someone tell you I was happy? That would surely account for your hasty appearance and intractable mood." *I'm getting the Victorian vernacular down pretty well,* she congratulated herself.

Gavin was frowning as he regarded her in the flickering glow of the lamps, his brandy like glowing amber in the firelight. "Since when do you use words like 'intractable'?"

"You wouldn't believe it if I told you," Katherine replied. Invisible St. Elmo's fire danced and crackled in the room, and she sensed that Gavin was as aware of the dynamic charisma between them as she was.

He took another sip of his brandy. "You'll be sorry to hear that your Jeffrey Beecham has lit out for greener pastures." The challenge was a quiet one, but nonetheless deadly.

"Good," she said, with light assurance. "I won't miss him." She swallowed, summoning up all her courage. "But I have missed you, Gavin. Very much."

His frigid gaze moved over her—she was wearing a cotton gown, a white background with small lavender flowers scattered over it—and her rich auburn hair was gathered up in a soft Gibson-girl style. When his Adam's apple moved, Katherine felt a certain tenderness toward him, as well as a captivation so powerful that she feared to think to what lengths it might drive her.

"Do not insult me with the inference that you cherish any wifely sentiments toward me," he warned. For all his words, for all that she was standing half a room away,

Katherine was woefully conscious of the hardness and heat of his body.

She sighed. She'd never seduced a man before, or been seduced *by* one, for that matter, and she had no idea how to proceed. She only knew that she had been thrust into this century, and the company of this particular man, because his soul was mate to hers.

"You want me, Gavin," she said simply. Quietly.

He turned away and tossed his brandy, glass and all, onto the fire. The glass shattered and the blaze roared up the chimney, but Gavin paid it no apparent mind. He stood with his back to her, his hands braced against the mantelpiece.

He hadn't given an inch of ground, and yet somehow Katherine knew she had the upper hand. "I'll bring you some dinner, if you'd like," she said in as normal a tone as she could manage. She'd been hoping and praying Gavin would come to the island all these weeks, and now he was here and she was more certain of her love for him than ever.

He was silent for a long, long time, but Katherine was just as stubborn as he was, and she waited.

"Bring the tray to my room," he said.

Her heart rushed into her throat. She was both terrified and joyous as she hurried to the kitchen. By the time she climbed the back stairway and entered the master suite half an hour later, after she'd laboriously reheated the leftovers from supper, she was trembling.

It wasn't fear of sharing her body with Gavin that scared her, although she had never been with a man in her life, despite having gone through the experience of childbirth. No, it was the possibility that he meant to reject her, to humiliate her, that frightened her so much.

Balancing the tray on one hand, she opened the door and stepped into the bedroom that had been hers alone these past weeks.

Gavin had built up the fire and was sitting in a wing-back chair, gazing solemnly at the flames. He'd taken off his coat and his collar, and his shirt gaped open to the middle of his chest.

Katherine wished she could believe he was looking so

rakishly handsome for her benefit, but it was more likely that he was completely unaware of the image he presented.

She set the tray on the small round table beside his chair, and he didn't raise his eyes to her or acknowledge her in any way.

She decided she'd read him wrong earlier and moved to the bureau, feeling both dejection and relief. "I'll sleep in one of the guest rooms," she said in a voice barely loud enough to compete with the storm outside and the crackling babble of the fire.

"You're my wife," Gavin said gruffly, still without looking in her direction. "You will sleep in my bed."

8

THE light of the bedroom fire flickered over Gavin's rain-damp clothes, glimmered on the polished leather of his riding boots, lent a crimson halo to his ebony hair. Katherine was stricken by the joyous love she felt for this husband she'd won by accident; it was as though some ancient wrong had been finally righted, after a long and difficult struggle.

Every tiny fiber in her body seemed to resonate, like the strings of some mellow old instrument that had been lifted from a musty trunk, tuned, and finally strummed with cherishing fingers.

Gavin set his strong hands on the arms of the chair and thrust himself wearily to his feet. When he turned to face Katherine, he took on an aura made up of firelight and the violent, golden lightning that flashed beyond the terrace doors.

Katherine could not read the expression on his face for

the shadows that cloaked him, but she felt the barely leashed power in his body, sensed the distant tumult of the battle going on within his spirit. The conflict, she knew, was between the mightiest of human emotions, love, and its twin, hatred.

For the first time since she'd landed in this place, she had hope of finding her way into Gavin's heart and making a lasting place for herself there.

Fearful that anything she said might tilt the delicate balance the wrong way, she kept her silence. She lifted her chin and stared straight at his face to show him she wouldn't be intimidated. For all that, the separate impacts of his physical presence, the warriorlike strength of his spirit, the laser-powered reach of his mind, practically overwhelmed her.

He took a step toward her, then another, reluctantly, as though resisting some elemental force every inch of the way.

His hand came to rest on her shoulder, and she turned and lightly brushed his knuckles with her lips.

"God help me," he whispered in the tone of one who expects no aid from any quarter, including heaven. He tilted his head back and closed his eyes, and Katherine watched the play of muscles in his magnificent neck for a long moment, then softly kissed the hollow of his throat.

She felt a shudder go through him, knew a sensation of homecoming that went far beyond the physical when he wrenched her against him. Her hair spilled down her back as he plunged splayed fingers beneath the little knot she'd pinned so carefully into place.

He spread his free hand over the small of her back, pressing her curvy softness against an opposing hardness. When he assailed her with his demanding, masterful kiss, it seemed to Katherine that the elegant room had suddenly turned to a vacuum, like outer space. Only her connection with Gavin allowed her to breathe; when he withdrew, her last contact with the life force would be broken. She would shrivel to a cinder and then disappear entirely.

Just when Katherine thought she couldn't accommodate another sensation, another dizzying emotion, without going into overload, Gavin thrust his tongue past her lips. It was symbolic of the conquering that would come later, she knew, and the sweet warning caused her knees to go weak.

She uttered a desolate little cry when Gavin lifted her into his arms, never troubling to withdraw his mouth from hers, and carried her to the bed. Only when he'd laid her on the coverlet did he draw back so that he could look at her as he stripped her of her clothes.

He made a slow ritual of that process, starting with her shoes. After rolling down each of her stockings, he kissed the tops of her insteps with light, fevered touches of his lips.

He pushed up her skirts and petticoats to bare her knees, and Katherine bit down hard on her lower lip to keep from pleading with him to go ahead and take her.

By the time she was completely naked, her skin glowed with perspiration and her hips twisted on the mattress, betraying her, seeking some contact with him.

He caressed one of her plump breasts as he began taking off his own clothes, and when he was finally bare, as she was, he stretched out over her, letting her feel his daunting manhood against her upper thigh.

Now, she thought, as hot shivers of desire streaked through her. Now, finally, he'll take me. I'll be his.

Instead, though, he slipped downward, his coarse chest hair chafing her breasts and stomach in an elementally pleasant way. When he took her nipple into his mouth, she cried out in helpless pleasure and arched against the steely strength of the body that spanned the length of her like a bridge over a flood-swollen stream.

At the same time, thunder and rain slammed against the house, and Katherine had a vague sense that no matter how loudly she called out in response to his attentions, no one else on the planet would hear.

She surrendered, completely and absolutely, reaching back to grip the underside of the headboard in desperate hands. Had she still possessed the faculties to speak, she would have begged, but she was far beyond that now. A storm had broken in her body and spirit, and she was at its mercy.

Finally, finally, when she wanted to weep with the force of her need, Gavin entered her in a long, slow stroke. He was looking into her suddenly wide-open eyes as he took her, watching her responses in the faulty light of the fire.

Katherine had never been so intimate with a man, not in her previous life, and in that other body she would probably have suffered pain. As it was, she felt only a tightness, then electricity as the tempest in her heart and soul gained momentum.

She clutched wildly at Gavin's shoulders, unable to ask for what she needed because she didn't know its name.

Fortunately, he seemed to know very well. He began to move within her, slowly, steadily, strongly, and while he moved, he nibbled at her lower lip, her neck, her earlobes, her jawline.

Each stroke made Katherine more desperate for the next one. Her breath quickened, and her nipples were hard buttons against Gavin's chest, her legs like a fierce vise around his hips.

Finally the pleasure reached an explosive pitch, and Katherine marveled even as her new body did its dance beneath Gavin, curving high to meet his hips. Her husky cries of triumph breached that last barrier of reserve he'd erected, and he uttered a raw shout and then convulsed against her, driving deep, spilling himself.

Gavin collapsed, his head resting against her breast, when it was finally over. His breathing was ragged, like Katherine's own, and neither of them was capable of speech.

Now that the harsh demands of his body had been met, at least for the moment, Gavin could think with some coherence again. And what he was thinking troubled him deeply.

People rarely changed in any lasting fashion. He knew that because of his Harvard education and his personal experience as a man and a doctor. Seeming alterations of personality were usually temporary, except in some cases of religious conversion.

He listened to the heartbeat of the woman whose luscious breasts cushioned his head, not as a physician, but as a man who drew a spiritual sustenance from the sound. This was Kathy, the woman he'd loved to the point of desperation, the mother of his child, the only bedmate he'd taken since his marriage. Yes, even after his wife had betrayed him, he had been faithful to her.

It did seem that Kathy had changed drastically since the day of Christopher's birth, though he feared to believe it. Her much gossiped about indiscretions had wounded him to the very wellsprings of his soul; he knew he could not endure such terrible pain again.

He closed his eyes, already feeling the temptation to turn his head and feast gently at her nipple, and a series of images flashed through his mind for the thousandth time.

Months before, Kathy had been defiant about her affair with Jeffrey Beecham. She'd said he was more attentive and affectionate than Gavin, more *fun*. She'd made no secret of the fact that she'd rather be Beecham's wife than his.

Since Christopher's arrival, however, she'd brushed the other man off like a speck of dust, and tonight she'd responded to Gavin's lovemaking as she never had.

There was a change in the way she spoke, too. Although her vocabulary had not been limited before, she had a much greater grasp of the language now.

Then there was the way she acted. Katherine was a devoted mother to Christopher, he knew that from what he'd seen and from Marianne's regular letters. And there were still other things.

According to reports from Maria, Kathy had taken to sitting in trees, reading. It was amazing enough that she would open a book other than her journal; it was incomprehensible that she was reportedly working her way through the Haven's well-stocked library. Furthermore, she'd never treated the help with such courtesy.

Gavin's long-starved body was not concerned with the speculations of his mind. He could feel himself going hard against the delicious cushion of Katherine's thigh, and the muscles in his hips and buttocks were flexing involuntarily, preparing themselves to thrust.

He wondered how she would receive him now, she who had never really cared for the strain and messiness of love-making—at least with him.

With a long sigh, Gavin turned his head and brushed a waiting nipple with his lips. The morsel immediately pouted, ready for capture.

He laid a hand on Katherine's belly, made slow, firm circles on the satiny expanse.

Kathy's fingers plunged into his hair, and she startled him by pulling him close for her kiss. Just before she raised her lips to his, she whispered breathlessly, "No preliminaries this time, Gavin. Just take me, hard and fast."

Her words intoxicated him as surely as a pint of good Kentucky whiskey would have done, and again he marveled as he positioned himself to give her what she wanted. What they both wanted.

The storm had passed when Katherine awakened the next morning, and Gavin had already left her bed. Indeed, Christopher was back, regarding his mother wonderingly over Maria's shoulder as she held him in the rocking chair.

The immediate sense of desolation that gripped Katherine at the realization that Gavin was gone was instantly displaced by the joy of seeing her son again.

"You're home from your travels," she chimed, sitting up and tucking the sheets underneath her armpits because Gavin had stripped her of every stitch the night before and never given her time to put on a nightgown.

Maria turned to smile. "Yes. I hope you weren't worried—we were safe with Aunt Nisa and Uncle Tie throughout the storm. Uncle brought us home this morning."

Although Katherine had definitely missed Christopher, she had had confidence in Maria's ability to take care of him, and she had not been overly concerned. "I trusted you completely. Now let me hold my handsome boy before I perish for the longing."

Gently, Maria handed the infant to Katherine, who cradled him against her breast and bent her head to kiss his fuzzy little crown.

"Have you seen Dr. Winslow around this morning?" she asked presently, hoping the question didn't betray too much.

A glance at Maria's face showed that the other woman had already divined the situation, probably from Katherine's lack of a nightgown and the pair of shiny riding boots sitting neatly beside the wardrobe.

"He's gone to the shore, I think," Maria said with a certain friendly smugness. "When something's troubling the doctor, he likes to come out here and walk along the beach while he works it through."

Katherine cuddled Christopher a little closer and stroked his back with her hand. Gavin had made thorough love to her the night before, unknowingly changing her forever, but he hadn't mentioned the word "love." She could only conclude that he was having doubts this morning, and maybe regrets, too.

"You look so sad," Maria said, coming to sit on the edge of the bed and squeezing Katherine's free hand.

A tear welled up in Katherine's eye. "I am," she answered. And then, because she knew this woman was a friend, because she couldn't keep the secret anymore, she poured out her story. Katherine told Maria about that other life, painted the freeway and the speeding sports car and the jackknifed truck into as understandable a picture as she could. She explained about the crystal bridge, the shock of waking up inside someone else's body—someone who was in the middle of childbirth—and the even weirder sensation that she'd known Gavin Winslow for all eternity, that her love for him was as primitive as the stars, and that she belonged with him.

When all the breathless, disjointed words had tumbled out of her mouth, Katherine sat tensing, holding Christopher and waiting to know if there was one person on earth who would believe her.

9

Maria carefully took the baby, who had fallen asleep against Katherine's chest, and laid him in the cradle.

Pressing the covers to her collarbone, Katherine scrambled to the foot of the bed for her paisley silk wrapper, which she hastily donned. She hoped Maria was remembering the day they'd come to the island, when they'd stood talking at the rail of the ferry and the other woman had said, *You are not mad. And you are not Katherine Winslow.*

When Katherine's friend turned to face her, there was a reassuring smile on her face. "We have many strange legends among our people," she said with a little shrug. "Besides, who is to say what is truth and what is not?"

Katherine was so relieved that she sagged to the edge of the bed. "Do you know what Gavin would probably say if I told him that same story? That I'd broken a blood vessel in my brain or suffered a psychotic episode."

Maria's pretty face crumpled with puzzlement. "What?"

"He'd think I was crazy," Katherine simplified.

"Tell me more about that other world. Is it better than this one?"

"In some ways," Katherine answered with a sigh. "There are lots of medical advances." She glanced toward Christopher, sleeping comfortably in his cradle, and felt fiercely protective. "Many of the old-time diseases like whooping cough and measles and smallpox have been almost entirely eliminated. People don't have to work as hard, and everything is much faster. For instance, here a letter

250

takes weeks to cross the country, but where I come from, there's a machine called a fax that will transmit—send— words or pictures anywhere in the world, in just a matter of moments."

Maria's mouth was open.

If there was one thing Katherine enjoyed, it was a receptive audience. "There are many other wonderful machines, too—airplanes, for instance," she went on, encouraged. "They're like a big metal ship, except that they have wings and fly through the sky instead of sailing on the water."

"I want to see this place!"

Katherine was filled with sadness. "That doesn't seem very likely to happen," she said gently, laying one hand on her friend's shoulder, "but don't worry. I have enough stories to last until we're both very old women. In fact, some of these things will be starting to happen by then."

"They must be written down, those things you remember."

Katherine agreed, and she couldn't help grinning. What a shock some historian would get when he or she opened a dusty old journal dated 1895, and found detailed descriptions of fax machines, computers, airplanes, and video cameras.

"In what ways is this time better than your own?" Maria wanted to know.

"I don't know that 'better' is the proper word," Katherine mused. "Things are generally simpler here. There isn't so much stress." She looked around at the sumptuous room. "It's very romantic, this life, riding in carriages, living in mansions, wearing long dresses that rustle when I walk. But I'm well aware that the vast majority of people don't enjoy this kind of luxury."

Maria's brow was furrowed with a frown. "Don't women wear long dresses in your world?"

Katherine smiled. "Only for very elegant parties and things like that. I spent most of my waking hours in jean— trousers."

"Women wear trousers there?" Maria's voice was soft with disbelief and wonder.

"Yes," Katherine said. "And they vote and own their own businesses and hold political office."

Raising the fingertips of both hands to her temples, Maria shook her head. "This is a lot to take in."

Katherine felt an even greater affection for her quiet, practical, steady friend. "Yes," she agreed gently. "But don't get the idea that I came from some kind of paradise. The human race still has a very long way to go."

Still looking a little dazed, Maria left her, and Katherine washed, dressed, and groomed her hair. Then, placing the baby in Marianne's capable care, she set out for the beach.

Katherine told herself she wasn't looking for Gavin, but when she spotted him sitting on a boulder in the distance, the salt-misted breeze ruffling his hair, she was overjoyed. She stopped to smooth the skirts of her bright cotton peasant dress with its lace-up front and to pat her hair.

"Good morning," she called when she knew she was close enough to be heard. With one hand, she shaded her eyes from the fierce sunshine, and behind her calm exterior trembled a woman who knew she was betting her soul on a longshot.

Gavin's gray eyes swept from her face to her hem then back again. He climbed agilely down from the rock, slung his lightweight tweed jacket over one shoulder. There was a remoteness in his manner that was even more disturbing than the hostility he usually displayed.

"Was I wrong in thinking last night made a difference?" Katherine asked boldly, facing him on the hard, rocky sand. The tide licked at the hem of her skirt, and the wind made coppery tendrils of hair dance around her face.

His expression was haunted, and Katherine felt an anger as deep as Puget Sound as she realized just how badly his voluptuous bride had wounded him. It was a bitter irony, having to pay the price for the other woman's sins.

"There are times," Gavin conceded after a long interval

of pensive silence, "when, if I didn't know better, I would think you are another person entirely."

Hesitantly, Katherine touched his arm, and just that simple contact started a sweet riot of sensation within her. She clung tenaciously to reason, to the sad truth that Gavin would merely think she was insane if she tried to explain how she had come to him. "Isn't it enough that I've changed, Gavin, that I'm genuinely sorry for whatever might have taken place in the past? Can't we go on from here?"

He raised his hand as if to touch her cheek, then let it fall back to his side. His grin was so brief and so sad that the sight of it wrenched Katherine's tender heart. "Yes and no," he finally answered, his tone ragged. "I want you in my bed again, and I want more children by you, but there will always be a part of my soul that I can't share with you."

Katherine longed to be welcome in Gavin's bed, and she wanted even more to bear him other babies, yet the pain his words caused her was so intense that it struck her dumb.

Gavin wanted to *use* her, like a stallion would a brood mare, and with no appreciable difference in concern for her feelings. He wasn't asking her to be a real wife, and he certainly wasn't offering her anything that remotely resembled love.

Her entire body trembled with the effort not to slap him across the face.

"I am not a bitch dog," she pointed out evenly, after a very long time.

Gavin hooked a finger under one of the laces at her bodice and brazenly traced the outline of a nipple, causing it to press toward him. "The response to that, my dear," he said, "is so obvious that I won't even stoop to it." He grew bolder then, flattening his palm against her breast, smiling as it swelled in his fingers, as ripe and succulent as a late-summer melon.

Katherine moved to twist away, her face crimson with

rage and humiliation, but he curved one iron arm around her waist and stopped her.

"At last," he said, "I've figured out how to deal with you, Katherine. You need a man who can play your body as deftly as an angel plays a harp, and we both know that, for some reason comprehended only by the gods, I have become that man. I will bed you often and well, and you will behave yourself in the interim or suffer the consequences."

Katherine's defiance drained out of her; she knew all the blood had left her face. "What consequences, Gavin?" The question was barely more than a whisper, for it took phenomenal effort to push the words past her constricted throat.

With an index finger, he lightly traced the line of her jaw, and she hated him for arousing such wanting in her with so innocent a caress. "Very simply," he said, with a regretful sigh, "I will divorce you and ship you off to live in a cottage somewhere, with a maid."

"And Christopher?"

"He would remain with me," Gavin said flatly.

Although she did not want to be sent away from Gavin and, admittedly, from the rich lifestyle he provided, she could have borne both those things. The thought of losing her son, however, filled her with desolation and terror. Where in her own century she would have been able to fight Gavin for custody, in the late 1800s, she had no more legal rights than her husband's favorite horse. She was his property.

"I couldn't bear that," she said, softly but proudly.

Gavin curved a finger under her chin and raised her face so that their gazes met. While his touch was certainly not painful, there was no tenderness in it, either. "Perhaps motherhood has redeemed your black little soul," he said. "We shall see." With that he walked away, in the direction of the house.

Katherine stood on the shore for a long time, feeling an explosive anger build inside her, fueled by frustration and, worst of all, desire.

It was probably despair that sent her rushing after Gavin to angrily grip his jacket, which was still slung casually over his shoulder.

"Damn you, Gavin," Katherine cried, "don't you *dare* drop a bomb like that and then walk away!"

His expression was one of bafflement, rather than anger, when he turned to look at her. "'Drop a bomb'?"

She sighed and shook her head. She had no patience for explaining about World War I and all the succeeding developments that would influence the language. "If you'll just open up to me, Gavin," she pleaded, holding his arm. "If you'll only give me a chance to prove I'm really different . . ."

"I'll visit you here when I feel the need," he said dismissively. "When I return to Seattle, I will live as I should have before."

Katherine's heart plummeted. "You're talking about taking a mistress, aren't you?" she breathed. "Maybe you've already done that, set up some bird in a gilded cage—"

He shook his head, not in denial but again in bewilderment. There wasn't a hint of confusion in his words, however; they were cutting and concise. "Don't tell me you have the gall to object?" he drawled.

She closed her eyes tightly and clenched her hands at her sides, struggling not to outscream the gulls whirling and diving against the blue sky. Finally she trusted herself to speak. "I do object," she said reasonably. "You are my husband, and I won't share you."

He touched her hair and offered her an indulgent little smile. "How refreshing," he said. "And how utterly unlike you." He bent his head to nibble lightly at her lips, but she knew the kiss was not a display of tenderness. It was a challenge.

Again he caught his finger under the laces of her bodice, nestled it in the velvety softness and warmth of her cleavage. "I'm going into the city today to attend to some of my patients, but I will return in time for dinner and your wifely comforts, my dear. Be ready for me."

Even as Katherine's mind shrieked rebellion, her body

ached for the pleasures of Gavin's possession. Her nipples yearned to nourish him, her hips and thighs to cushion his weight. In her own time, the talk shows covered problems like hers, but since Sally and Phil and Oprah and Geraldo had yet to be born, she would just have to deal with it on her own.

They separated then, and Katherine went to one of her favorite refuges, a tiny chapel set back in the woods. It was complete with pews, stained-glass windows, and candles to light, and the place seemed somehow eternal, neither of this century nor of her own.

Before her accident and subsequent mystical experience, Katherine had not been particularly religious. She still wasn't too clear on her theology, but she had encountered Someone near that shimmering glass bridge, and she knew now that the universe was not the random place it had once seemed to be. There was a distinct order and logic to events, though for the life of her she couldn't see how her own situation fit into the scheme of things.

As she sat in the soothing silence of that place, a tear slipped down her cheek. Every day her old existence in modern-day Seattle seemed farther and farther away, more and more like a fantastic story she'd read somewhere. This life, here and now, was real and vital, the one she truly wanted to live, and yet the emotional distance between her and Gavin seemed too vast to bridge. They were in accord only when they were making love, and that simply wasn't enough.

10

GAVIN did return to the island house for dinner that night. He made love to Katherine later, in the privacy of their room, just as he'd promised to do, and even though her ego demanded it, she hadn't the strength to resist.

Gavin transported her, taking her to new levels of pleasure with every conquering, swallowing her cries of stunned ecstasy so that the whole household wouldn't know what was going on. Between bouts of passion, he kissed and caressed Katherine back to a state of such fevered wanting that she murmured in frantic distraction until he satisfied her.

When Christopher cried, Gavin got up, lit a lamp, and changed the infant, then brought him to bed and watched, propped up on one elbow, while Katherine nursed their son. Never, in this life or the other, had she ever treasured the miraculous secrets of her womanhood as she did then.

She put Christopher back into his cradle when he was full and sleepy again, and stood watching him in quiet awe for a long time. Her body was naked, her wild auburn hair tumbling down her back.

"Katherine."

She turned and watched as Gavin tossed back the tangled sheets on her side of the bed. Incredibly, he wanted her again.

She went to her husband without hesitation.

She was different. The stubborn thought nagged at Gavin as he stood at the railing of the boat as it chugged across the water toward Seattle. Before the great change, which seemed to have come with Christopher's birth, Kathy had avoided his lovemaking. She'd said he was too big, too fierce, too insatiable.

Yet the night before, she'd bucked beneath him like a mare in springtime, flinging back her head so that the muscles in her neck corded when she climaxed. He'd kissed her to stifle the cries that vibrated from the depths of her moist little belly and burst from her throat to batter against his. Once, while taking her in the way that went back to earliest man, he'd muzzled her with his hand. She'd taken one of his fingers into her mouth, and Gavin had closed his eyes and delved deep, and there had been no one to muffle his moan of triumphant surrender.

Gavin sighed. According to Mrs. Hawkins, Katherine regularly visited the chapel in the woods behind the house, and that was another mystery. The Kathy he knew had recognized no deity other than her own self.

The way Marianne told it, Katherine would spend hours on the sunporch with Maria, laboriously recording "stories." That was another thing that baffled Gavin; the woman he'd married wouldn't have drawn up a laundry list, let alone penned reams of prose.

He shoved a hand through his hair. Katherine wanted him to believe she'd changed, he concluded. It was all just an elaborate scheme to regain his trust, to keep her hold on the sumptuous lifestyle she admittedly loved.

How ironic it all was, he reflected. Just when he'd stopped caring, Katherine had become everything he'd convinced himself she was, back in the days before their marriage. Gavin now thought of that era as a time of foolish bliss; he'd been ensnared by his own illusions, and he had no intention whatsoever of repeating the error.

The passenger ferry came into port, and crew members shouted to one another as they tied the vessel to the pilings and put down the plank. It was a bright, noisy, blue-skied day, and instead of going ahead of him, to the hospital and the patients who awaited him there, Gavin's mind strayed back to the island, and the woman. She had watched him go with red-rimmed eyes, her chin at a proud, obstinate angle, and he knew the image would haunt him until he saw her again.

The door of an especially fine carriage popped open as he passed, intent on finding a cab, and Caroline Raynes peeked out, beaming. "Gavin!"

He wasn't wearing a hat—he hated them because they made his scalp sweat—but he touched a nonexistent brim anyway. Caroline, the niece of the very forward-thinking Dr. Elliott Raynes, a colleague of Gavin's, was a beauty with blond hair and flirtatious brown eyes. She'd offered herself to Gavin on more than one occasion, as though her favors were of no more consequence than a platter of sweetmeats and exotic fruits.

He'd always meant to help himself—some other time. Now, just returned from a fresh baptism in the fires of physical pleasure, Gavin was only too aware of his vulnerability to Katherine, and he knew he'd better do something about it.

Fast.

Dr. Gavin Winslow had finally decided to take a mistress—not because he really wanted or needed anything more than the cataclysmic pleasure Katherine gave him in his own bed. No, what he needed was a defense against the wiles of his lovely wife.

"Hello, Caroline," he said, and returned his smile.

"On your way to the hospital?" Caroline's voice was like chiming cowbells, and Gavin wondered why he'd never taken notice of that singularly annoying fact before.

He nodded, and she offered him a ride, just as he'd known she would. Seated across from her in the elegant, tufted-leather interior of the carriage, he studied the slender lines of her figure.

Katherine was plumper, especially since she'd had the baby, he thought, but he liked feeling her softness beneath him, like a scented featherbed.

"Gavin?" Caroline sounded petulant, and Gavin steered his wandering attention back to the matter at hand.

"I don't think I've ever seen you looking lovelier," he said.

* * *

"I'm going back to the city," Katherine announced, two weeks after Gavin had left the island. In that time, she hadn't had so much as a terse note from him, let alone a visit, and her mind was filled with all sorts of dreadful visions.

"Gavin hasn't sent for us," Marianne pointed out, as though that settled the whole issue. It was a rainy afternoon, and the two women were seated on the sunporch, Marianne stitching a sampler, Katherine writing. She'd been recording memories of her other life as fast as she could, and it was a good thing, too, because with every passing day she could recall less of the place beyond the crystal bridge. Before long, she guessed, she would probably forget it entirely.

"Of course he hasn't," Katherine muttered furiously. "He's too busy entertaining his mistress!" The social column in that day's issue of the *Seattle Times* had linked Gavin with Caroline Raynes, and Katherine had been in torment ever since she'd read it.

Marianne didn't even look up from her sewing. "All men have mistresses, Katherine," she said. "It's a fact of life."

"It isn't going to be a fact of *my* life," Katherine countered. Then she marched upstairs, prepared Christopher to travel, packed her own things, and sent the caretaker around for the carriage.

When the ferry left that afternoon, Katherine was aboard it, along with Maria and Christopher. It was time for action; Katherine loved her man, and she meant to fight for him.

She arrived at the mansion overlooking the harbor only to find that preparations were being made for an elaborate yard party. Colored Chinese lanterns hung from wires, and ribbon streamers decorated the rose arbors and the garden benches. Tables had been set up, and extra servants bustled back and forth, carrying chairs and food and more decorations.

At first Katherine was delighted. Then she realized she not only hadn't been invited to this party, she wasn't supposed to know about it. Her temper bubbled up like mercury in a desert thermometer.

"Take Christopher upstairs, please," she said to a wide-eyed Maria, who obeyed without question. After tossing her gloves onto the marble-topped table in the entryway, Katherine started for the kitchen.

Katherine was not surprised to find Caroline Raynes there, consulting with the cook, and yet her emotions were as volatile as dry gunpowder in hell. "What are you doing here?" she demanded.

The cook backed away and then fled through the dining room doorway, rightly sensing the approach of disaster.

"I might ask the same thing of you," Caroline responded coolly. "It was my understanding that Gavin had consigned you to the island, where you couldn't get into any trouble." She smiled with acid sweetness. "You know. Like you did before."

"Get out," Katherine said with quiet menace.

Caroline evidently sensed Katherine's determination, for some of the color drained from her cheeks, leaving her rouge to stand unaided. "But the party—"

"There isn't going to be any party, Miss Raynes," Katherine broke in. "And you may interpret that statement as you see fit."

"Gavin will have something to say about this!" Caroline snapped, but, nonetheless, she snatched up her little beaded handbag and headed for the door.

"He certainly will," Katherine replied. She was thinking of the eighteenth-century dueling pistols that hung on the wall of his study over the fireplace, and wondering where a person went to buy musket balls. Or whatever they fired.

When Katherine got her wits about her again, she noticed the big cake on the counter, and everything fell into place. Of course. It was Gavin's birthday, and as his wife, she should have known that. *She* should have been the one to plan a celebration.

When Gavin entered his study half an hour later, he looked more than a little surprised to find Katherine seated at his desk, solemnly pondering the dueling pistol she'd taken down from the wall.

"Happy birthday," she said pleasantly, still simmering. Then she frowned at the gun in her hand. "Tell me, does this thing still work? If so, I'd like to change your gender right about now.''

Gavin didn't comment. He simply approached the desk and lifted one of the pages from her journal that she had laid there, the one describing the Space Needle. "What's this?"

"Proof that I'm not the same person you knew," Katherine answered, hoping her voice wasn't shaking. "Look at the handwriting, Gavin. Did she form her letters like that?"

He lowered the page to look at her, and she realized she'd gotten through by the stunned expression in his gray eyes. "No," he said, and the word came out hoarse and broken. Here was something Gavin couldn't explain away with scientific babble, and Katherine could see that he was troubled. "Katherine . . ."

She laid the pistol on the desktop and stood to face her husband with tremulous dignity. "Did you sleep with Caroline, Gavin? Is she your mistress?"

He was still staring at her, as though she were some kind of freak. He seemed to be stricken speechless, and Katherine marveled that she hadn't thought to show him samples of her handwriting before. Maybe, she reasoned, she hadn't wanted to, subconsciously, until she was ready to make a full commitment to this time, this place, this man.

"Gavin?" she prompted.

"No," he said. "I planned to, but it just never happened."

Katherine laid her hands on his lapels. "Good, because I love you with my whole heart and soul, Gavin Winslow, and I plan to keep you so well satisfied that you won't need another woman. Ever. And you can trust me, because I'm not the Katherine you knew, and I'll never hurt you."

She felt his powerful shoulders move under her hands in an involuntary shudder. His jawline clenched as he struggled visibly to control his emotions, and once again Katherine was filled with tenderness, thinking how he'd suffered.

"Tell me who you are . . . where you came from . . . how such a thing could happen . . ."

She touched an index finger to his lips. "Not now, Dr. Winslow. At the moment, you have a birthday present to unwrap."

A smile lit his eyes, and he took her hand. "That's scandalous Mrs. Winslow. After all, the servants are around and there's about to be a party."

"The servants are all deaf," Katherine responded teasingly, "and if there's a party, why, that's all the more reason to celebrate."

They climbed the stairway hand in hand, aware only of each other. Gavin lifted her into his arms and carried her over the threshold of the master suite, his lips already tasting hers.

This encounter was unlike their earlier couplings, however, for there was no leisurely pleasuring, no tempting and teasing. The hunger was simply too great, because of their long separation and their newfound accord, and there could be no waiting.

Somehow, fumbling, now laughing under their breaths, now kissing playfully, they managed to undress each other. Then Gavin laid Katherine gently on the side of the bed, positioned himself between her thighs, and glided into her.

For Katherine, the sensations were far more profound than mere pleasure; this experience was spiritual as well, something that had been preordained at the conception of the universe. She gave a primitive, guttural cry as Gavin lunged, withdrew, and lunged again, and when her body began its dance of release, it seemed that her mind soared free.

She found herself standing on the crystal bridge again, felt a deep and abiding fear because she knew she could be called away from Gavin forever. Behind her was 1895, Gavin, Christopher, Marianne, Maria. Ahead was darkness, and that was when Katherine realized her old body had died.

"The other Katherine," she asked of the shimmering light. "What happened to her?"

She is at peace, the light answered, without words.

Katherine was relieved. "Let me go back to 1895," she

pleaded. "Please. That's where I belong, where I've always belonged."

You have made your choice, the light replied.

Katherine found herself in Gavin's bed again, her face wet with tears, her body still trembling with the aftershocks of her release. Gavin was breathing hard, his muscular back moist under her palms, and she rejoiced because she had a lifetime to make love with him, plenty of time to tell him about the crystal bridge and the world on the other side.

"I love you," he said.

Katherine kissed the top of her husband's forehead. It might have been his birthday, but she'd been the one to get the gift.

Linda Lael Miller

At summer camp, I loved the chillingly delicious late-night stories my cabinmates told of ghosts, goblins, and escaped maniacs with hooks for hands. To this day, I adore (forgive me) sinking my teeth into a good vampire story. Give me a weird and wonderful tale every time.

So it is that I offer you *That Other Katherine*.

Have a hairy, scary Halloween.

Enchantment

Christina Skye

The wild hawk to the wind-swept sky,
The deer to the wholesome wold,
And the heart of a man to the heart of a maid,
As it was in the days of old.

—"Gypsy Song,"
as cited by Rudyard Kipling

*To Maggie Lichota, who has the rare gift of imagining;
And to Kathe Robin, who enriches us all with her vast
knowledge and deep love of our genre,
With heartfelt thanks*

Prologue

HE sat in sullen shadows, staring pensively at his own portrait. Dark-eyed, velvet-clad, he stroked a great gray cat, which drowsed on his knee.

Around him the granite house seemed to sleep, intensely quiet, caught in wistful, yearning dreams.

So different, the man thought sadly. How could the same house be so very different?

He frowned, realizing that no one would notice him here. Here he was just another shadow in the darkness, just a still figure slumped in a faded damask armchair, studying his own proud features with self-loathing.

Once it had been different, of course. Once the house had rung to his shouted orders, and an army of servants had scuttled to anticipate his slightest bidding. Once *she* had walked here, and to look upon her had been his greatest joy.

But times change; he should have known that better than anyone.

No, the figure in the chair thought, he liked this graceless age not at all. But then liking was not what had brought him here. Love perhaps, but not liking.

His long pale fingers tensed and halted their rhythmic stroking of the cat. "Ah, Gideon, it is hard, much harder than I'd thought, this business of coming back."

269

In his lap, the cat arched slightly, nuzzling the man's cold hand.

He smiled bitterly. "Nothing is as I expected. Everything feels wrong. Too slow. Too heavy. Too clumsy. Too—"

He thought for a moment. *Solid.* Yes, that was precisely the word. And that sense of solidity was what bothered him most.

At the cat's sharp meow, the black-clad figure looked down, and his hands resumed their lulling movements; a deep purring sound spilled from the animal's throat.

"Yes, old friend, it will be hard—dangerous even. Should I fail, my torment will be magnified a thousandfold. But we knew that already, did we not?"

The cat's hair seemed to bristle for a moment. His tail arched and flicked sharply from side to side.

"Very true. But what choice have we?"

Gideon's eyes narrowed, gleaming golden from the darkness.

The ghost of Draycott Abbey merely frowned and shook his head. "That would not be permitted, I'm afraid."

For a moment anger boiled up in him—savage and lethal. Around him the room seemed to grow chill, the darkness to heave and tremble.

Then with a ragged sigh, the man closed his eyes, struggling vainly to forget how far his jealousy had driven her and how much he had hurt her.

His beloved stone walls were intact, at least. Down to the last capstone and merlon, they stood inviolate.

And they were still his. That much had not changed.

Nor would it ever, the ghost vowed grimly. In the shadows, his proud, gaunt features seemed to gleam and shimmer, suddenly merciless.

1

Later on, after the fear had fled and the hurting stopped, she would realize it was the house that she had fallen in love with first. But for now Kacey Mallory could only stare, speechless and dreamy, at the towering walls of weathered stone before her.

Lichen-covered, with climbing roses spilling color over its ancient gray towers, Draycott Abbey was a vision of heart-stopping beauty.

Even more jarring, it was somehow familiar.

In some strange way, she felt as if she were coming home. But that was impossible, of course. Home was three thousand miles away, where a small clapboard saltbox nestled amid the rolling hills of western Connecticut.

And this vision before her was a universe apart from that—a granite Jacobean moat house whose crenellated roofs and twisting chimneys floated like a summer dream over the Wealden Hills of southern Kent.

Kacey felt her breath catch. The sun was going down behind her, pouring golden light over the valley, painting the mullioned windows a fiery crimson.

To be here at last. To feel so strangely at home, as if she were returning from years of wandering.

Frowning, Kacey tossed back a wind-blown lock of honey-colored hair. What in the name of heaven was wrong with her? This massive granite structure was no more hers than was Balmoral Castle!

And yet the dark feeling of familiarity persisted. Along with something else—a hunger so tangible that it hurt.

Abruptly she dropped her canvas bag and rubbed a slim hand across her weary eyes. The blurring was only to be expected after twenty-two straight hours of traveling. Yes, of course—that must be the source of this strange disorientation.

She closed her smoky-green eyes, then warily reopened them.

Nothing had changed. Just as before, the abbey gleamed back at her.

Like a jewel, Kacey thought. Set within an emerald ocean of manicured lawns. And flowers everywhere, a scattering of pinks, sweet alyssum, and madonna lilies.

Something had told her there would be lilies.

A shiver ran down her spine.

"Next thing, you'll be following a white rabbit right down its little hole, Katharine Chelsea." Still muttering, she tossed her bag up over her shoulder and crossed the last feet of lawn onto a narrow graveled path that wound up to the house.

So this was Draycott Abbey—or what was left of the medieval structure. Built in 1255. Nearly burned to the ground in 1645 during the "troubles" with Cromwell. Partially restored a year later, and entirely refurbished in 1793, after the eighth Viscount Draycott made a number of clever investments in the Orient.

Kacey could have gone on forever about this house, quoting chapter and verse of its long, rich history—right down to the ghost of an ancient ancestor who was said to pace the battlements on moonless nights, sad-eyed and travel-weary, a rose crushed between his long fingers.

Yes, she knew the gray granite structure by heart, from its Jacobean long gallery on the fourth floor to the fine stained-glass windows on the north front facing the quiet moat.

It was an imposing house. A magical house.

A house of many secrets, she suspected.

Once again, a shiver worked its way down her spine.

But it was not the house she had come to see, though that alone would have been the dream of a lifetime. No, it was a different task that brought her to this small corner of England—equally the dream of a lifetime to an art conservator like herself.

Somewhere inside the abbey was a newly discovered canvas carrying the signature of James Whistler. An uncatalogued canvas that appeared in none of the artist's correspondence. A painting unseen since the day it was completed. Ever the temperamental artist, Whistler had ordered it destroyed along with all the other pieces he felt were inadequate to bear the scrutiny of posterity.

If the canvas actually *was* by Whistler, Kacey reminded herself sharply. It was far too soon to hope, especially since the odds of its being real were very small.

Yet a part of her dared to hope. The canvas had been discovered two months ago by the present owner of Draycott Abbey. Wrapped in linen, it had remained unseen and forgotten for over a century. Kacey's job was to verify the painting's authenticity and to undertake any restoration that might be required.

Her pulse quickened at the thought of such a discovery, and at her rare good fortune in being involved in the recovery of such a masterpiece.

Not that luck had much to do with it, of course, for Kacey was one of a mere handful of experts who specialized in Whistler. After completing her doctoral work, she had gone on to further study in pigment and canvas restoration at the Louvre.

Her own articles on Whistler had soon become widely circulated, provoking a good deal of controversy. Perhaps it was because K. C. Mallory's passion for Whistler shone through every word she wrote. Or perhaps it was just that she seemed to have a skill for seeing beyond the layers of color right into the heart of the canvas, sensing the unspoken motivations of the painter's soul.

For whatever reason, Whistler had been her life and love. And now here she stood, wind-blown and weary, at the foot of an awesome stone edifice, surrounded by a scene of timeless pastoral beauty.

In the shadow of Draycott Abbey.

Almost within reach of her long-dreamed-of Whistler.

Nocturne in Lavender and Silver: Southampton Pier. An unseen, unrecorded masterpiece by probably the greatest American painter of the nineteenth century. Along with the canvas, the present viscount had discovered a scribbled note, apparently from Whistler himself, directing his assistant to destroy the canvas.

The slim beauty frowned, worrying her full lower lip with her teeth. *Authentic*? Or simply another one of the Whistler hoaxes so common in the last decade, since Japanese collectors had driven the prices sky-high? The painter's spare brushstrokes and flat washes of color made him damnably easy to forge, after all.

Kacey tried to calm her racing pulse, knowing that in a few hours she would have her answer. Gripping her bag, she started toward the gatehouse perched just outside the silver moat.

As she walked, she flung back a handful of honey-gold hair, entirely unaware of the way the sun gilded her high, fragile cheekbones to a warm, glowing porcelain. Entirely unaware of the way her hair flashed like liquid gold upon her slim shoulders.

Had she known what was waiting for her just beyond the crenellated stone gatehouse, Kacey Mallory might never have taken another step.

Too late . . . too late . . .

He could feel it even as he jumped from his horse and lunged up the cold marble steps to an unlit house. He knew it even before he threw open the heavy door and plunged into the leaden shadows.

She had gone, taking the child with her. Sweeping away all his hope, all his chances to atone for his unforgivable stupidity.

With a harsh curse, he turned and stumbled back into the lashing wind, his eyes narrowed on the dim line where the chalk escarpment fell away six hundred feet to meet the frigid swells of the English Channel.

She would have taken the old path along the cliffs. That way she would be least likely to encounter anyone who would try to stop her.

Like him . . . .

Dear God, out there on the cliffs—in such a storm!

Tossing his greatcoat about his shoulders, he plunged forward, shouting her name wildly.

But no sound drifted back to him. Only the wind wept a shrill answer, its fierce blasts whipping black strands across his face. As he struggled south the last frayed edges of sky bled from indigo to black far out over the channel.

Too late, the wind keened.

All gone.

And then he heard another sound, more like the wild shriek of a bird than any human cry. The sharp stiffening of muscles along his neck and the twisting stab of fear in his stomach told him that could be only one person's voice.

"Katharine!" he screamed, pounding forward blindly. "Wait for me! Let me—"

A second later, the earth tore free. With a muffled explosion, a thousand tons of chalk and granite smashed down toward the narrow shingle, drowning out her last, shrill cry.

And then only the long darkness.

"Nooo!" His heart pounding, Nicholas Draycott jerked upright in the chill silence, sweat-soaked and heartsick, listening to the telephone ring. After two days of insomnia, he'd finally fallen into a ragged sleep, only to be shaken awake by the old nightmare.

Just a dream, he tried to tell himself. Just an illusion, like all the others. It was the quiet that did it, or maybe it was the drinking and the endless stream of late nights.

At his sides, his strong fingers clenched into fists. He stared into the room's shadows, fighting a choking wave of loss and regret. Let it go, he told himself harshly, listening to a branch whip against the window. Put it behind you— it's only a damn dream, after all.

Once again, the phone rang; Draycott made no move to answer it.

That, too, was over, he told himself harshly.

But there were some things a person never got over. And a ten-month hell of jungle captivity in southeast Asia was probably one of them.

A muscle flashing at his jaw, the hard-faced Englishman reached across the bed for the pack of cigarettes on the side table.

At that moment, the phone again began its insistent ringing, the sound echoing loudly in the deathly silence of the house. On and on it rang, shrill peal after shrill peal.

Draycott didn't move. His silver-gray eyes narrowed, studying the receiver.

The ringing stopped for a few moments only to begin anew. Slowly the Englishman bent down and lifted the receiver, not saying a word.

"Ah, Lord Draycott. You respond at last. Have you given any more thought to our proposal?"

Nicholas did not answer.

"Still stubborn, are you? Such a pity, that." The voice was flat and faintly accented.

Just like all the other callers.

Murderous visions burned through Draycott's brain, but he knew that expressing them would only give these men what they wanted. So he held his silence instead, making the most of the lessons a year in hell had taught him.

"So. You have made your choice, Lord Draycott. That makes my own choice so much easier." The man on the other end of the phone chuckled. It was a cold sound, harsh with finality. "There will be no more warnings. You have four days, Lord Draycott. The next time we will not miss, I assure you."

A second later, the connection broke off into scattered static.

Draycott's left hand slowly tightened, crushing the cigarette package into a shapeless mass. A muscle flashed at his temple. In the gathering dusk, his face looked very hard.

Goddamn the man with the voice like sandpaper. Goddamn the people who came spying, day after day.

Goddamn them all!

But the twelfth Viscount Draycott knew that the man had spoken the truth. Unless he came up with a miracle by Friday, he was a dead man.

Awkwardly, he came to his feet and tossed the crumpled cigarette pack down onto his dresser. The muscles at his chest rippled as he rubbed his neck tiredly, then bent down and tugged on a pair of charcoal trousers.

In the darkened room, the scars at his left thigh were barely visible. No more than a phantom network, they radiated from his pelvic bone to the outside of his knee.

He barely noticed them now, beyond a stiffness when he overexerted himself. His silver eyes narrowed. Someday maybe the rest of the scars from Bhanlai would fade, too.

Frowning, he strode to the telephone and punched out a number.

"Six-two-one-five," came a clipped voice at the other end.

"Inspector Jamieson. Nicholas Draycott calling." His face dark, Draycott stared down at the crumbled cigarette pack.

"Lord Draycott? Has something—"

"Nothing new, inspector. I merely wanted to see if you'd got anything on the men who took my Turners."

"I'm afraid not, Lord Draycott. These were no amateurs, unfortunately. We're tracking our regular sources just in case the stolen paintings surface, but it could take weeks . . ."

And time is the one thing I don't have, Nicholas thought grimly. "What about Trang? Anything new there?"

From the other end of the line came the rustle of papers. "There has been some revived activity in his part of Burma. A few munitions purchases, the usual opium deals. Nothing significant, however. The villagers swear they saw this man Trang cut down in the barrage after your release and that he is buried in the hills outside Bhanlai. Which leaves me wondering why you'd doubt their opinion. Is there perhaps something you're not telling us, Lord Draycott?''

For a moment, rage darkened Nicholas's vision. There was a bloody lot he wasn't telling the inspector—but only because it was none of his damn business. And as for Bhanlai's grimy little dictator—Nicholas, too, had seen him fall in the gunfire when he was rescued. And yet who else but Trang could be behind the harassing phone calls he'd been getting? Who else but Trang knew the details of those last desperate days at Bhanlai and a woman who had betrayed him?

One of the warlord's men, perhaps? Or one of that motley horde of a hundred different nationalities who drifted around Trang, men of no allegiance to anything except themselves? And what did they want from him anyway?

Nicholas's hands tightened as he felt the old gnawing sense of powerlessness begin to choke him.

''Lord Draycott? Are you there?''

''I'm here, inspector.''

''Are you going to answer my question?''

Draycott's eyes were unreadable. ''Just call it an instinct. Trang and I got to know each other pretty well up there in the jungle. I guess it's often that way between captor and captive. And lately I've had the feeling . . .'' *That I'm being watched. That I'm walking right on the edge of a precipice.*

But Nicholas didn't tell Jamieson that. It would only bring another horde of police flocking down to Draycott Abbey, and all he wanted now was to be left alone.

''Just a feeling, Lord Draycott?'' The inspector's voice was sharp with disbelief. ''You won't be more specific than that?''

''No.''

''Did you know that Trang was supposed to have buried a fortune in jewels somewhere in those hills? Not one piece has ever been recovered, as a matter of fact.''

''Are you calling me a liar, inspector?''

There was a silence at the other end. ''Not a liar. Not quite. But I think there's a damn sight more that you're not telling us, my lord.''

''I can't remember, damn it!'' Draycott's hand clenched

and unclenched at his side. Even this much he hated to reveal.

The inspector's next words were slow and careful. "There are ways of remembering, you know. Relaxation techniques. Hypnosis." A momentary silence. "Drugs."

Draycott cursed low and graphically. "And have my brain ripped open all over again, so that some stranger can pick through whatever bits he finds interesting? Thanks but no bloody thanks, inspector. I'm done with Bhanlai. All I want now is to get on with my life!" Nicholas's fingers whitened on the receiver. *If I ever can.*

"I'm sorry to hear that, Lord Draycott. Because I'm afraid there is very little we can do for you in that case. Not until you give us something more concrete to go on."

Nicholas's jaw hardened to a rigid line. He'd expected nothing more than this, of course. Were he in Jamieson's shoes, Nicholas supposed he'd have said the same. But time was running out, and he was nowhere nearer to an answer than before.

"Of course, inspector," he said flatly. "Good night."

After cradling the receiver, he stalked to the window and pulled aside the curtain. To the east, the valley was tinged with purple shadows, while the distant Wealden Hills beyond shone vermillion in the setting sun.

And that's when he saw her—a long, cool column of womanhood poured into a pair of expensive designer denims so favored by the bloody Americans. A mane of blond hair spilled about her shoulders. On her feet were a pair of lavishly hand-tooled leather boots.

A muscle flashed at Draycott's jaw as he watched the woman move around to the side of the house. In the slanting sunlight, her hair shone honey-gold, the color of the finest Burmese silk.

He cursed, long and savagely. So she was another gossip hunter. Another maggot come to feed off the wounds of Bhanlai. When would they learn that his privacy was not for sale? That he refused to see his story become cheap copy to fuel tabloid sales? Photojournalists! A fancy word for voyeurs, he thought angrily.

But this one would be no more successful than any of the others who'd come in search of a story, he swore, even though she was stunning.

Trust Edward Armistead, one of Fleet Street's most ruthless gossip peddlers, to find someone like her. Armistead was an expert when it came to acquiring gossip, and he never stinted on money or personnel when tracking down a story.

Furious, Draycott turned from the window, a wild plan already forming in his head. Yes, the woman deserved exactly what she got, he decided.

For right now, Nicholas Draycott was no longer a gentleman. No longer the hero of Bhanlai.

Tonight he was only a man—a man who had reached the end of his rope.

2

THE air was still and heavy, rich with the scent of thyme and hyacinth as Kacey moved forward into the cool shadows of the stable. She called out several times, but no one answered.

Frowning, she tried to gather the few scraps of information she'd been given before leaving New York.

"Lord Draycott is an unusual man," Kacey's employer, Cassandra Edwards, had announced. "He's intensely protective of his privacy. Obnoxiously so, in fact. You'd do best just to keep out of his way. I imagine his staff will provide you with anything you need. The man probably won't even be in residence at the abbey—he has homes all over England, did you know?"

As it happened, Kacey hadn't known, but that suited her

just fine. The last thing she wanted was a nervous owner hovering about while she examined the would-be Whistler canvas.

And with several million dollars riding on her decision, she couldn't blame an owner for being a little nervous about her findings.

Still, she hadn't thought the earl would be quite so eccentric as to leave the house closed up and silent, with no one at all to meet her. After all, he had stipulated this weekend as the best time for her to arrive.

Kacey pulled her case higher on her shoulder, frowning. Perhaps money and pedigree did that to a person—made him cold and careless of others. She made a mental note to avoid the viscount at all costs.

Inside the stables, the air was still and cool, little motes of dust dancing across the last golden beams of sun slanting down through the high windows.

Kacey's breath caught. Even here, the sense of timelessness, of being caught in a dream, lingered, for the stalls were all empty, pooled with shadows.

So where was everyone? she wondered crossly. She had been punctual to the dot. The bus had dropped her at the foot of the home wood, as the driver referred to the dark expanse of beeches and elms. He had provided her with careful directions to the abbey, but his look, Kacey recalled now, had been frankly curious.

And faintly hostile.

Her brow creased in thought, she dropped her canvas bag and sat down on an upturned wooden crate. She tugged off her right boot, massaging her cramped and blistered toes.

Her gaze wandered up to the ceiling, crisscrossed by massive overhanging beams. That was when she first noticed the meticulous carving atop the first stall—three horses in full gallop, tails flying, hooves aloft.

On an impulse, she unzipped her bag and extracted her camera. Unless she missed her guess, that detail was an eighteenth-century masterpiece, perhaps the work of Grinling Gibbons himself! Quickly she switched on her flash and began to shoot. She would ask the viscount for permission when she saw him, of course, but meanwhile, this was just too good a chance to pass up, especially since Cassandra had just received a commission to restore a pair of sculptures by Gibbons in Cheshire.

In the excitement of her discovery, Kacey forgot that she should be looking for the man who belonged to that sleek black sports car parked outside or tracking down a place to sleep. Already the sun was melting over the treetops.

Instead, she saw only the fine details of wood and plaster, intent on capturing them on film.

Concentrating on her documentation, she didn't notice the tall shadow which separated from the darkness of the front court.

Nor did she see the glittering eyes which scrutinized her, harder than burnished steel.

"Nice . . . very nice," a hard voice growled. "And it's about bloody time you got here."

Her breath checked, Kacey spun about.

He stood well over six feet, broad-shouldered and lean, eased into a battered tweed jacket and form-fitting charcoal trousers. His face was a fascinating play of angles and shadows in the darkness of the stables.

His eyes smoldered.

Dangerous, she thought dimly, sensing an aura of power about him that fairly crackled.

And made her own skin tingle in response.

Frowning, Kacey tamped down her rioting pulse. "Who—" To her fury, she found she had to swallow before continuing. "Who are you? You nearly terrified me."

The man continued to study her in silence, a lock of black hair fallen across his brow.

Her frown grew. "Lord Draycott? But I thought . . ." For the first time, Kacey noticed the faint silver scar running across the man's cheekbone.

It gave him the cold look of a pirate—a modern-day pirate, the sort who would raid corporations rather than coastal settlements.

One dark brow slanted up, mocking her.

The sight made Kacey lift her chin and stare back coolly, her green eyes glittering.

"Don't let them intimidate you, love," Cassandra had warned her back in New York. "These wretched blue bloods will walk all over you if you give them half a chance. Don't forget, it's still the sixteenth century as far as they're concerned."

Only Kacey wasn't about to be any man's doormat.

Her lips tight, she shot him a challenging look. "I'm K. C. Mallory. Cassandra Edwards sent me."

The man's expression did not change. "Cassandra Edwards?" He seemed to find the name unfamiliar.

His voice was dark silk, and it made Kacey's skin tighten and prickle. The sight of that dark hair shadowing his open collar was doing equally strange things to her pulse.

Get a hold of yourself, Kacey girl.

"I've come about the—" She started to say "the Whistler," then recalled that Lord Draycott had stipulated that the project be kept totally secret. "About the research work," she finished carefully.

His eyes slid from her windblown hair to the tips of her boots, missing no detail. Finally his full lips curved in the ghost of a smile.

"Nice. Yes, very nice, indeed. I shall have to thank— Cassandra, did you say her name was?" He moved a step closer, his face made even leaner by the shadows.

"Cassandra Edwards," Kacey repeated impatiently, trying to ignore the sudden trip beat of her heart. She saw his lips tense in a hard line, as if he were struggling to retain his control.

Dimly, Kacey found herself wondering just what it would take to make him lose that control, to melt the ice in those wintry eyes. She shivered slightly, her pulse jerky. "You *are* Lord Draycott, aren't you?"

"Does it matter?"

Kacey frowned. What was wrong with the man, anyway? "I'd like an answer. *Now*. If you are not Lord Draycott, then I'm wasting my time here."

"Oh, you're not wasting your time, my dear. I assure

you of that." Smiling, the man moved a step closer, so close now that Kacey could feel the heat of his hard body. "The Cassandra Edwards in New York, is it, by any chance?"

"Of course it is. She received your cable last—" Kacey had time for no more. Somehow his fingers were cradling her face, his thumb tracing the curve of her cheek.

She froze. "What do you think you're—"

"First things first, my dear," he murmured, moving closer, so that she felt his heat in earnest, along with the barely leashed power of his lean body.

Until she wanted to feel much, much more.

What in the name of heaven was happening to her?

As she stumbled away from him, his lips quirked in a mocking challenge. "I shall have to assess your qualifications before we talk business, my dear."

Kacey took another step back. Her pulse was wild, her heart slamming against her ribs. Something was very, very wrong here.

"Cassandra sent my *vita* ages ago," she snapped. "Or are you having second thoughts because I'm a woman?"

"Oh, I wouldn't have it any other way, my dear," he said silkily.

Their eyes locked, slate-gray to jade-green. The force of the contact was enough to make her jump.

Kacey's jaw set in a mutinous line. The man was a bastard, no mistake about it, but this job was too important to risk losing. *Steady, kiddo. Show him that it takes a damn sight more than one insolent Englishman to frighten you away!*

She was just getting ready to tell him so when his hand curved around her shoulder, slipping deep into the warm hair at the back of her neck. Her eyes widened in shocked inquiry. She tried to speak, but her throat was suddenly too dry.

"Very nice indeed," he murmured. "Kacey, did you say your name was? Let me see—personable. Intelligent. Open to new ideas. Everything I requested. You are all those things, aren't you?" His voice, just beside her ear, was low and darkly intimate, as if they were sharing a private joke.

"Yes, I suppose so," Kacey began impatiently. "But—"

And then his mouth came down on hers, darker than the shadows gathering through the stable. As electric as the bright, jagged bolts playing out over the channel.

As fiercely erotic as any of those forbidden thoughts she had been trying so hard to ignore.

His mouth opened, urgent and persuasive, demanding a response. And somehow Kacey gave it, her lips softening beneath his.

His breath hissed out in a hot growl of triumph.

He wanted her, she thought dimly.

And, dear God, she *wanted* him to want her. Suddenly it seemed as if her whole life had been no more than a prelude to this moment.

She didn't move, dizzy with shock. *What was happening to her?* For wild heartbeats, she stood paralyzed beneath his touch, aware of a thousand different sensations at once.

The cold still air on her face and neck. The lingering smell of hay and old leather. The distracting tickle of his tweed collar against her neck.

And always there was the raw awareness of the man himself. His mouth hot against hers. His fingers, powerful and demanding, where they teased her neck to electric awareness. His restless tongue exploring the locked barrier of her lips.

He moved over her like a man with a mission, and dimly Kacey realized that right now she was the mission.

She caught back a moan. Suddenly she was dizzy and spinning and nothing else in the world mattered but that he stop.

And that he *never* stop.

His ribs crushed her chest, and his taut thighs backed her against the cool wall. She blinked, stunned by the hardness of his body pressing against her softness.

A raw, choked moan escaped her dry throat. Was she mad? She drew her palms up to his chest, meaning to push him away.

But he caught the sound of her moan between his open

lips and answered with a hoarse groan of his own. He seemed to sense exactly where to skim her neck to drive her wild, exactly how to stroke her tongue until she was shivering with need.

And somehow Kacey seemed to know the same. How to smooth the hard, corded muscles at his shoulders. How to feather her fingers through the black hair at his temples. How much he enjoyed it when she tightened her lips around his restless tongue and drew a ragged moan from him in turn.

Not *if*, but *when*. As if she'd done this all a thousand times before.

Her fingers tensed at his chest. *But you have touched him like this before,* a dark voice whispered. *And he's touched you just the same. Until you begged him for more—much more—than this.*

Dark, heated images swept over her.

Images of hard thighs and soft, yielding hips.

Images of his long fingers, sure and urgent, feathering over her naked thighs, parting her softness. His body rising over her.

Kacey's breath caught in a ragged gasp. *Madness!*

"St-stop!" she hissed, even then feeling the pull of those erotic images. She balled her hands into fists and shoved desperately at his chest. "Let—let me go!"

But her protests came too late to be believable, and they both knew it.

The next minute, she was swept up in his arms and tossed facedown over his shoulder. Blood surged in hot waves to her head as she fought her way through the drugging storm of passion he had aroused so unerringly. Furiously, Kacey flayed at his back and shoulders, kicking her booted feet wildly. All the time, she cursed herself for being the worst sort of fool. "What in the name of heaven do you think you're—"

The next minute, she was spinning through space, landing with a sharp jolt in a mound of sun-warmed hay. Far above, a ray of fading sunlight slanted down through a mullioned window, one faint golden gleam amid the shadows.

He had tossed her down in one of the stalls! Was the man completely insane?

Or was *she*?

With trembling fingers, Kacey pushed up onto one elbow and swept a tangled mass of hair from her eyes. She'd had more than enough of this fool and his arrogance—and more than enough of her own strange reaction to him!

"I don't know who you are or what you think you're doing, but I'll see that you're struck from Cassandra's client list. You'll never get another researcher down here ever again, I promise you that! So your precious Lord Draycott can just kiss off any other restoration projects he might have in mind. Believe me, when I'm done, you won't be able to find a restorer in Timbuktu who'd work here!"

The man's only answer was a sardonic smile. In horrified silence, Kacey watched his long fingers drop to his belt.

A deep red blush stained her pale cheeks. "Just what in the name of hell do you think you're doing now?" she demanded.

The slate eyes narrowed. His belt slid free with a soft hiss, darkly intimate in the confined space of the stall. "Doing, my dear? Why, I'm getting ready to screw you, of course."

3

THE silver eyes narrowed, smoldering. "That *is* how you say it on your side of the Atlantic, is it not? If you can supply a better word, of course I'd be happy to use it." His hard fingers tossed the belt to the stable floor. "I don't believe I've ever had an American before. I find I'm rather looking forward to the experience."

White-hot fury exploded through Kacey's veins. None of this could actually be happening, could it?

But the tingling of her lips where his mouth had savaged hers told Kacey this was no dream. The urgent tension of her skin, clamoring for more of his heat, told her the same thing.

She pushed unsteadily to her knees, brushing wildly at the errant bits of straw clinging to her hair and face. "Now just wait one damn minute! You can't really believe—" Her voice died away sharply when she saw his fingers fall to his zipper.

"We can discuss your terms later. Of course they will depend on just how well you . . . perform for me."

Kacey's heart slammed against her chest. "Perform! *T-terms!*" she croaked. Her breath was coming in jerky little gusts now. "Listen—this is some kind of joke, right? You can't possibly believe that—"

Wide-eyed, she stared at the place where his hands worked. The fabric was stretched taut, she saw.

The realization of just why it was so tight sent a wave of crimson shooting through Kacey's cheeks and neck.

Her heart was hammering so loudly she could barely hear. "Well, you—you can just take your fine title, your expensive car, and your fancy belt and—and—stow them where you sit!"

His only answer was a dry chuckle.

And then, with a sharp metallic snap, his zipper slid free.

Kasey's eyes fixed in horrified fascination on that tight square of charcoal wool. "You—you wouldn't *dare*! You couldn't—"

Hard, work-callused fingers began to pull the zipper.

Down.

Lower and lower.

The fabric parted slowly, inch by inch, to reveal more bronzed skin, sprinkled with springy black hair.

Hungry skin. All aroused male.

Kacey's tongue was wedged in her mouth. Her pulse was out of control. That's when it hit her.

There was nothing beneath the cloth—nothing but taut

bronzed skin and a mat of dark hair, a denser version of that shadowing his open collar.

And in a few more seconds he would—

Suddenly the man's fingers went still. "You *are* the call girl I phoned for, aren't you?"

Kacey's eyes widened. A firestorm of fury ripped through her at his cold question. Dear God, he thought she was a—

She took a ragged breath, focusing her fury on his mocking eyes. Even now she found it difficult to forget that tantalizing V of bronzed skin beneath his hard fingers.

"Get this through your thick skull because I'll tell you only once," she hissed. "I'm an art restorer, damn it! Cassandra Edwards sent me to see Lord Draycott. About a project *he* requested."

The man's eyes narrowed, running thoughtfully over her heaving breasts, noting the taut nipples clearly outlined against the fine lawn of her shirt.

Exquisite, Nicholas Draycott decided. And even more dangerous than he'd thought.

Almost too damn hot to handle.

Almost, he told himself grimly. "What sort of project?" he drawled, clearly skeptical. "A project of Edward Armistead's perhaps?"

"I'm not at liberty to discuss it," Kacey countered. "Only with Lord Draycott," Kacey countered.

The slate-gray eyes narrowed. "Indeed. Only with Lord Draycott, is it? Well, I'm afraid he's busy. As his estate manager, I'm the one you'll have to deal with."

"You *were* his estate manager," Kacey hissed. "When I'm done with you, no one will even open a door to you."

"So, the little cat has claws, does it?" Draycott moved closer. "At least we're getting down to the truth."

"Call Cassandra, if you doubt my word. Or call that bloody procuress in London and—"

"Procuress. How quaint."

"Oh, I'm sure *you* know all the proper terms. Having never had dealings in such things before, I confess to complete and total ignorance on that score. My work is rather different, you see. It's honest work. Work performed out of love rather than greed.''

"You—an art restorer? Come, come, my dear." His mocking words hit her like a knife. "When was an artisan ever so lovely? So seductively packaged? No, no, let's just dispense with the charade, shall we? I didn't ask for any particular erotic fantasy. I thought I made that very clear to your employer. Simple sex, that's all I require. Maybe later we can try something more—''

Kacey threw back her head and screamed. The gambit had always been useful in silencing her younger siblings when their bickering reached intolerable proportions.

It had the same effect on the Englishman now.

"Now you listen to me, you—you bacon-brained, bone-headed pile of horse dung." At least she had his complete attention, Kacey thought.

"A mixed metaphor to say the least," he said dryly. "Obviously, English isn't your strong suit."

"No, *art* is, damn you! Now are you going to move back and let me out of here or not? Lord Draycott," she added a moment later, crossing her arms mutinously at her chest.

"Didn't fool you, eh? What a pity." His keen eyes scoured her face. "And the answer's no. Not on your goddamn life, Miss K. C. Mallory."

Kacey's lips tightened as she fought to salvage her rapidly splintering control. Suddenly she went very still, a plan creeping into her head. An outrageous plan. Something entirely out of character.

And then Kacey found herself smiling, a tiny smile that began at the corners of her generous mouth and worked up to glint from her jade eyes. Yes, it would be the perfect thing. And she would get her look at the Whistler, too.

Slowly, she sat back in the straw, studying him through lowered lashes. *Careful now, Katherine Chelsea*, she told herself. *This man's no fool*.

Her tongue gently swept her upper lip.

Lord Draycott's silver-gray eyes narrowed, fixed on the sight. "What the devil—"

He never had time to finish. His breath caught in a rush

as the woman in the straw smiled up at him with wanton promise.

Her upper lip was too full. Her forehead was too wide, her neck too long. She had straw scattered all over her hair, for God's sake, Draycott told himself sternly.

And in spite of that she was blindingly beautiful. So beautiful it made him ache.

The sight of her smile was like a fifty-thousand-volt electric current plugged directly into his heart.

Or into his groin, to be more precise.

Her slim fingers moved to the top of her shirt and slipped the first button free.

Slowly. Teasingly. With total awareness of the infinite torture it was causing him.

Draycott growled a curse.

His jade-eyed temptress merely smiled and moved on to the next button.

Suddenly Draycott was on fire, in a way he hadn't been for months. With a pain that had nothing to do with burns or reconstructive surgery.

It was a fire of wanting, of needing. A fire for total possession.

Just as he had possessed this woman long before.

Nicholas frowned, wondering where that crazy thought had come from. Perhaps he was farther gone than he'd realized, cooped up out here in the country. Yes, maybe this idea of paid companionship was something he should have considered sooner.

Then his lips twisted in distaste. It was always for payment anyway. There was invariably a price—it was simply paid in different ways.

And then his mind went blank, for the woman's hand was at mid-chest and a pink expanse of skin mocked him along the faint shadow between her breasts.

Two buttons more, Draycott found himself thinking. His breath was coming strangely heavy now, and the pain at his groin didn't even bear thinking about.

The woman smiled slowly, her head tilting back. Showing

him she knew damn well what she was doing. And was enjoying the effect thoroughly.

"How do you like my performance so far?" Kacey murmured huskily, her voice as rich and textured as the erotic currents flowing between them.

To Draycott's infinite disgust, he had to clear his throat before he could answer. "Just—fine. But I think I'll suspend judgment . . . until I've seen everything you're offering."

Strange, he thought absently—her hand seemed to quiver for a moment at his words. But then the next button slipped free, and he forgot everything but how the full upper swell of her breasts beckoned, gently shadowed in the growing twilight of the stable.

Dear God, don't stop now, Draycott found himself praying, only to tamp down the thought a moment later. It was never meant to go this far, after all. Just far enough to scare her off.

And to see that she scared off anyone else with similar plans.

Only now, with her before him like this, half-clothed, her smile warm and inviting, Nicholas was finding it hard to breathe, much less to think clearly.

"Oh, you'll like it," the woman whispered, rising slowly to her feet. Deeply V-ed, the white fabric strained against her breasts, lovingly cupping the lush curves beneath.

Draycott felt beads of sweat break out on his brow. "Perhaps we should discuss terms now, after all," he muttered, unable to tear draw his eyes away from that erotic shadow.

From the dusky, upthrust nipples tormentingly outlined against the thin lawn.

"Oh, not yet, surely. I've so much more to show you, my lord. And you *will* show me that pretty painting of yours in return, won't you? I've heard so much about it." Kacey managed a husky giggle. "I just can't wait to tell all my friends I've seen it!" Her fingers slipped lower, tugging the white shirt free of the waistband of her jeans.

Draycott had to struggle to hear anything she was saying. Painting? Good sweet Jesus, she was the painting! A perfect

Botticelli masterpiece. He could look at her forever, he thought dimly.

"You do remember the painting," Kacey prompted, her voice a sultry caress. "In the long gallery, isn't it?"

"The painting," he repeated mechanically. "On the fourth floor." He had to tell her to stop, Nicholas thought.

He had to tell her *not* to stop.

Her full mouth curved in a blinding smile, and the sight was like a shaft of sunlight plunged right into his heart.

He wanted to see her smile like that always, the Englishman thought. When she awoke, her hair tousled on his pillow. When he slipped off her clothes and plunged deep inside her.

When he felt her convulse in wild, breathless passion beneath him, whispering his name.

Dear God, what was wrong with him? Had he lost the last ragged shreds of his sanity?

"Now you listen to me, young lady," Draycott began, feeling priggish and a complete fool.

She didn't listen.

Instead, her slim hands drifted down to the last, tantalizing button of her shirt. A secret smile on her face, she began to inch toward him. "Oh, I'm listening, my lord. You have my total attention, I assure you."

Draycott couldn't have moved even if the stables were on fire and the roof falling on his head.

Which in a way, they were, at least as far as his screaming senses were concerned.

Her eyes challenging, the beautiful intruder slipped past him. One hand trailing across his tensed shoulders, she teased the bunched muscles at his neck. The faint scent of gardenias rose from her warm skin, inundating his senses. Tightening muscles already taut past enduring.

She was all woman—all soft, yielding desire. She was the fire that lit his restless nights, the dream that tormented his lonely days.

His breath hissed out with the nearness of her. He felt her slip around him, then draw close to his back. He was on fire with wanting her; he was driven by an infinite need to touch her.

In every way that a man had ever touched a woman—and then some.

He was—

Falling?

With his next heartbeat, Draycott was spinning down, his legs kicked straight out from under him. Gasping, he hit the cold cobblestone floor, breaking his fall with knees and wrists. What in the name of bloody everlasting hell?

He cursed harshly, struggling to stand, fighting the raw agony radiating from his kneecaps. He was still cursing when he heard the doors to the stall slam shut behind him. With a sharp thump, a piece of wood was wedged between the handles on the outside of the door.

"Enjoy your evening, Lord Draycott," the woman outside said sweetly. "I'm afraid it will be rather colder than the night you had planned, but maybe you'll learn something in there—not that I count on it overly much. Oh, and don't hold your breath waiting for Cassandra to send down another restorer. You've had your chance, and frankly, you've just blown it."

Fury swept through Nicholas—fury at his own stupidity. Fury at her cunning.

Fury at how much he wanted her still, in spite of everything.

What would the little bitch do now?

Exactly what she'd come here to do, of course. And like a fool he'd told her exactly where to find the Whistler.

Kiss it goodbye, imbecile. If it's the Whistler she's after she knows how to get it. If it's information she wants she can get that, too. And she'll be long gone before you can even work that bloody door free!

The viscount's eyes rose, smoking with rage, assessing the twelve-foot walls around him with disgust.

Bloody blazing hell, Nicholas Draycott thought grimly.

How could he possibly be such a damn fool?

Again.

4

KACEY was gasping by the time she reached the front of the stable. Just beyond, sheer granite walls beckoned across a silver sheet of water, shadowed and smooth in the gathering darkness.

Somewhere to the south, heat lightning dug phosphorous fingers into the channel, but she barely noticed.

He must have come out this way. There had to be a wretched door here somewhere! Breathlessly, she ran over the narrow two-arched stone bridge that spanned the moat. And then she saw the door, tucked behind the base of a chimney, painted gray to blend in with the granite walls.

Kacey's heart raced. Did she dare? What if she met someone—a servant or a relative?

A wife?

She resolutely ignored the faint sliver of emotion that pricked her at that thought, seizing the doorknob and twisting violently.

The door slid open smoothly before her, revealing a long corridor of spotless, sparkling marble. She stopped, turning back to listen to the night.

No noise, no angry shouting. Good, he must have given up. Now to find the stairway.

Warily, she slipped inside, feeling a shiver work down her spine as the silence of the abbey's interior fell over her like a cool, enveloping cloak.

Welcome, the house seemed to say. *We've been waiting for you . . .*

Kacey caught her breath, fighting her dark fancies. Too much traveling, she told herself. Too little to eat.

Of course—it was all so simple. There was nothing wrong with her that a decent meal and a full night's sleep wouldn't cure.

She stopped only long enough to tug off her boots and tuck them under one arm. Then, soundless and graceful, she darted off toward the stairway and her waiting Whistler, determined to have at least one sight of the tantalizing canvas before she turned her back on this place forever.

Never say forever, the house seemed to whisper.

Forever has a way of happening. In places and ways you haven't begun to imagine.

That dim warning, too, Kacey ignored, gripping her lip between her teeth and telling herself to get on with this wild escapade and then get the devil out of here.

It took her only seconds to find the massive oak staircase. She looked neither right nor left, denying herself the pleasure of that rare and ancient house. Somehow she knew she must close her eyes to its beauty, that if she dropped her guard even once she would never find the strength to leave.

And now there was a clock ticking in her head, telling her that a silver-eyed predator was only minutes behind her. Driven by sheer adrenaline, she found her way to the top floor.

And there she forgot her fear. For now the luminous canvas was before her, shimmering in the first faint rays of moonlight spilling through the long gallery's tall windows.

There Kacey made her last, and most deadly, mistake, which was to underestimate the man with the voice like silk and the eyes like beaten silver.

Eyes that she seemed to have known forever.

He found her at the south wall of the long gallery, seated before the great canvas. Her long legs were tucked beneath her, and her eyes were radiant.

The Englishman's face filled with awe at the picture she made, her long hair gleaming silver in the moonlight, her whole being suffused with love for the canvas before her.

Suddenly he was ripped by jealousy at the warmth that

glowed from her eyes, angry that he wasn't the one who'd put it there.

Suddenly he wanted to be an artist so he could paint her.

A poet so he could capture her in exquisite words.

Most of all, he wanted to be her lover so he could know her warmth always and in a thousand intimate ways.

And then, like a dirty tide, memories of Bhanlai washed over him. Memories of betrayal. Memories of deceit and the blinding pain and rage that came in its aftermath.

Memories of the other woman for whom he had also wanted to be all those things—a woman who'd taught him everything there was to know about betrayal.

Draycott's jaw clenched. In the moonlight, the muscles at his neck stood out clearly. He fought down the urge to stride through the gallery and shake her. He shook beneath a fierce need to touch her—to crush her against the wall and bury himself deep in her heat and softness.

Unaware of the brooding presence behind her, the woman came slowly to her feet. She shook herself slightly, as if fighting the spell of the great canvas. Her eyes were fixed still on the dim, phantom boat that rocked in timeless silence beneath a lavender moon.

Her heart filled with its beauty, Kacey breathed a silent song of thanks for this rare gift she'd been given.

For having glimpsed such a masterpiece, even once. Most of all, for the knowledge, deep in her heart, that it was indeed from Whistler's hand.

A tear slipped down her cheek. For long moments, she didn't move, struggling with nameless regrets and disturbing memories, shadowed fragments that clamored up from some dark place inside her, so deep that she had never before guessed they existed.

Go now, Katherine Chelsea. Go now, or you'll never go!

One hand to her lips, she spun about and stumbled toward the door. In her desperation to be away, she didn't notice the tall shadow unmoving amid the other shadows of the silent room.

Her trembling fingers rose, sweeping her eyes blindly, and then she was gone.

* * *

Hidden in the shadows of the long gallery, Nicholas Draycott stood frozen, his hard fingers clenched into fists. His head spun as he tried to grasp what he'd just seen. She hadn't taken the painting after all. And that meant—

Abruptly his expression hardened. *It means nothing, you fool. It means that she wants photographs and juicy gossip, not canvases. She probably doesn't even know what the hell she's looking at.*

Draycott reminded himself what she'd said back in the stable. She'd called the canvas a pretty picture, for God's sake!

But try as he might, he couldn't forget her hesitation and the dreamy look on her face. Right now, every sense was clamoring that he was wrong about her.

In spite of that instinct, something made him hold back, waiting silently in the shadows outside the door.

Merely the logical need to learn her real intentions, he told himself coldly. Merely a natural desire to see that she took nothing with her when she left.

By the time she reached the front staircase, he was gone, melting back into the darkness, where an ancient rear staircase ran down to a hidden passage leading out to the gatehouse.

Just in case she stole something else on her way out, Draycott told himself.

But he knew that, too, was a lie.

The first fat drops of rain had just begun to fall when Kacey jerked open the side door. Her shoulders slumped as she stood staring out into the night. A long sigh escaped her tense lips.

So this was it—no way out except to walk to town. So be it. She absolutely refused to go back and ask that misbegotten swine in the stable for anything, not even if her life depended on it!

She tossed her bag firmly over her shoulder. At least these wretched boots might actually prove to be of some use, she thought, smiling grimly.

She turned up her collar, then tugged the top of her trench coat up over her head, fighting to see through the slanting sheets of wind-driven rain.

Far to the south, ghostly fingers of fire ripped the sky, and a tremor snaked through her. Fear? Or was it regret?

No, something else, she decided.

But then Kacey had all she could do to keep herself upright as she tottered over the rain-slick grass. Unused to the new boots she was wearing, she tripped painfully and often. Each time she bit her lip against the pain and forced herself forward into the rushing darkness.

It couldn't be more than five miles to town, after all. Her bus ride from the village had taken no more than fifteen minutes, surely.

But in the night and the lashing rain, five miles seemed like the other side of the world.

Which means you'd better get started, she thought. At least she would have the memory of the painting to warm her. Yes, that memory would last her for a very long time.

Fifteen minutes later her hair was plastered to her ashen cheeks and her lips were blue-tinged, even though she hadn't reached the bottom of the hill. The lightning was much closer now, her only beacon in the sullen darkness of the storm.

She would be dangerously exposed out here in the middle of the sweeping lawns, Kacey realized. Soon she'd have to cut west, toward that dim line of beeches, silver against the darkness.

She stumbled again and bit back a moan of pain, feeling her ankle swell.

Surely no more than four miles to go, she told herself optimistically.

Suddenly she stiffened, listening to the wind howl through the trees. Somewhere a branch ripped free and plummeted past her.

She frowned, tugging her coat tighter over her head. She was just asking herself how she'd gotten into this mess when she heard the other sound.

It came from nowhere and everywhere, and the hands

were from the fabric of night itself, jerking her around and holding her rigid.

Kacey screamed.

His face was a cold mask of anger, etched by deep lines at his forehead and cheeks. But then Kacey saw something else—the buried traces of anxiety and concern. For *her*, in spite of what she'd done.

For a wild instant, she felt a primal desire to brush the lines from that brooding face. To set the fires of passion aglow in those silver eyes once again.

His fingers bit into her shivering shoulders. "Just where in the name of God do you think you're going?" he growled, struggling to be heard against the wind.

"Back to Alfriston," she cried. "Back to sanity. Back to civilization. Anyplace that's away from *you!*"

A muscle flashed at the granite line of his jaw. His fingers tightened. "It's eight miles to the village. You'll never make it in the dark."

"Why not? I happen to like walking!"

His smoldering eyes settled on her mud-stained boots. "Especially in *those*, no doubt," he said disgustedly.

"Then I'll just have to take them off, won't I?" Kacey jerked free and bent down to tug at her boots. One came free and went flying, hitting him in the knee. He winced, she noticed happily. A moment later, the other spun off, sailing into the darkness.

Catching back an angry sob, she plunged forward toward a bleak cluster of yew trees, trying to ignore the paralyzing cold seeping into her bare feet.

"You crazy, headstrong—" With a ragged curse, Draycott seized her and swung her up over his shoulder.

"Let me go! Put me down this instant, you bastard!"

But the Englishman's hard, pounding gait did not slacken. Her bag bouncing over the grass, he set off over the rolling lawns to the house.

Gasping, Kacey hammered his sodden back, tugged at his hair, and lashed out with her bare feet, all without the slightest apparent effect.

"Put me down!" she screamed. This time, her voice was ragged with fear.

Draycott went absolutely still. "You promise not to bolt if I do?"

Her heart thundering, Kacey considered her answer. She could lie, of course, but somehow she felt it necessary to meet him head on, with total honesty. "I won't run. Not yet, anyway."

Grim-faced, Draycott pulled her from his shoulder. The next instant Kacey was sliding slowly down his rain-slick body.

He was all hardness, bone and muscle against her softness. And Kacey felt his need revealed clearly in every taut, wet inch.

Her feet touched the grass, and his eyes fell to the small dark crests upthrust against the near transparency of her wet shirt.

Draycott's breath checked. The pain at his groin returned, far worse than before.

"Dear God, who are you?" he said hoarsely. "What are you doing to me?"

Kacey stared back at him, equally dazed. His words drove straight into her heart, echoing the same turmoil she was feeling.

The storm around them paled to insignificance beside the savage, wordless emotions that rocked them both.

Their eyes locked. She felt all his need, his shock, his fury . . .

His vulnerability, no matter how hard he tried to hide it.

Around them, the air shimmered, supercharged, crackling with electricity and the relentless force of their opposing wills.

Time shuddered and then ground slowly to a halt.

Above them, the wind raged on, hurling sheets of rain down onto their frozen bodies. Lightning split the sky, sending an ancient beech smoking to the ground. The world seemed to cry out and twist on its axis, unable to endure this confrontation of relentless opposites.

And then suddenly there was no world and no time, only

the two of them. Only the naked need that swept out of some other place to engulf them.

Kacey shuddered, rain sliding chill and forgotten down her face.

Draycott frowned. "You're freezing," he muttered, almost to himself. "You'll catch pneumonia out here." Unconsciously, his grip softened, his fingers cupping her shivering shoulders. "Come back to the abbey with me, Kacey Mallory. Let's begin again." There was a note of desperation in his voice. "I'm afraid I've been a bloody fool. You don't have to be one, too."

Kacey could barely breathe for the intensity of the feelings flowing over her. For the touch of his hard body from her neck to her knees. For the need to feel him far closer still, bodies bared, skin pressed inch to sweat-slick inch.

As they slid into passion's raw center.

When had everything changed? she asked herself dimly. When had she become this strange new person, this wanton creature of hot desire and reckless need?

Dear God, what was happening to her? His touch was too keen, her need too raw.

Settle down, Katharine Chelsea. It's just all those female hormones talking. Maybe you've gone too long without listening to what they had to say.

And they were certainly talking right now—with a vengeance, she thought.

"Kacey?"

One word, but the way he said it, slow and uncertain, nearly pushed her over the edge.

"I—I can't go back." Her words were no more than a whisper. "I won't. I can't ever go back. Not *there*—not with *you*!"

"You must. The Whistler's waiting for you." He paused, studying her tense features. "I saw you in the long gallery, you know. You loved looking at it. You adored it with your eyes. No, don't try to deny it, Kacey. Your eyes couldn't lie—not about a thing like that."

Another shudder ripped through her. It was madness even to consider what he asked. She knew instinctively that she had to get away from this place, from this man. Yes, far away—before she did something crazier still. "Please . . ."

"Think of it," Draycott whispered, his lips feathering over the chill curve of her ear. "No one else has even seen the canvas for one hundred years. You'll be the first to touch it, to learn its secrets. It's waiting there right now, Kacey. All you have to do is come back with me."

It was the lowest sort of bribe, but Nicholas Draycott didn't care. He couldn't let her go—not this way. Not yet. She was either his sweetest dream or his worst nightmare, and he had to find out which.

Kacey gnawed at her bottom lip. Her body shook, from the cold and the struggle to control some dark, nameless yearning.

But she was losing. Nicholas could feel it in the quiver that ran through her shoulders.

"*Now*, Kacey."

"Oh, all right. Yes, damn you. *Yes!*"

His smile was dark triumph itself. But when he took her hand and tried to pull her back toward the house, Draycott found it was going to be a little more difficult than he'd thought.

Scowling, Kacey dug in her heels. "On three conditions," she shouted against the wind.

"Name them," he yelled back.

"First, we call New York and verify my credentials. I want no more questions on that score."

"Done."

"Second, you move my things—such as they are—into the gatehouse."

Draycott's response was slower this time. "Very well."

"Third, you give me the gatehouse key. No, make that *all* the gatehouse keys."

The Englishman's eyes darkened. "I can't do that," he countered flatly. "There are reasons—"

Kacey spun about and began to stride over the downs toward the village.

"Oh, all right, damn it! One of us has to be sensible about this."

Muttering darkly, Draycott searched for her boots and bent down to shove them on her feet. Scowling, he shrugged out of his coat and pulled it over her head. In the process, his arm encircled her shoulder. Her breast grazed his rib.

They froze, while the rain hammered down on his makeshift tent. For long breathless moments neither moved, caught in the warmth and darkness beneath.

Her hip nudged his thigh; her chin brushed the naked skin at his neck.

Draycott muttered a curse.

You think you're safe, but you're not, Kacey Mallory, his eyes warned from the darkness. *I'll have you. I'll have you every way there is to have a woman. You couldn't stop me if you wanted to. And you don't.*

Somehow she heard his silent challenge, attuned to him as she had never been to any other man. *Not now*, her jade eyes answered. *Not ever, Englishman. You can look forever, but you'll never find me.*

With a little gasp, Kacey broke free and stumbled forward over the grass, knowing no danger could match that of being caught in this man's arms.

Almost immediately she slipped in the wet grass and fell to her knees. Without a word, Draycott swept her up into his arms and strode forward across the glistening sweep of lawn.

Somehow her hands slid around his neck; somehow her fingers combed through his wet hair.

Kacey felt him shudder.

And then the shuddering was hers.

The gatehouse before them, Kacey raised wild, dazed eyes. In the darkness, the towers stood stark and forbidding. The house seemed almost to watch them, a thing of power and tangible will.

Determined to hold sway forever over these ancient acres. In spite of whatever frail, hapless humans might stumble across its shadowed paths.

Kacey frowned, trying to ignore the chill tendrils of fear that swept down her spine. Trying to ignore the angry power of Draycott's tensed shoulders beneath her hands.

How did I ever consider this place comforting? she wondered as the brooding Englishman carried her beneath the stone arch into the silence of the abbey's watchful, waiting walls.

The storm passed on to the north soon after their return. In careful silence, a white-haired butler showed Kacey to a room on the gatehouse's second floor. After reminding her to lock her door, he walked downstairs. A few moments later she heard him lock the ground-level entrance door.

Somehow the sound did little to reassure her.

She walked slowly to the bed and was asleep by the time her head touched the large and ornately embroidered feather pillow.

Twice she came awake during the night, her breath jerky, her muscles tense. But each time, the room was just as she'd left it—velvet bed curtains half pulled, behind a damask wing chair that had seen better days.

Moonlight spilled through the casement windows.

Rat-a-tat-tat-tat. Rat-a-tat. Rat-a-tat.

So that was it! Kacey felt a surge of relief. Just the wind shaking the glass. Just the wooden window frame creaking.

She lay back slowly, holding the bed linens protectively against her neck. It was cold for a June night, and she found herself wishing once again for her bags, which had been lost on the flight from New York. Back at Heathrow, she'd requested that they be shipped on to the abbey, when they were found.

She was reminding herself to phone the airline once again in the morning when her eyelids grew heavy. Her fingers twisted in the pristine sheets, monogrammed with dragon-entwined coronets.

How good it feels to be home again, she thought dimly just before her eyelids closed for good.

In his bedroom, Nicholas tossed down the agricultural journal he'd been reading and began to pace. The article had been boring enough—he should have fallen asleep hours ago. But sea-green eyes drifted before him, and a vision of tawny-colored hair.

Lips soft and proud by turns, and a body sweet beyond imagining.

With a low curse, he tried to fight the haunting pull of her, to forget the dreams.

But it was no good.

He knew without the slightest hint of a doubt that *she* was the woman in those dreams.

And he the man.

When finally he could pace no more, Nicholas sank tiredly into a chair by the window. The moon was thin and chill, like cobwebs on his face.

He slept—and was tossed instantly into dreams.

Thunder. The slash of rain and wind.

His hands fought the empty air. "Katharine! Come back—you must not go!" *His eyes were stark, desperate with fear.*

The wind swept back her cloak, and he saw her face. Green-eyed, chiseled beauty at cheek and chin. Her porcelain skin glazed with tears.

Guilt wedged in his throat. He had driven her away. He and Adrian, with their constant quarreling and their everlasting jealousy.

And then her wild, shrill scream, twisting his heart into a thousand pieces.

"*Nooooooo!*" His pulse thundering, Nicholas jerked upright in the chair. At the window a tree branch scraped the glass.

Only the dream, he told himself, trying to steady his breathing. Only an illusion.

But tonight the pain was far worse, because tonight Nicholas had sensed that it all might have turned out differently if he hadn't been so bloody stupid.

He stared out into the silver night, choked by a wave of regret, realizing that this dream was more real than anything he'd ever known.

* * *

Silent and silver, the moon rose over moat and meadow, dappling yew forest and hedgerow in ice and shadow. Beneath its molten light, the walls of the abbey seemed to shimmer and change, rendered faint and then finally insubstantial.

Like a paper castle in a paper landscape.

An owl cried once from the dark stand of yews at the brow of the hill. A night creature rustled and scurried through the dense shrubbery lining the moat.

Wrapped in a timeless dream, like a sleeper waiting to be kissed back to life, the ancient stones slept on.

The eyes were keen and clear in the moonlight.

Dark and bottomless, they studied the home wood, then swept down to the darkened windows of the turreted gatehouse.

There, the motionless figure thought. So close.

And yet she might just as well have been an eternity away.

The eyes clouded, harsh with regret. But regret was a useless thing. "Regret is life's bitterest poison." Hadn't he read that somewhere, eons ago?

Noiseless, the figure glided across the clipped lawns. The night seemed to hold its breath, the wind to still. As if of its own accord, the oak door swung open.

No light was lit to guide him, nor did the dark figure require any. He found the bedroom by feel and memory alone. He had memories enough for a hundred lifetimes, after all.

And then the moon met him in greeting, poured in a luminous pool on the bare wooden floor. Almost as bright as her hair spilling over the white linen pillow, he thought. Almost as beautiful as her smile, faint and soft and infinitely sweet now in sleep.

The darkness trembled. Will became being. Emotion turned to brooding substance.

A shadow fell over the sleeping woman's face.

Outside the wind rose, shaking the casement, tossing gravel and broken twigs against the gatehouse.

Dreaming still, she twisted restlessly, dimly sensing nature's distant warning.

The glass panes shuddered, and the shuddering turned to rapping. Then the rapping, too, changed—became low, urgent drumming. Beside the window, the thick damask curtains rippled and flared out, with the slow grace of an underwater scene.

The brooding eyes swept over the sleeper's face, issuing a silent command.

Wake up, they whispered. *We have waited long for you, and now the time for sleep is past.*

The phantom eyes waited, raw with hunger.

But for now, seeing her was enough. There would be time for all the rest in the long dreaming midnights of summer yet to come.

Since, of course, she could never be allowed to leave this place again.

5

THE sun shone from a cloudless sky the following morning as Kacey halted at the door to a sunny dining room overlooking the moat and western lawns.

His face expressionless, Nicholas Draycott held out a chair for her. "I trust you slept well, Miss Mallory."

He was clean-shaven and perfectly dressed, and the sight only made Kacey angry, since she had been reduced to wearing the same rumpled shirt and creased jeans from yesterday. "Perfectly, thank you," she lied, sliding into her seat, knowing full well that the dark circles under her eyes must belie her words.

"In that case, let's get right down to business," Draycott

said in that abrupt, intense way that Kacey was coming to see was a habit with him. "As I see it, we have two choices."

"Aren't you forgetting something?" Kacey countered.

"I don't believe so."

"You agreed to call New York."

"Ah." Draycott paused, his eyes unreadable. "It seems that Ms. Edwards is unavailable. Her answering service said that she had gone on holiday."

Damn! Kacey looked down. Cassandra hadn't told her she was planning to go away. It complicated everything! Frowning, she looked back at Draycott. "Well?"

"Well what, Miss Mallory?"

"What are you going to do about it?"

"Since I can't very well summon Miss Edwards back from her vacation, we'll just have to proceed as planned— until she returns, at least. I'm prepared to do that much."

Kacey was prepared to do that much, too, but she wasn't about to like it. But what choice had she, really?

Partly to avoid those piercing silver-gray eyes, Kacey looked out the window, where bright morning sunlight streamed through emerald velvet curtains worked with a dragon crest and an entwined D.

The Draycott coat of arms, no doubt, she thought sourly.

In the aftermath of the storm, the air was crystal clear and the lawns hung with diamonds of dew. From somewhere over the hill, she heard the distant bleating of sheep. Today even the sheer granite walls seemed less forbidding—sun-warmed, dappled by scattered patches of lichen.

Almost protective, somehow.

Yes, in the bright light of day Kacey could almost convince herself that yesterday had been a bad dream.

Until she looked up into Draycott's piercing eyes, that was. Into his chiseled, brooding face, which quickly reminded her that what had happened in the stable was anything but a dream.

There was no way to forget how those eyes had stripped her bare. How his hard body had felt when he'd swept her up and carried her back to the gatehouse.

Her throat turned dry; heat swirled through her.

Just simple, low-grade lust, Kacey told herself flatly. *He's one damn handsome man, and it's been far too long since you've had a good case of lust.*

Dark and unreadable, his eyes grazed her lips. Suddenly Draycott smiled as if he'd read her guilty thoughts.

Heat swept across Kacey's high cheekbones, staining her face and neck. At that moment Draycott's daunting butler entered bearing steaming trays of eggs, crisp bacon, toast points, and an array of condiments.

''Ah, Marston. Thank you.'' Nicholas settled back in his chair, waiting for the servant to finish before resuming the conversation.

In the interim, Kacey studied the room. Everything was exceedingly civilized. Fine old china. Gleaming crystal. A blinding array of silver—all sporting the Draycott dragon crest, of course.

The butler served discreetly while the earl murmured polite suggestions to Kacey. But by the time the servant withdrew, she was feeling very much the interloper, the clumsy colonial upstart. She knew she had faint shadows under her eyes, and her coloring was just short of cadaverous. Her hair must have looked a total disaster. She sat in the blinding sunlight, feeling like a grubby schoolgirl summoned before the lord of the manor, who sat infuriatingly neat and crisp in a white shirt, tailored wool pants, and a much-worn wool jacket in a muted gray tweed.

Kacey began to toy with her eggs.

''You may eat them, you know. They're neither drugged nor poisoned, I assure you.''

But at that moment she couldn't have swallowed anything. ''I'm—I'm not very hungry,'' she lied. Unfortunately, her stomach chose that precise instant to growl—quite loudly.

Draycott's brow slanted upward. ''Indeed.''

There it was again. That irritating word which could mean a thousand things—or nothing at all.

''As I was saying, we appear to have two choices, Miss Mallory.''

"Indeed," Kacey said silkily, managing to force down a spoonful of eggs.

Something flared deep in Draycott's eyes for a moment, but he ignored her mocking imitation. "One is for you to leave today, as you seem so dead-set on doing. That would hurt both of us. You, because you'll never get to see the Whistler again, and me, because something tells me I'll never find another conservator with even half your skill."

His calm assessment stunned Kacey. "And the second option?" she asked, somewhat breathlessly.

"Is that you stay on here at the abbey. I'll see that you have free access to the painting, along whatever materials and tools you require. Your hours will be entirely your own. That, my dear Miss Mallory, would be to both our benefits."

It was tempting, Kacey had to admit. By daylight, the man looked almost human.

Almost, she reminded herself quickly. *He tossed you over his shoulder like a caveman yesterday, remember? He thought you were a call girl hired for a night's pleasure.*

"So which is it to be, Miss Mallory?" Draycott's gray eyes taunted her. "Or do you perhaps feel unequal to the job?"

Kacey stiffened. "I'm more than up to any job you can give me, Lord Draycott." Her jade eyes glittering, she shot him a furious look. "And don't you have a real-life name? We Yanks have never cared much for ranks and titles, you know."

The dark brow slanted higher. "Nicholas is my given name. You may use it, if you prefer, since my title seems to make you uncomfortable. But if it's not the work you're afraid of, then perhaps it's something else." His slate eyes narrowed. "Me, perhaps?"

"In a pig's eye!"

"Yourself then? After all, your performance last night was quite convincing. One might almost say you put your heart and soul into the act. Perhaps *that's* what's really troubling you, Miss Mallory—the thought that you're just not up to the temptation of staying at Draycott Abbey. With me," he added.

"Don't flatter yourself, Lord—Nicholas! Resisting you will be the easiest thing I've ever done!"

"In that case, I fail to see any reason for your reluctance. It will be a simple business proposition, nothing more."

Kacey frowned. He was right, of course. There was no reason for all this anxiety. Her days would be spent in solitude up in the long gallery, doing the work that she loved best.

Her frown deepened. *But there'd always be the nights,* a voice whispered. *And you're not half so immune to this man as you'd like to believe.*

She looked down at her plate, all fruit and florals coiling against a pink porcelain background. Like everything about this house, the china was old and tasteful and colossally expensive.

In tense silence, she pushed the plate away.

So what's the problem? she asked herself. Just say no and be done with it.

Her lips moved. To her total shock, the words that tumbled out sounded strangely like "All right, I'll do it."

A hint of emotion flickered over Draycott's chiseled features—a look that was too hard for relief and too wary for triumph. "I'm pleased to hear it. I'll have a suite prepared for you on the second floor. Marston will see to whatever you require in the way of materials and supplies, although I expect you will have brought most of that sort of thing with you. And if you need anything else, just—"

"Impossible," Kacey said flatly, already regretting her moment of weakness. "No suite—not here in the main house. It's the gatehouse or nothing at all."

Draycott eased back in his chair. The sun on his white shirt was very nearly blinding, enhancing the dark bronze of his neck and face.

His eyes began to glitter dangerously. He took his time about answering, studying the wave of crimson that swept her cheeks. "That would be entirely out of the question, I'm afraid," he said flatly.

"Now, how did I know you were going to say that?" Kacey snapped. "In that case, our arrangement is off, too."

She tossed down her napkin and pushed up from her chair. "Good day, Lord Draycott. I wish I could say it's been a pleasure."

The Englishman's eyes narrowed. "Are you always this irascible, Miss Mallory? Or is it merely I who have the dubious honor of being able to provoke you to fury?"

Dimly, Kacey realized her behavior was totally out of character, but she wasn't about to admit that to this insufferable egotist!

Draycott's dark eyes mocked her. "I see. In that case, I must remember to stay well out of your way in the future."

It was a complete and total lie, of course. Nicholas Draycott only intended to get closer and closer to her. For some reason, that challenge had become at least as important to him as the restoration of the Whistler.

Kacey's fingers gripped the back of her chair. "That will hardly be necessary. For we have no future, you and I. That, I promise you!"

Draycott looked down. "I see I shall have to tell you the truth. You see, in the last weeks there have been several . . . incidents here at the abbey. Oh, nothing serious—a rake disappearing here, a chair there. Nothing to worry about." His eyes turned hard. "Until last week, that is."

"And then?"

"Someone broke into the gatehouse—ransacked the place royally. One very fine Turner landscape was slashed and two more were stolen. No one was hurt, thank goodness."

"Was the thief caught?"

"Unfortunately, no. The police have had a look, but the culprit was damnably thorough. No prints. No clues of any sort."

That was not quite true either, Draycott thought. There had been clues—if a person knew what to look for.

"Can't you just replace the locks?" Kacey demanded, clinging stubbornly to her original plan.

"They had been changed the day before the robbery. The man—or men—simply broke through the gatehouse windows. It's far enough from the main house that we could hear nothing." Draycott's face hardened. "So you see it would be quite out of the question for you to stay out there. Not now at any rate.''

Kacey's breath caught as she realized there was something he wasn't telling her. ''And you expect whoever it is to return, don't you?''

For a fleeting moment, Draycott looked startled. ''I do. Especially now.''

''You mean once the news of your Whistler starts trickling out.''

He nodded grimly.

''Perhaps it already has.''

''The thought has crossed my mind, too.''

''Is that why you were so suspicious of me last night?''

''That reason—among other reasons,'' Draycott answered cryptically.

''How do you know that I'm not? One of *them*, I mean?''

''I don't,'' the Englishman said bluntly. ''But I mean to find out very soon. And if you are—one of them, as you put it—I'd rather have you here where I can see you than somewhere else,'' he added.

''I see.'' Suddenly Kacey did see. That his performance last night was simply to smoke out a thief. That his passion had been no more than a clever ruse.

She refused to consider why the idea should leave her with a lingering sense of regret. Meanwhile it seemed she had no choice but to do as Draycott required—if she wanted to see the Whistler again.

Her fingers twisted back and forth on the chair rung. ''Very well. I'll stay here in the abbey,'' she said at last. ''As long as *you* agree to stay out of my way while I'm working.''

His eyes followed her, dark with challenge. ''And the rest of the time, Miss Mallory?''

''The same condition applies.''

Very carefully, the earl dropped his damask napkin on the table. He uncoiled his tall frame slowly and came to his feet, his eyes never leaving her face. ''Then of course I must not interfere in your work. Beyond that—I promise to do nothing you don't wish me to do, Kacey Mallory.''

A faint flush swept her cheeks, but he was gone before she could tell him that the only thing she wanted from him was to be left alone.

Damn the man's arrogance! If he thought she was open to a casual flirtation, he'd find himself snapping at thin air.

Yes, I'll see you in hell first, Nicholas Draycott, Kacey swore silently.

Behind her, the air seemed to shimmer and tremble. A shadow fell across the corridor. *That, too might be arranged, Katharine*, the darkness seemed to whisper. *For there are many different kinds of hell, and a great many are right here on earth. Hell is wanting what you can never again have. Hell is facing something that was once yours and knowing that you destroyed it wantonly.*

So speak that word carefully, the darkness murmured. *Lest you find it sooner than you think.*

And the ghost of Draycott Abbey had reason to know that particular lesson better than most.

Thirty minutes later, Kacey closed her mind to the viscount and every other concern, settling down to her work.

In the daylight, the painting was even more magnificent than it had appeared the night before. Now every subtle stroke of muted gray, lavender, and turquoise was clearly visible.

A masterpiece of design, the canvas showed a river scene captured at jewellike twilight, with a single gray figure standing at the end of a shadowy pier. In the distance rocked a phantom ship, lanterns lit, agleam from empty masts.

But was it a genuine Whistler? Kacey asked herself. Her heart said yes, but her mind warned her to stay cautious as she considered a thousand questions of pigment, brushstroke, and canvas treatment.

From somewhere outside came the crunch of feet on gravel, then the creak of a car door opening. A motor roared to life, smooth and powerful.

The sleek two-door number in black, no doubt. Kacey had to fight an errant compulsion to peek out the window.

With an explosive roar, car and driver were gone, gravel skittering in their wake.

Kacey felt her heart give a little lurch. Silence fell once more, heavier now. She tried to tell herself everything was the same, but somehow without Draycott, the house felt different—hushed, waiting. Without fire or heart.

Just as she waited?

Forget him, will you!

Suppressing an irritated sigh, she carried the bulky painting to a chair near the window. Carefully, she tilted it back to catch the full rays of the midmorning sun. Despite modern technology, there was simply nothing like natural sunlight to reveal faint details in painting.

The canvas was clearly fragile, weakened by the hard treatment Whistler was famous for meting out to his paintings. Never content with a single stroke, he often scoured the cloth, digging with brush and file to soften the background for the muted subtlety he prized.

But a few hours of exposure would not harm this one, Kacey decided. There seemed to be little damage beyond a slight buckling of the wooden struts and some crackling of the paint near the signature. In several spots, the pigment appeared to be losing tone—a constant problem with works by Whistler, who grandly ignored every rule of chemistry and artistic practice in mixing his colors.

Her green eyes lit with excitement, Kacey pulled out her jeweler's loupe. There by the window she knelt and began meticulously inspecting the canvas, inch by inch.

Kacey was still hunched in that same position two hours later when Marston came to inquire if she would care to take tea downstairs.

At first his soft question did not register.

She blinked, squinting through the small frame of the magnifying lens. The question came again.

Frowning, Kacey looked up, her eyes vague and confused. Only then did she register the butler's presence. Slowly she sat back, rubbing her sore back and shoulders. Unfortunately, she had discovered long ago that aching muscles were an occupational hazard for a restorer.

Yes, it was definitely time for a break, she decided, trying to fight the excitement bubbling up inside her. The pigments were of the correct composition, range, and period; the canvas preparation appeared entirely in keeping with Whistler's practice. With any luck at all, this just might turn out to be the lost Whistler she so hoped it was!

"Might I suggest the front salon?" the butler murmured as she tucked back a long strand of tawny hair and flexed her shoulders wearily. "That room is very pleasant this time of day, with the light reflected from the moat."

A few minutes later, he pushed open a polished wooden door and stood back while Kacey entered a bright room filled with chintz, Chinese blue and white porcelain, and freshly cut flowers. At the center of the far wall, an unbroken expanse of leaded windows opened onto the glittering sweep of the lily-strewn moat and the dark woods beyond.

Kacey caught her breath at the beauty of the scene, moving to the window for a closer look.

Somewhere nearby, a telephone pealed shrilly.

A flicker of annoyance—and something more?—crossed the butler's face as he excused himself to answer.

He returned far sooner than she'd expected. "You have a telephone call, Miss Mallory. You may take it across the hall in the library."

Kacey followed him to a book-lined retreat whose French windows overlooked the rolling lawns to the south and the faint blue haze of the channel. Marston held out a telephone, then retired silently.

"Hello? This is Kacey Mallory."

"Any luck?" It was a low dark murmur, just as if they'd picked up their conversation after a lapse of mere seconds.

"Luck?" Despite her firmest intentions, Kacey's heart lurched uncomfortably. "Oh—you mean about the painting." Of course Draycott meant the painting! "I'm afraid it's far too soon to say anything definite. I thought I explained that to you this morning, Lord Draycott."

"Nicholas."

Kacey plunged ahead, ignoring him. "The choice of subject is quite acceptable, the brushwork extremely good. Masterful even. All of that is very promising, of course, but I must remind you that there are still any number of tests to be done—chemical analysis, canvas inspection, possibly even U-V photography.''

"*Is it or is it not a forgery, Miss Mallory?*" he asked impatiently. "Or aren't you capable of telling me that?''

Kacey's face went white with fury. "No, I can't tell you that. Not yet, at least. No reputable appraiser could, without doing one or two tests. And anyone who tells you otherwise is a damn charlatan! *Lord Draycott*," she added furiously.

A faint whisper of sound crossed the line. A sigh? And if so, was it of relief, of regret, or of exasperation?

"Very well," the viscount said. "We dine at seven. Try to be prompt, if you please." With that brusque utterance, the phone went dead in her hand.

Kacey put down the receiver, seething at this latest insult. She was still standing that way when the phone rang again.

So now he meant to apologize, did he? Her lips set in a line of sheer stubbornness. This was one apology she wasn't going to miss!

She jerked the phone to her ear. "Draycott Abbey," she purred.

Silence met her—five seconds, then ten.

"Hello?" Kacey repeated irritably. She was nearing the end of her patience with this infuriating man!

"Tell Lord Draycott that my patience is nearly at an end. He now has two days left." It was a male voice, low and clipped.

English with a faint touch of something else, Kacey thought. "Two days? What do you mean?"

"Draycott will know what I mean. I wonder if he will die well. I shall enjoy finding out, I think. And . . .'' There was the faintest calculated pause. "Enjoy your stay at the abbey, Miss Mallory.''

Kacey's heart began to pound. The last two words were spoken slowly and very precisely, as if the person at the other end wanted to make it clear that he knew every detail of what went on at the abbey.

Was this Draycott's thief? she wondered wildly. "Who—who is this?" The line went dead.

Her fingers gripped the receiver, white with tension. Suddenly Kacey felt painfully vulnerable and exposed.

Most of all, she found herself wishing that Nicholas Draycott was a great deal closer at hand.

Teatime came and went, then dinner. Lord Draycott was nowhere to be seen.

In the end, Kacey took her dinner on a tray in the long gallery, where she could enjoy the beauty of the golden-tinged Wealden Hills.

The food had been excellent, the setting exquisite. And yet she'd eaten almost nothing.

She returned to work, weary and on edge. Several times she spun about, certain she was being watched. But there was no one behind her—nothing but shadows.

And the taste of her own fear.

Finally, her nerves drawn taut as a bowstring, Kacey angled the mounted canvas back against the wall and stood up. So far, every detail had been absolutely accurate—the physical details, at least. Pigment, backing, canvas, and stroke detail—all appeared correct.

But most of all, the painting *felt* real. Of course, Kacey was wise enough to admit that she *wanted* the canvas to be genuine. And that was very dangerous, because experience had taught her that skepticism was her only true friend when it came to the exacting work she did.

A cool draft brushed her cheek, lifting a long strand of honey-gold hair. Kacey frowned, feeling her muscles throb in the aftermath of her meticulous work.

And yes, God help her, with expectancy and an excitement she could barely contain.

The laugh came at her ear, low and dark with triumph. "You just can't keep away from it, can you, Kacey Mallory?"

6

Kacey went totally still, her fingers clenched on the wooden slats of the painting. Every muscle leaped to aching attention. Every inch of feminine skin flushed with tense awareness.

Until she could calm her rioting pulse, she refused to turn around.

But that just might be never, with this man around you, a mocking voice whispered.

His warm breath teased her neck, playing over her unbound hair. She felt the force of his silver eyes sweep over her, and the power of it made the tiny hairs at the back of her neck tingle.

"Go away," Kacey said flatly. "I'm working, and you are most definitely bothering me."

Draycott made a muffled noise somewhere between a laugh and a curse. Slowly he pulled the frame from her fingers, then titled it to rest against an antique armchair with gilt legs.

What a ridiculous chair, Kacey thought, her eyes stubbornly glued to its spindly gold legs.

"Stand up, Kacey."

She didn't move.

"Look at me." It was a husky growl.

She tried to ignore him. With every straining fiber of her body, she tried. But it was useless.

His hand fell to her shoulder, and the touch was like a jolt of raw energy. Kacey flinched, her muscles throbbing.

In places she shouldn't even be aware of. In ways she shouldn't be imagining.

The long fingers curved over her skin and then slowly tightened. As if he felt her stiffness, Nicholas began to smooth the taut muscles aching from a day of painstaking detail work.

His thumb hit a knot of angry, corded muscle. Kacey gasped softly. Instantly his fingers stilled. "Kacey? What is it?"

She wouldn't face him. Somehow that would make this moment, these feelings, all too real.

Draycott's mouth was at her ear. "Look at me, damn it! Tell me what's wrong."

As if in a dream, Kacey angled her head, staring up at him through a curtain of tawny lashes, her long legs tucked useless and immobile beneath her.

The sight of her creamy skin and wide, haunted eyes stunned Draycott, even though by now he should have become used to her beauty. But something told him he would never become used to the sight of her, nor ever take this woman for granted.

And then hunger was a tangible thing, a painful thing, twisting through every inch of his body. Suddenly he was restless and hungry.

For her. Somehow it had always been her, Nicholas Draycott thought dimly. "Did I hurt you?" he demanded.

Oh, you hurt me all right, Kacey thought. *You hurt me the very first second I laid eyes on you.*

Maybe even before.

"It's—it's my neck." Her eyes fell, wide and smoky, riveted to his hard mouth. She blinked, trying to forget what it felt like to be flush against him, his lips hard and seeking. His body hot, hungry with need. "It—it always happens. When I work. No time. I—forget—"

She was babbling, but she couldn't seem to stop. Besides, Kacey realized if she stopped she might do something really crazy.

Like pull him down to kiss her. Like comb her fingers through that dense black hair teasing her from the opening of his white shirt.

"Let me touch you, Kacey." It was an urgent command, raw with infinite hunger.

Her heart slammed against her ribs. She couldn't have spoken if she'd been drowning.

Which she was, suddenly. In the dark, hard textures of him. In the heated memories his closeness provoked.

Draycott smothered a curse. With one swift, fluid movement, he came down to kneel beside her, his slate eyes never leaving her face.

Beautiful cheeks, he thought dimly. Beautiful mouth. Beautiful everything. "Don't worry—I'm simply protecting my investment," he murmured, trying hard to believe it himself. Before she could protest, he pulled her between his thighs and drew her back against his chest. His fingers cupped her shoulders and dug smoothly at the knots of tension, splaying and contracting rhythmically. "You're very expensive, Yank, in case you didn't know it."

Kacey's eyes closed, then jerked open sharply as she fought the power of those masterful fingers. "Oh, I do— know it. But . . . something tells me—ummm—you're very good at . . . protecting your investments."

Draycott laughed huskily. Strong and certain, his hands played over her shoulders while pleasure lapped through her in drugging waves. "Tell me how it feels, Kacey." His voice was a dark caress against the lobe of her ear.

"Good," she whispered, barely realizing she'd spoken. "*Too* good." Her eyelids fluttered down, and this time they did not reopen.

Nicholas's mouth curved up. Soon I'll make it feel even better, he promised silently.

His hands followed the slim line of her neck downward, picking out the exact inch of skin where a cluster of muscles screamed in agony. With practiced skill, he circled the tense center, gradually narrowing the circle. Long weeks in the hospital had taught him a great deal about physical suffering, after all. Now he knew all there was to know about pain and the thousand ways of releasing it. In the weeks after Bhanlai, physical therapy had helped him survive and restored his sanity.

"How did you know? Who . . ." With a sigh, Kacey gave up trying to talk, her question forgotten midsentence.

Draycott's laugh was a dark, intimate thing. "You work too hard, Connecticut. It's unhealthy, too much work, don't you know that?"

Kacey's eye cracked open. "Who—who told you I was from Connecticut?" she muttered.

Draycott's fingers paused for a fraction of a second. "Your address was there in your letters of recommendation. I looked them over this morning."

"Oh." Kacey's frown faded and her eyes closed once more. "And now I suppose you're going to tell me—ummm—that you're the very person to teach me how to relax?"

Draycott's smile widened. "However did you guess?"

She tried to scoff, to tense, to push him away. But she couldn't, because his fingers were heaven itself. Dear God, her bones were turning to jelly, and Kacey realized she would do anything to ensure that he didn't stop.

For the span of a heartbeat, he hesitated.

Her soft protest tumbled out before she knew it.

Even before that, Draycott had felt the exact moment she stopped fighting him. The instant her mind let down its barriers, and her body surrendered to his pleasure.

He knew, and the knowledge stabbed him with hot, primal, male triumph. *First round to me, Kacey Mallory.*

Her head fell back, cradled against his forearm and chest. Her breath escaped in a sigh—soft and husky and endlessly female.

Mine, Draycott thought. Every silken inch, every sweet sigh mine. And suddenly he felt a reckless need to make her sigh that way again. But this time with a woman's pleasure.

At that moment, a high-pitched hum swept the room, followed by a faint click. A second later, every bulb in the long gallery flickered and went out.

The bloody power was out again, Draycott realized.

He looked down at the woman in his arms, his eyes already adapted to the darkness. Her eyes were closed,

Draycott saw, her head tilted back. Her hair spilled like a warm honey cloud over his chest and shoulders.

Fire pooled heavy in his groin. He felt himself harden and swell with a passion he hadn't known for months. But he didn't move, wanting to savor the sweet, aching need.

She hadn't noticed the sudden darkness, he realized. Right now, she felt nothing but the dark power of his kneading fingers. Right now, she was intensely vulnerable, infinitely female.

And that realization gave Nicholas Draycott stunning pleasure.

When her fingers moved a moment later, cupping his taut thigh, he felt it right down to the tip of his toes, right out to his fingernails, right up to the fevered pleasure centers of his brain.

So this is what it's supposed to feel like, the hard-eyed Englishman thought in wonder.

Wanting—a thousand kinds of wanting.

Needing—in ways that hadn't even been invented yet.

And through it all, feeling that somehow he had done all these things before.

He didn't notice her stiffening until her breathless gasp caught him short. Suddenly her fingers were hard on his thigh—and this time she was pushing him away.

"L-let me go!"

"Kacey, don't—"

"Right now, damn you!" She twisted back and stumbled to her feet, blind in the encompassing darkness. "You arrogant bastard! You misbegotten slime! What have you done with the lights?"

What have you done to *me*? Kacey screamed inwardly.

Draycott's jaw tightened. He had an advantage over her, knowing exactly where he was in spite of the darkness. Right now, for example, she was only inches from a sixteenth-century marquetry card table.

He smiled faintly, the movement a slash of white against the darkness. "I did nothing. The electricity's merely gone out again. The construction teams nick a cable every few weeks. They're in too much of a rush to bother reading utility maps.''

He heard her stumble, then curse beneath her breath. A moment later, the card table crashed to the floor.

''Aren't you going to do something?'' Kacey demanded irritably.

''I thought I was. And very nicely, too.''

He was laughing at her! Kacey thought. Damn the man! How could she have been so stupid as to trust him? To let him touch her, to allow herself to feel so—so safe in his arms?

It's only lust, Katharine Chelsea. Only a matter of hormones. After all, it's been almost a year since—

She closed her mind to that particular avenue of thought. ''Well, if *you* want to sit here like a fool, then go ahead. But I'm going down to find a candle.''

''You'll never make it in the dark.''

''Wanna bet?''

''It's three flights down to the kitchen.''

''Ask real nice, and I might bring back a candle for you. No, on second thought—''

''You'd bloody well try it, wouldn't you? And in the process, you'd stumble and break that stubborn neck of yours. Then, no doubt, you'd try to sue me for aggravated assault. No thanks—you're going to stay right here while I go and get the candle. Then I'll see you safely to your room. And you'll damn well stay there until the power is restored.''

She heard him turn, his soft soles padding over the wooden floor.

Kacey's fingers clenched into fists. The man was a complete throwback to the Dark Ages! ''Now just wait one minute!'' She started after him and promptly stumbled. The next second, she felt hard fingers grip her arm.

''Has anybody ever told you you're too bloody stubborn for your own good, woman?'' Draycott growled.

''A few times. How about you?'' She expected him to snap back a denial, and so his silence surprised her.

His fingers tightened. ''Only once. It was a very long

time ago." His voice hardened. "I didn't listen then, either."

A thousand questions sprang to her lips. Questions Kacey knew she had no right to ask.

Questions, she reminded herself grimly, that she hadn't the slightest interest in having answers for!

The Englishman muttered something under his breath and pulled her along after him. "Come on then. At least I can keep you from breaking your bloody neck!"

At that moment, he sounded as if the prospect of getting rid of her held definite appeal.

In the engulfing silence, their footsteps echoed noisily. Every breath was sharp, every rustle intensified. And the infuriating man knew exactly where he was going, Kacey soon realized.

"Stop," she hissed. "I can't keep up! It's pitch-black in here, remember?"

Draycott muttered something beneath his breath and slowed his pace.

Reaching out, Kacey felt the banister beneath her fingers, velvet-smooth with centuries of beeswax and careful polishing. Five hundred years ago, the house must have been much the same as this, she thought. No lights, no whirring machines. Only this total, encompassing silence.

Down the stairwell they went, and to Kacey, it was as if they'd found the path straight into the house's heart. The ancient walls seemed to hum and close around them, as if welcoming them down a long corridor.

Of time. Of dreams.

To a place they both dimly remembered.

"Don't you have a generator or something?" Kacey asked irritably, to cover her growing uneasiness. "After all, this *is* the twentieth century."

They were at the second-floor landing. Draycott led her confidently to the right, his fingers hard on her wrist. "Marston will be on to it already, I'm sure."

She frowned, trying to tug free, only to feel his fingers tighten. "Stop fighting me, Kacey. You'll never win."

"That's where you're wrong, Nicholas Draycott!"

He stopped so abruptly that she stumbled into him. Without a second's hesitation, he twisted back against the wall, taking her with him. His arms slid to her ribs and crushed her against his chest.

The next moment Kacey found herself captured between rigid thighs.

"Do you really believe that?" he asked. "Let's find out, shall we?"

Disoriented, she reached out blindly in the darkness. The hard contours of his shoulders flexed rigid beneath her searching fingers.

Somehow her hands curved, digging into those taut muscles.

Somehow his hands shifted, burying themselves in her silken hair.

"Katharine—sweet, soft Katharine." His breath hissed free in a dark, erotic groan.

The sound went straight to her heart, setting off sensual explosions that jolted bone by tiny bone all the way down Kacey's spine. "St-stop, Nicholas."

His mouth cut off her half-formed protest. He kissed her urgently, unthinkingly. All his calculation was gone now—all that remained was raw male need. He took without asking, commanded without speaking.

He shaped her mouth, then remade it in his desire, and he didn't stop until her lips softened beneath him and her breath fled sharply.

Only then did he part her lips and fill her with his heat.

Perfectly.

Agonizingly.

Until the kiss seemed to go on forever, blinding in its power and sweetness.

When he released her at last, her mouth was throbbing, and the old Kacey was gone, swept away forever. Now a new Kacey burned in the darkness, consumed by yearnings she had never before known.

The Englishman just smiled. Without a word, he turned and tugged her after him into the darkness, moving noiselessly and with total certainty. Dimly, Kacey heard a door open, then felt a chair probe the side of her knee. A moment later he pushed her down into a stiff-backed wing chair.

"Stay put. I'll be back in a few minutes."

"Nicholas, wait! Let me—"

Too late. She heard him move away.

Her heart was pounding. Only anger, she told herself and tried to believe it.

Later she was to wonder why she hadn't been more afraid at that moment. Oddly enough, she wasn't, though she was sitting in utter darkness in the middle of a strange room in an unfamiliar house.

As her eyes gradually grew accustomed to the dark, she began to make out faint details. The rectangle of gray at a window. The dim, gleaming oval of a clock face, its hands at eight o'clock.

Since it was too late to go after Nicholas, Kacey decided to pass the time trying to imagine what the room looked like. Vaulted ceiling? Tall bookcases? Paintings covering every inch of its silk-lined walls?

She frowned. The image came to her suddenly, without warning or prethought.

Oak paneling. Gleaming brass wall sconces and a great crystal chandelier. Floor-to-ceiling French windows hung with sapphire velvet curtains.

A gilt desk with claw feet. A vast canvas of Henry VIII, fisted hands on his hips, dominating the room from the opposite wall.

Kacey shook her head, but the image persisted. No, somehow more than an image. *A memory.*

Now the silent shadows mocked her, no longer friendly.

Without warning, she felt a current of air brush past her feet. She stiffened at the sound of faint scratching near the floor. Two eyes gleamed up at her from the darkness. A moment later, warm fur rippled past her ankle.

Just a cat, she thought, smiling unsteadily. A very clever cat, however, to find its way in past bolted doors and locked windows.

"I wonder what *your* name is?" she mused, her fingers curving over the soft fur.

The amber eyes shifted up to study her, unblinking in the darkness. The cat meowed once, deep and fluidly.

Kacey relaxed in her chair, enjoying the low hum that radiated into her fingers. The cat shifted slightly, maneuvering closer against her leg.

Gideon.

The word just popped into her head. Somehow she knew with perfect certainty that if she spoke the word, the cat would slant his head and meow softly at her.

Enough, Kacey! she thought, scrambling to her feet, her thoughts reeling.

And then, with a click and a faint pop, the power returned. The room filled suddenly with warm, golden light.

She saw with relief that there was no gleaming chandelier before her.

No gilt desk with claw feet.

Only pamphlets and ancient leather volumes rising in a haphazard mound atop a massive desk—rosewood surely? A bronze bust of George III cheek by jowl with a little ormolu clock. A row of cut-glass tumblers and a decanter alongside a collection of sherry and whiskey bottles.

A very lived-in room, full of that cheerful clutter her countrymen liked to call the English country house style.

Then Kacey's breath caught in her throat. Her eyes widened.

For now she saw the oak paneling—just as she'd imagined it. The brass wall sconces gleamed back at her—shoulder-high, just where she'd envisioned them.

And there was the lusty monarch himself, swaggering from a gilt frame just above the darkened fireplace.

She sank down slowly, her fingers digging into the padded damask arms of the wing chair.

At her feet the cat shifted and meowed softly.

Slow down, she thought. *You've got a good, healthy imagination, but this is just too weird. Madame Blavatsky you're not.*

But the proof was right there before her, tangible and irrefutable.

Blinking her eyes did not make it go away.

She frowned, looking at the large gray cat with ink-black paws. The amber eyes seemed to narrow, staring back at her intently.

"What am I looking at *you* for?" she asked shakily. "I'm not likely to be getting any answers from you!"

She took a deep breath, trying to calm her racing pulse. Perhaps she'd seen the room before in a guidebook. The abbey must have been photographed often, after all. Yes, that must be the answer!

But something told Kacey that the abbey's hard-faced owner would refuse to allow anything but the public rooms to be photographed for publication.

Which left her right back where she'd started. In the middle of a strange, unsettling house with a sinking feeling in the pit of her stomach.

And the total conviction that she had been in this room before.

Trying to deny the dangerous course her thoughts were taking, Kacey jerked to her feet, sending the cat running. Then her eyes flickered across the cluttered desk. They said you could tell everything about a person by what he read. So what would this desk tell her about Nicholas Draycott?

She riffled a leather-bound volume of *Richard III*, lying atop the latest thriller by Tom Clancy. Nearby were four thin gardening manuals. She lifted one and glanced inside the front cover. Published by the Royal Horticultural Society, no less.

A pile of letters—opened and unopened.

A children's book with wildly colorful pictures.

Kacey's brow wrinkled. So Nicholas Draycott had eclectic tastes, did he? She moved closer, pulling a file folder out from beneath the slim leather volume of Shakespeare.

"Armistead," the file was labeled.

Her eyes narrowed. Hadn't Draycott said something about that name last night in the stable? Her curiosity piqued, Kacey opened the folder, resolutely pushing away a pang of guilt at poking into what might be private papers.

But there were no letters inside, only carefully clipped newspaper articles. From the lowest and sleaziest of the

English tabloids, judging by the lurid headlines and sensational photographs.

And then her fingers froze. A caption screamed out at her.

"English Diplomat Freed in Burma." A gaunt face stared back at her from a newspaper clipping, the eyes oddly flat and unfocused.

Nicholas Draycott's face—forty pounds thinner and a hundred years older. A face dominated by the savage will to survive, even when logic dictated that all hope should have fled.

Her eyes had just flashed to the smaller text below when the lights flickered. Kacey smothered a curse as the room was flooded with darkness once more.

Scowling, she carried the file to the window and pulled aside the curtain, hoping for enough light to read by. Outside, the wind had risen to a wild, steady rush, and the moon hung huge and silver above shuddering trees.

Kacey shivered, feeling a chill seep across the room, and with it a nearly tangible sense of sadness.

Moonlight glittered on the carpet, pale and cold as frost. Somewhere in the house, a clock chimed. Far away in the distance, across the Wealden Hills, she heard the echo of other bells, low and faint. Something about the sound was infinitely disturbing, as if they did not belong to this world.

And Kacey could have sworn they chimed thirteen times.

Her fingers tightened on the file.

She squinted down at the dim lines of script, barely visible in the moonlight.

Without the slightest sound, the French doors slid open before her. The curtains began to flap wildly.

Cold air lashed her face, making her take a step back.

The file in her hands fell forgotten to the carpet as the curtains surged up, then parted to reveal broad shoulders encased in black velvet, long legs eased into breeches and knee-high boots.

His cascading ruffles gleamed white beneath a flowing beard, and his raven hair was cinched in a long queue. Kacey tried to speak, but only a raw squeak emerged.

Hard and shadowed, the man's eyes watched her, his broad shoulders almost filling the doorway. "At last! I've managed it well and truly. About bloody time."

The words coursed across Kacey's skin in the chill wind, a rich current of sound. "Wh-who are you?" she stammered, sinking away from the door.

Her heart pounded as he strode past her to the unlit fireplace. Without a word, he stripped off his cloak and bent down, his face taking on a fiery glow.

Bathed in the light of a fire that did not exist.

Phantom steam began rising in thick clouds from his sodden cloak as he tossed it over the nearby chair. Briskly, he held his hands out to the dark grate.

"Cold, as usual. I see I shall have to—" His voice halted abruptly. He seemed to stiffen. "Sit down, Katharine Mallory," he commanded, not turning. "I'm afraid I haven't a great deal of time."

Kacey pinched her palm to see if she was dreaming.

The laugh from the fireplace was deep and harsh. "No, you're not dreaming. Not unless *all* life is a dream and death its waking. Some philosophers would have it so, I believe. Now do sit down," he added sharply. "You're making me deucedly uncomfortable standing there with your mouth hanging open, looking for all the world like a beached mackerel."

Had she walked into a madhouse? Kacey wondered. Her heart racing, she glared back at the dark figure.

Once more, the curtains fluttered. Through the open window glided a second shadow—sleek and gray, legs capped with black paws.

"Ah, Gideon, there you are. All clear?"

The cat made a low purring sound.

"Excellent. Now perhaps *you* can do something to convince her."

Kacey gaped as she watched the sleek creature steal with noiseless footfalls across the thick carpet. With a sharp meow, the animal jumped into an armchair near the fire and curled up in a ball.

And there, his intelligent head slanted at an angle to study her better, the cat began to purr. As if summoning her.

Gideon. So she had gotten the name right after all.

Hard on the heels of that wild realization, Kacey began to tremble. She bit her lip, fighting down her fear. ''Now wait j-just one d-damn minute.''

The bearded head turned, one brow raised, black eyes snapping. ''I'm afraid I've no time for your hysterics, Katharine. So you will oblige me by taking yourself in hand, sitting down, and listening.'' He pointed to the armchair where Gideon sat studying her. ''*Now*,'' he barked.

Without thinking why, Kacey found herself moving where he pointed. Immediately the cat shifted, then settled in her lap. The room seemed to shimmer, picking up the light of a dying fire.

A fire that did not exist.

Kacey bit back a moan. Dear God, she was going totally mad, without the slightest hint of a doubt!

The man at the grate came slowly to his feet. His face was lean, filled with shadows. Somehow it reminded her of Nicholas's face. ''Not mad, my dear, or even dreaming. Had we more time, I would try to explain this the slow way, the patient way, but—circumstances . . . prevent that.'' He frowned. ''You're still thinking about that bloody file of my brother's?''

''Brother?'' Kacey croaked. So that explained the similarity of proud nose and angular jaw. The familiar curve of the sensual lips. She hadn't realized that the viscount had an older brother, but then she was no expert on the Draycott family tree.

''His twin, to be exact. Fraternal twin. Unfortunately, I had a bit of an accident when I was seven years old. We were exploring along the foot of the cliffs, and I was trapped in a cave when the tide came in.''

He studied her for long seconds, his eyes as black as Gideon's paws. ''My brother managed to escape, but I, unfortunately, did not.''

Kacey's eyes widened. ''I b-beg your pardon?''

''Drowning isn't really such a bad way to go, all in all. First the cold, then the gradual numbing. And then—'' He seemed to catch himself. "But I digress. My brother's labors over that generator will not keep him away much longer, and he had better not find the two of us here when that happens. It would raise all the old jealousies . . ." The shadowed mouth curved in a faint smile. "Not that he would see me. He never does. But it would make things deucedly unpleasant for you to be seen speaking to thin air, my dear Katharine."

A thousand wild questions flew to Kacey's lips. In her lap, Gideon began to purr softly, and somehow the noise only made her more uncomfortable. "You—you can't really expect me to—to believe—"

"That I'm a ghost?" he finished for her. "No, I suppose I don't expect you to believe that. Not yet. But I do expect you to listen. For a man needs your help this night. Two men, in fact," he muttered, turning to stoke the fire that was not there. Warming his long fingers at flames that did not exist.

Kacey started to protest, to hurl a barrage of cold, hard questions at him, but his head turned just then. His eyes changed, naked and vulnerable now. "Once again it is the three of us, just as it was all those years ago. You can remember none of it?"

Kacey shook her head blindly, fighting down the beginnings of hysteria. "I don't know who you are or what you want, but—"

The figure smiled rather sadly. "I am Adrian, Nicholas's brother, Katharine. Just as I was his brother then. And what I want is to help you."

A raw laugh escaped her locked lips. "A ghost? Just grand! You're telling me I'm talking to a *ghost*?"

"Please, my dear—just listen. Do it for Nicholas. Do it for me. Most of all, do it for yourself." The man's gaze swept her face, chill and light as fingers of mist. "Between us, we tore you apart, Katharine. Neither one of us could let you go, even though we should have seen what it was doing to you."

Unable to speak, Kacey only shook her head. It must be

some sort of joke! Of course she couldn't be sitting here conversing with a—.

The man at the grate frowned. "I see it will take something more to convince you, stubborn one." On the floor, the forgotten file fluttered open. Suddenly the pages began to turn.

Soundlessly. By hands unseen.

All at once, images began pouring through Kacey's mind, images of lush rice fields, of ancient stone cities hidden beneath an emerald jungle. She saw Nicholas Draycott— young, ambitious, and driven.

Then the walls closed in, and the darkness began to crush her. The silent screaming began.

Bhanlai. The word hissed down, burning like acid into her head. She understood it all so clearly now.

For she saw—no, she *became* his past, tried it on like a coat, felt it ripple and surge over her like a river of light and sound.

Now she knew why Draycott was hounded by the tabloids for his story. Now she understood the ghosts that returned, night after night, haunting him, shaking him tense and screaming from sleep.

An ambitious Englishman trying just a little too hard to do his job. A Golden Triangle drug lord flexing his muscle. A dirty little war in a dirty little village in a very dirty little corner of Asia.

And Nicholas Draycott had landed in the middle of the crossfire as three countries scrambled for the pickings. Tossed in a dark, muddy hole, he had become the symbol of everything Trang wanted to destroy.

Stunned, Kacey stared at the man beside the fire, tears sliding down her pale cheeks.

"He's a lucky fool, my brother. I only hope he realizes that in time. If things were different—if I had the chance— I'd take you away from him," Adrian Draycott said fiercely. "Just as I did *then*." His face turned shuttered, and he seemed to give himself a shake. "But things aren't different, are they? And it's his chance now, not mine," he muttered bitterly.

Kacey could only stare at him, aghast, unable to believe what he was saying.

For a moment his face burned with the dark flares of remembrance. "There was never anyone else like you, Katharine. No one who even came close, though you refused to believe that. That was always your greatest mistake, in fact—underestimating yourself."

Kacey shivered. Why did he say her name just so, as if there were a lifetime of feeling behind the word? And why did it affect her so strongly?

She raised a trembling hand, trying to fight the chill that gripped the room. She felt a sudden, gnawing premonition that he was about to reveal some frightening truth.

His gaze burned over her.

Suddenly he stiffened, his eyebrows raised in imperious slants. "Good God, woman, what are those unspeakable things on your feet?"

Trancelike, Kacey looked down. What was wrong with her boots?

She gave herself a mental shake. Who was he really? A relative of Draycott's who'd come to play a little trick on the visiting Yank? Or merely a neighbor who'd had too much to drink?

"No neighbor. No relative. Draycott has none left, poor fellow. Not alive, that is."

Kacey stiffened. She hadn't *said* anything, only thought it. "How—"

"A simple enough thing, actually. For one of *us*. And one of the bloody few vices we're still permitted."

Suddenly Kacey pushed to her feet, grim-lipped, paying no attention as she dumped an irate Gideon hissing to the floor. "I—I won't listen, do you hear? It's all a trick!" she cried wildly. "An illusion. I'm leaving now, before you can toy with me any more!"

Slowly, Adrian Draycott rose and braced his long body against the mantel. His eyes narrowed. "How would you like to know Whistler's favorite pigment? Shall I tell you the exact proportions to match that *Nocturne* upstairs?"

Sheet-white, Kacey took a step back. "Stop it! I refuse to listen to another word!"

The strange eyes darkened. Across the room, they seemed to seek her out, to glow and widen, fire-flecked. "You *must* listen, Katharine—before it is too late. You are in gravest danger here, as in my stubborn, arrogant brother. No, don't interrupt—I can only manage this materialization for a few more minutes, I fear."

Gasping, Kacey spun about, refusing to listen. Immediately she felt a faint stirring of wind across her shoulders. Her neck began to prickle, almost as if shot through with static electricity.

"Maybe it's because I loved you once," the dark voice continued. "Or maybe it's because of the harm I did you both then." The sound moved closer, low and rough and bitter. "Damn it, perhaps the whys aren't important. What *is* important is that I've been given the chance to come back. To warn you both, so that things do not end as they did before—out there on the cliffs in the slashing wind. So heed this warning well, my dearest heart. There is greed and great hatred at work here, along with something even darker."

Dimly, Kacey felt herself fall beneath the dark rhythm of his words, pulled deep into his spell. Even as she fought him, his voice rippled over her, became part of her. "It was never suicide, though they found your bodies together at the base of the collapsed cliff. No, if anything it was murder—and *I* was the murderer." His voice caught for a moment. "But I never thought you'd take it so hard, Katharine. And I couldn't marry you, don't you see? I had the estate and the Draycott name to think of. You were just a village girl—and an artist's model to boot."

Kacey heard him curse, and then, feather-light, a current of air rose and skimmed her cheek. "You *can* remember what happened then. It is with you even now. All you lack is the desire to know."

Even as he spoke, Kacey had a queer vision of silver cliffs above a leaden sea, of horse's hooves pounding through the rain-swept night.

And then raw terror as the ground fell away beneath her and she plummeted down . . .

Down . . .

Into darkness.

She froze, rigid with fear.

Suddenly the scent of roses surrounded her. "But now I must say goodbye, my beautiful Katharine," the wind whispered, combing through her long hair. "I can come only once more. And it must be through *you*, since Nicholas refuses to see me or allow me in. The rest is up to the two of you. Until then . . . tell my brother not to grieve about what happened in the cave all those years ago. Tell him it was—necessary, for many, many reasons. Had I lived . . . well, I am just coming to understand all of that myself."

The rich voice wavered for a moment. "Just tell him Adrian found the pirate treasure after all, though it cost him dear. I pray to God he will not make the same mistakes that I did. As for you, my beautiful Katharine—trust in Nicholas. Help him trust in himself. He loved you very much then— far more than I did. He deserved better than what he got. *My* fault, again."

The words seemed to fade. And then out of the darkness behind her came the whisper of fluttering curtains.

Her heart slamming against her ribs, Kacey summoned her courage and slowly turned.

The dark figure was gone.

Only a quiet room remained, and a file that lay closed on the rug, exactly where she had dropped it long minutes before.

Only a locked door and tightly drawn curtains.

Only a dark fireplace and a chill room, with no one in it but her.

7

A RAGGED cry ripped from Kacey's throat. White-faced, she moved to pick up the file, which lay forgotten on the carpet.

At that moment, the door burst open behind her. Nicholas's face was outlined against the bright rectangle of light from the doorway. "The bloody power's still out, and I'm afraid the generator won't—" Suddenly he stopped, his silver-gray eyes narrowed on the file Kacey clutched to her chest.

A vein beat at his temple, and the scar at his cheekbone gleamed silver in the light of the desk lamp.

Suddenly Kacey saw the image of a different man in that doorway—a man taller and slightly leaner, clad in sapphire velvet. In his hand, he carried a single candle that flickered in a ceaseless play of light and shadow over his deeply lined face.

A beloved face. The face of a man who loved too much . . .

And then her breath snagged as she had a keen image of those strong, callused fingers loosening her long gown.

Gown? she thought, frowning.

Next, her lace-edged chemise and a boned undergarment of some sort opened, and then his naked skin met hers.

She caught back a moan, feeling the touch of his hand at her breast, the steely length of his thigh. Pleasure shot through her—*remembered* pleasure. Kacey realized that she knew just how to make this man groan with ecstasy, just when to stop to make him wild with desire.

Could it possibly be true? Had she and Nicholas really

been lovers in some other time? Had they somehow managed to find each other again, haunted by a tragedy that had separated them two hundred years before?

No, it couldn't be! She was a nice, normal person; things like this didn't happen to *normal* people!

Kacey shivered in the chill grip of hysteria. She started to offer the file to him, only to feel the string closure snag on her blouse. With trembling fingers, she ripped it free, sending a button flying onto the carpet.

But she barely noticed. Suddenly she had to know for certain whether Adrian had spoken the truth. Her hands clenched, and she studied Nicholas's face. "You really should stop feeling guilty for what happened . . . back in that cave. It was meant to be."

The only sign that Draycott heard came in the tensing of his fingers on the door frame. "Cave? I haven't the faintest idea what you're—"

"There were just the two of you." Kacey watched his face for a response—and saw none. "The tide came in. You didn't notice until the cave was half covered."

Suddenly, just as before, images began to flood into her mind, like slides clicking in a swift, ceaseless flow across a bright screen. First came the image of two boys, dark-haired and slate-eyed, scrambling over a beach of white sand. She could hear their high, reckless laughter above the crash of the surf.

"It was a dare. His dare." She frowned, concentrating—and then tried not to concentrate as she discovered it was best just to let the images flow over her. "It was your—your seventh birthday. You were sick from too much cake. Plum cake—it was always your favorite, though Adrian—"

Draycott's breath exploded in a curse. "You bloody little liar!"

Kacey flinched beneath the force of his anger, but she had come too far to stop now. Most of all, she had to have an end to this terrible uncertainty. "You called and called, but he wouldn't come away from the tunnel he was searching. And then the tide surged."

"Don't do this, Kacey," Nicholas rasped. "I can't take much more tonight, I warn you."

And then she saw it all, as clear as the pages in a book. "Dear God, you just managed to get out and—and Adrian didn't."

Draycott's curse cut her off. "Who told you those things? *Who,* damn you?"

"*He* told me."

"He? Armistead, you mean?" Nicholas pounded across the room, seizing her shoulders in a hard grip. "How much did he pay you to—"

"Can't you stop looking for villains? I didn't say anything about Armistead. It wasn't Armistead who told me. It was—" Kacey took a quick, unsteady breath. "It was . . . Adrian."

A muscle flashed at his jaw. "Stop this bloody charade, Kacey. My brother has been dead for almost thirty years."

"I didn't believe it either. Not at first. But I saw him, can't you understand? He was standing right there by the French doors, his cloak steaming, his shirt fluttering in the wind. He said . . . he said we were both in danger."

Nicholas's mouth twisted. "In danger, are we? So that's where all this is leading. How much? How bloody much do you expect me to pay you?"

"Stop it, Nicholas. Just listen to me!"

But he didn't stop. Grim-faced, he pressed her back, step by step, until a ridge of books bit into her spine.

Struggling vainly, Kacey closed her eyes, trying to ignore the fire of him, the searing steel of him, desperate to make him listen.

"Do you think that you're the first to try this scam?" the Englishman growled. "Over the last ten years, dozens of helpful mediums have written to offer their services so that I might escape a terrible fate that's supposedly hanging over me."

Kacey's shot open. "And you paid no attention?"

"Half of England must know the story of the Draycott ghost. Any one of those people could tell you that the ghost appears only when a member of the family is in danger.

Why should I listen to every crackpot who—''

''But you must! There's a reason the ghost is appearing, don't you see? If we don't listen, he said it will happen all over again. Dear God, the storm—the cliffs—'' She swayed as the dark images flashed over her again: lashing wind, ragged lightning, the explosive fury of collapsing earth.

And then the thunder was beside her, in the growl that ripped from Nicholas's throat. In the savage force of his body wedged against hers.

''How did you know, Kacey? No one but Adrian and I knew those things! And did you guess the rest of it—that I was jealous of Adrian? Dear God, maybe I even . . . wanted him to die.''

Suddenly Nicholas stiffened. His glittering eyes seemed to look right through her. ''So you think you know the whole of it, do you, my sweet?'' He laughed mildly, mirthlessly. ''You never could let it alone, could you? You just couldn't accept the fact that Adrian and I were enemies, and you the cause of that enmity. No, you always had to be about your infernal meddling, determined to smooth over what could never be set right.'' His fingers tightened on her wrists. ''He doesn't love you, Katharine, haven't you realized that by now? Adrian is incapable of love—except for himself. And perhaps for that great gray cat of his!''

Kacey's breath caught. She had the riveting sensation that she was looking into the blank eyes of a stranger.

The man he had been two hundred years ago?

Nicholas's eyes smoldered silver, scouring her face. ''But you're mine, do you hear? You were always meant for me. I won't let Adrian hurt you anymore, and I'll see to it that you have the things he would never give you. I'll give you the security of my name—a home. A family.'' His voice turned raw and hoarse. ''Oh, God, Katharine, how I want to see you heavy with our child.''

His eyes narrowed on her face, and Kacey had the feeling that he was more than a little mad at that moment. Desperately, she lashed out with her foot and struck him soundly in the ankle.

Draycott flinched. With a start, his eyes refocused. For

long moments, he simply stared down at her, frowning. "What did I—" He shook his head sharply. "Do you still think you're the only one with questions, Kacey? There are other kinds of ghosts, you know. Do you want to hear about those?"

"Let me go, Nicholas," she gasped, trying to ignore the heat seeping through her shirt. Trying to ignore the hot hard length of his body, which was doing crazy things to her pulse.

"Not until you answer a few questions for me, I think."

"*Now,* Nicholas. I'm tired of these games. I've an immense amount of work to complete tomorrow before—" A tiny, breathless sound escaped her drawn lips as his thumb rose to trace her cheek.

Once again, Kacey caught the fleeting scent of roses. The air around her seemed to hang heavy with regret and the acrid bite of sadness.

He is your life now, the darkness seemed to whisper. *Let the rest go. Forget how it ended all those years ago. Teach him to trust you, Katharine. Then take this happiness and never look back.*

Kacey shivered as Nicholas's finger slid along the arch of her lower lip. "Why do you fight it? Is there a boyfriend waiting somewhere back in the States?"

Kacey stiffened instantly.

"Ah. A no. Are you married?"

"Never!"

"Now that, my sweet Kacey, would be a terrible waste." His eyes fixed on her lips.

"What in the—are you—" She swallowed and tried again. "Just what do you think you're doing?"

"Doing? I'm asking some questions of my own, Kacey. Like how you can feel so bloody soft. How that sexy mouth of yours can rip me apart. And I'm going to find out just what excites you in turn." Even as he spoke, Nicholas's thumb teased the locked line of her lips.

Kacey shuddered. First had come Adrian's revelations. And now she was caught in dark sensations stronger than anything she'd ever known. Were they *both* going mad?

"Get—get away from me," she whispered, her mind reeling. "You promised not to—"

"I promised to do nothing you didn't want me to do, Kacey. And you've been wanting me to touch you like this since the first moment you got here. Which is just as long as I've wanted to do the touching," Draycott added hoarsely.

"That's a lie!"

"Is it?" he growled. His fingers brushed the line of crimson staining Kacey's cheeks. "This heat says no." His hands moved to the pulse point just behind her ear. "This skittish pulse says the same." His eyes searched her face. "There's no need for lies between us, Kacey. We're both adults. I'll make it good between us—incredibly good. I've thought about this since the first moment I set eyes on you. Maybe even before that," he muttered, half to himself. "Maybe I've been waiting my whole bloody life for this moment."

Kacey tried to steady her plunging pulse. What was he up to now? Or was this Adrian's doing?

With a groan, Nicholas splayed his fingers open over her ribs, measuring her resistance ridge by ridge before coming to a halt just beneath the yearning swell of her breasts. His mouth was at her ear, low and hard and hungry. "I want to see you wrapped in moonlight, Kacey. In warm moonlight and cold shadows and not a stitch of anything else." Each word was a fierce, erotic rasp, punctuated by the sleek velvet stroke of his tongue against her neck. "I want to hear you when I fit myself all the way inside your heat. I want it to be *my* name you whisper, *my* shoulders you dig your fingers into when you go spinning away into space. And, by God, it'll be *my* body you want deep inside you when the pleasure shatters you into a thousand pieces."

One by one, the dark images triggered shock waves down Kacey's spine. Too late, she realized he had freed her shirt from her jeans. Moving across her naked skin, his hard fingers subverted her last vestige of stubborn resistance.

Dear God, why do I want those things, too? Gasping, Kacey tried to break free, realizing clearly that with this man things could never be halfway or halfhearted. Yes, this man would sweep inside and claim her very soul.

And she would welcome his fierce claiming, which could bring her only searing pain and loneliness.

For whatever was happening between them was too strange, too powerful to be real or lasting. "*No*, Nicholas. This is all wrong!" Kacey caught back a moan. Her hand broke free and flattened against his chest. When she felt hot naked skin and crisp wiry hair beneath her fingers, a shudder stabbed through her.

Nicholas smothered a curse. "You're trying to tell me you don't want this, Kacey?"

"No, I—I don't!"

A dark light flashed in his eyes and then disappeared. Kacey watched a hard line settle over his jaw.

"Then you'll have to prove it to me, because I'm afraid I just don't believe you."

In taut silence, Nicholas's silver gaze stripped her bare. He had to find out how far he could push her, and not just for the painting. He had already accepted the fact that there was more than the Whistler at stake here.

"I don't have to prove anything, damn it!"

"Try to tell me you haven't felt it too, Kacey. Tell me you haven't had the crazy feeling that this has all happened before between us. You know *exactly* how it feels when I kiss you, when you wrap your sweet legs around me and take me all the way home inside you."

Kacey heard the desperation driving his words, since it mirrored her own. Her breath caught sharply. So he *had* felt the same thing she had. Something naked and visceral. Something terrifying familiar.

She shivered as his warm breath teased her neck. She felt his body tense.

She looked down to see his gaze smoldering across the closing of her shirt, where white cloth had parted to reveal one perfect, upthrust pink nipple.

"Good sweet Jesus," Nicholas muttered hoarsely. "You're so beautiful that it hurts, Kacey Mallory." Rough and heated, his gaze swept over her silken skin. Abruptly his voice dropped. "You have a birthmark on your right breast, just where the lace edge of your gown ends. It's small and smoky and crescent-shaped. You've got another one—"

Kacey's breath caught. "How—"

He went on hoarsely, as if she hadn't spoken. "—at the base of your neck. You tuck your right hand beneath your chin when you sleep. You never use a pillow. And you always sleep without a stitch, just the way you were born, my sweet Kacey." As he spoke, Nicholas made no move to touch her, only gazed down, his face dark with an endless, tormenting hunger.

Kacey's face turned white. How did this stranger know such things about her? "It's—it's another trick! You're just—"

A muscle flashed at Nicholas's jaw, the only movement in his rigid body. "Is it, Kacey? Then tell me you haven't the birthmarks where I said." His voice dropped lower, husky with arousal. "Better yet, show me."

Kacey swallowed, fighting a wild urge to do just as he asked.

"Tell me that I don't remember every detail of how it feels to love you. That the dreams haven't haunted me for weeks, starting at Bhanlai. God, I almost wish I didn't know how your eyes darken with passion. How your breath comes and goes in soft little gasps. The way you moan when I fill you."

Kacey bit back a gasp. He was frightening her now. "St-stop, Nicholas. If this is some sort of joke—"

"It's no joke, Kacey. From the first second I saw you, I knew you were the one, even though in the dreams I never could quite make out your face. Maybe that was why I fought the knowledge so hard, why from the beginning I found the sight of you so damn frightening."

"You're lying!"

"Am I, Kacey? You've felt it too, haven't you? The pooling heat. The sweet, aching restlessness."

She shook her head wildly. "You're stark, raving mad,

do you hear? Whacko. Crazy as a loon. Definitely unhinged!''

A vein began to hammer just above the jagged scar over Draycott's cheekbone. ''Now *you're* lying, Kacey. I can see it. I can *feel* it.''

''And you're one prime, grade-A bastard, Nicholas Draycott. A miserable, rotten egotist. Can't you get it straight? Whatever you're feeling is all in your own head, and has nothing to do with me!'' Her desperation made the lie convincing.

Or it would have, to anyone except this man, who knew her as well as he knew himself.

''Then why is your voice shaking, Kacey? Why is your breath so jerky?''

''Because I'm scared, damn it! *You* scare me—with all this ridiculous talk!''

Draycott went completely still, his eyes fixed on her face. ''So you still refuse to admit it?''

Kacey nodded her head mutely.

''No matter, I remember enough for both of us. I remember enough for a whole lifetime—and maybe even *more* than a lifetime. And what I remember most is wanting you, the way I want you right now. With your honey hair tangled across my chest. With your emerald eyes glazed with passion when I bury myself inside you—as far as a man can go. Until you're wild, my sweet Kacey—as wild as a woman can be.''

There was something more—something Nicholas should have remembered, but couldn't. Something that seemed important.

Then Kacey shivered against him, and the elusive thread of thought was shattered. Hunger tightened; need threatened to overwhelm him.

Silence fell around them, tense and brittle.

Very slowly, as if in a dream, his head slanted down, raven hair lying thick and straight against her ivory skin as he worshipped the pink bud that furled beneath his lips.

Pleasure coursed through her, hot and achingly familiar.

Just as his mouth was hot and familiar against her. After all the long, lonely nights and empty years.

Why only with *him* all these intense feelings? Kacey asked herself over and over. Why only with this man, who was a complete stranger?

She had her answer a moment later. It came in the fierce rush of heated images. He and she, bodies intertwined.

Frenzied and reckless. Not as strangers but as lovers, skilled and intimate with the secrets of each other's pleasure. Knowing every curve and lithe movement until each body was simply an extension of the other.

Kacey began to tremble. "St-stop, Nicholas." It was a plea and a silent admission.

An end and a beginning.

"Never, Katharine," he whispered, his lips hungry against her flushed skin. "Not until you tell me that you feel it too. Dear God, whatever I have is yours—whatever I *am* is yours. Just tell me what's happening to us."

Kacey's eyelids fluttered as his lips closed around her, fierce with a velvet fury that strained to break free of his rigid control.

His strong fingers swept her neck, easing the shirt down until it balanced precariously at the very edge of her shoulders.

But no lower. Not yet. Nicholas Draycott wanted to make this moment last forever. He wanted to make her feel every inch as hungry as he was.

So that she'd never think about leaving him again.

"I don't understand—it isn't—" Kacey swallowed audibly. "Nicholas, we can't—"

Nicholas raised his head. His eyes raked over her, dark with need. Suddenly Kacey saw a pair of entwined bodies reflected there.

Their bodies. In that moment, she accepted the fact that she'd loved this man a thousand times. But she knew she could never tell him that, because then he'd never let her go.

Warm and wet, his lips traced the swell of her breast. "Don't be sensible, Kacey. Not tonight. Tonight just forget sense and logic. Forget anything else but us.'' His fingers curved over her hips, drawing her flush into the heated line of his arousal. ''Dear God, forget anything but this.''

Kacey felt his need burn through her clear up to her forehead. Right down to her toes.

Most of all in her heart, which was naked and vulnerable.

For him alone, deny it as she might.

Nicholas gasped, reading the dark shimmer of passion in her eyes. The sight of it made his breath snag and his body catch fire.

Then it was Kacey who gasped as his teeth limned her breast. Her head fell back, the slim column of her throat revealed as pleasure flowed over her like a river.

Like a tide of dreams, a current of beauty.

And with the pleasure came a dark, swift flood of memories.

Memories of him. Of her. Of all the other times they'd touched and moved and loved, just like this.

Each one different and yet somehow the same.

Driven always by a love that didn't die, only surged and frothed and tumbled forward in a forever twisting course, spilling over its banks from one life to the next, its molten ripples gleaming down through time.

Nicholas felt her answer before he heard it. It was there in her soft, jerky gasp. In the restless shifting of her hips, which sought his heat. In the hot tide of crimson that stained her chest and neck.

Dear God, she was more beautiful than the silken petals of any rose. And though it was hell, Nicholas made himself wait, desperately afraid that this dream would suddenly end, just as all the others had done.

He held himself still, hoping—no, *aching* for her to say the words he'd waited two hundred years to hear.

''Don't—don't ask this of me, Nicholas.''

''I must, Kacey. Just once,'' he said hoarsely. ''Dear God, it's driving me crazy, don't you see? Dreaming of this—of *you*—was the only thing that kept me going through those long months in captivity. Now I've got to find out if it was nothing more than a dream. I've got to know if I left my sanity back there in Bhanlai, along with everything else.''

His body shifted, his hips teasing and then mastering in turn as they flexed in the ancient, drugging rhythms of passion and seduction.

He eased open her shirt with his mouth, then slowly traced the soft swell of her breast. Her breath caught when he coaxed the tight bud at its center even tighter.

Inch by smooth inch, the fabric slipped down her shoulders, one more exquisite texture among so many.

Suddenly Kacey was drowning in sensation—the rough velvet of his mouth, the sleek thrust of his tongue, the hot granite of his rippling thighs.

When he loosed his belt and let it fall to the floor with a raw, sensual snap, she caught back a restless moan. When his teeth nipped her naked shoulder, she arched wantonly.

She felt Nicholas shudder. And then his hard fingers eased the cloth lower until it wedged over her arms, holding her captive.

''N-Nicholas!''

''Hush, my love.''

He found the birthmark at the base of her neck and traced it lovingly. With a growl of triumph, he found the other on her right breast, which he suckled reverently.

Too reverently for the way Kacey wanted his claiming now.

Her hips shifted, seeking his heat, pleading for it.

He tugged her zipper free and eased her jeans lower. A moment later, his callused fingers glided over her ribs and her belly, settling on the wild tangle of hair at the joining of her thighs.

Slowly he coaxed an entrance, then slid in search of her heat. Deep, so deep.

Unforgettable . . .

''Tell me, Kacey. Tell me that you want this—that you want *me*.''

Kacey shuddered beneath his exquisite caress, overwhelmed by need and raw sensation. How could it all be so familiar?

"Do you feel it, Kacey?" Nicholas demanded hoarsely. "Can you remember every sweet detail as clearly as I do? Oh, God, tell me I haven't lost my mind!"

Kacey heard the catch in his voice and realized he was as overwhelmed as she. Words, that was what he wanted. But how could she speak, how could she begin to explain the storm of memories breaking over her all at once?

Words?

She tried to find them, digging deep, down below the fires of desire fanned by his expert touch, down below the hard-built layers of defense, deep down into the dark silence of remembrance, where words did not exist or ever would.

No use. Nothing could reflect the intensity of what she was feeling right then.

So, forsaking words, she found emotion and shaped it into movement. With movement she answered him, and every movement was a discovering, every sigh a claiming.

Her senses bold, she ventured out with her answer and prayed it would be enough. As she sensed that the last time, two hundred years ago on the eve of tragedy, it had not been.

Her fingers found his hair and slid deep. Her mouth found his shoulder and nipped urgently. Her eyes found his, and her gaze was open, wanting, infinitely vulnerable.

For you, Nicholas, her eyes promised. *Only and ever*.

Desire slammed through him. Heat exploded to his groin. In that instant, Nicholas Draycott learned a thousand new meanings of word "torment."

But he wanted that sweet torment from her, too. And he wasn't about to be rushed in anything he did this night. "Look at me, Kacey," he rasped.

She only tossed her head, arching restlessly.

"How long has it been?" His voice was raw with passion.

She mumbled a mindless protest, half lost already, seeking the heat of his hand.

"Since you've had a man, sweetheart."

Her head rose at that, her beautiful eyes flashing open, dark and unfocused, hazy with passion.

So beautiful, she made Nicholas grimace with new pain.

"A man?"

"A lover, Kacey. How long?" he repeated urgently, nearly unhinged by her honest, open need.

For him, only him.

Slowly comprehension tightened her features. "I—six months. A year, maybe . . ."

Her answer nearly unmanned Nicholas, even though it was no more than his first touch had intimated. All of which explained why she was so sleek and tight against his fingers. Sweet Jesus, just thinking of it nearly drove him over the edge.

Her, narrow and sleek.

Him, big and painfully hard.

Nicholas's jaw clenched savagely. Dear God, he'd tear her apart, he thought dimly.

And then he smiled, a dark, primal twist of lips. He turned and swept the desk clear in one wild, powerful stroke and then lifted her up into his arms. A moment later, he arched her back onto the cool, smooth wood.

Gently, gently, his mouth traced a hot path down her chest to her navel.

"Wh-what—"

"Trust me, love," he murmured thickly. "Just trust me. It will be good, I promise."

"Nicholas, what are you—"

With a rich, sensuous whisper, the last barriers of cloth slipped free of her arms and hissed to the floor. Kacey's skin burned beneath him, glowing with an inner fire.

The fire of love, Nicholas thought, awed beyond words. Knowing his own skin burned the same way.

In that moment he knew that all his life, he'd somehow been a taker. But now all he wanted to do was give. To atone, with body and soul, for a mistake he couldn't even remember.

And somehow Nicholas realized that this would be the very last chance he would be given.

Then he thought not at all. All heat and hard planes, his body glided down her nakedness. His head slanted forward.

"Nicholas—" Kacey gasped, restless, totally urgent. She tensed, realizing his intent.

"No, don't stop me, love," he said roughly, aflame at her sultry beauty. At the sight of her burnished golden fur. Wanting to taste every sweet inch of her. "It's been a long time since I've been a knight—in shining armor or any other sort."

She started to disagree, to say that wasn't the way she'd heard the story of Bhanlai from Adrian.

But then she froze. Fear ripped through her. "I—I can't, Nicholas! I promised myself—never again. Not unless it was on *my* terms. By my own choosing. Safe—and it can never be safe with you."

"It's never safe, my love, don't you see that? It's only good when you give it all, when you've got everything to lose. It might be easier the other way, but it would be a damn sight less interesting," he muttered.

And then his mouth traced the softness of her thigh.

Kacey tensed.

"Smooth and easy," he rasped. "Let it happen, love— just feel it. Me wanting you. You needing me."

His lips teased aching skin. His tongue found her flowering need.

Gently, then not so gently.

"I love you, Kacey." His voice was a raw blur of sound. "Feel me loving you."

And then conscious thought shattered as Kacey's body spun away, raw and desperate, awakened to infinite pleasure.

Her heart trembled and convulsed. Her spirit leaped free. She cried out wildly.

And because it was Nicholas, and the night silence was lush with promise—because his touch was nothing but magic, pure, primal magic, she let the last wall topple and fled the bonds to find paradise breaking over her.

At the window the curtains rippled faintly. Wind growled and tapped at the pane.

Outside, Gideon floated comfortably in space one minute,

then tensed abruptly and hit the ground with a muffled thud.

A low curse split the night air. "So sorry, old friend. I fear I've—miscalculated—once again." The voice was gruff. "This whole thing is damnably awkward. It's been thirty years, after all. And two hundred before that. One forgets . . ."

There was a faint shimmering just beyond the glass windows, where a pair of shadows arched, then slid together into one. The air hung chill and sullen for a moment.

"One forgets a great deal. And now, seeing her again, like this—" The pale fingers clenched convulsively for a moment. "Yes, far better for me to go. But keep watch, old friend. On her. On them both. If it comes, it will be soon. That much I can feel. These men of Trang's are desperate."

The gray cat meowed once, his long tail high and arched. Then Gideon turned and trotted obediently to the ancient wall, where he jumped noiselessly to a high perch. And there, his sleek body simply another shadow on the dappled stone, he lay down to wait.

Beyond the window, out in the darkness, the air spun wildly, rising in a vortex of twigs and fallen leaves. Then, slowly, the currents subsided and the shimmering began to fade, bleeding away into a silence that was night, and no more than night.

Until finally only the faint, lingering scent of roses remained in the chill air.

He held her while her breath stilled, stroked her while the tremors ebbed.

Lifetimes later she shifted, breathless, dazed.

Nicholas's eyes smoldered silver above her.

"Are you protected, my love?" His voice was raw silk.

Kacey's eyes cracked open dreamily. "I . . . I had all the shots before I left New York. The usual—smallpox, gamma globulin."

She felt a sudden spasm work across his broad chest. "Nicholas?"

The rumble reached his throat and burst free in dark

laughter. "Sweet, soft Kacey. Where have you been all my life?" Draycott turned and reached for the pocket of his pants.

Kacey's cheeks flamed as she saw the small packet in his hands. His eyes smoldered over her face, one dark brow raised. "This is hardly the eighteenth century, after all. But I can and will protect you, my love. Every way I know how. Remember that."

Kacey's heart lurched and sank into the dark current of his eyes. Even now he thought of her, he wanted to be sure—

Like a great effervescent bubble, joy burst through her.

And then she gasped as Nicholas molded her against him, skin to naked skin. Hands dark and hungry.

Discovering passion, in all its infinite variations.

For a ragged infinity, he let her feel him—wanting her. He made her feel herself—wanting him back.

He eased her down onto the soft carpet. "I warn you, Kacey, the knight's gone now, and all that's left is the man. Tonight he's hungry. He's dangerous, I promise you. Because he's remembering all the things he's had before and all the things he's never gotten to have. Things he never even dreamed existed until now. If your mind's in a different place, then you'd better get away as fast and as far as you can, because in a few seconds, the man's going to be beyond stopping. He's going to do something crazy. And completely irreversible."

"Take me, Nicholas." Kacey's voice was breathless, husky with her own need. "Now. Beneath you. With you. I don't want to wait another second to know how you feel inside me."

And when she looked up at him then, love-dazed and passion-slick, skin turned inside out, heart shining on her shoulder, he found his way home inside her, all the way home.

Heaven, Kacey thought, and told him so.

"Sweet love—ahhh. So bloody good . . . so tight." He tensed suddenly. "I'm not—oh, God, Kacey—hurting you, am I?"

She moaned breathlessly beneath him, adrift in dark, mindless currents of pleasure, past and present like a split image suddenly focused into one.

"*Kacey?*" he muttered hoarsely.

"More—now. Oh, please . . ."

His smile was a fierce, feral thing, full of the heat of conquest, dark with triumph. A moment later, he did just as she wanted. As they both needed.

With a raw groan, he caught her to him and slid deep, rocking her to the very center of her soul, shaking himself to the roots of his being.

Crying out her name when he felt her silken contractions begin again.

Gripping him infinitely. Dragging him off to paradise.

Just the way it always was when he loved her.

Above them, half-shadowed in the gentle glow of the room's single light, the portrait of Henry VIII seemed to wink and smile down benignly.

8

THEY fell asleep there on the carpet, Kacey's long hair spilling golden over Nicholas's bronzed chest, his hard hand molded protectively around her thigh.

Once and then twice more they awakened in the long night, lips urgent, breath fled, fingers sure and swift, drawing each other to wordless, shattering passion.

Until Kacey sank down with something between a laugh and a breathless moan, and Nicholas began to have serious doubts about whether he would ever walk again.

But he merely smiled.

After all, giving up walking was a small price to pay for the exquisite pleasure he'd just experienced in her arms.

* * *

The call came in the last chill hour before dawn. The sharp peals shook Draycott awake as he drowsed somewhere between sleep and dreams, body and soul satiated in a way he had never before imagined possible.

The Englishman frowned, making no move to answer. Her cheek to his chest, Kacey stirred restlessly, mumbling a protest at the intrusive noise. When the shrill ringing continued, her fingers tensed on Nicholas's thigh.

At last the insistent peals stopped.

Draycott watched Kacey's eyelids flutter, relieved that she did not wake.

And then the ringing began again.

With a smothered curse, Nicholas slipped from beneath Kacey's warm body, twisted across the desk, and jerked the receiver to his ear. "Who is it?"

Silence.

And then from the other end of the line came the faint hiss of indrawn breath. "Dreaming again, Lord Draycott? Such a pity. But perhaps the American will ease your painful memories. Is she good in bed, by the way? Does she make you hard with desire? So different from Su Win, of course, for *she* knew how to pleasure you in the thousand ways of hand and tongue."

Not Trang, Nicholas thought, but who? And what was Trang's part in all this?

"Leave me alone," he snarled.

"So sorry, Lord Draycott, but that is quite impossible. You have something of mine, you see, and I'm afraid I need it back." Silence fell for a moment, punctuated by another sharp hiss of breath as the caller's lungs again filled with smoke.

"I don't have anything of yours. I took nothing with me from Bhanlai, you bastard. You should know that better than anyone!"

A soft chuckle. "Really, Lord Draycott, do you think me such a fool?" And then the soft voice dropped, ruthless beneath its silken timbre. Ruthless as only one who has

lived long amid the poverty of Asia can be. ''You have one
more day to give me what I want. If not, you die. And your
death will be the old way—the hard way. The way you saw
all the others die at Bhanlai. And your American lover, she
will die too. Just as Su Win died—after she betrayed you.''
The chuckle that followed was low and coarse.

A vein began a wild staccato throb at Nicholas's temple.
Anger roared through him, along with the ragged edge of
fear. Who, damn it? Who was it this time?

It could be any number of people, of course. The warlord,
Trang, had had dealings with many nations. He must have
double-crossed them all at one time or another—Russian,
American, and Chinese. Even the British had had their
reasons for approaching the ruthless warlord on occasion.

And Trang would deal with anyone for hard cash. His
trade was infinitely accommodating—any commodity of
worth to the buyer. Information. Poppy. Planes.

But it was the human trade Trang liked most. And he
was very good at it.

Bloody, sodding dung-eater!

Lips clenched, Nicholas waited for the cold, precise voice
to finish, fighting his rage and saying nothing because he
knew that this would goad his caller most.

Long minutes later, his face a mask of unrelenting fury,
he lowered the telephone back to its cradle.

Slowly. Very carefully.

Trying to ignore the wild, ragged laughter that erupted
in a shrill din just before the line clicked dead beneath his
fingers.

One more day to give them what they wanted.

One more day—and then they would kill him and everyone in the abbey.

Something warm on her cheeks. Something soft at her
breast.

Sweet fatigue and dark, silken memories.

''Mmm.'' Smiling dreamily, Kacey curved her body into
that heavenly softness. Her fingers moved, seeking the
warm, muscled length that had pillowed her, teased her,

and coaxed her to wild abandon throughout the long night.

But her hands met only cold cloth.

"Nicholas?" she cried, jerking upright, her eyes fixed on an unfamiliar room. Heavy velvet draperies on a huge mahogany four-poster. Spare, bold prints on pale silk walls.

Nicholas's room. Nicholas's bed . . .

She remembered all of it now and couldn't help smiling even as her cheeks reddened at the memories of the night before.

But where was *he*?

She frowned, sensing a strange emptiness. The air did not hum or the room shimmer as it always did when he was near.

Slowly she lay back, wincing at the protest of hidden muscles. Where had he gone? Was he already regretting last night? Had something happened to him?

Unbidden, a new image sprang to her mind.

Lightning over a jagged silver shore. A riderless horse, hooves pounding out of the darkness. "Wait!"

And then a scream, ragged with terror.

Her scream.

Kacey tensed, feeling the fear slam through her even now. What was wrong with her? Was this the dream that shook Nicholas from sleep night after night? Was this the past that Adrian had warned her would be repeated?

Was there was a curse on this house, after all? Or was it perhaps *she* who was cursed?

She slipped from the bed, her eyes widening as she took in the dress and lacy lingerie laid out on a nearby chair. She picked up the accompanying note, its lettering angular, elongated and bold. Nicholas's writing—there could be no doubt about that.

My sweet Kacey,
    Had to go out. Ought to be back in good time for lunch. Meanwhile, try this on. It was my grandmother's, and I rather think it will fit you. There's a brooch of hers on the dresser. Wear it, won't you?
                                                                Nicholas

P.S. Did I tell you that you snore? Low and soft—very erotic, actually.

P.P.S. Did I tell you that I love you? I do, you know.

Her eyes glistening, Kacey lifted the silken dress, mesmerized by the way the soft mauve folds fell about her, as smoothly sensual as Nicholas's hands had been the night before. A collar of handworked lace framed the old-fashioned square neck—richly feminine with just a hint of sensuality.

Oh, yes, trust Nicholas Draycott to choose well, she thought.

Her carry-on bag lay on the dresser, and she realized Nicholas must have put it there before he left. Deftly, she fished out the pink ballet slippers she had packed for comfort on the long flight.

Then, fully dressed, she smoothed down her long skirt, feeling every inch a princess or a heroine in an old novel.

Feeling, best of all, like the woman Nicholas loved. Which was all she wanted to be, anyway.

There was a soft tap at the door. "I beg your pardon, Miss Mallory." It was Marston's voice, low and acutely uncomfortable.

Kacey opened the door. "Yes?"

The butler's eyes were carefully averted, and a hint of color streaked his cheeks. *So you're not accustomed to seeing strange women in Nicholas's bed, are you?* Kacey's heart, already humming, took a serious, high-voltage leap at that realization.

"Lord Draycott was called out some two hours ago, Miss Mallory. Before going, he left instructions that you were not to be disturbed." The splash of red across the butler's cheeks darkened.

God bless you, Marston, Kacey thought. But she was careful to keep her thoughts from showing. "And?" she prompted, sensing that there was more.

"As it happens, there is a police officer below requesting

to speak with you, miss. I asked the nature of his business, but he declined to say. Shall I . . . ?'' The servant's voice trailed away suggestively.

''No, of course I'll speak with him.''

The broad-shouldered officer was waiting before the mullioned windows in the salon. He turned as Kacey came in, his eyes blue and very keen, his smile expectant. He was much younger than she'd expected.

Marston left them, closing the door softly.

''Ah, there you are. Miss Mallory, isn't it? That Marston chap's always so tight-lipped. One can't ever get a bloody thing out of him.'' He took her hand in a quick, brisk grip. ''I expect you'll be wondering why I've come. Business, I'm afraid.'' His eyes flickered over her face, assessing her reaction. ''But I haven't even told you my name. How silly—'' He extended a hand a second time. ''Detective Chief Inspector Gerald Parks, Hastings Police. But perhaps . . . yes, I think you'd better sit down before I continue.''

Kacey paled. ''Go on,'' she whispered, sinking into the nearest armchair.

''Yes, well, there's been an accident, I'm afraid. Or at least we believe it was an accident. We found Lord Draycott on the coast road slumped over his steering wheel about ten miles from here. Engine still running—but the Alfa was pretty badly banged up. Before he passed out, the viscount muttered something about another car trying to run him off the road.''

Kacey felt the room begin to spin. ''Is he—dear God, will he—''

''I expect he'll pull through, Miss Mallory. They've taken him to hospital in Hastings. We've an excellent staff there— no need to fret. But before he went under, Lord Draycott asked . . . for you.'' The policeman's blue eyes were kind.

And very curious.

But Kacey barely noticed, already lurching to her feet. ''What are we waiting for, inspector?'' She ran to the door. ''I'll just tell Marston where I'm going and—''

The inspector's eyes narrowed. ''I'd prefer that you didn't do that.'' It was soft, but an order just the same.

Kacey looked back, frowning. "Why not?"

"The fewer people who know about this, the better, Miss Mallory. Lord Draycott was being harassed and . . . well, it's strictly on a need-to-know basis, I'm afraid. The only reason we're telling *you* is because he specifically asked. You do understand, don't you?"

Kacey didn't understand, not entirely, but she nodded anyway, desperate to get to Nicholas.

The young inspector nodded approvingly, then patted her shoulder—a quick, professional touch. "You're very brave, you know."

Kacey bit her lip. She didn't feel brave. Right now, all she felt was wobbly and sick and horribly afraid. Somehow she managed a bleak smile before following the inspector outside to a dusty blue Mini with a badly rusted fender. An older man, dark-haired with a creased, lived-in face, nodded to her from the front seat.

"My partner," the inspector explained. "Right now he's got a nasty case of laryngitis. Too many late nights, eh, William? When are you going to learn it's no good burning the candle at both ends?"

The older man shrugged, smiling grimly.

The next moment the engine coughed to life and they were bowling down the long, twisting drive. Kacey's eyes blurred, and she had to resist an urge to turn and stare back at the abbey's ancient walls, warm and mellow in the morning sun. Suddenly it seemed as if the last two days had been a dream. Nicholas, the Whistler, Marston even—all a dream.

Why did she have the odd feeling that when she returned, it would all be gone?

She gave herself a shake, fighting down a sick stab of fear. "Have you—have you had any luck with your search?" she asked, trying vainly to think of anything but Nicholas lying white-faced and silent in a hospital bed somewhere.

"Luck?" The blue eyes flickered to her face in the rear-view mirror.

"With the search for the thieves. Nicholas—Lord Draycott—mentioned what happened to the gatehouse.''

''Not much, I'm afraid. No trace of the paintings. In fact, no clues of any sort.'' The inspector frowned. ''Damn good, these fellows.''

Kacey barely heard him. *Hold on, love. You can't get away from me now—not when I've just found you. I'm coming, Nicholas . . .*

''How about you?''

''Me?'' Kacey blinked.

''With the painting Lord Draycott discovered. It's become quite the focus of local gossip, you know. Down here, everyone knows everyone else's business.''

Remembering Nicholas's insistence on secrecy, Kacey bit off what she'd been about to say. ''Not yet. It's still too soon to say.''

The driver nodded. ''I suppose your work is rather a lot like ours, in the end. Chasing down clues, sorting through all the possibilities. And something tells me you're very good at what you do, Miss Mallory.'' The keen eyes studied her in the mirror. ''The very best, in fact.''

Kacey managed a vague answer, staring blindly at the landscape hurtling past. There was a time when she would have said that being the very best at her job was the most important thing in her life.

But now she would have traded all her skill, all her experience, to have Nicholas here beside her, safe and sound.

''You're very fond of him, aren't you?''

Kacey dropped her head, brushing furtively at her eyes. *Fond?* The word didn't even begin to describe her feelings for Nicholas Draycott.

The driver nodded. ''Not that I'm surprised. Quite a few people hereabout feel that way about Viscount Draycott. With his wealth, he can do a great deal of good for the area.'' Abruptly the inspector's voice hardened. ''Unfortunately, not everyone feels the same way that you do.''

Kacey's eyes fixed blindly on the window as the road dipped and twisted past thatched, timber-framed cottages and grand estates hidden behind stone fences.

The young inspector drove quickly and efficiently, just the way he did everything, she imagined. In fact, he drove rather too fast for comfort, but then he must know these narrow roads well. Out of the corner of her eye, Kacey saw the inspector's partner click open a lighter.

Dear God, he wasn't going to smoke! She would be sick, she knew it! Quickly she leaned forward and rolled down her window.

A little better.

Breathing deeply, she watched the earth flatten and empty, trees gone now, houses too. The ground stretched away to right and left, a myriad rich shades of green. Here and there was a nearly black tangle of gorse, orange-blossomed now in summer.

But all Kacey *really* saw was the image of Nicholas's pale face, his body shattered and unmoving.

Somewhere in the distance came the glint of water. The channel, she thought. To the west rose the treeless slopes of the Seven Sisters, their white cliffs bared to the ceaseless hammering of the sea far below.

The road was empty now, and they began to pick up speed. On and on the man in front smoked until the car was thick with fumes and Kacey felt her stomach lurch.

They slowed at a small intersection, and Kacey noticed a point jutting out into the channel. But that had to be Beachy Head! And that meant they were going west, while Hastings lay to the east.

"Excuse me, inspector but—haven't you made a mistake? This *is* the road to Eastbourne, isn't it? Hastings would be the other way, surely."

The inspector's clear blue eyes met hers in the rearview mirror. He nodded briskly. "Quite right. This road loops about though, and with less traffic we'll make better time."

Kacey managed a faint smile, feeling rather foolish.

"You know the area then, Miss Mallory?"

"Not really. I took the bus from Hastings on the way to the abbey, though, and I remember the route." Her voice trailed away and she found herself blinking back tears. How long ago that all seemed—how different she had been then.

A tear slipped down Kacey's cheek, and then another. *Oh, Nicholas, hold on!*

It was a moment or two before the sound penetrated her consciousness—very soft, like a sigh.

A sound she'd heard before . . .

Her eyes narrowed. She sat up straighter.

Then the realization slammed into her like a fist. Her heart began to pound. Dear God, she hadn't even asked for any identification. They hadn't let her tell Marston that she was leaving . . .

"Did you . . ." Kacey swallowed, trying to steady her voice. "Was Nicholas's wound better when you saw him?"

"Wound?" The blond brow framed in the rearview mirror slanted up.

"On his cheek. He fell when the power was off last night. It was quite a bad cut."

"Ah." The driver nodded thoughtfully. "No, there didn't seem to be any bleeding." His tone was faintly apologetic. "I can't say for certain, though, since the bandage was still in place."

Through the wild hammering of her blood, Kacey managed to smile naturally and nod. Dear God, it was true then. Nicholas had no wound on his cheek, of course, or any bandage. If these men had seen him, as they claimed, they would surely have known that.

Again came that faint hiss of air . . .

Now Kacey knew without any doubt that the man in the front seat was her unknown caller of yesterday!

Her fingers locked in her lap. At least they didn't know she'd found them out—not yet. *Think, Katharine Chelsea—think!* If they didn't have Nicholas, then where was he? And what would he want her to do?

Escape.

The word simply dropped into her mind, then hung there, resonating faintly.

Kacey blinked. And how exactly am I supposed to do that?

She didn't realize she'd asked the silent question until an answer flashed back to her.

There's a door right beside you, my dear, the voice said dryly. *I suggest you use it.*

Only he didn't speak in words, of course. He communicated in quick bursts of meaning, in bold, concrete pictures.

And the speaker was most certainly a *he*. She could feel the dark force of him most clearly.

Adrian? she queried.

None other. But you must make haste.

That's easy for you to say, Adrian Draycott! You're a ghost—you can walk through walls! came Kacey's angry, silent answer.

Static ripped through her thoughts for a moment, and then the voice in her mind returned, needle-sharp this time. *Now, Katharine! Before they realize you've seen through their desperate little masquerade. Get out of there!*

Still wearing a crooked smile, Kacey moved her fingers down in search of the door handle. They were going about forty miles an hour, she estimated—enough to do quite a bit of damage to whatever part of her anatomy hit first. At least she was on the left side of the car, which meant she would land on grass rather than pavement.

For a long, breathless moment, she fought down wild laughter.

And then, with a gasp, she yanked open the door and dove from the Mini.

The ground exploded toward her, a swirl of green, and she heard the driver shout. "She's bolted, damn it! Stop her!"

Dimly, Kacey heard the shrill scream of braking tires. An instant later her vision filled with shards of light and then went blank as the darkness claimed her.

She heard a shrill whine. Her head felt huge and heavy. Savage hammering split her left temple.

What . . .

And then Kacey heard the dim scream of grinding gears.

Run, Katharine! Cross the fields to your left, toward the cliffs.

Kacey brushed a shaky hand across her temple and frowned to see it covered with blood. She must have hit her head on a rock when she'd jumped from the car.

Now, woman! the voice broke in, harshly this time.

Wincing with pain, Kacey stumbled to her feet and began to weave toward the distant slash of silver, where the cliffs turned to chalk below the green turf of the downs.

Nicholas? she queried wildly.

Unharmed. But he'll need time.

Kacey no longer even wondered at this strange, wordless form of communication. In fact, all she heard was the first word. It burned through her with a rich glow, giving her the strength to plunge ahead.

Good girl! That's it, steady on—now to the left.

Abruptly the voice receded, as if Adrian had moved away.

Kacey fought down a feeling of fear at the sudden severing of their unspoken contact. Not human contact, she could accept that now, but contact with someone who had once been very dear to her.

Gasping, she ran over the flat green earth, her eyes fixed on the distant azure glint of the channel.

And then she heard a low growl, felt the ground begin to vibrate. Still running, she turned her head and saw the blue Mini swerve sharply and head off the road onto the grass.

Coming directly toward her.

Adrian! What do I d-do now?

No answer.

Kacey swept her hair from her eyes, fighting the razor-sharp pain in her head. Something slipped into her eye, blinding her, and she brushed it away roughly.

Sticky. More blood . . .

Just like *that* night, when she'd run away toward the village, unable to bear the pain of being caught in the middle any longer.

Kacey shuddered as the growling behind her grew louder. She heard the muffled thump of tires and the metallic creak of the car frame protesting as the Mini took bump after bump far too fast.

It came to her then, with total, blinding clarity. She'd never make it. She could never hope to outrun the car, not on this flat downland, without trees or any place of concealment.

Adrian's warning had come in vain after all.

A wave of despair slammed into her, black and suffocating. It was not for herself that she grieved, but for the love severed fragile and newborn, like a green shoot trampled just as it pushed free of the earth.

"No!" Her wild, angry cry split the air. She had to think—there must be something she could do! Time, that's what Adrian had whispered to her.

And then she saw it—a narrow, gorse-fringed basin dotted with boulders at its lowest point.

Enough gorse to slow a car. Enough stones to savage the car's underbody and perhaps even destroy the engine floor. And if she circled around gradually, the basin would be totally invisible from above, until one was almost upon it . . .

Kacey's breath was coming ragged in her ears when she shifted course. Behind her, the motor droned louder.

"Stop, you fool. You can't hope to outrun us!"

Sheet-white, she closed her mind to the angry shouts. It must be the other man, the smoker. The man who had phoned the abbey yesterday expecting to reach Draycott with his warning.

Oh, Nicholas—hurry!

Her throat was raw and her knees shaking as she stumbled down the slope toward the basin, calculating the remaining distance. Twenty-five feet, with luck. Maybe a little more.

Behind her, she heard the man curse. A second later a bullet whined past her head, and she ducked reflexively.

Dear God, not a gun too!

Fifteen. Twelve.

Her heart felt like it would explode from her chest.

Ten. Nine. Eight.

And then the roar was beside her. From the corner of her eye, Kacey saw a door swing open. They meant to ram her!

Somehow, at the last second, she managed to dodge and stumble to her knees, then right herself drunkenly. A moment later she felt the sharp arms of the gorse spear her ankles. Just in time she jumped across and dropped out of sight, flat against the ground.

A stream of curses ripped the air. An instant later the Mini came sailing over her head, tires spinning uselessly, engine whining, only to land with an explosive crash atop the rugged line of boulders at the center of the green crater.

Without a backward look, Kacey pushed to her feet and lurched back up the incline, away from the muffled shouts, a silent prayer fixed in her head.

She had just cleared the gorse when she heard a shrill crack. White-hot metal bored through her shoulder. Gripping her forearm, she tried to fight back tears.

Adrian . . . where in the name of heaven are you? Now would be . . . nice . . . very nice . . .

She swayed, closing her eyes to the tears and pain, feeling hysteria weave its seductive web around her. She caught back wild laughter. Asking help from a ghost, no less!

When her tear-streaked eyes opened, she saw a gray shape dart over the slope, moving downhill.

Kacey squinted in disbelief. "G-Gideon?"

But the cat was gone, no more than a slash of gray as he surged down the hill out of sight. From the hollow came angry curses, grunts, and the whine of spinning wheels.

Go, Katharine. Head east! The voice took her by surprise. She stumbled to the left. Adrian?

No, east, to the right. That's it—steady now, love.

Her hair tossing wildly about her face, Kacey did as the voice bade her, too tired to wonder at his return, too tired now to think of anything but escape.

Panting, she wobbled up the incline, trying to focus on the cloud-dappled earth stretching flat to Eastbourne and beyond that rising sharply to the ruined battlements of Hastings.

Her eyes glazed with tears, Kacey didn't see the dark shape at first. Only gradually did the shadow resolve into an oval, then into a horse with flying feet—and a rider.

"N-Nicholas!" she cried raggedly, lurching over the

grass, one hand to her shoulder, the other scrubbing away tears of pain, now turned to tears of joy.

Such fierce joy that she didn't hear the low, feral purr until the Mini was nearly upon her.

Turn! The raw order rang out in the depths of her mind.

She moved by pure instinct, just as Nicholas's hoarse warning filled her ears a split second later. Horrified, she watched a blue door go whipping past, only inches away from her knee. If she hadn't moved, it would have broken her kneecap—and possibly much more.

This time, however, the car kept going, picking up speed. Dear God, they were heading straight for Nicholas!

In mute horror, Kacey watched the two adversaries surge together on a collision course, car and rider implacable. She caught a glimpse of Nicholas's face, dark with fury, before he pulled his mount aside at the final instant, barely managing to avoid impact with the Mini.

He pounded past her a moment later, shouting a question. "—all right?" she heard.

"Yes! Be careful! They've got a gun!"

But he was already gone, streaking toward the coast. In that instant Kacey felt her stomach wrench as she realized his intent.

To save her, he meant to draw them off, toward the cliffs.

Be careful. Oh, be very careful, my dearest love. At first, she didn't realize that she'd spoken with her thoughts rather than with speech. Raw static filled her mind for an instant, and with it came a burning sensation like acid. Like bitter sadness and aching regret . . .

She turned, her legs wobbling, her lungs aching. Horrified, she saw the Mini wrench about in pursuit of Nicholas. As if caught in a nightmare, she watched the car streak after horse and rider. In the bright sunlight, the jaws of the cliffs gleamed silver above the sea, and Kacey realized that this deadly game of cat and mouse would soon be pushed to a bloody conclusion.

Help him, Adrian! Please, if you love me—if you ever loved me, help him now! Tears spilling from her eyes, Kacey put all the force of her yearning heart into her plea.

Suddenly the swirling static receded; now only chill silence remained. Kacey tasted the sick-sweet tang of fear on her tongue as the two shapes began to converge.

They were gaining on him! It was only a matter of yards to the edge now! Nicholas kneed the horse in a sharp turn, but the car followed, its angry wheels jolting over the earth.

"Dear God, no!" Kacey's shrill scream echoed across the downs.

And then out of nowhere came the gray blur, flashing from behind the gorse and streaking over the flat earth. Only feet from the Mini, he lengthened stride and leaped into the air, legs flexed, a study in grace and power.

A second later, the cat lay flat against the windshield, his black paws braced against the wiper blades as he clung to the glass.

Kacey never knew exactly what happened next. It would always remain a blur of noise and movement interwoven with the sound of her own screams.

An angry shout. The wild neighing of a horse. The scream of grinding gears . . .

And then the dark rectangle of the car, rising as if in slow motion and arcing in sudden, dreamlike silence over the ragged edge of the cliffs to plunge out of sight into the snarling waters six hundred feet below.

"N-Nicholas . . ." Kacey never finished her hoarse cry. Already swaying, she felt her legs give way. That was the last thing she felt before crumpling slowly to the ground.

9

*I*T is done. I must go now, Katharine.

Kacey frowned, hearing—no, *feeling*—the words slip down to the dark place where she floated, mind asleep, thoughts closed off to the outside world.

A-Adrian?

Yes, my heart. I'm here.

Thank you—for saving him.

Silence, bleak and total, for long moments. In those empty seconds, Kacey realized exactly how much he loved her.

And just how much he regretted having to give her up.

Suddenly the scent of roses filled her mind, along with the gentle kiss of spring wind. *Nonsense*, the voice whispered. *It is no more than I came to do. Now you, my stubborn woman, must rest. There will be time enough for all the other things. For now, just rest . . .*

Kacey tensed, caught up in the terror of those last, chilling moments. But—Gideon? He was—

Gideon will be with me, which is where he belongs. And then, as if he'd seen her frown, *No, don't fret, Katharine. Not for what you cannot begin to understand . . . just accept this thing I tell you.*

Then . . . thank him, at least.

A smile. She could feel it crinkle through her, warm and slightly chiding. *No need, sweeting. Gideon has already heard. You might try the aquamarine, you know. Whistler vows it was always his most difficult pigment in the Nocturnes. And be bold—add ocher to your aquamarine and lavender to your grays, then dilute the lot with a liberal dash of turpentine. This is his way of thanking you for caring. But then you were always a rare one for caring, weren't you, my love? Even while Nicholas and I tore you in two . . .*

The scent of roses lay heavy upon her, almost like a lover's caress. And then Kacey's thoughts began to scatter, exhaustion overtaking her, the fragile thread of contact beginning to unravel, *Adrian?* she asked drowsily.

Sleep. It was a brisk command, almost paternal now.

She felt the last thread break, then slipped deep into a cloud of dreams.

Into forgetting. Just as Adrian had intended.

Goodbye, my heart, the voice in her mind whispered softly, knowing she could not hear. Regret hung heavy on him as he began the last difficult step of easing the contact which had become the sweetest thing in his long and very tattered existence.

His bitter sigh mingled with the wild channel winds. *My three visits have been given and used. There can be no more, my love.*

Someday, perhaps, you will remember—when the pain has faded and this day is no more than a faint shadow in your memory. And on that day, perhaps you will remember just how much I loved you, Katharine, though my damnable pride always got in the way.

Until then, forget me and everything about me. Just forget . . .

The voice fell away, ebbing into a raw swirl of noise for a moment.

He collected himself, but only with great difficulty. *Until then, mind my roses, if you will, sweeting. Them I have loved full well. But not as much as I have loved you, Katharine. And always will love you . . .*

Then the voice melted away, buffeted by the chill currents from the sea, swallowed up by the cry of gull and curlew.

Soon even the scent of roses was swept away on the churning channel winds.

* * *

Something prodding—squeezing her fiercely.

Go away!

"Kacey!"

No more—leave me alone. World surging in, and all she wanted was forgetting—no, *remembering*, in a way more intense than any waking thought.

"Sweet God, Kacey, wake up!"

Once again the probing fingers. This time they shook her, then slapped her cheeks.

She started to reach out with her mind, then stopped short, frowning.

Reaching out for what? For whom?

No answer came back from the chill shadows around her. Only sheer blackness, like a slate washed pure and clean.

"Kacey, can you hear me?"

Something about the raw plea in that voice pierced the dark veil of her thoughts. She opened one eye warily, wincing at the light that flooded in. Her head immediately began to throb, and pain broke over every inch of her body.

It was a hard face Kacey saw above her then—eyes smoldering silver, lips full, tense now with fear. So very tense . . .

Slowly she reached up and traced the taut line of that mouth. A beloved mouth. A beloved face, she realized.

In one sharp stroke, recognition burst over her, and the lingering traces of her dreams were swept away.

"N-Nicholas? Is it really you?"

The hands tensed and crushed her to his chest. "Thank God," Draycott muttered thickly, his fingers buried in her hair, his breath warm on her cheek. A faint line of moisture worked down his face.

"You came," Kacey whispered. "I hoped . . . I tried to believe . . ."

"Of course I came. I'll always come, my brave, sweet love."

Then no more words, just two bodies crushed together, heart to wild heart, breaths raw with thanksgiving. And then, as the fear slowly ebbed, they were caught up in feelings far different . . .

Driven by a need too long unassuaged.

Driven by a need that felt two hundred years old.

He would have taken her then, fiercely, out of a raw desperation to prove that they were both alive, with a future yet to share. But at that moment Marston tapped at the door and entered, followed by a tall, gray-haired visitor.

The Englishman with the silver eyes smothered a curse. Not yet, it appeared, were they to have their moment of peace.

It was a strange scene, even in this room that must have witnessed many strange scenes in its time. The golden-haired woman, pale still, propped against the flowered chintz cushions, an ice bag on her temple and a bandage wound around her forearm.

The dark-haired man on the sofa beside her, his eyes tense on her face, full of the consciousness of how close they had both come to dying.

The butler, stealing discreet, sidelong looks at the other two, holding back a smile, content with all he saw.

Last of all was the irritated police inspector, who plunged a hand through his disheveled gray hair, understanding nothing at all. "But I still don't see how you knew where they'd gone, Lord Draycott," the inspector began, moving directly to the question that had been bothering him the last two hours. "The coast road could have taken them any number of places."

Nicholas's eyes fixed on Kacey's face, drinking in the beauty of her smile. He muttered a curse, desperately wishing the officer would go away.

Draycott said nothing about the voice he'd heard, of course. Nothing about the swift, sharp images or the absolute certainly he'd had of her location. No, that would be for another time, he decided. Preferably after he'd come to understand it more himself.

Inspector Jamieson muttered something beneath his breath as Draycott bent and feathered a soft but very thorough kiss across Kacey's parted lips. The officer scratched his gray head, distinctly ill at ease, but determined to have some answers all the same. There were forms to be completed, after all. Forms in bloody triplicate! And this was one case he wanted closed—once and for all! "I'm terribly sorry to intrude, Lord Draycott, but I really must ask—"

Nicholas sat up slightly, his lips curved in a dark smile. "I'm afraid I haven't the slightest idea, inspector. Just a lucky guess, perhaps."

The officer gave an exasperated sigh. If only the man would concentrate for a moment . . .

Then, as he saw the radiance that filled Kacey's eyes, saw the blinding force of her answering smile, Inspector Jamieson began to understand exactly why Nicholas Draycott was having trouble breathing, or of thinking about anything else right now.

But business was business, the officer told himself firmly, squaring his shoulders. "I don't believe in guesses, Lord Draycott. It's hard work that solves crimes." Jamieson frowned for a moment, considering his next words. "Shall I be frank?"

"Of course." Just as long as you make it quick and then leave us bloody alone, Nicholas thought, his irritation growing more pronounced by the second.

"Special Investigations knew that Trang had secured a movable fortune somewhere close at hand for a fast escape. It was there all along, hidden in the mud of your cell—an ancient Buddhist reliquary urn set with a fortune in cabochon gems. And inside was a microfilm list of all Trang's contacts—in Asia as well as Europe. That's what your two friends were after." The inspector's eyes narrowed. "They'd been involved with Trang long enough to learn about his little stash, and when the choppers came in for you, Lord Draycott, they were already scrambling for the urn. They never found it, though, because by then soldiers were swarming everywhere and they didn't have a clear chance to look. By the time things settled down after Trang's death, the urn had disappeared. That's where SI came in. They found out about the contents of the jar last week and grew distinctly uneasy when . . ." The inspector cleared his throat, clearly uncomfortable. "That is, just in case . . ."

With a sharp curse, Nicholas jerked to his feet. "Just in case what, inspector?"

"In case Miss Mallory might be, er . . ." The officer's eyes flashed to Kacey's face, and he cleared his throat again.

"Go on, spit it out, man!"

"Well, be working with one of those fellows from Bhanlai. Someone up in London was worried that—"

Draycott plunged across the room toward the telephone, muttering a long and very graphic stream of curses with every step. "The bloody, interfering imbeciles! What have they got, oatmeal for brains? Someone's head is going to roll for this, by God. Just see if it doesn't!" His hand was on the receiver when Kacey's breathless protest brought him to a halt.

The inspector never did see what passed between them, as Nicholas's back was turned. Ever after, he was to puzzle about that.

But whatever it was, the effect was swift and totally persuasive, for a moment later Draycott ran a hand through his unruly hair and slowly came back to his seat. Silently, Kacey reached out, drawing his hand to her cheek. That much Inspector Jamieson did see, and the jolt of naked longing he'd seen on her face was enough to stun him speechless.

His discomfort increasing by the second, the inspector plunged ahead. "By the way, the two of you were bloody lucky out there on the downs today. That's a damn unstable stretch of cliffs. It could have given way any moment, especially with the weight of the car." Jamieson's brow creased. "Good God, didn't one of your ancestors fall from the cliffs somewhere near there, Draycott?"

A closer ancestor than you'll ever know, Nicholas thought grimly. And luck had absolutely nothing to do with the events that took place out on the cliffs today, he added silently.

No, love and not luck had saved them today. Love along with trust. And perhaps a little help from Draycott Abbey's proud and stubborn ghost . . .

Nicholas's fingers tightened as he felt Kacey shudder.

Jamieson saw, too, and that more than anything else decided him it was time to leave. His only regret was that he wouldn't get a chance to interrogate those two ruffians in the Mini, particularly that fellow with the acrid cigarettes and the arrest record stretching from here to Brighton.

But neither of those men would be talking to anyone—ever again. And that left the urn in limbo.

Too bad, that. Still, someday Draycott might remember exactly what had happened to it. Until then, SI would just have to wait.

Jamieson smiled grimly at the thought of those tight-lipped bureaucrats up in Whitehall waiting patiently for anything.

Yes, nothing else needed tending to here, the gray-haired officer decided. "I expect I'll be going then. Tomorrow one of my men will pop round with the Turners we recovered, Lord Draycott." He darted a last, sidelong glance at the pair of oblivious lovers. "On second thought, perhaps next week might be a better idea," he revised softly.

When he took his hat and left the room, Marston, efficient as usual, was waiting to show him out.

"Bloody strange business," the inspector muttered, half to himself.

"But it ended well for all that, I believe."

Jamieson merely frowned, cramming his hat down on his head with unnecessary force. "A lucky guess indeed! What kind of fool does the man take me for?"

Still muttering, he walked into the courtyard. "It's going to look damn odd on the paperwork, I can tell you that!"

The inspector was still frowning when he got into his car and slammed the door.

"You were shameful with that poor man, Nicholas." Kacey shot the viscount a chiding smile. "No, we were *both* shameful," she added ruefully.

"Nonsense. The bloody fellow should have left hours ago. Anyone could see we had other things on our minds than police business."

"The inspector was only doing his job. And we certainly

didn't give him much help." Kacey's eyes darkened, probing his face. "How *did* you know—where they'd taken me, I mean?"

Nicholas ran the pad of his thumb tenderly over her brow where a white bandage covered the lacerated skin at her temple. He gave a soft sigh. "Something told me you were going to ask that . . . Hmmm—let's just say that a bird told me."

"Indeed." Kacey's brow rose in a devastating imitation of the viscount's own arrogant gesture.

"It's the only answer you're going to get from me. After all, who are you to complain? You claim to have conversed with a ghost," Draycott growled, bending down for another kiss, this one long and devouring, not nearly as gentle as the last.

Long minutes later, when they finally began to resurface, Kacey slanted her head back, frowning. "Ghost? I don't believe in ghosts."

It was Draycott's turn to look skeptical. "No? Very well then, let's just drop the whole business, shall we? But one day I'll work it all out of you, I promise. And I can be most persuasive when I wish to be, Kacey Mallory."

Kacey's tawny brow arched. "Prove it," she whispered silkily.

With a low growl, the Englishman did just that, leaving no weapon in his vast arsenal unused.

When Kacey's breath was ragged and her pulse beat a wild staccato, Nicholas slid forward and drew her head onto his lap. He twined her slim fingers through his. "I love you, Kacey," he said huskily. "You know that, don't you?"

Her eyes radiant, Kacey nodded up at him, too full of emotion to speak just yet, still floating on the rich currents of the love that surrounded them.

The brisk tapping at the door barely registered at first. When neither answered, the door opened.

"Excuse me, your lordship, but it *is* nearly noon. Shall I serve luncheon now?" Brisk and correct, Marston stood just outside the door.

Draycott smothered a very graphic curse.

Marston's face remained entirely impassive. "I take that for a no. In that case, will you be requiring me for anything further?"

"Take the night off, Marston." Nicholas's smile widened, decidedly wolfish now. He did not take his eyes from Kacey's flushed face. "On second thought, take the whole bloody month."

The butler's lips twitched, but to his credit, he did not give way to the smile sneaking over his mouth. "Thank you, my lord. You are very generous. And may I be the first to wish you both happy?"

Nicholas turned at that, shooting Marston a grin that was swift and lopsided, making the viscount look boyish and slightly uncertain.

It was a smile that made Kacey's heart ache. A smile that made her vow to see that he looked like that often.

"Always on the mark, aren't you?" Then, turning to Kacey, "Yes, I rather think you *may* wish me happy, Marston."

"By the way, your automobile has been repaired, my lord. I've taken the liberty of returning it to the garage."

"Ah. Thank you for the loan of your Alfa."

There was a decided glint in the butler's eyes as he caught Kacey's look of surprise. "His lordship is rather conservative when it comes to automobiles, Miss Mallory. You might as well learn that now. The Alfa Romeo is mine, in fact. The Land Rover is his—and a greater pile of junk never existed. If I may say so, my lord," he added smoothly.

Nicholas's grin widened, but he still did not turn, enjoying Kacey's confusion. "No, you may *not* say so, Marston."

The butler merely nodded. This argument was clearly one of long standing between them. "Very well, my lord. Consider the remark unsaid." His eyes still glittering, Marston turned and left them then, closing the door softly behind him.

"That gorgeous sports car—it's Marston's?" Kacey couldn't keep the incredulity from her voice.

"Quite a first-rate amateur in the racing circuit is our Marston. Rather the ladies' man, too."

Kacey could only shake her head, amazed.

And then Nicholas shifted, bending down and sweeping her into his arms.

"What . . . whatever are you doing?"

"I'm carrying you upstairs, my heart. I find I've had entirely enough talking for one day."

"P-put me down this instant, Nicholas! I'm perfectly able to walk."

"Ah, but I like carrying you, Kacey Mallory from Connecticut. I plan on carrying you quite often, as a matter of fact. Up my steps. Over my threshold." His voice grew taut. "Into my bed. And right now I have a very important question to put to you, but I mean to render you entirely mindless with lust before I risk it."

Kacey smiled. Her fingers eased deep into his dark, unruly hair. "Indeed." It was a perfect imitation of his own imperious tone.

Nicholas's laugh was silk over steel. "You dare to provoke me? For that you'll pay most dearly, I warn you. Do you know that my aunt has been calling all morning? I really should throw you to the wolves, you know. She's just itching to get her hands on you—she's got an attic chock full of art up at that ruin of hers in Yorkshire. But I told her you'd be tied up until after the honeymoon. We've decided on Lake Como, by the way."

"Have we indeed? And what else have *we* decided upon?" Kacey demanded silkily, her voice low and very provocative.

Nicholas's eyes narrowed to silver slits. The pain at his groin was growing worse by the minute. "That it must be soon." His eyes closed as her fingers eased open the top button of his shirt. "Oh, God, very soon," he muttered thickly.

Kacey merely smiled, her lips following a moment later, teasing a hot, wet trail down his neck.

Nicholas's fingers tightened on her hips. "I'll never get enough of you, Kacey, I warn you here and now. In fact,

I probably won't let you out of my bed for a week.''

The smile she gave him was instant and breathtaking. "Promises, promises.''

"And just in case you change your mind at the last minute, I have a little bribe for you, my dear Miss Mallory. It's upstairs in the long gallery. Would you care to see it?''

Kacey nodded dreamily, thinking the only bribe she needed was him—the things he did to her, the cherished way he made her feel.

He carried her upstairs, then lowered her gently to the ground before the door to the long gallery, frowning. "That's odd. I could have sworn I left that door closed this morning . . .''

He glanced quickly through the room. The curtains were drawn now, as Kacey had instructed, to protect the fine old tapestries and Oriental carpets from the damaging effects of the sun. The quick inspection told Nicholas everything was as he'd left it.

With a faint shrug, he took Kacey's hand and led her to the canvas propped on a chair by the far wall. "It's yours, my love. That's the least I can do. Without it, I might never have found you. Although sometimes I wonder . . .''

A startled protest broke from her lips. "Nicholas! You can't! I *couldn't*—it's far too valuable for—'' Kacey's breath caught. "It's genuine, you see. I should have told you yesterday, but—''

He stopped her with one finger soft upon her lips. "All the better, my heart. The perfect bribe, isn't it? My only condition is that it not hang in *our* bedroom.'' His eyes darkened. "I want neither distractions nor onlookers when I have my way with you, woman. Or shall I take you back to the stables, perhaps?''

Kacey decided not to argue with him about the canvas now. Instead, she slanted her head and studied him through half-lowered eyelids. "Indeed, your lordship? The way I remember it, *you* were the one sizzling like a lit stick of dynamite back there in the stables.'' Her hands climbed slowly to the buttons at her collar. "Maybe I should . . .''
The first came free, and then the second. Her fingers slipped

lower, freeing a third. "And what about when *I* have my way with *you*, my lord?" she purred.

Nicholas's eyes darkened, shot through with molten specks. "Promises, promises," he whispered thickly.

Clear laughter spilled around them, dispelling the gallery's lingering shadows, along with any ghosts that might have haunted that ancient room. Nicholas pulled her to him, easing her between his taut thighs until she felt the hard evidence of the passion she had so skillfully provoked.

Kacey's hips shifted against his thighs, restless and sweetly urgent. Her eyes darkened, fixed on his hard mouth. It was a silent plea, and one which the Englishman resolutely ignored. This time he would make her wait, Nicholas vowed, firing her need until it was just as great as his.

His hand dropped, gliding over her ribs until his fingers skirted the full swell of her breast. He didn't even try to resist the urge to move higher and palm her rich, seductive curves. Fire shot through him when he heard her breathy sigh, saw her eyes close, felt the nipple bud sweetly beneath his touch.

"God, Kacey . . ."

"Please, Nicholas . . ."

Fingers laced, hearts meshed, they moved unsteadily to the door. They were almost at the threshold when Kacey stiffened, staring at the massive portrait that hung beside the entrance. "Do you see it?"

"See what, love?"

"There—the portrait!"

Draycott studied the gaunt figure of his ancestor impatiently. Clad in velvet and lace, the eighth viscount wore a faint, sad smile on his proud lips. "Am I supposed to see something?"

"Adrian . . ." Kacey seemed to hear a faint humming in the air around her. With it came the drifting scent of roses. She frowned, trying to place something—something about that smell. Something that seemed very important.

Her eyes narrowed. "I could swear there's something different about it. The face . . . the stance, maybe." After a moment more, she gave up, shrugging. "Oh, I don't know. Maybe I'm just imagining it. This house has always done strange things to me."

"I was hoping you'd say it was the house's *owner* who did strange things to you," Draycott muttered, oddly jealous of the portrait that had captured all her attention.

Suddenly with a little cry, Kacey pointed lower. "There—that's it! The rose. He didn't have a rose before, I'm sure of it. I worked here for a whole day and I never before saw that rose!"

Nicholas studied the portrait more carefully this time. The figure carried a single rose in full bloom, not a modern hybrid but one of the old, wide-petaled varieties. Just the same sort as those growing over the stone face at the front of the house. "*Cuisse de nymphe*—maiden's blush. One of the old reprobate's favorites." He frowned. "To tell the truth, I never paid much attention to the portrait before. Of course, all of these have been reproduced in some collection or another. We'll have a look in the library and check on it."

Kacey was still staring at the portrait, a crease working across her brow, when Nicholas pulled her around to face him. "*Tomorrow*, that is. Right now, I've got other things on my mind than paint and canvas, no matter how old or cleverly executed."

With a tremulous smile, Kacey turned into his embrace, combing her fingers through his thick hair and then rising to brush a kiss across his lips. Hard-faced, fierce with a need that was hunger and far, far more, Nicholas swept her up and strode down the hall to his bedroom.

A vein throbbed at his forehead as he laid Kacey back against the sapphire coverlet. "How right you look there."

A muscle flashed at his jaw when he slipped the buttons of her dress free and tossed it away, feasting on her pure ivory nakedness.

In a wild flurry of rustling, he tugged his shirt from his pants and fumbled at his zipper with fingers suddenly unsteady.

Seconds later—seconds that seemed like an aching eternity—his clothes went flying atop hers. Slowly Nicholas laced his fingers through hers and stretched her arms above her, every movement deliberate as he covered her with his hard body. "Marry me, Kacey Mallory," he ordered huskily. "Spend the rest of your life making me hungry, happy, and very crazy. Ferret through my mail. Sneak files out of my desk. Knock over my plants. Lock me in my own stables." His eyes darkened, searching her face for her answer. "Make me the happiest man on earth, in short."

"Yes—a thousand times yes, my love." As Kacey spoke, a tear worked from the corner of her eye. Her love poured over him in a golden flow, nearly tangible.

At last some of Nicholas's fear began to ebb. His head dropped, and he tongued one furled pink nipple to exquisite arousal. "Are you sure, Kacey? Are all the ghosts gone now? There's room for only two in this bed, you know." His fingers shifted, seeking her sweetness.

Jade eyes dazed with passion, Kacey stared up at him. "I—I told you I don't believe in ghosts, Nicholas."

"What *do* you believe in, green eyes?" he muttered, sliding his fingers deep, shifting his hips against her until she was mindless and gasping with the pleasure he brought her.

"*You*, Nicholas Draycott. Oh—"

"Prove it," he muttered, arching his back and filling her with the steel of his own need.

Instantly Kacey's fingers dug into his back. Her legs wrapped around him. "Please, Nicholas . . ." she moaned.

The Englishman's face darkened with the strain of control. "God, Kacey, I wanted to make it last . . . but—ahhh—I don't think I can. No, don't touch me or I'll—"

Her hands moved. Her soft, breathy gasps rocked through Nicholas like an explosion. He felt her tighten, convulsing around him, her eyes dazed as she pleaded for him to follow.

With a raw groan he did, sliding deep, oh, so deep, until time shimmered and wove its glowing strands around them, long spirals crossing and then meeting again, past, present and future caught together in the beauty the lovers wove with hearts and minds and bodies one.

* * *

Somewhere far out over the downs, a church bell rang twelve times—and then once more, one could have sworn, the last peal low and faint but clearly audible. A freak of nature, the experts called it. The product of high humidity and low temperature—or perhaps the opposite. Experts could never agree about such things, of course.

But the locals only shook their heads, knowing it was something very different. They knew the work of a ghost when they heard it—the work of the Draycott ghost, to be exact, signaling his presence with that phantom thirteenth stroke.

Upstairs in the long gallery, a dark portrait began to shimmer in an errant beam of sunlight from a not quite closed curtain. Golden light played over the man's lips, carved in a proud, bittersweet smile.

In his hands, the blush-pink rose seemed to gleam, its petals slowly unfolding while rich perfume filled the air.

One petal moved, detached from the corona, and fell dreamlike to the floor.

And then, as the sun moved behind a cloud, the beam shifted and the portrait was cast back into shadow, resolving into a flat plane of oil and canvas once more.

From the end of the hall came the creak of wood, followed by soft, breathless laughter.

"Again?" Kacey's voice was startled. "Nicholas, you wouldn't—I *couldn't possibly*—"

"Wanna bet?" It was a low, primal growl, dark with triumph, rich with promise. "Sweet Jesus, you make me feel like a randy sixteen-year-old, Kacey Mallory. Like a man's who's got two hundred years to make up."

Which, in a way, he did. Perhaps they both did.

So it was no surprise that neither noticed the sleek gray form ghosting past the door and down the corridor. On velvet paws, the cat found the long gallery and came to rest before the portrait of Adrian Draycott.

His long tail arched, the great creature sniffed at the fallen rose petals, then turned to stare up at the painting.

For a moment, the air seemed to hum.

The cat fell back, legs tensed, tail high. He jumped . . .

Up, and then higher . . .

Right into the portrait, which shimmered and seemed to open as the gray body sailed inside, then disappeared from view completely, to the sound of low, welcoming laughter.

Christina Skye

A descendant of Revolutionary War hero Adam Helmer, CHRISTINA SKYE was born in Dayton, Ohio. She holds a doctorate in classical Chinese literature, has travelled back and forth ten times to the Orient, and is the author of four acclaimed books on Chinese art and theater. She speaks fluent Chinese, along with French and Japanese.

But her first love is England, in particular, the glittering Regency era. "While researching my first novel, *Defiant Captive*, I visited the fog-swept English coast near Rye and slept in the medieval, timber-framed inn on charming, cobbled Mermaid Street. Talk about magic! That hypnotic visit plunged me headlong into *The Black Rose*, my second novel.

"Did I forget to mention the dashing ghost?

"I hope not because one thing led to another and somehow I found myself staring up at an imposing oil portrait of a proud, but sad-faced aristocrat. Just beneath the painting sat a huge gray cat whose amber eyes studied me with disconcerting force.

"Magic *does* happen, believe me. Just ask Adrian Draycott!"

Forever Yours

by Katherine Sutcliffe

1

London, England
November, 1888

LORD Byron Rothschild gripped the young man by his coat lapels and slammed him against the wall of the manor house. "You've been a naughty vampire again, haven't you, Johnny? Show me your teeth. I said, show me your teeth. Aha. Just as I thought."

"It's not what you think, my lord."

"No?"

"I . . . it's . . . chocolate. That's it. I supped some cocoa down on Westminster . . ."

"Your face is flushed, Johnny. Your flesh is warm. You don't look like a vampire half starved for his nightly ration of blood. You look like a man who's just made passionate love to a woman and experienced the most triumphant climax of his life. Johnny, we both know that *we* don't attain that blush from carnal bliss. That kiss of color on your cheeks and lips could be put there in only one way. You've bitten someone's neck."

"I didn't! I swear—"

"You know that such an idiotic action is a flagrant disregard of our laws. Johnny, such a crime is punishable by death. Must I describe again for you what we do to vampires who bring this sort of trouble to our select society?"

"No, my lord!"

"Allow me to refresh your memory. We have three basic rules here. We call them the Three Commandments. One: *Thou shalt not bite the neck and drink the blood of any living human being.* Can you tell me why, Johnny?"

"Be-because it's murder."

"Correct. Murder is such a ghastly business, and totally unnecessary, given our special circumstances. Aside from that, such brutalization brings unwanted attention to our existence. What do you think would happen if the good citizens of London were to discover that there was a society of vampires living among them? Naturally, they would descend upon us with hammers and wooden stakes, their eyes bulging in rampant hysteria. I've seen it before, and it's the nastiest and most unappealing display of human terror that you could ever imagine in your pea-sized brain, Johnny. I witnessed such a nauseating riot last century, and it was enough to curdle my cold blood. I barely escaped with my cursed life, if one wishes to call this wretched existence life. It is not—I repeat, not—something I wish to experience again.

"Two: *Thou shalt not flaunt thy handicap in public.* In other words, Johnny, if you're possessed by the overpowering urge to flash those sharp white teeth to a skittish passerby, say, just because you're in the mood for a bit of hellraising, you must refrain from doing so. Children cry, women scream, and old men die of heart attacks. And then we come back to the topic of pandemonium. We don't like pandemonium, do we, Johnny?"

"N-no, my Lord Rothschild."

"Three: *Thou shalt never lure anyone onto these unhallowed grounds.* Why is that, Johnny?"

"To do so would risk exposure."

"Then we would be forced to dispose of the hapless trespasser. Another nasty business, grave digging and all that. I was never one for manual labor."

"Of course not, your lordship, you being highborn and all. With a gifted mind and the looks to make every fair lady swoon. Had I only been so luck—"

"Shut up, Johnny, and listen closely. I'm not happy. And

we all know what happens when I'm not happy. I fear I'm cursed with a hellish temper that is occasionally beyond my ability to control. 'Tis a shortcoming, I confess, but there you have it. The last vampire who thought to run amok through London and indulge himself in bloodsucking met a most gruesome demise at my hands. Would you like me to explain in detail what I did to him, Johnny? No? Oh, please; humor me. It was simple, really. First I chained Sir Richard out back of the house. You never heard such howling and snarling and hissing. It really wasn't befitting his station in life to behave in such a manner. He had been a knight in King Henry V's court, after all, and should have shown a bit more restraint and courage when meeting his end. But I digress. Have you ever seen what the sunlight does to a vampire, Johnny? They melt. Disintegrate. They go *poof*! All we found of Sir Knight was a scattering of rusty dust and the bone of one finger.''

"Oh, Lord.''

"Gruesome, isn't it? About as gruesome as it was for the poor sod you feasted upon tonight to have his throat gashed. Now, be a good lad and tell me what you did with him.''

"Her.''

"You bit a woman? Johnny, Johnny, Johnny. It's bad enough to go bouncing off the jugular of some strapping young man. But a helpless woman and . . . good God, surely she wasn't a child?''

"No, my lord. Just some gypsy trinket seller I followed from Houndsditch.''

"*Just*, you say? My good boy, do you feel that because she was *just* a trinket seller her life was any less worthy than yours?''

"I'm sorry, my Lord Rothschild. I won't do it again.''

"That's what you said last time, Johnny.''

"I swear it this time.''

"And tell me why I should believe you.''

"I—I try, my lord. It's just so bloody hard to control the urge when I'm hungry.''

"Are we not providing you with enough sustenance for

survival? Or could it be that you're simply too weak of character to rein in your baser urges?''

''Sir . . . I'm only eighteen. Surely you can remember what it was like being eighteen. I have these . . . needs that cry out for fulfillment.''

''Then grow out of them.''

''I cannot, my lord. You know that as well as I. We are all damned to exist forever in the identical state in which we died.''

''Died? We're not dead, Johnny. That's the crying shame of it. We surely live—cursed existence that it is. We walk. And talk. We breathe the air and feel emotions—''

''How can you possibly call this existence living! Sleeping in tombs meant for worm's meat and depending on some wretch from London Hospital to provide us our supper— foul blood drained from fresh cadavers. Bah! It is like eating rancid meat, Rothschild. Tell me why I should subsist on garbage when London's streets are teeming with the warm, sweet, and ambrosial nectar of living beings. I did not ask for this contemptible fate.''

''None of us did.''

''Then why preach this abstinence from violence? Why should we not hit back at a population who would crucify us without a moment's thought of our misery and guilt?''

''Survival, my dear young man. That's what it all comes down to. For as vile and grievous as this life is, there is not one of us who doesn't fear that black unknown called death. What's out there, Johnny? Heaven? If we are to believe in some spiritual life everlasting that is bestowed only on the righteous, then where does that leave us, hmmm? Where do the damned go when they die and rot into dust? If we believe in heaven, then we must also believe in hell. Are you prepared to writhe for eternity in some burning perdition, Johnny? Are any of us brave enough to risk that?

''Alas, no. Therefore, we have come together and formed a society of vampires who no longer wish to associate with the ghoulish maraudings of those night stalkers who thrive on terrorizing the innocent. We have existed comfortably in this state for seventy-five years by following three commandments. Those who don't follow the rules are eliminated for the benefit of the rest of us.''

"Please, my lord. Have mercy, and I promise I'll try harder.''

"What did you do with the female? Did you kill her?''

"No. I barely touched her. I swear it! I had no more than sunk my teeth in her neck when a lot of drunken laborers came lumbering down the street.''

"And . . . ?''

"She was unconscious. I dragged her off into the bushes at the back of the property and hid her there.''

"Therefore, there is now a victim wandering around out there who, even as we speak, could be shrieking out her story of bloodsucking vampires to the nearest constable.''

"She was unconscious when I left her, my lord. Perhaps she's still there.''

"For your sake, Johnny m'boy, she'd better be. Rosie!''

The rotund little maid materialized from the shadows. "Aye, yer lordship?''

Rothschild released his grip on the young man, smoothed Johnny's coat into place, then turned to the maid. "Bring me my cape and see that Sir Varocher accompanies Johnny to his tomb. He is to be sealed in his coffin for the term of forty-eight hours and no less. By the time he's released, he'll drink the 'garbage' Ruth supplies us and think it sweet as the dew from heaven.''

"Aye, m'lord. I take it ye'll be goin' out then? Need I remind ye that the sun'll be up in another hour?''

"I realize that, but I've little choice, have I? We certainly can't afford to have some woman's mutilated body found hidden in our bushes. Especially in light of the gruesome murders going on in Whitechapel.''

"Oooh, aye. It were a ghastly business, them killin's. Scotland Yard is bumpin' into walls tryin' to find that Ripper.''

"Exactly. If they so much as sniff blood in the vicinity of these grounds, they'll not leave a stone unturned in their investigation. The last thing we need is a lot of police rummaging through our basements.''

''Yer cloak, m'lord.''

Rothschild swept the flowing black garment around his shoulders. ''Thank you, Rosie. Once the others have returned, please inform them of the circumstances. All precautions must be taken. We can't be too careful.''

''As you say, sir.''

Leaving the house, Rothschild hesitated on the porch steps, breathing in the cool damp air of the autumn night, his eyes taking in the gray images of trees, shrubs, and the meticulously tended flower gardens lining the driveway. Damn young fool, he thought. What could Johnny Delacorte have been thinking to succumb to such an idiotic weakness? Then again, why should he be surprised? Johnny was a product of his times, and the times left much to be desired. Crime and poverty in London were rampant. Rebellion among the Socialists was escalating every day. Christ, what was the world coming to? In *his* day people respected their king, and each other. No doubt about it, London had been a gentler city one hundred years ago. People went home to sleep in their beds at night instead of carousing about the gas lit streets inviting butchers to slay them and delinquent vampires to bite them.

Where had Johnny hidden the girl? She must be somewhere on the grounds, but the grounds stretched for five acres. There wasn't time to search beneath every shrub and bush. The only way to locate her if she was still on the premises was to use his supernaturally keen senses. He didn't relish the idea. The process was an excruciating ordeal. And besides that, it weakened his resistance against the very cravings to which Johnny Delacorte had succumbed.

What a bother.

Still, although the prospect of rectifying the unseemly situation both infuriated and nauseated Rothschild, he knew the deed must be done, and with haste.

He walked to the edge of the copse and paused. He gripped the trunk of a tree on his right as he prepared for the inundation of sensations. Since that fateful night a century ago when he'd fallen into the clutches of a Parisian beauty with blood lust in her eyes, he had finely tuned his ability to block out his vampire's heightened response to sight, sound, smell, and touch. He'd grown adept at limiting the shriek of traffic or a simple bird song to nothing more than a dull and distant buzzing, no more irritating than an insect. Though his vision had been magnified a thousand times, he'd learned how to focus his view down to a pinpoint, which was just as well. In his world of eternal darkness, there was very little beauty.

"So be it," he murmured to himself, then closed his eyes. Little by little, the throb of the night creatures grew to a pulsating drone, and the scant breeze expanded to the intensity of a typhoon, both in sound and feel, roaring and lashing like some primeval monster, making Byron stagger and groan. Around him, the darkness rolled back, and the moonlight beat upon his skin like white night fire, making him sweat and shake, making his stomach turn. The smells of the city rolled over him: rotting garbage, pungent horse dung, the nauseating stench rising from the paved streets. And the beast inside him roused like an awakening dragon in its lair.

The smell of human flesh and blood overwhelmed him. Hunger. Oh, sweet God, the rising of his disgusting need made him tremble.

He turned his head into the breeze and did his best to block out the stirring of the leaves that sounded more like the crash of ten thousand cymbals to his ears, concentrating instead on the rich scent that was as sweet as nectar to his expanding senses. Spilled blood. Fresh. Fragrant. Intoxicating.

He moved without a sound, with no rustling of the bushes or snapping of twigs, toward the clump of faded anemones in the distance. A rabbit scurried from its burrow and froze in its tracks, ears laid back and body quivering, heart sounding like a tiny soldier's drum rat-a-tat-tatting in fear within its chest.

He continued walking down the slope, glancing now and

again through the canopy of limbs and noting the dimming of the stars, the slight intrusion of light on the darkness of the night sky. Speeding his pace, he wound his way around a patch of eyebrights, through the cluster of sweet William, focusing his senses on sound and scent . . . There! The faint but unmistakable beat of a human heart . . . yet . . .

How thin it seemed. And irregular.

Blast the young vampire for his foolishness! Johnny had obviously wounded the woman more than he—

"Good God," Byron whispered as, stepping through the shrubs, he looked upon the victim's face. "Bloody idiot, she *is* a child!" But . . . no. No child. A young woman. No more than eighteen. He dropped to one knee beside her and allowed his gaze to wander the contours of her thin face, which was unnaturally pale. He touched her hair, a fall of black richness that had sprayed over the ground like ink when she fell. He noted the punctures in her neck. They were very small and shallow, and she had lost very little blood. The wounds were not so serious as to cause this form of shock and unconsciousness.

What now?

Obviously, he could not leave her here. Although the bite wasn't serious, there could be no denying what it was.

Yet, dare he move her?

Dare he *touch* her?

He had not embraced another living human being for seventy-five years, since he had last vowed to never—ever—take another life to quench his filthy, perverted lust for blood. What folly even to imagine it!

Ah, but the little wench was beautiful, though bedraggled in her tattered clothes and worn shoes. By the looks of her slender torso, she was greatly malnourished. No doubt sales from the cart of trinkets and glassware haphazardly buried in the bushes was her only means of support.

His fingers touched the warm red blood on her throat, and his pulse quickened. His nostrils flared, and he groaned as desperate need flooded through him, turning his body rock hard and his flesh to fire. The transformation came upon him with a swiftness that staggered him, wrenched and twisted and stunned him with an explosion of blinding pain. With a roar of fury, he flung himself away from the sleeping gypsy, stumbled against the nearest tree, and covered his face with his hands.

"No," he groaned. "For the love of—"

The girl stirred and moaned. He slowly turned.

Dawn palpitated around him like heat from an oven. The roaring of blood in the gypsy's veins and the uneven beating of her heart thundered in the silence until he was forced to close his eyes and fight back his overwhelming need for the sweet oblivion that the taking of her young life would bring him.

She rolled her head from side to side, then lay still again, her white throat exposed, her pulse beating against the translucent skin as weakly as a dying butterfly's wing. He moved to her again, eased down on one knee, and brushed a tendril of hair from her neck, fingers hesitating as he thought aloud, "What fate is this for one so lovely and young? But what should I do? If I leave you here, I risk the lives of others, and . . ."

Her eyelids flickered, then opened. Raising his cape to cover the lower portion of his face, he gazed down at her and watched her moist red lips turn up in a weak smile. "Kind sir," she whispered, "will you help me? I . . . fear I have fainted again . . . and hit my head. I . . . don't recall . . ."

The words were like music. Gentle bells. Harmony amid the discordant racket of the distant helter-skelter world.

Could it be that she truly didn't remember Johnny's attack? What was it she had said? That she had fainted . . . again?

Looking past her through the trees, at the shadow of the house looming in the distance, he did his best to make sense of the situation. He could leave her here, and perhaps she would eventually awaken and actually believe she had fallen and hit her head when she fainted. But something wasn't right. Her condition wasn't solely the result of Johnny's attack. Her pallor wasn't normal. Nor was her frailty. And when he concentrated hard, he could detect the irregular beating of her weakening heart.

The girl was dying.

A blast of warm air swirled around him, and, glancing up through the trees, he noted the graying of the night sky, the first red-hot streak of sunlight piercing the darkness. Time was short. A decision must be made . . .

With a muttered curse, he effortlessly scooped the girl up with one hand, grabbed the trinket cart with the other, and made for the house in a rushing, whirling cloud of scattering leaves and wind. By the time he reached the front door, Rosie was waiting.

"Hurry! Hurry!" she cried. "The sun be crestin', m'lord, and . . . oh, lud, sir. What the blazes will ye be doin' with that one?" She pointed to the girl.

"We'll put her in the blue bedroom—"

"But, sir, ye said yerself that it's against the rules—"

"I know what the devil I said. But she's still alive, and we can't take the chance of her going to the police."

"Well, pardon me fer sayin' so, sir, but ye're only askin' for trouble by bringin' 'er here. The others—"

"—will know nothing about it if you'll only keep your mouth closed."

"Give over. You know wot they're like when they first leave their coffins. They'll be fiercely hungry, and—"

"Then make certain Ruth is on time with dinner."

"She does the best she can."

Having reached the top of the stairs, they hurried down the carpeted corridor, to the farthest bedroom. Rosie opened the door. Rothschild carried the unconscious woman to the bed, waited while the tittering maid pulled back the covers, then laid the girl on them.

"She's a right bonny lass, isn't she?" Rosie said.

"Yes."

"She certainly looks peaked."

"She's ill, Rosie. Very ill. She could be dying."

"Did Johnny—"

"It wasn't Johnny's doing, although his idiotic descent

into bestiality didn't help. I think it's her heart.''

"All the more reason why ye shouldn't bring 'er here.
Ye know what weakness does to a vampire. They can sense
a person's infirmities a mile away. It's a bit like wavin' raw
meat in front of a starvin' wolf.''

Rothschild eased the coverlet up to the girl's chin. In the
silence, her breathing sounded shallow. Her skin looked
like white wax in the gloomy chamber.

"M'lord," came Rosie's urgent voice. "The sun is nearly
up! Make haste to the crypt while there's still time!"

Pulling his gaze from the gypsy's face, Rothschild focused on the pale gray light slanting through the part in the
window curtains. Already the heat pressed down on him.
The blood pulsated in his veins like water simmering over
a low fire. The strength that had earlier enabled him to lift
both the girl and her entire cart of trinkets evaporated like
a mist, and it took all his effort to turn away from the bed.
Rosie regarded him with panic as he leaned weakly against
the bedpost and dug a key from his waistcoat pocket.

"Keep that door locked. Allow no one but yourself to
enter this room. See that the lass is . . . taken care of. Give
her food . . . drink . . . all necessities to keep her comfortable.''

"Aye, m'lord, never fear. Rosie's never let ye down.
Now hurry!'' She dashed out of the room, preceding Rothschild down the stairs and along the corridor, where she
hurriedly tugged the brass ring in the stone lion's head
mounted on the wall of the gallery. The door slid open with
a grating noise, allowing the cool, damp darkness of the
underworld to yawn before them.

Rothschild stumbled down into the black void, legs weakening, heart pounding, and blood heating. Before him,
Rosie occasionally materialized out of the darkness, momentarily illuminated by the gas sconces on the stone wall.
He stumbled. She turned and, quick as a nymph, flew back
to him, wrapped his arm about her shoulder and, huffing
and puffing, continued their hurried descent deep into the
bowels of the earth.

He had grown accustomed to the dank and musty odor of decay long ago, but tonight the rankness seemed asphyxiating and vile, and for the first time in nearly a century he yearned to howl out his fury and self-disgust over his cursed circumstances.

Reaching the threshold of the crypt, Rothschild paused, gripping the cold, slick marble column as Rosie scurried to the ornately carved, burl wood coffin and shoved open the lid. "Quickly," she beseeched him. "The sun will be up any moment, m'lord, and—"

"Ah, God, to be human again." He closed his eyes and pressed his hot forehead to the marble.

"But ye ain't, sir, and if ye don't mind me sayin', sir, ye won't be no vampire either if ye don't move it. Now get into the bloody casket before I'm forced to sweep yer noble dust up and pot a periwinkle in it like I did with Sir Richard's. That's a good lordship. Steady now. Too bad ye didn't have time to change into yer nightclothes, but never mind. Ye'll sleep well enough, I suppose."

He dropped down into the coffin and sank onto the mattress; his head rested on the satin-lined pillow. Raising his arm with great effort, he caught the lid before Rosie could close it.

"The girl," he whispered. "Take care of the girl."

Rosie smiled into his eyes. Then the lid clicked shut, obliterating his consciousness.

2

LORD Rothschild knew there was trouble afoot before he emerged from his coffin and did his best to shake the wrinkles from his clothes. Rosie had failed to lay out a clean suit. His dinner repast was missing. He had a horrific headache.

No doubt about it. This wasn't going to be the best of nights.

He hurried down the tunnel and up the stairs, impatiently yanking the lever on the wall and running his fingers through his thick black hair as he waited for the wall to swing open. He felt gaunt with hunger, and the familiar trembling of his hands and the dryness of his mouth aggravated the pounding in his temple.

Stepping into the carpeted corridor, he stopped short. The girl—the gypsy—wasn't in her room; he sensed it immediately.

Rosie looked around as he entered the drawing room. The maid stood near an armchair, her portly figure blocking his view of the girl sitting there. Around them were scattered the curious characters who made up a small portion of the select vampire society.

"Ah!" cried Mercutio. "He is finally among us, friends. But what? Wait. By heaven, methinks his mood is foul this eve. Quickly! Pluck some petal of patience from this thorny stem of discontent and cast it to his feet!"

"What did he say?" came the whisper-thin voice from the chair.

" 'E said 'is lordship ain't happy and that means trouble," Rosie replied without taking her gaze from Rothschild, who continued to regard them all from the doorway.

"God's blood, 'tis as if he had but seen some demon dropped into his midst." Sir Varocher moved gracefully across the room, his armor squeaking and clanking in the quiet. He slapped a gauntleted hand on Rothschild's shoulder. "Smile, sire, lest we think something is amiss."

"Amiss?" Brutus bellowed from his perch near the hearth. Leaping to his feet and tugging up the hem of his toga, he paced around the chair. "Amiss, good soldier? Ha! He speaks in understatements. Amiss? What grandiose rules have been set to stone and then broken by the very hands who chiseled each syllable into the marble. Bah! Kings and dictators are but puppets who enjoy tugging their own strings."

"What does he mean by that?" came the small voice again.

" 'E means 'is lordship should practice wot 'e preaches," Rosie responded with a frown and a sharp nod of agreement.

"What the blazes is going on here?" Rothschild asked.

"Dinner!" Mercutio declared.

"Good God, you haven't—"

"Over me dead body!" Rosie cried.

"That can be arranged, good lady," Brutus said with an authoritarian lift of his chin.

Leaning forward in her chair, the girl peered with wide blue eyes around Rosie's rounded belly. Her black hair framed her white-as-porcelain face like a cloud. Her lips were red and smiling in a charming, impish manner. "Is this Rothschild?" she asked.

" 'Tis he," Mercutio answered, then leaped to his feet and pranced across the room in his colored stockings, mandilion, and flat brocade slippers. "Or as my very dear friend, Bill Shakespeare, would have said of this man: 'I am Sir Oracle, And when I ope my lips, let no dog bark!' "

"Sit down and stop prattling," Brutus said to Mercutio. "No one here cares that you were befriended by Shakespeare."

"Not just befriended, friend. It was I who inspired the fictional character who played so crucial a note in the trials and tribulations of Romeo and his fair Juliet. And what did Shakespeare do in return?''

"Killed you off in Act three, scene one.''

"I was originally supposed to woo Juliet away from Romeo. But never mind. 'Tis water under the bridge. Our concern lies not in past transgressions, but in our present dilemma.''

"True enough," Sir Varocher said. "What say you, sire? Mayhap this is some test of our loyalty or strength of character? Or mayhap she is only—''

"Dinner!'' Mercutio repeated with lighthearted laughter.

"Rosie?'' Rothschild said.

She regarded him with her lips pursed.

He crooked his finger at her. "Come here.''

"Yes, m'lord.'' She waddled toward him, wringing her pudgy hands. "Yes, m'lord?''

"I thought I told you to keep her abed with the door locked.''

"I did, sir. She found a key inside the room and let 'erself out.''

"And the others? They are . . . aware?''

"Aye.''

"And there's been no attempt to—''

"No, sir. Not after I told 'em they'd be soil for me periwinkles if they so much as sniffed 'er.''

"Where is Ruth?''

"She ain't here yet, m'lord.'' Smiling, Rosie added, "She's a right delicate little thing, is Dawn.''

"Dawn?''

"That's 'er name. Ironic, ain't it?''

Dawn smiled at him again with her rosebud lips, and her wan face brightened. "Yes,'' he replied softly. "Very ironic. And so very . . . beautiful.''

"Ye're right though, sir. I fear she ain't in the best of health. Why, it took all 'er strength just to make it down them stairs. She hardly had any breath left in 'er at all by the time she got here.''

"What about Johnny's attack? Does she remember it?''

"No, sir. She says all she can recall is that she became

dizzy as she was on 'er way home from Houndsditch.''
Lowering her voice even more, Rosie said, "Sir, if ya don't
mind me offerin' me own tuppence worth of wisdom, I'd
say Johnny come upon the lass after she fainted. I think 'e
found 'er unconscious and decided to take advantage of the
situation. So what do we do with 'er now, m'lord?''

Rothschild scanned the others' faces. Their flesh looked
bloodless; the pupils of their eyes were taking on a pinkish
tint, a certain sign that if Ruth didn't arrive from the hospital
with their dinner soon, the girl might well be in danger. He
shuddered to imagine what he himself looked like at that
moment, and he cautiously ran the tip of his tongue across
the edges of his teeth. So far so good.

For a moment he stood there undecided, watching the
girl speak quietly to Mercutio, who regarded her from a
safe distance, his mouth looking somewhat pinched, his
earlier humor rapidly evaporating as his gaze strayed more
frequently to her pale, slender throat. Mercutio then prof-
fered a bow and exited the room, only to return seconds
later pushing her cart of trinkets which clinked and tinkled
in the intensifying quiet.

Stepping around Rosie, Rothschild moved toward the
dark-haired gypsy, who had yet to leave her chair but
seemed intent on the welfare of her cart of treasures, which
Mercutio placed beside her. Only when Rothschild had
stopped before her did she look up and bestow upon him a
beaming smile.

"My lord, it is a great pleasure to meet you at last, and
to thank you for saving my life.''

He bent over her extended hand and pressed his mouth
to it. "My sweet young woman, I'm not certain I've done
you a favor.''

"Oh, but you have!'' She leaned toward him, and the
richly sweet scent of her flesh and blood swirled over him.
"I might have died out there, yet you brought me into your
magnificent home. Your kind maid has bathed me and fed
me and kept yonder fire in the hearth blazing brightly to
render me warm. No one, sir, has ever treated me with such
compassion. And your friends . . .'' She laughed lightly,

and the men pacing around her like dogs on a tight leash stopped abruptly, their gaunt faces disconcerted. "What delights they are!" she exclaimed. "What I would give to witness their performance on the stage."

Rothschild raised one eyebrow. "Stage?"

"They explained to me why they dress this way. They are actors!"

"Ah, yes. Of course. And brilliant actors, too."

"I was just telling Mercutio that I would like to repay each of you for your philanthropy."

"That isn't necessary."

"Of course it is." Leaving the chair, she swayed, and Rothschild caught her easily in his arms. How fragile she felt! And warm. He heard her heartbeat escalate as she turned her face up to his.

"Steady," he said. "You're obviously very weak."

She stared at him, her lips parted, her breasts rising and falling shallowly against his chest. At last, and with tremendous effort, he righted her on her feet, refusing to release her until she had regained her equilibrium.

A hodgepodge of assorted goodies crowded the pushcart: old jewelry, satin and velvet ribbons, feathers, lace doilies, and glassware. Dawn rummaged through her supply, speaking quietly to herself as the vampires ventured closer, only to be brought up short as Rothschild waved them back with a sharp motion of his hand and a threatening flash of his black eyes.

Where the blazes was Ruth?

"Sir Varocher?" Dawn called.

The knight clanked across the floor, his helmet tucked under his arm. "At your service, fair lady," he replied.

"I noticed the plume on your helmet is missing. Perhaps this will suit you."

"Why, what a splendid comb!" he cried, accepting the bright pink ostrich feather.

"And for Brutus. This brooch should help keep your gown—"

"My dear girl, generals wear togas, not gowns."

"Oh, I do beg your pardon, General Brutus." She offered

him the brooch encrusted with gemlike beads of colored glass. "If pinned at your shoulder, I'm certain it will keep your toga from dragging on the floor and tripping you."

Mercutio leaned over her shoulder. "You've not forgotten me?" he asked.

"Of course not. I recently traded a very fine pair of practically new slippers for this hat. The green color will suit your lovely blond hair and hazel eyes, I think."

Accepting the full-crowned, flat-brimmed hat of emerald velvet, he gave her a delighted smile. "Why, it suits my doublet exquisitely!"

"I thought so too. Now, for Rosie. This lace collar will look lovely over her uniform. Don't you think so, Lord Rothschild?"

"Smashingly so, dear heart," he replied with an amused laugh.

She looked over her shoulder at him, her countenance serious. "I haven't a thread of cloth or glass bauble that would complement his lordship's extreme handsomeness." She chewed her lower lip in contemplation, then, digging deeper into her treasures, she withdrew a sizable wooden box and placed it on the floor. With utmost care, she lifted the lid, revealing a set of six crystal long-stemmed wine-glasses. "Yes, I think this will do." On her knees, she lifted the box to him. "Will you accept this as a token of my appreciation, my lord?"

He stooped before her and put his hands alongside hers, their fingers brushing as his closed around the box. "A gift isn't necessary . . ."

"You don't like them? Perhaps I can find something better—"

"Dear heart, they are the finest glasses I've ever seen. But you should keep them. They could bring you a great deal of money."

"I shan't be needing them, I think." Her voice sounded weary; her lashes lowered briefly, shielding her enormous eyes. But when she gazed at him again, she smiled. "Ofttimes since I inherited the glasses, I've imagined bestowing them on some worthy individual. Someone who would cherish them as much as I. Please, sir . . .'' Her face paled, and she appeared to waver. He caught her hand, offering support as she did her best to focus on his face and finish, ''You would do me a great honor by taking them.''

''Then of course I accept. Rosie!''

''Aye, m'lord?''

''Please put these away in a safe place while I see the young lady back to her bed. I fear she's in need of rest.''

Dawn fainted then, into his arms. For a moment he simply cradled her small head against his shoulder and caressed her hair. Nearly a century had plodded by since he'd last touched hair such as this. Not since the night in Paris when he'd seduced a very beautiful demimonde down to the River Seine, then proceeded to sacrifice her in the name of his survival.

The others moved closer, drawn to her vulnerability like a magnet to iron. Their pleasant facades turned ugly and feral in the blink of an eye. They breathed loudly as the crush of their hunger bore down on them, and their restraint grew as fragile as finely spun glass.

''Stand away!'' Rothschild demanded, hating the hoarse sound of his own voice, despising the perverted lust for blood that flailed at his diminishing willpower.

''Sire, you bring a human into our midst and expect us to ignore her. 'Tis folly, and you know it.''

''It is a blatant disregard of the commandments,'' Brutus stated.

Mercutio spoke softly as he went to his knee beside Rothschild. ''Friend, an error in judgment is quickly remedied by sound logic. Take the lass out of here before damage is done to us all.''

''She's ill.''

''All the more reason that she cannot remain here. You must try to understand—''

''Do you forget what I am, Mercutio? I'm no different than you.''

'' 'Tis true. If you could but see yourself, you would understand that you are no more immune to these base desires than the rest of us. 'Tis not easy to accept such a bleak and loathsome reality. We are men, yes; and being men we cannot help but share men's needs. But are we human? Nay, my lord, we are but beasts masquerading in human form. Deny it to the girl if you must, but soon the truth is bound to surface; it is as inevitable as the sun rising in the morning.''

"But it doesn't rise, at least not for us. Our only light is the moon, and, like truth, it is inconsistent and occasionally obscured. Now, I'm going to put the girl to bed, and if anyone of you thinks to harm her in any fashion, you'll answer to me.''

Sweeping the girl into his arms, Rothschild exited the room and did not hesitate until he laid her on the sheets of the massive four-poster bed. How white was her skin, and how transparent. The veins ran like infinitesimal blue threads just below the skin and throbbed at each pulse point.

Closing his eyes, he forced himself to turn away, to cover his face with his hands, hating the monster hidden behind his trembling palms. The cursed pain in his mouth pounded up both sides of his face and pressed at his temples. Piercing fire erupted in his eyes until he was forced to throw back his head and tear at his hair as he struggled with the overwhelming need to howl out his fierce agony.

He stumbled from the room, repeating to himself, "Don't look back. Keep going and don't look back." Slamming the door closed, he jammed the key in the lock and twisted. Rosie appeared at the end of the corridor, and as he staggered forward, he thrust the key at her. "No one is to get into that room. Do you understand me? No one. I hold you personally responsible for her welfare, Rosie, and—''

"M'lord, Ruth has arrived.''

"It's about time," he snarled and pushed past her.

"She were detained in traffic," Rosie said behind him.

"I grow weary of her excuses. I grow even wearier of your excuses for her.''

"She's me sister, sir. I wouldn't like to think ye'd harm 'er.''

He stopped abruptly and turned. Rosie's eyes were wide,

her hands clenched in despondency. "Have I ever lifted a hand against either of you?" he demanded.

"Nay, m'lord, but ye know wot yer temper is like. And when ye've been so long without feedin'—"

"For the love of God, don't talk to me as if I'm an animal whose appetite can be assuaged by a slab of raw meat."

"Oh, sir, I didn't intend such a thing. It's just that ye've been under a great strain lately, and wot with the gypsy bein' 'ere in the house and all . . . well, sir, if ye could only see yerself . . ."

He frantically touched his hand to his face.

"And there's been all that trouble with Johnny, not to mention the Yard's investigation of them Ripper killin's. London ain't a safe place for humans, much less vampires." She ventured closer. "Wot'll ye do if the girl's family comes lookin' for 'er, as surely they will, sir? Ye can't keep 'er 'ere forever, ye know."

"I have no intention of it."

"Well then, sir. If ye don't mind me sayin', get shut of 'er now. We can have Ruth take 'er to the hospital, if that's wot ye want. At least there they can better deal with 'er illness."

"And what if she's only pretending that she doesn't recall Johnny's attack?"

"Oh, sir, there ain't a dishonest bone in the lass's body."

He stared at her for a moment longer, then turned on his heel and proceeded down the stairs. By the time he reached the drawing room, the others had finished their dinner and were nowhere to be found. Only Ruth remained, trembling by the fire in anticipation of his anger.

"What the blazes took you so long?" he snapped. When she refused to move, just stood like a statue and regarded him with round eyes and sagging jaw, he sneered, "Pray tell, madam, has the devil stolen your tongue? Or is something about my appearance bothersome to you?"

"I—I beg yer pardon, sir. It's just that I ain't ever seen ye like . . ."

He dropped into a wing-back chair and crossed his legs.

"Like what?" he demanded softly.

She lowered her eyes.

"Like a vampire?" he said. "Lest you forget, madam, that's what I am."

"Ye're so pale. Yer skin looks so thin, and yer eyes . . . they're *red*, m'lord."

"Yes, indeed they are. Why don't you look into my eyes, Ruth? That's a dear lady. Now try and look away. You can't, can you?" He left his chair and approached her slowly, his gaze locked on hers. The fire in the hearth grew brighter, the flames hotter, gyrating back and forth as if pummeled by wind.

He smiled, and though she gasped and quivered, she did not look away. "Let's not forget the teeth," he taunted. "Very nice, aren't they? Notice how sharp they are. They only get this way when I'm starved or aggravated beyond my means to control myself. Have you any idea how painful they are for me? Having these atrocities contort my mouth so grotesquely is like having red-hot icepicks shoved up through my cheeks and into my temples. The agony alone is enough to make me want to strike out at anything or anyone. The only way to make it go away swiftly is to feed the monster what it demands."

Sliding his hand around he old woman's nape, he tipped her head to one side with his thumb. Ruth's heart boomed like a drum in the stillness. Yet she didn't move. The breath wheezed in and out of her constricted lungs, sounding like wind forced through a fissure.

"I could take you now," he whispered. "And there wouldn't be a thing you could do to stop it. You wouldn't even be fully aware of what was happening. In the tiny corner of your mind that was still capable of rational thinking, you would hear yourself scream in absolute terror; after all, who among us doesn't fear death? But mostly you'd succumb to the erotic beauty of the moment, the dizzying rush, the sense of soaring through the heavens and bursting like fireworks upon eternity. And at that precise moment, I could bring you back, or I could push you over the precipice and end your existence."

"Please, m'lord," came Rosie's voice behind him. "Ye wouldn't do such a terrible thing to 'er."

"Wouldn't I?" Looking over his shoulder at the maid, he watched as she threw up a hand to shield her eyes. Cautiously, Rosie hurried to the tea table and reached for the silverplated kettle. Her hands were shaking badly as she poured the thick, warm red liquid into one of the glasses that the gypsy had given him earlier.

"Please, sir," she beseeched him as she extended the glass. "Ruthie does the best she can. She's simpleminded, ye know."

A moment passed, then he released Ruth. She sank to the floor and gazed in drowsy confusion around the room while her sister clucked her tongue and helped her to her feet.

Rothschild raised the goblet before him, watching the light dance off the crystal in brilliant, heart-stopping colors. He saw the gypsy's face again as she had offered him the set of glasses—the innocence of her smile, the flash of appreciation in her eyes . . . dear God, the trust in her naive soul.

"Ah, to be human again," he said softly. Then, closing his eyes, doing his best to ignore the pain in his body and the ferocious hunger to take in the sustenance too quickly, he tipped the glass against his mouth and drank.

Vile liquid!

" 'Tis the blood of a child!" he roared.

"No, m'lord—"

Whirling on the cowering women, he shoved Rosie away and gripped Ruth by the front of her hospital uniform, lifting her effortlessly off the floor. "Are you insane, woman? Have I not told you repeatedly that in no circumstance are you to bring us the blood of a youth? And don't stammer at me with lies. There can be no denying the overwhelming richness of a child's blood!"

"It were a slow night at the hospital, m'lord. There were only one death . . . a lad who was run down by an omnibus."

"Then bring me the blood of a dog or a rat, but never, *ever*, the blood of a child. My God, to be forced to partake in this depravity is torment enough. To taste the blood of one so innocent and precious as a child is more than I can endure. If you do it again I'll kill you! Do you understand me?''

''Aye, m'lord!''

''Now get out of my sight. Both of you!''

The women scurried from the chamber. Alone, Rothschild stared down into the glass, doing his best to contain his mounting fury and disgust, knowing that even as he imagined hurling the appalling elixir against the wall, he couldn't do it. The fiendish hunger inside him was too strong.

He drank, and gradually the storm inside him diminished. The inferno subsided. The pain slackened to a subtle throbbing of discomfort. Weakened, he took hold of the chair back and steadied his breathing, waiting for the monster to slither back into its black hole and disappear. Then he gently placed the empty glass on the table and quit the room.

3

DAWN wasn't certain that she had ever known a man as dynamic, as kind, or as handsome as Lord Rothschild. Or as mysterious. His comings and goings at odd hours confused her. She'd learned quickly during the last days that if she cared to spend time with him, or his wonderfully quirky friends, she must get as much sleep as possible during the day—for they arrived to socialize only after the sun went down.

Not that she was bothered by the unusual hours Rothschild kept. She had spent most of her life moving from one village to another, living wherever her father could find work. Folk had always called them gypsies, and in a way they had been. Many of their nights had been spent dancing and singing around campfires or crowding around her grandmother, who gazed off into the dark and spoke in whispers about myths and legends and things that went bump in the night. At dawn they would crawl into the rear of their wagon and sleep until the moon came up again.

Since her arrival at Rothston Hall, Dawn had often thought that Lord Rothschild could pass for a gypsy with all that glorious black hair and those black eyes . . . oh, those eyes. They did strange things to her, just as his smile did. She lived for that smile, for his company; the instant he entered the room, her lethargy vanished, her soul felt cleansed. In truth, she felt . . . reborn. Just as now. As he sat in a chair next to her bed, so breathtakingly handsome and debonair in his splendidly tailored suit, his pristine cravat tied meticulously about his neck, she felt positively weak with happiness. Simply speaking seemed to require a supreme effort.

"I grew up in East Anglia," she said. "When my father died, my mother and I moved here to London in hopes of finding employment." She smiled up at Rothschild as he poured her a second cup of tea, then laced it with sugar and a touch of milk. He returned her smile but did not meet her eyes.

Returning to his chair, he crossed his long legs and, with a lift of one hand, motioned her to drink the hot beverage. She did and enjoyed the delicious warmth that stole through her shivering body. It seemed that she could no longer stop her trembling.

"How long have you been ill?" Rothschild asked.

"For as long as I can remember. Even as a child, I was frail. I was never able, or allowed, to run and play with my friends. If I did, I lost my breath and fainted."

"Are you warm enough now?"

"Yes." She nodded. "Thank you. You and the others have been so very kind. There isn't any way I could possibly repay you for bringing me into your home and caring for me these last days. I can't recall when I last slept in a decent bed or ate a decent meal.''

A look of irony passed over Rothschild's features. "Nor can I," he muttered to himself. But before Dawn could question the strange statement, he went on. "You're welcome to remain here for as long as you like. However . . . aren't there some family or friends you would care to contact about your welfare?"

"No, my lord. I have no family since my mother died two years ago. And while I have a great many acquaintances, there are few friends who would even notice my absence in the East End.''

"A despicable place. I cannot imagine one so fair and frail residing there. Precisely where do you live?''

"Near Mitre Square.''

His dark brows drew together in concentration. "I've recently read of Mitre Square in the *Times*.''

"An acquaintance of mine was murdered there. Catherine Eddowes. She was the Ripper's latest victim.'' Sighing, Dawn put her teacup aside. "I saw her not long before her murder. You see, I occasionally work nights in a pub. As I was leaving work early that Sunday morning, we bumped into each other at the corner of Houndsditch and passed a few minutes of conversation. She was a bit drunk and was complaining of having been in police custody for a while. As it turned out, it would have been far better for her to have remained there all night. She was murdered only three-quarters of an hour after having been released from jail.''

Settling more comfortably against the pillows, Dawn studied her host's face as he lounged in the high-backed Queen Anne chair. Then Rosie entered the room and hurried to collect the tray of biscuits and the tea service.

"I don't be meanin' to interrupt," she said to Rothschild, who regarded her with an amused lift of one eyebrow, "but that mischiefmaker, Johnny Delacorte, is at it again. 'E's about worn the carpet through waitin' for ye to come down to the drawin' room.''

"What, pray tell, does he want with me now?''

"Ye think 'e'd tell me?'' She sniffed and said to Dawn,

"'E's a troublemaker, is that one. Gives me the willies just to be in the same room with 'im. No, sir, I wouldn't trust 'im as far as I could throw 'im with me little finger . . . 'specially in light of wot 'e done to—''

Rothschild cleared his throat, and Rosie, her eyes suddenly round with apparent consternation, snapped her mouth shut.

Leaving his chair, Rothschild moved to the bed and covered Dawn's hand, which lay atop the bedcovers, with his own. "I'll return shortly. Then perhaps you'll feel more like venturing downstairs. I'd love to show you around Rothston Hall.''

"I'd like that very much," she replied somewhat breathlessly as she regarded his hand on hers.

He remained a moment longer. The corner of his mouth turned up slightly as he appeared to study each detail of her features, and Dawn felt her heart flutter; this time, however, the sensation had little to do with her wretched malady.

"Later," he told her softly, and squeezed her hand.

Dawn watched as he quit the chamber, then closed her eyes amid a rush of sensation that left her mind reeling and her body tingling. "Oh, Rosie, have you ever known a man so kind and gentle and handsome?" She looked at the maid, who was still staring at the door, her chubby face concerned. "How long have you worked for Lord Rothschild?" Dawn asked.

"Forty years," the maid answered absently.

"Surely not forty. He told me himself he was only thirty-four, and—''

"Oh, lud! Wot I mean is, I've worked for the *family* for forty years," Rose explained a bit anxiously.

"How very fortunate for you! Imagine spending your entire life associated with such a wonderful, generous man. Tell me, Rosie, why hasn't his lordship married . . . or perhaps he has . . . or perhaps there's someone he's interested in romantically?"

Without waiting for the woman to respond, Dawn tossed back the sheet and counterpane and swung her feet over the side of the bed. She felt giddy and flushed all over. In truth, she hadn't felt so vibrantly alive for as long as she could remember.

As Rosie plunked down the tray and jumped to assist, Dawn waved her away. She slid her feet to the floor, stood there wobbly-kneed for a moment while the room took a slow rotation around her, then moved to the window and gazed out at the night-blanketed landscape. The distant lights of the city twinkled back at her through the interlocking branches of trees. An impending storm danced in spears and sparks behind mounting rain clouds, and thunder rumbled in the distance.

"Well, Rosie? *Has* he some lady in his life?" Rosie's face looked pinched as she wrung her hands.

"Oh," Dawn whispered. "I can assume by your silence and nervousness that he does. But of course he does. How silly of me even to imagine that one so blessed would be without a lady's love."

Rosie moved up behind her. "Please, miss, don't let it distress ye. Ye need all yer energy to get stronger. Don't waste another minute frettin' over what can never be with 'is lordship. Believe me, it's better for ye just to concentrate on gettin' well and leavin' here as soon as ye can. Here now, sit ye down in this chair and I'll brush yer pretty hair. That's a good lass. We'll just lift up this here mirror from the dressin' table so ye can see how pretty ye're lookin' this evenin'. There's a lovely blush to yer cheeks, and yer eyes are twinklin' like sapphires."

Dawn watched Rosie's quick hands brush the tangles from her hair and adroitly sweep it back from her face and affix it with combs. She recalled Rothschild's hand caressing her own, the tenderness with which he had touched her, yet . . . what strength there had been in so simple a motion! It had been as if a current of electricity had passed through her, as potent and vibrant as the lightning outside. For a moment—a brief blink of an instant—the malaise within her had vanished.

"Ye're charmin' as a picture," Rosie told her. "Just like a fairy princess."

Managing a smile, Dawn met Rosie's understanding eyes

in the mirror. "If I were a fairy princess, I'd be fit enough for someone like Rothschild. But I'm not, Rosie, and I never shall be."

Johnny Delacorte paced before the fireplace, his hands opening and closing in agitation, his face twisted into its usual pugnacious expression as he glanced with narrowed eyes, first toward Mercutio, who sat reading a copy of *Knight's Excursion Companion*, then at Sir Varocher, who perused a voluminous edition of Pliny the Elder's *Historia Naturalis*.

"Daft buggers," Johnny grumbled, and both men looked up. "You're constantly reading about those silly villages as if you were really going to visit them," he told Mercutio. "And you." He pointed to Sir Varocher. "What rubbish do you glean from reading that?"

"Quite good rubbish actually," Sir Varocher replied. "Did you know that attaching crocodile teeth to the right arm will act as an aphrodisiac?"

Shaking his head, Johnny turned toward Rothschild, who watched him from where he stood by the mantel. "The gypsy is mine, you know," Johnny said in a voice seething with sarcasm. "I seen her first. I took her first."

"You took advantage of her, you mean. You came upon her after she'd fainted—"

"So what? All the better, ain't it? I mean, she don't remember what happened. You got no right to condemn me, not in light of what you're doing, keeping her locked away and all. Keeping her to yourself. I mean, it's perverted what you're doing."

"I'm doing nothing more than allowing her to rest and regain her health. And even if I were, it would be no business of yours."

Johnny laughed. "Right. He who makes the rules is the first to break them. Why ain't I surprised? You're always putting yourself up on some pedestal, as if you think you're better than the rest of us, or that we ain't got the brains to blunder our way out of our damn coffins. You saunter around here in your finely tailored suits and pristine white shirts and silk cravats and think you're the king of England just because you were born with blue blood. Well, I've got news for you, guv. You're no more human than the rest of us. You take your dinner just like me.''

"I don't murder innocent girls in the process."

"No? Then what are you doing with the lass? Or could it be that you've taken a fancy to the little wench?"

"Don't be stupid."

"That's it, isn't it? Why, the great Lord Rothschild has been smitten by a gypsy trinket seller."

"Johnny, Johnny. You're sorely trying my patience."

"As if mine ain't been tried. See how you like being locked up in a box for forty-eight hours for some menial crime, only to get out and learn the victim has been brought into the house and is being treated like a bloody queen. You're endangering our lives, you know. I can't imagine why all of them ain't raising hell over it." He motioned toward Mercutio and Sir Varocher, who watched in growing consternation. "The first minute she gets wind of what's up, she'll be scurrying off to Scotland Yard and we'll all be murdered in our beds. I say get rid of her. If you ain't got the stomach for it, then let me do it. It'll be slick and clean. She won't even know what happened."

Rothschild stared down at the smaller man, who regarded him from beneath pale brown eyebrows. Johnny's face was flushed with color, his brown eyes feral. "If you so much as look at Dawn as if you want to harm her, I'll crucify you," Rothschild declared.

"I say let's put it to a vote," Johnny said. "Majority rules. If the rest of us want her to go, she goes. I vote her out!" he cried.

Mercutio threw one leg over a chair arm and snapped his book closed. "Oh God, that men should put an enemy in their mouths to steal away their brains."

"Cast your vote, you bloody puffter."

"What's in a name? That which we call—"

"Vote, I say, and make it count lest you find your Elizabethan bones dust within a fortnight."

"Well . . ." Mercutio drummed his fingers on his knee,

then flicked off a piece of lint. "He has a point, my lord. You've admitted it yourself. 'Tis folly to keep her here. She is bound to stumble on the truth eventually. Then what? You'd have no choice; you'd be forced to eliminate her."

"Then you vote for turning her out!" Johnny shouted.

"Not so fast, you loathsome little piss ant." Tossing the book aside, Mercutio left his chair and walked to the window, where rain shimmied down the glass panes. "Methinks I should consider the matter for a while."

"Did you know, knaves," Sir Varocher began, "that fat melted down from a camel's hump is a most stimulating aphrodisiac once rubbed on a maiden's body?"

Johnny stormed across the room and snatched the book from the knight's lap. Sir Varocher leaped to his feet, his mail clattering.

"You're all a lot of buffoons," Johnny said. "Had you a single backbone between you, you would be out there now drinking in the blood of this city. We could all become omnipotent!"

"I vote that she stays," Mercutio called out.

"I second that vote," Sir Varocher added as he continued to regard Johnny down his narrow nose.

"Not that it matters," Rothschild said. "Only one vote counts in this house. Mine. And I say she remains as long as she wants."

The doors opened behind them. Rosie stepped in. Behind her came Dawn, her lush black hair spilling over the pale pink dressing gown the maid had provided her. Swiftly and gracefully, Rothschild moved to greet her, Mercutio and Sir Varocher close at his heels.

"Fair maiden!" Mercutio sang. "What splendid flower has taken root within thy breast and burst forth with such radiance upon thy splendid cheek?"

"Bloody heck, what a performance," Rosie muttered, then tipped her head toward Dawn and explained, " 'E says ye've got right nice color in yer cheeks tonight. But then, I already told ye that in words ye can damn well understand."

Sir Varocher took up her hand and kissed the air above it. But it was to Rothschild that she smiled.

"My lord, I hope I haven't intruded. I felt much stronger after you left, and you mentioned that you would happily show me around Rothston Hall."

"Better not show her too much," Johnny said from across the room.

Dawn looked at him, surprised. Rothschild noted the slight, momentary narrowing of her eyes as she watched Johnny approach.

"Fe fi fo fum." Johnny grinned. "I smell the blood of a human. Shall we dine, good fellas?"

Dawn took a step back, her gaze flying to Rothschild, her hand reaching out to grip his arm.

"Don't let him frighten you, dear heart," he told her. "He's only a bully who enjoys tormenting children. We really don't like him, but, alas, we're stuck with him . . . for the time being. Be a good boy, Johnny, and find something worthwhile with which to occupy your time. Else I'll be forced to occupy it for you. Now, if you'll excuse us, I promised the young lady a tour of the house."

He smiled down at Dawn. Her eyes twinkled up at him, and for a moment, just a moment, he felt happy, and so very human again.

They ended the tour of Rothston Hall in the original structure of the two-century-old house. The soot-smudged sconces on the walls barely reflected the flickering light of the candles within them. The towering ceilings and mahogany walls added to the gloom that hung like a canopy above them.

"The house is lovely, my lord, and so very grand. I've often seen its gables peeking above the trees and wondered who lived here. It's a very odd setting for such a house, if you don't mind my saying so."

"Oh? How so?"

"To have these vast grounds and gardens plunked amid these busy streets, I mean. And your property backs up to Thrawl Street Cemetery."

"My grandfather worshipped his privacy. The cemetery assured him of that."

"He must have been very eccentric."

Smiling, Rothschild crossed his arms over his chest and leaned one hip on the windowsill. "A slight understatement, I think. But then, I come from a family who thrived on controversy."

Gazing out the window, Dawn watched lightning brighten the turbulent sky. Rain fell hard against the panes, and the wind whipped the treetops back and forth as she tried her best to calm the timid racing of her heart.

Turning to look at Rothschild, she said, "Forgive me if I seem somewhat overwhelmed, my lord. Never did I imagine that I would ever be rescued by such a charming prince."

"I'm far from a prince, dear heart. I can't claim to be charming, either."

Dawn blushed as the intensity of Rothschild's gaze increased; his smile became all the more gentle, yet oddly wistful. Then he quickly lowered his gaze in the same odd and curious way he had the last few days, as if he were afraid to meet her eyes directly.

What prompted her to reach out and touch his hand she didn't know—normally, she would never have been so bold. She did it without thinking and was stunned as he quickly moved it away.

He turned from her. With his hands in his trouser pockets, his black suit coat caught behind his wrists, he walked to the far side of the immense room, where he paused before a monstrous cabinet housing a collection of seventeenth- and eighteenth-century antiques. Shrouded in shadows, he stood in silence. How remote he seemed now, as if he had forgotten her presence entirely. His features took on a haggard look that made him appear much older.

"My lord, is something wrong? If I've said anything to displease you, I apologize."

He said nothing.

"My lord?" she called softly, and moved toward him, only to be brought up short as his dark head turned and he fixed her with eyes that were like fires burning.

"You really shouldn't be here," he said quietly.

She couldn't move or speak, and as a cold wind came from nowhere to swirl around her, she could do nothing but stare into his magnificent face and eyes, and feel as if she were suddenly tumbling helplessly down some bottomless black abyss.

His words floated to her as if in a dream as he said, "Come here, dear heart."

She obeyed.

Standing half a head taller than she, Rothschild lay his hand against her face, traced the outline of her cheek with his fingertip, and smoothed the pad of his thumb across her lower lip. Dawn quivered. Her breath became fast and her mind drowsy. Catching his big hand in hers, she cupped it against the side of her face, only vaguely acknowledging the coolness of it as she was swept by the familiar potency of his touch.

How intensely he watched her with those odd, mesmerizing eyes. She could not conceive of what he might be thinking, but in that moment it didn't matter. Adrift in a tide of emotion that she had never before experienced, she knew only that she felt very queer, light-headed, and absurdly foolish.

"I must be insane for bringing you here," he said, his voice a husky whisper. "But it's been so long . . . so very, very long since . . ."

"Since what, my lord?"

Closing his eyes, he pulled her nearer and, sliding his hand around the back of her head, pressed her cheek against his chest and gripped her tightly. "Will you . . . hold me, dear heart?"

She closed her arms around him and listened to the heavy throb of his heart against her ear. She allowed her senses to soak up the smell of his skin and the texture of his coat against her cheek.

"Oh, my God, you feel good," he murmured in her ear. His fingertips slowly, so slowly, skimmed down the length of her neck. "You smell good. I can only imagine how you must taste."

Her head fell back, and she looked up into his eyes.

"Don't," he whispered urgently. "Don't dare look at me with such invitation. Don't trust me, for that matter."

"Because you're in love with another woman, my lord?"

"Another woman?" He stared up at the ceiling, at carved likenesses of fire-breathing dragons. "What gave you that impression?"

"Rosie—"

"Ah. Of course. I should have known." His gaze came back to hers, drawing her again into that familiar vortex of breathless confusion that left her mind and body spinning out of control. "Of course she would tell you that for your own good. No doubt she encouraged you to get well and leave here as soon as possible." Suddenly his hand twisted in her hair, and he pulled back her head. "I should encourage you to leave, but God help us both, I can't do it. It's as if a ray of sunshine has entered this bleak house since you came here."

"My lord, you seem so sad."

"Yes, I'm sad. I'm sad that I didn't meet you long ago, when I believed—or was allowed to believe—in love and happily ever after. Back then I was an incurable romantic and trusted that everything was possible if one only had faith. Now . . ."

He lowered his dark head over hers, and the intensity of his eyes became like a blinding light that both repelled and entranced her, enchanting her and terrifying her too. For an instant she longed to back away from his arms, to turn and run from the room; indeed, from this house as fast as she could.

But she couldn't move, mesmerized as she was by the transformation going on before her eyes. Little by little the soft lines of his face were growing harsher, the grip in her hair more fierce.

Then, with no warning, he flung her away and backed into the deeper shadows. Covering his face with his hands, he cried, "Get out of here. Quickly! Oh, God, that I was such a fool to bring you here. I said, get out!"

She backed away. "My lord, if I've displeased you—"

He spun on his heels to face the wall.

"My lord, are you ill?"

"Go back to your room and lock your door. Have Rosie stay with you. She's not to leave you until . . ." Groaning, he moved farther into the cavernous room, toward the enormous fireplace that stood black and empty on the far wall. "Tell her to send for Ruth. Yes, yes. Quickly, dear heart, before . . . Run, I tell you, and whatever you do, don't look back. Stop for nothing and no one, no matter what you see or hear. I beseech you, Dawn!"

She backed toward the door, then, spinning on her heels, ran from the room. The corridors were long channels of shadows and cold drafts that brushed her shivering skin as she fled along the rugless floors. Odd how the same hallways that had earlier impressed her with their majesty now seemed as dark and damp and dreary as the stinking alleyways running the length of East End London. She tried to cry out for Rosie, but the sound wouldn't come. Only the deafening explosion of each heartbeat seemed to ricochet from the walls and crash against her ears like discordant cymbals. No, there was something else there—some noise that sounded like the panting of an animal, and the hot, almost fetid stench of sour wind whipping around her shoulders, lifting her hair like warm, clammy fingers caressing her throat. Some presence was there, pressing nearer. She could sense it; dear God, she could feel it, just over her shoulder, and—

Turning down yet another corridor, she stopped abruptly. Corridors spread out to her left and right. Which one to take?

The hand came from nowhere and clamped on her shoulder. Spinning around, voiceless with fear and breathless with the fierce agony that suddenly gripped like claws about her heart, she spun around just as a crash of thunder erupted above the house.

"Lass!" Rosie cried. "Wot's 'appened? Ye look as if ye've just seen a ghost!"

4

"MY Lord Rothschild, I wish I had happier news, but, alas, I must confirm your worst fears. The young lady is extremely ill."

"Is she dying?"

"Yes."

Rothschild closed his eyes. "Is it her heart?"

"Neither of us needs my stethoscope to tell us that."

"How long does she have?"

"Honestly, I don't know how she's lived this long." Dr. Leland Bradley closed his black bag as he continued to gaze down on Dawn's pale face. "Tell me, your lordship, does she know about us?"

"No."

"Then I suggest you get her out of here as soon as possible. Word of her presence at Rothston Hall has already traveled in our circles throughout London. I don't mind telling you, there are a great many of our friends who are growing extremely nervous."

"What am I to do? Turn her out on the street? For God's sake, Leland, you just told me yourself that she's dying."

"Surely she has a home—"

"Some rat hole near Mitre Square. If I sent her back there, she'd be dead within days—if not from her heart defect, then from some maniac killer."

The physician released a sigh, and easing down into the chair near the bed, he withdrew a flask from his coat pocket, uncorked it, and turned it up to his mouth. He sighed again, this time in pleasure. "Ruthie's outdone herself tonight. This one was a Frenchman. He was drunk and attempted

427

to climb Big Ben. Fell on his head, poor sod. His blood was very rich. By gosh, it leaves a warm glow in the pit of my belly. Remind me to thank Ruth before leaving.''

Sliding the bottle back into his coat pocket, Dr. Bradley glanced at Rothschild. ''You know your having the girl here is forbidden, Byron. It goes against the commandments you yourself drew up. Need I remind you that you've condemned others to death for doing just this sort of thing?''

''No,'' he snapped. ''You needn't.''

''Are you certain that your philanthropy is due strictly to your concern for her health?''

Picking up the pink dressing gown Dawn had been wearing when she fainted into Rosie's arms, Rothschild ran his fingers lightly along the satin ruching on the sleeve.

''Are you in love with her?'' the physician asked.

''Don't be silly. I'm a vampire, for heaven's sake.''

''And where is it written that a vampire cannot fall in love, my lord? 'Tis true that this fiendish malady has robbed us of our ability to exist as humans do, but, as we all know, our malady has not stolen our emotions.''

'' 'Twould have been better if it had.''

''I won't argue with that. Still, we both know that daydreams of love and commitment are merely fantasies. But all that is beside the point. The young woman has only days, if not hours, to live. If you insist on allowing her to remain here, try your best to keep her as comfortable as possible. And no more scares like the one that sent her into this faint. The next one will kill her.''

Rothschild moved to the bed and touched his fingers to Dawn's pale forehead. Her breathing sounded thin and raspy in the quiet; her heart beat an uneven rhythm. ''It isn't fair,'' he said. ''She's so very young and gentle.''

''Life and death are rarely fair. We learned that centuries ago when each of us became victims of our circumstances. But we learn to go on. We have little choice.''

''Oh, we have a choice, my good doctor. Just like any human, if we grow weary of going on, we simply end it. Some of us have been strong enough to do it: Charles Fleet, Henry Glen, and others. They grew weary of facing eternity without love and walked off into the sunrise. It was as simple as tumbling off Big Ben.''

Dr. Bradley placed a compassionate hand on Rothschild's shoulder. ''You sound weary, Byron. There are lines of fatigue on your face that I haven't seen before.''

''I haven't been resting well.''

''I'm not surprised. Having the girl here must have put an unimaginable strain on you. I'm amazed that you've managed not to succumb to her. I'm not certain I could have been so strong.''

Rothschild walked to the window and looked out into the rain-drenched night. Lightning flashed and thunder rumbled as he pressed one hand against the pane.

''My lord,'' the doctor said softly. ''Why not allow me to remove the girl?''

''And take her where? To that stinking, miserable hospital? What can they do for her there?''

''Nothing.''

''Right. Nothing. Remember what it was like to die, Leland? I recollect lying there alone in the dark in a puddle of blood and watching my life dwindle to a pinpoint. I remember fighting for that last breath. I recall the memories that flashed one after another through my mind's eye. I can still see my mother's and father's and brothers' faces as they paraded through my memory, and I can yet feel the terrible stabbing sadness as I realized that I would never see or touch them again. I wanted so damn badly to tell them goodbye.

''For the last century, I've hidden in the night shadows and watched my family grow old and die, my brothers' families as well. Do you know what it was like to be forced to lurk in the darkness outside my father's death room, hearing his last dying words? He said, 'Thank God, I'll be joining my dear Byron at last.' Oh, my God, Leland, if he only knew . . .''

He took a long, weary breath and turned to regard the sleeping woman. ''I can't allow her to die alone, Leland. No one deserves that.''

Dr. Bradley, his face sad, nodded in understanding.

''What do I tell her?'' Rothschild asked.

"By the comments you said she's made, I suspect she is already aware of her circumstances. I doubt that you'll find it necessary to tell her anything."

They walked together to the bedroom door. Pausing, Dr. Bradley regarded Dawn for a long moment. "She'll have questions about tonight. If she has any intelligence at all, she may well begin to put two and two together. Are you prepared for that, Byron?"

"I may consider telling her the truth . . . if she asks."

"What then? What if she runs screaming from the house and to the police?"

"If she'll allow me to explain—"

"She'll think you're insane, or a monster. You know humans are terrified of anything they don't understand. Look at the pandemonium the Ripper is causing. How do you suppose the people would react to us? For that matter, look how she reacted to you. You practically frightened her to death." Rothschild frowned, and the doctor softened his tone. "Take my advice. Do yourself and the young woman a favor. Stay as far away from her as you can get."

Dawn awoke from her deep sleep feeling remarkably refreshed, considering the terrible pain she had experienced the night before. Still, her thoughts were more than a little fuzzy as she tried to recall the reasons for her attack. There had been tremendous fear. But fear of what?

Surely not of Rothschild, though, in truth, he had precipitated her initial panic with his unusual behavior. Dear God, what had possessed him to act so strangely? To cause him to change from a charming admirer one moment to an angry, desperate stranger who wanted no part of her the next?

The house was as quiet as a mausoleum as Dawn eased down the winding flight of stairs, pausing momentarily to peer out an oriel window whose leaded glass splintered the late afternoon sunlight into streaks of red, blue, and yellow. She stood there for several minutes, allowing her body to soak in the warm rays while she studied the landscape stretching out before her.

How very peaceful were these surroundings. The gardens were tended with meticulous care. She could imagine that in the spring and summer the flower beds would be brimming with great drifts of vibrant colors and the air would be scented with the blooms' perfume.

She continued down the staircase and discovered the house was empty. Not that she was ever given the impression that Rothston Hall teemed with servants. In truth, she had never seen any domestics, other than Rosie and Ruth. With the exception of the cleaning crew that had come in two days before and dusted furniture that had already been immaculately clean, she had seen no one other than Rothschild and his friends—and that had been only *after* the sun had gone down.

She sat in a chair in the lavender drawing room, staring up at an oil portrait of Rothschild. Only it wasn't *her* Rothschild. It must have been his grandfather, for the date in the corner read 1788. Still, the resemblance was stunning enough to keep her staring at it in fascination and growing unease.

Her mind kept drifting back to the nights she had spent with her grandmother, when the bright-eyed old woman had spoken softly of beings who ventured out into the world only after dark. Her grandmother had sworn on the grave of her mother that she had once known a man who claimed to be a vampire. Dawn's father had chastised her for spinning yarns that gave the children nightmares. There were no such things as vampires! Yet, while other children huddled under their sheets and shivered with fear of imagined creatures with sunken faces and fangs who devoured bad little girls and boys, Dawn crept into her grandmother's bed and begged her to tell her more about her friend the vampire.

Was he ugly?

No.

Did he have big teeth?

She never saw his teeth, and besides, they grew long only when he was angry or hungry.

Did he skulk about the night biting people on the neck?

Only if he didn't like them.

How old was he?

Three hundred years old.

Older than you?

Cheeky child.

How long does a vampire live?

Forever.

Living forever would be very nice.

Sitting in Rothston Hall's spacious drawing room, Dawn frowned and shook her head. Believing in such incredible stories when she was a child was one thing . . . but to succumb to them at her age . . .

Still, there was something very, very strange about Rothschild and his friends, and this house, for that matter. Even the potted plants placed about the rooms were unusual. One on the window ledge was called Sir Richard. Another in the vestibule was known as Charles, and Rosie called still another Henry. Numerous times Dawn had heard the servant speaking to the plants as if they could understand her. And if that wasn't enough, the blooms opened only *after* dark.

Just for a moment, what if she allowed herself to believe that her new dear friends were vampires . . .

That evening she felt strong enough to join Rothschild for dinner. Except she was the only one eating. While she dined on roast beef and potatoes, he sat back in his chair and watched her with those incredibly searching eyes. The fact that he had chosen to stay home with her, instead of joining his friends at the theater had breathed heat into the ember of hope that she had tried so hard to deny the last few days.

"My lord, the food is wonderful. Why don't you eat?"

His mouth curved in a smile. He raised his wineglass as if in toast. "I am."

"That's hardly a decent meal for a man, sir."

His eyes never leaving hers, he said, "I'd like it very much if you called me Byron."

She felt the blood rush to her face, and Rothschild shifted in his chair. She watched his fingers caress the glass with a sensuality that made her breath catch.

Surely it wasn't desire she saw in his look, in the way

his long black lashes lowered as he contemplated the glass in his hand—one of the very glasses she had given him. His generosity stemmed from nothing more than kindness and compassion—or pity. By now, he must be aware of her progressing illness.

Sitting back in his chair, Rothschild regarded her thoughtfully. "Are you feeling stronger?" he asked.

"Yes, my lord." She took a drink of water.

"Is there anything I can do to make your recuperation more comfortable?"

"What I would like, sir, is to be shown about the gardens. Perhaps . . ." She met his intense gaze and smiled. "Perhaps you would walk with me about the grounds tomorrow."

He didn't blink. The slight curve of his lips barely faltered, but she saw it. A long minute passed before he responded.

"That won't be possible, I'm afraid. I have obligations that take me away from the house during the day. But perhaps Rosie—"

"What sort of obligations?" she asked.

He nudged his glass away and lightly drummed the table with his fingers. "This and that," he finally replied.

"I often wonder when you find time to sleep, considering you come and go so frequently throughout the night."

When he made no further response, she pushed her food away and sat back in her chair. "Where do you go during the day?"

"Dear heart, I think you're a little too curious for your own good."

Rosie entered the dining hall and refilled Rothschild's glass. Dawn watched his face as she said, "I wouldn't mind a touch of that wine myself."

Rosie regarded her with round eyes, her carafe suspended over Rothschild's glass.

Dawn glanced back and forth between them. "A doctor once told me that red wine would build up my blood."

"Did he?" Rothschild raised the glass to his lips.

Still, Rosie didn't move. Her face turned whiter.

"Very well," he finally said, and motioned for Rosie to

fill Dawn's glass. The maid hurried to the task, then stood back with the decanter gripped to her breast as Dawn peered into the red liquid with a puzzled frown.

"Is something wrong?" Rothschild asked.

She shook her head and cautiously sampled the liquid. It was a robust claret. "I hope you don't mind," she continued a trifle more hesitantly, "but I wandered about Rothston Hall today."

"Did you?"

"I discovered there were chambers that you didn't include on our tour last evening. Like the west wing. Obviously, it's an area that has yet to be renovated. It seems so dark and forbidding.

"And you don't care for the forbidden?"

She smiled and squared her shoulders. "I confess that I've always been intrigued by the forbidden, my lord. After all, the forbidden is so much more stimulating."

He turned his smile up to Rosie and lifted one eyebrow. "And where were you while our guest was roaming the house unattended?"

"Fetchin' meself a copy of the *Times*, m'lord. In case you ain't heard, the Ripper has struck again."

"Yes. A nasty business. A young woman named Mary Kelly. Did you know her?" he asked Dawn.

She shook her head. As Rothschild watched her over the rim of his wineglass, he noted the soft color of blood in her cheeks and forced himself to avert his gaze. It wasn't easy. Like the night before, her mere presence sensitized every nerve in his body. The air grew warmer by the minute. The fact that she continued to regard him in that curious manner, with heavy lids and her soft mouth innocently petulant, stirred the discomfiture in him . . . as it had the night before.

Rosie cleared her throat, bringing his and Dawn's attention back to her. "There was witnesses who said they seen a man fittin' the Ripper's description runnin' by Thrawl Street Cemetery. Word is that an Inspector Chesterton will be contactin' ever' one who lives in this vicinity."

"I'm certain you'll be able to handle the inspector, should he show up on our doorstep."

"Course I will. Still and all, I wish they would catch the fiend who's killin' these poor wretches. The streets ain't safe for a woman to wander anymore, 'specially after dark. They say this Ripper always strikes after midnight, and that 'e has an uncanny way of appearin' and disappearin' just like that." She snapped her fingers.

Rothschild left his chair, moved around the table, and helped Dawn to stand. "I'll see you back to your room," he told her.

"But I don't wish to return to my room. The night is early, and we still have so much to talk about."

"Such as?"

"Such as what happened last night."

As they entered the foyer, the front door opened and Johnny Delacorte entered in a swirl of wind and leaves that swept in a rush across the floor. "Well, well," he said. "Look who we have here. If it ain't the lovely gypsy of Rothston Hall. Ain't she looking nice and flushed this evening?"

Rothschild took Dawn's arm and directed her toward the stairs.

"Tucking her into bed again, my lord?" Johnny said behind them. "One would think that to be an enviable task . . . for any *normal* man."

Ignoring the taunt, Rothschild paused long enough to sweep Dawn up into his arms. She laughed.

"My lord—"

"Byron."

"Sir . . . I'm perfectly capable of climbing the stairs on my own."

"Please allow me. It's been a very long time since I've been allowed to play the gallant."

"How sweet," Johnny called from the bottom of the stairs. "Will you kiss her good night, my lord? If you've forgotten how, I'll be more than happy to instruct you . . . if the lady permits."

"I don't like him," Dawn whispered.

"Neither do I."

"Then why do you allow him to come here?"

"Perhaps I'll tell you someday." ·

"I can't shake the feeling that I've seen him before."

His step faltered, but he smiled. "Best not to trouble yourself with Johnny. He's a mischiefmaker and not worth a moment of your consideration."

Reaching the bedroom, he lowered Dawn into the bed, raising one eyebrow as she wrinkled her nose in displeasure.

"I'm not sleepy, my lord. Or tired. You really shouldn't coddle me so. I'm not yet at death's door."

The words jarred him.

Her dark eyes regarded him thoughtfully, and she placed her hand against his cheek. He jerked away. "Don't," he said, backing from the bed and lightly touching his face, which still tingled from the warmth of her fingers.

"Don't what, sir? Don't touch you?"

"Don't speak of dying. You're not dying."

"Of course I am. We both know it. Perhaps not tonight, or tomorrow, but someday soon. I don't dwell on it. What good would that do me?" Kicking away the covers, she slid from the bed and walked to the dressing mirror where Rosie had placed her brush and ribbons. Easing into the chair, she began to brush out her hair. It spilled black as night and soft as silk over her shoulders.

Dear God, she was beautiful. And innocent. And brave. Far braver than he had been when he'd realized his life was draining from him into the street. He had tried to scream. He'd wept. He'd fought out of desperation for that final gasping breath.

At last, she put her brush down and turned to face him. Her cheeks were pink and her mouth was red. Her eyes gazed at him in fascination.

"If I were not here, Byron, what would you be doing tonight?"

"Wandering the London streets. Visiting my friends. Frequenting the opera or theater."

"The opera? How fascinating! Tell me about it. *All* about it. I use to stand outside the opera house and watch the beautiful people arrive in their fine coaches and beautiful clothes, and I'd dream that someday I would see a performance.''

"Perhaps . . ." He laughed at the absurdity of the idea. Imagine him sweeping this innocent out into his world of darkness and mystery and danger. She'd be appalled. If she learned the truth, the shock would kill her.

Ah, but to introduce her to the London he had grown to love. The lights. The uncrowded streets. The wonderful men and women who, like him, had been plunged into this existence through no fault of their own, but who, like him, had chosen to make the most of this eternity.

"Perhaps . . . you would allow me to escort you to the opera," he said.

Her eyes widened in disbelief. "I couldn't possibly. I wouldn't know how to act. I wouldn't fit in. I have nothing to wear!"

"That, of course, can be remedied. And as far as your fitting in . . . Dear heart, you would be the most envied woman there."

She stared at him, her white hands gripped in her lap, her small teeth nibbling her lower lip. Then she leaped from her chair and threw her arms around him.

The dressmaker's name was Paulette, and she stood no taller than Dawn's shoulder. Her white hair lay coiled at the nape of her neck as she peered up at Dawn through wire-rimmed spectacles.

"The young lady is very pretty," Paulette murmured to Rothschild as she tucked and pinned the dress to Dawn's figure.

Dawn glanced at Rothschild, who stood near the rear door of the dressing room, his arms crossed over his chest, his shoulder resting against the door frame. How different he seemed in these surroundings. Not so formal. Certainly more relaxed.

As a bell tinkled at the front of the store, Paulette hurried for the door, paused briefly, and looked around, her face pinched with unease as she regarded Dawn, then Rothschild. "My lord," Paulette said. "What shall I tell them?"

"That everything is under control."

"But they'll sense immediately—"

"*Everything* is under control," Rothschild repeated more forcefully and with a lift of one dark brow.

With a formal bow, the dressmaker quit the room. Dawn smiled at Rothschild, who had not stopped smiling at her since the moment they had entered the shop.

"She seems a very nice woman," she said.

"She is."

"She's a bit pale, however."

"Perhaps she's overworked."

"She needs to get out more. In the sun."

Rothschild shrugged and shoved away from the door. He moved gracefully across the floor, impeccable in his black suit.

Moving up behind Dawn, he gently touched the hair she had braided and pinned in a coronet to the back of her head. "I'll tell her," he replied softly, so softly the words were little more than a breath upon her ear.

Closing her eyes, exhilarating in the feel of his fingers lightly brushing the curve of her throat, she swallowed. "My lord, the dress is beautiful. I've never owned anything so lovely."

"What a shame. We'll have to do something about that."

She turned to face him. Her head tipped back as she gazed up into his deep-set eyes. "You've been far too generous. What can I do to repay you?"

"Nonsense. Besides, you already gave me the crystal glasses."

"But they couldn't possibly compare to this."

"Dear heart, just having you smile at me that way is reward enough."

"Might I kiss you? There?" She touched his cheek with her finger, and he stepped back. His gaze locked into her eyes with an intensity that rocked her. As the sound of voices rose and fell in the other room, punctuated by an occasional laugh and the racket of traffic on the street, she watched a myriad of emotions sweep his features: desire, concern, fear. Still, the ferocity of his observation of her didn't waver. She felt as if she were slowly losing consciousness, as if her soul were gradually being drawn from her. She could not look away from his eyes, no matter how hard she tried. They were burning. Hypnotic.

Gathering her courage, she went up on her tiptoes and lightly brushed his lips with hers. He tensed. He buried his hands in her hair and tipped back her head. Yet he didn't kiss her, but lowered his mouth to just above hers—so close she could feel his cool breath brush her cheek—and hesitated.

"Don't you want me?" she asked.

"Of course."

"Then take me."

"Foolish girl. You don't know what you're offering."

"Of course I do. I've known for certain since last night."

His eyes narrowed. The grip on her hair became harsh.

"You're a vampire," she said, feeling the first twinges of fear and anticipation as his features went from desirous to threatening. "The mirror," she rushed on. "You stood behind me as I brushed out my hair. I saw only my reflection in the mirror."

He moved away suddenly and turned for the door just as Paulette scurried in. The little woman stopped abruptly, and as Rothschild lifted his hand in dismissal, she pivoted on her heel and exited the room.

"She's one too, isn't she?" Dawn demanded. "All these people who have come and gone here the last hours have been vampires. Mercutio. Brutus. Sir Varocher—"

"Obviously, you have a very vivid imagination, dear heart."

Dawn moved up behind him. She gently placed her hand on his back and felt his body go hard as stone. He slowly turned. His face looked flushed. His chiseled, masculine features were indescribably beautiful and full of unspoken emotions. And his eyes—his marvelous eyes . . . For the first time she experienced the full impact of their unworldly mastery, and she understood why he had refused to meet her gaze directly until now. Like the sea surging under the invisible power of the moon, her body and soul lifted to some frightening height on a journey she was helpless to control. She felt drowsy. The peripheral world faded to a swirling gray fog that seemed to wrap around her and shrink her consciousness to a finite point of light that was filled only by him—Rothschild—whose voiceless words reached inside her mind and caressed her thoughts as softly and gently as the lyrics of a love song.

Come to me.

Let me love you.

I've waited an eternity just to hold you.

"Yes," she murmured, and swayed against him, clutching his coat as her eyes drifted closed and her heart beat in rhythm with the cadence of his words and the tingling stroke of his fingers on the feverish flesh of her throat. "Take me," the odd, husky voice inside her pleaded.

Through the fog she watched his head lower, felt his mouth breathe against hers, experienced the first flush of hot desire as he pressed his cheek on hers and whispered something incomprehensible against her ear. Her head fell to one side, offering up her pale throat, and with a groan, he slid his tongue down the cool white column and skimmed the transparent skin shielding her palpitating pulse, first with his tongue then with his teeth as a low animallike growl rumbled in his chest, and hot air blew around them.

"Kiss me," she heard the frantic stranger that she had become beseech him.

"Little fool, you don't know what you're asking."

"We can be together forever . . ."

His closed his hands in her hair, and the pain on her scalp felt torturous. Tears rolled down her face as he forced her to look in his eyes. They were different now. Red and burning. For the first time, she became frightened, not just of him, but of her own actions—her inability to fight the inevitable outcome of the moment.

Suddenly he shoved her away. Backing into the shadows of the cramped chamber, he bumped into a table laden with spools of thread and trays of needles that tipped over the edge and sprayed the floor like tinkling icicles. With the lamplight gyrating on the wall, Rothschild covered his face with his hands and pressed his body into the corner, his back to her. But when she thought to hurry forward and console him, he shouted, "Get away from me! Don't touch me. For the love of God, run from this place before it's too late for us both."

"Then it's true!" she cried. "I was right. You're a vam—"

"A vampire? Yes!" He spun on his heels, causing the curtain nearby to billow. Transfixed, she stared into his transformed face, the gauntness of his cheeks, the whiteness of his skin, the elongated teeth that shone like dim gold in the poorly lit room. Yet his eyes hadn't changed. They swam with pain and distress as he watched shock sweep her features.

"Go on," he snarled. "Run screaming for the police. Turn from me in repulsion and terror. But for the love of God, don't stand there and pity me."

"Pity you? I don't pity you, my Lord Rothschild. I envy you."

"How can you envy this?" He shielded his mouth with his hand and, closing his eyes, turned his face away. "I'm a monster," he said, "and if you know what's good for you, you'll flee from this place and never look back."

"And go where?" She took a step toward him. He threw up his hand as if erecting some invisible barrier. "What's out there for me, my lord? Only a society teeming with squalor and pestilence. How many times have I fainted along the very street on which you found me? No one but you stopped to offer me comfort. In the five years I've struggled to survive in this city, no one, aside from you, has offered to feed me, clothe me, wrap me up when I was cold or sponge my brow when I was hot. The people of this city are killing one another like animals, yet within the confines of Rothston Hall I've experienced nothing but peace and harmony. *They* are the monsters, my lord. Not you."

"What do you want from me?" came his soft, deep, and masculine voice as he stared at her over his upraised hand.

"To stay with you forever."

"Impossible."

"Don't you like me?"

"Like you?" His lashes lowered. His head bent, and his broad shoulders sagged, if only slightly. His sad laughter tugged at her frantically racing heart. She suddenly felt limp with love and an impossible longing. "*Like* you," he repeated, as if sounding out the words for his own ears. "An understatement, I think. Yes, I like you. I like you very much, dear heart. Too much to stand back and watch you grow old before my eyes and die."

"I shan't grow old. We both know that. But you could help me, my lord . . . you could make me a vampire."

His gaze flew back to hers. His eyes were stunned and disbelieving as he swept his arm down, revealing his cursed teeth. He laughed, a sharp, ugly sound as he walked in leonine strides to the far side of the room. Without turning to address her directly, he toyed with a length of black satin ribbon draped over the shoulder of a mannequin. "You've just asked me to murder you. Do you realize that? You've asked me to condemn you to an eternity of darkness, of constantly looking over your shoulder for fear someone will recognize you for what you are. It is a life of relying on crazy old women servants to deliver your food and fearing that if they don't arrive your willpower will snap and you'll revert into some bloodthirsty fiend who would stalk down the most innocent child to assuage his hunger."

"Could that life be worse than what I'm living now?" she demanded.

"Yes. A thousand times worse. My world is one unending colorless shadow. It reeks of decay. You would never again look a human being in the eye and not fear that you'd somehow be discovered. It is . . ."

"It is what, my lord?"

"Never knowing love again."

Silence.

At last Dawn moved up behind him. She placed a hand on his back and heard his breath catch. His body seemed to draw in on itself. "I fear you presume too much," she said. "For I have fallen in love with you, my Lord Rothschild."

His head turned a little, and his hand came back to catch hers. "Impossible," he whispered in an aching voice. Then, spinning on his heels, he fled the room, leaving Dawn alone and staring after him.

5

THE hunger overwhelmed him. It knotted his stomach and made his head pound. As he lay in the dark and stared up at the lid of his coffin, he groggily tried to reason why he should be suffering so feverishly with the need to feed immediately. He hadn't felt this desperate in seventy-five years—not since the first twenty-five years of vampirism when he'd done his best to scare the living hell out of London. Back then he'd been lusty with power and anger— just as Johnny Delacorte was now. But eventually he'd learned to control it. He'd realized that it had been his own foolishness—not the world's—that had brought him to this sorry existence.

Yet he had awakened tonight filled with the old audacity. Even as he closed his eyes again and did his best to relax and breathe evenly, he felt the changes taking place in his body. Clenching his hands, he tried to concentrate, to bring calming images to his mind that would relieve the stress. The thoughts that paraded through his memory were far from soothing, however.

The woman would have to go.

Everyone had tried to warn him, but, alas, he'd refused to listen. He'd foolishly allowed himself to become smitten—no doubt falling in love with her innocence and the mere fact that she represented something he could never be again. He'd stupidly believed that by associating with her he could once more experience the joy of living . . . and he had. Dear merciful God, he had. Her laughter had filled him with sunshine. The smell of her skin had cleansed his senses of decay and replaced it with the scent of spring rain and roses. And her eyes . . . violet one moment, sapphire the next. They reminded him of the sky just before dusk. Before nightfall crashed its black fist down on the earth. In Dawn's eyes, he could experience a little bit of heaven amid his tumult.

But she would definitely have to go.

She knew about them. If the others found out, he couldn't assure her safety, and he certainly didn't wish to be put in the position of having to protect her. No doubt about it; he'd kill any vampire who thought to harm her. But all that was beside the point. The innocent creature had actually pleaded with him to make her a vampire. The appalling thought occurred to him that she had come very close to succeeding. What had he been thinking to invite that sort of closeness between them? Had he become so weak—so starving for a human's love and compassion, for the mere touch of the girl's hand—that he had allowed himself to make the most dangerous of mistakes?

Could he trust himself to see her again?

No. He couldn't. She was the reason for this insatiable need for nourishment. Nearly a century had passed since he'd last experienced this sort of desire—the kind that turned him hard and throbbing for repletion. The ache was enough to make him forget about his need to eat, to concentrate instead on the memories of what it was like to make love to a woman. To feel her hot, tight, wet body surround him and drive him mad and panting and urgent for release.

When it became evident that his body's upheaval would not be assuaged by simple concentration, Rothschild shoved up the lid of his bed. Upon sitting up, he knew immediately the reason for his discomfort.

Dawn stood near his mother's catafalque, her face white in the gloom, her eyes appearing sunken with illness and fear—no, not just fear, but terror. The smell of her flesh and blood washed over him in a staggering wave.

"What the blazes are you doing here?" he roared, and the words rebounded off the marble walls. Dawn stumbled back and covered her ears with her hands. She said nothing; it was as if she had been struck dumb.

He leaped from the coffin with ease. But then, he was always at his most powerful when his hunger was at its peak. No obstacle existed that could stop him from taking what he wanted . . . and the beast in him wanted her: the life in her veins; the warmth of her body that would melt away the ice in his.

"What are you doing here?" he demanded again. This time his voice sounded thin and vicious.

"You know why I've come," she told him, even as she backed away, one pale, slender hand gripping her neck.

"I could kill you. Don't you understand that? The line between death and the life of a vampire is so thin, I could guarantee you nothing. You could slip over the edge, and I would be powerless to save you."

Dawn drew her slender shoulders back the best she could. She tried to breathe, but the sound was ragged. "I had another attack this morning. Worse than the last. My heart feels as if some fist has taken hold of it and won't let go. I'm dying!" she cried. "If you love me, you'll save me."

"For this?" He swept his hand toward his coffin. "And this?" He glanced around the catacomb where generations of Rothschilds were entombed.

"But we would be together. Would that not make for a difference, my lord? Could we not meet our destiny with greater dignity and bravery if we had each other to lean on?"

Her frailty drove through him like a stake. It reached inside him and, little by little, opened the dragon's cage until the fire of hunger threatened to consume the last semblance of rationality. As the world turned into a fiery red haze, he spun toward the door, intent on putting as much distance between them as possible before he succumbed to his repugnant appetites.

With the little strength she still maintained, Dawn flung

herself against him. "What are you afraid of?" she beseeched him.

Closing his hands about her arms, he easily lifted her from the floor and shook her in anger and frustration. "I won't condemn you to this cursed life. Don't ask it of me, Dawn!"

"Then you condemn me to die. Even as we stand here arguing, I feel my life growing dimmer. 'Tis only a matter of days, if not hours, before it's finished. I love you," she cried. "I know you love me—"

"Look at me." He shook her again. "Are you blind, woman? Is this what you wish to become? Some fiend—"

"No fiend!" she argued hotly. "No monster! Were you a monster, you would have given no thought to ending my life. Here you stand, tortured by some overwhelming hunger to take me, yet you refuse. My Lord Rothschild, you're more human than most of the men who inhabit the world outside the gates of Rothston Hall."

He stared down into her face, her eyes, her lips, the dainty curve of her chin, and the delicate sweep of her dark eyebrows. He watched the flush of rising blood paint her cheeks and minutely darken the throbbing artery in her throat.

With a curse, he buried his hand in her hair and pulled her head back. Then he crushed his mouth down on hers with a fierceness that made her gasp. Ah, sweet nectar! His body shivered, and as his tongue glided around and around in her mouth, the sleek, hot, and silken texture of her being made him groan with desperate need.

She yielded, pliant against him, folding her slender arms around his neck; her small breasts pushed hard against his chest. Awash with the taste and smell of her, he ran his hands over her curves and swells that were barely hidden behind the transparent nightclothes. When he dragged up her gown and stroked her thighs, higher and higher, she twisted and sobbed with the pleasure of it.

"Please," she whimpered.

"Please what?" he demanded in a pained and breathless voice. "Please make you a vampire? Don't ask it of me,

Dawn. Please make love to you? Dear heart, I'm not even certain that I can. I haven't since . . ." He dragged her nearer, if that was possible, until his body and hers seemed to meld and the beating of each heart drummed like an echo of the other. Perhaps . . .

Yes, perhaps it would work, his making her into a vampire. Imagine their living out eternity together—an eternity that might not seem so terrible if she was at his side.

"My lord!" came Rosie's voice from the tunnel. "My lord, come quickly!"

The moment was shattered; the foolishness of his thoughts reared up before him and slammed home the ugly realities of his—their—circumstances. Still, Dawn clung to him until he was forced to shove her away.

"My lord," Rosie whispered from the shadows. "The police have come."

"Police?"

"Inspector Chesterton. 'E wishes to look around. 'E wants to ask ye a question about them Ripper murders."

Forcing his gaze from Dawn's wan features, he turned for the door. The maid materialized through the dark, her concerned eyes darting from him to Dawn. "Have you brought it?" he demanded harshly.

She lifted the container of liquid. He snatched it from her hand, sloshing the blood over the cuff of his shirt sleeve. Dawn's eyes grew wide and her face white as he raised the glass to his lips, hesitated, and smiled coldly at her. "Here is your eternity, dear heart. Your elixir of forever. In your desperation, you've turned me into some man of your romantic imagination. That man doesn't exist—hasn't for the last one hundred years. The man you think you love is no more than an illusion—a facade to hide this despicable hideousness that I've become. A toast, my love, to the bestial ugliness of my existence."

Throwing back his head, he allowed the sweet liquid to pour down his throat. In an instant, heat radiated throughout his body, surged to every nerve, and incinerated the numbness of hunger that left him cold as death. Savoring the familiar, delicious languor the sustenance brought him, he leaned weakly against the wall and closed his eyes.

Rosie removed the emptied container from his hand and replaced it with a napkin. "The inspector is intent on seein' ye, sir," she said quietly.

Opening his eyes, he regarded Dawn thoughtfully. Her face appeared strained. There were dark circles under her eyes. She stood back in the shadows, shivering.

" 'E came by earlier," Rose continued. "I put 'im off until tonight. 'E's bound to speak with ye, sir."

"What about the others?"

"They've all scattered. All 'cept Johnny, that is. 'E's skulking about the place with that idiotic smirk on 'is face. Looks like the cat what swallowed the canary,'e does."

Rothschild took a deep breath and, with some degree of hesitation, held his hand out to Dawn. She had witnessed all the ghastly truths about his life; now was her opportunity to turn from him in disgust.

Yet . . . she didn't. Accepting his hand, she walked with him down the black tunnel.

Dawn sat in a chair before the fire and did her best to concentrate on the conversation between Rothschild and Chief Inspector Chesterton of the CID going on behind her, but the tremors wouldn't leave her. The cup of steaming tea Rosie had supplied her did nothing for the chill that had settled throughout her body. Keeping her eyes open required tremendous effort.

Johnny Delacorte sat nearby, his long legs crossed, his head cocked in its typical arrogant manner. His gaze had not left her since she and Rothschild had entered the drawing room nearly half an hour ago. Nor had the smirk on his mouth.

Odd how his presence could so unsettle her. Here was evil in its purest form, the dark side of this apparent salvation that Rothschild could offer her. Yet there was something else, some greater reason for her discomfiture over his presence than just the fact that he was a vampire with no scruples.

Inspector Chesterton walked to the fireplace and, with his

hands clasped loosely behind his back, stared down into the
flames. The fingers of one hand were bandaged, and as he
glanced over his shoulder at her, she noted his face appeared
to be bruised.

"I can appreciate your thoroughness," Rothschild said
as he moved into Dawn's line of vision. "But I assure you,
inspector, no one in this house would know anything about
the identity of your murderer."

Chesterton turned to face him; his features appeared haggard. "Still and all, my lord, you do understand that we
can leave no stone unturned. There were witnesses who
claimed to have seen a man running in this direction soon
after Mary Kelly was killed."

Several policemen entered the room; each shook his head
at the inspector.

Johnny left his chair and, hands in pockets, offered the
inspector a dry smile. "I was under the assumption that you
had discovered the identity of the Ripper some weeks ago.
The headlines were screaming about some magician . . ."

"For a time our investigation centered on a number of
suspects, a Mr. Dominick D'Abanville among them. He
was cleared of the charges and now resides in Paris."

"I also read that there was some question of a satanic
cult being involved."

Chesterton regarded Johnny with sharp interest. "You've
certainly followed this case closely, sir. Yes, for nearly six
weeks we believed the Ripper might have been killed in the
explosion of Greystone Hall, where the cult carried on its
gruesome activities. Being extremely involved in that particular case"—he held up his bandaged hand. "—I had
rather hoped that we had seen the end of our friend Jack.
Alas, we haven't. I shan't rest until I've apprehended the
bloodthirsty fiend. I intend to expend every ounce of energy
to discover his identity."

Johnny turned his gaze down to Dawn. She gripped the
hot china cup tightly in her trembling hands as she experienced another wave of apprehension—as she had every
time she found herself in his presence. Odd, but somehow
the disquieting feeling had less to do with what he was than

with the fact that there was something creepily familiar about him.

"Perhaps," came Johnny's words to her, "this young woman could help you. Before coming to Rothston Hall, she lived in the East End."

The inspector's eyebrows rose in interest. He glanced toward Rothschild, whose entire being tensed. Rothschild's face turned dark, his eyes ominous as he skewered Johnny with a look that spoke volumes.

"You don't say," the inspector said. Moving nearer to Dawn, he smiled at her with a degree of compassion. "Tell me, my dear, were you acquainted with any of the women who were killed?"

She nodded. "I've already told the police that I saw Polly and Catherine not long before they were murdered. Other than that, I could offer no new clues about their deaths . . . except . . ."

"Yes?" the inspector said.

Frowning, Dawn concentrated on the hazy memory of that bleak night weeks before, when she had bumped into Catherine Eddowes just moments before she was murdered. But to think clearly was becoming more and more difficult. The effort left her exhausted.

Rothschild moved up beside her. He took the cup from her hand and placed it on the chairside table. Closing his fingers around hers, he squeezed reassuringly, but it was to the inspector that he spoke.

"My young friend has been very ill. I fear this questioning has left her more than a little fatigued. Will you excuse us, inspector?"

"Certainly, my lord. However, will you allow me to encourage the young lady to come forward should she recall anything more about those evenings?"

"Of course, inspector."

The chief inspector then nodded to his uniformed companions, and with a brief nod to Dawn, he left the room.

Having gone to his knee beside her, Rothschild gently caressed her cheek. His eyes were dark with concern.

Nestling her face against his palm, Dawn smiled. " 'Tis

better when you touch me," she said softly. "The pain isn't so bad, or the weakness either. I sometimes fancy that if you held me long enough, I might recover completely."

"A most delightful possibility, dear heart."

"Now ain't that sweet," Johnny joined in.

"Methinks I smell trouble afoot!" cried out Mercutio from the hallway, then came the squeak and creak of Sir Varocher's armor, followed by Brutus's blustering commands to stand at attention since a general was entering the room. Dawn's heart lifted at the prospect of seeing her friends again.

Mercutio swept his cap from his head and bent in an exaggerated bow. His eyes, however, coming back to hers, showed distress. "My lady appears frail, my lord. What plagues her?"

"She's overtired, I think. Rest should help."

Sir Varocher perched on her chair arm and, having removed his helmet, waved the feather she had given him under her nose, making her giggle and sneeze. "I can not tell you how many compliments I've received regarding this plume," he informed her with pride. "The entirely of ol' England has fairly swooned with envy. I declare, I've been forced to joust no less than half a dozen times in order to keep it."

"As I have my brooch," Brutus announced with a puffing out of his chest. "I haven't tripped a solitary time since I was given it."

"You're all a lot of enraptured buffoons," Johnny remarked.

"'Tis true, I confess." Mercutio lifted Dawn's hand to his lips and pressed a kiss upon it. "You've brought a spot of light into this glum world of ours, lass." He looked at Rothschild. "Her hand is chilled, my lord."

"Stroke the fires!" Brutus bellowed at Rosie, who dallied near the door.

Plunking her hands on her broad hips, the servant scowled. "Ye best be holdin' yer toga, ye pompous popinjay. I take me orders from one master here, and don't forget it.'' She sniffed and addressed Rothschild. ''M'lord, I've prepared the young lady's bed.''

''But I don't want to go to bed,'' Dawn replied. ''I want to stay here with you—with all of you.''

Rothschild smiled and eased his arms around her, lifting her from the chair. ''They'll be here when you awaken, dear heart.''

''Of course we will,'' Mercutio said, waving at her over Rothschild's shoulder.

''Where else would we go?'' Sir Varocher added as he brushed her cheek with one finger. ''Good night. Good night. Parting is such sweet sorrow—''

''Here now, that's my line!'' Mercutio cried.

Laughing, Dawn rested her head on Rothschild's shoulder and closed her eyes. He easily carried her up the stairs and into her bedroom, but he did not lay her in the bed. Instead, he sat down in the chair nearest the fire and cradled her in his lap.

They sat in silence, Dawn relishing the serenity his nearness brought her.

He listened hard for her every weakening heartbeat, counting the pauses between each.

Finally she raised her head and gazed up at him. ''My lord,'' she whispered, ''is that a tear I see in your eye?''

''Is it?'' His mouth curved in a smile. ''My, my, so it is. I didn't realize I was still capable . . .''

''Are you sad?''

He nodded and held her more tightly.

''Because I'm leaving?''

''I don't want you to leave.''

Smiling, Dawn kissed him lightly on the cheek. Then she saw the stunningly beautiful dress Paulette had delivered just after dark. ''My lord, do you know what would make me happiest tonight?''

''What, dear heart?''

''To spend it as if we were healthy and normal. To visit the opera, as we had planned.''

Rothschild traced her cheek with one finger. ''I still have the tickets, but should we chance it, darling?''

"I'd like to try."

"Then so be it."

He watched Dawn's face brighten, noted the soft color that stained her cheeks and the light of anticipation that brightened her blue eyes. The idea was ludicrous; he knew that. He could be risking her life. But he could deny her nothing. Nothing except her greatest desire: to join him in his cursed existence as a vampire. If he remained here any longer, burning with this desperate hunger for her, he would surely capitulate.

Once he had made her comfortable, he told her that Rosie would be up soon to help her dress. Then he proceeded from the room at a quick pace. His friends still lounged about the drawing room, their faces sad, their thoughts introspective. They perked up, however, upon hearing of Rothschild's plan.

"We'll bring the coach around!" Mercutio cried with fresh enthusiasm.

"I'm driving!" Brutus shouted.

"Dear Brutus," Mercutio said. "Thou will make worm's meat of us all!"

Laughing and slapping one another on the back, they exited the room. All except Johnny. He stood in the shadows, his features sullen.

"You're a lot of fools," he said. "She knows about us."

"Does she?"

"I wonder what the others will think of this once I tell them."

Rothschild poured himself a sherry. "Is that what you intend to do, Johnny?"

"They'll stake you to the nearest crucifix for endangering our society."

"The young woman is no threat to our society."

"I don't think the others will see it that way."

Gently, Rothschild put his glass down, then he turned on Johnny with the speed of a striking asp and slammed him up against the wall. "You young bastard, are you blind? If she was going to reveal us, don't you think she would have spoken up to the inspector?"

"Your infatuation with the little trinket seller is a humiliation to us all. She's human, Rothschild, with all the human frailties and weaknesses that makes them lower than worms."

"Need I remind you that you were human once?"

"But I'm not now. And neither are you. No amount of fraternizing with the gypsy is going to change that. If you're smart, you'll get shut of her now before she topples everything you've accomplished the last seventy-five years. Or perhaps . . ." His pale eyes narrowed. "Perhaps the reason for your interest in her is not so philanthropic. Maybe you have designs on something besides her beautiful little throat. Maybe it's what's between her legs that has you so enraptured."

"You disgust me, Delacorte." Rothschild flung the younger man away. "Get out of my sight while I'm still rational enough to keep from killing you."

Smirking, Johnny straightened his coat. "Perhaps I haven't given you enough credit, Rothschild."

"I said to get out."

Johnny offered a slight bow. "As you command, my lord. But don't say I didn't warn you."

Johnny left the room, closing the door behind him.

Due to Dawn's shortness of breath, they were forced to leave the opera at intermission. But it didn't matter. The performance had lived up to everything she had ever envisioned: the music, the singing, all the beautiful and elegant men and women in the audience. More than once she'd caught the ladies glancing enviously at her gown, and at the striking couple she and Rothschild made.

They took a light repast at a restaurant off King William Street, called Romano's. They were greeted by an Italian waiter with flashing black and knowing eyes.

"Is he one?" Dawn whispered in Rothschild's ear.

He pretended to frown. "I fear you'll start suspecting every man you meet after sundown, dear heart."

"He is, isn't he? And what about all these people?"

"What people?"

She poked him in the ribs, making him grin. "They're all looking at us, my lord."

"They must think you a ravishing little creature."

"More likely they're seeing dessert," she retorted, and he threw back his dark, handsome head in laughter. In truth, he laughed often throughout the night. The sojourn through London appeared to have lifted Dawn's spirits. Her cheeks were bright and her eyes twinkled. But for her spate of breathlessness during the opera, she seemed little affected by her malady . . . until the waiter served them cherries jubilee. She watched in fascination as the Italian set fire to the luscious concoction. She gasped and clapped and bounced in her seat as he spooned the delicious sweet onto her plate.

"Oh, Byron," she said, laughing. "Isn't this wonderful?"

She turned her shining eyes and smile on him, and all he could think of was that, at last, she had called him Byron. That and the fact that she was the most beautiful woman he had ever known in this or any lifetime.

Then her smile faltered. The light in her eyes appeared to fade. He watched her small white hands twist the tablecloth in desperation.

"My lord," she whispered. "I fear . . . I think we should go now."

He swallowed and did his best to shove back his chair as calmly as possible. Mercutio, Brutus, and Sir Varocher hurried from a nearby table and helped her to stand.

"Gently!" Rothschild snapped, finding he was shaking too badly to offer assistance.

Mercutio departed briefly and brought the coach around. Soon Dawn was settled in beside Rothschild, her head resting on his shoulder as he cradled her in his arms, brushed the hair from her cold, cold forehead, and kissed her temple. Her hands lay limply on her lap.

"Talk to me, dear heart," he said to the dark.

"Sleepy . . ." she replied.

He held her tighter and closed his eyes. "We'll come back for the cherries jubilee tomorrow night. Perhaps we'll even try the opera again. I can get tickets any time. The lead tenor is a friend of mine ... Talk to me, sweetheart.''

There was nothing but the fast clattering of the horses' hooves on the pavement. Focusing as hard as he could, he could barely make out the faint beating of her heart.

As the conveyance pulled up before Rothston Hall, Rothschild kicked open the coach door. Rosie greeted them, her eyes wide with distress to see Dawn unconscious in his arms.

He sprang up the stairs, and upon reaching the bedroom, he laid Dawn gently on the bed. Looking over his shoulder at Brutus, who stood in the doorway wringing his hands, he barked, ''Get Dr. Bradley, and be quick about it.''

Sir Varocher stepped in, his features composed but crest-fallen. ''My lord, you know nothing can be done.''

Rothschild turned to Rosie. ''Help me undress her. The clothing may restrict her breathing.''

They undressed her, but it mattered little. As the hours dragged by, it became apparent that she would not awaken, and though her small heart fought valiantly in her breast, it weakened with each tick of the clock.

His anger and desperation mounted.

By the time he became aware of Rosie crying his name, the clock in the hallway was striking the hour of six.

''M'lord, ye've got to come away now. The sun will be up soon.''

Blinking, he gazed down on Dawn's face. How cold and lifeless it was! Oh, sweet Lord, to think that she was as beautiful at death's door as she was vibrant in life.

''Byron.'' It was Mercutio, trying his best to ease Dawn from his arms. ''You must come away. You can stay here no longer.''

''No.'' He shook his head, spilling a long strand of black hair over his brow. ''I won't leave her.''

Sir Varocher lowered himself to one knee beside the bed. He looked Rothschild in the eye. ''Sire, the girl yet lives. Mayhap she'll survive the day.''

''But ye won't if ye remain here,'' Rosie joined in.

Mercutio eased Dawn away, and Sir Varocher gingerly

coaxed Rothschild from the bed. Glancing at Brutus, Mercutio said, "Help us get him to the tomb."

The soft command jarred Rothschild from his stupor. With a roar of fury, he struck out at his friends, to no avail. They sprang at him from every direction, pinning his arms back and grabbing his legs. He twisted and flailed and cursed them.

They managed to wrestle him to the floor outside the bedroom. The pressure of the dawn bore down on them all, robbing them of strength. His chest heaving, his body sweating, Rothschild pounded the floor with his fist.

"You'll pay for this," he cried.

"No doubt," Sir Varocher replied as he clanged and banged his way to his feet. "But fault us as you may, sire, we are friends enough to want to help you."

"Then be a friend and leave me alone."

"How far that little candle throws his beams! So shines a good deed in a naughty world!" cried Mercutio.

"Shut up," Rothschild snapped, and swung his fist at Mercutio's jaw, missing him by inches.

Brutus, fighting his way free from his tangled toga, peered up at Rothschild with a scowl. "If you so wish to spend your miserable eternity with the gypsy, then make her one of us. 'Tis simple enough."

"There is simplicity in virtue," Sir Varocher declared, sweeping his helmet and plume from the floor and sliding it over his head. Then he flipped open the visor and cocked one eyebrow. "He is more frightened that she should come to hate him for making her thus." He swept his arms open wide. "Frankly, I find nothing so repugnant about us. Are we not noble, honest, forthright, and virtuous?"

Standing, Mercutio offered Rothschild his hand. "Perhaps you love her only because she's human."

"Don't be daft."

"Could—would—you love her less if she were a vampire?"

"Of course not."

"Then I fear, friend, that you love not wisely, but too well."

Falling back on the floor, Rothschild covered his face with his hands. "Bloody coward," he muttered.

"But chivalrous to a fault!" cried Sir Varocher, then he bent and, with Mercutio's and Brutus's help, lifted Rothschild from the floor.

T HE dream awakened her. Opening her eyes, Dawn tried to focus on her surroundings. Rosie sat dozing in a chair nearby, her cap sliding over her brow with each bob of her head.

How odd she felt, as if she had somehow become almost but not quite detached from her body. As if she were balancing on some tenuous tightrope over the yawning mouth of a black abyss, and below her stretched oblivion. This was death. She recognized it. She'd watched it pluck her parents and grandparents from her over the years, and now it was reaching its all-powerful hand up through that Stygian well of forever to drag her down.

Not yet. Not yet. She would fight the grim reaper for a while longer.

Sunlight poured through the western window in a dim stream. The day was drawing to a close. Dusk would settle on the house at any moment, and soon her darling Byron would join her again. She would try one last time to persuade him to help her, to convince him that her desire to be with him in his life was not merely to live forever, but to exist for always as his wife.

Falling back onto the pillow, she closed her eyes, yet refused to allow her thoughts to slide again into its storehouse of memories. Throughout the night the events of her life had paraded before her mind's eye. They had been neatly arranged in chronological order, from her childhood to her womanhood, each display bringing her closer to her present destiny. There had been family, friends, acquaintances—anyone who had somehow touched her life and changed it for the better, from a young farmer's son who had once given her a puppy, to Catherine Eddowes, who, just moments before her death, had slipped Dawn a penny for a potato because she'd not sold enough trinkets that day to pay for her supper.

There, however, the recollections had snagged. The imagery had grown murky and disturbing. With a frightening reality she had remembered being on that street corner again with her friend, exchanging whispers of concern as they tried to see through the pea-soup fog that had rolled over the city just after midnight. They had bid their goodbyes, then Dawn had continued to push her cart down the street toward home.

The man had materialized through the fog, knocking her aside in his haste. She'd become angry because he hadn't bothered to apologize for his clumsiness. He'd been wearing a cape and had a hat pulled low over his brow, so she'd managed to catch only a glimpse of his face before he hurried toward Catherine, who still dallied beneath a streetlamp. Only moments later, her friend had been brutally murdered.

It was the man's face that rolled repeatedly through Dawn's mind, and she realized that, even on that bleak night, a flicker of a thought had occurred to her that she had seen his features before . . . in late August . . . with Polly Nichols . . . the Ripper's first victim. That face belonged to Johnny Delacorte.

Dear God. *He* was Jack the Ripper!

Forcing open her eyes, Dawn rolled her head toward Rosie. The servant's snores sounded softly in the quiet. Her generous bosom rose and fell with each deep breath. Dawn tried to speak, but she hadn't breath enough to form the words. With a weak, trembling hand, she reached for the cloth covering the bedside table and, twisting it in her fingers, tugged it as hard as she could, bringing books and an empty glass tumbling to the floor with a crash.

Rosie jumped upright and grabbed her cap as it slid all the way to her chin. "Lud! Wot—" Her eyes widened. She leaped from the chair and grabbed Dawn as she lay partially off the bed. "Gum, lass, wot the blazes d'ye think ye're doin'?" Laying Dawn back on the pillows, she smoothed her hair from her brow. "Lud, 'is lordship'll 'ave me 'ide if he learns I fell asleep. Oooh, I'm a daft woman."

"Rosie."

"Wot is it, luv?" Rosie lowered her ear to Dawn's lips. "Tell Rosie wot's wrong."

"Johnny . . . the Ripper."

Rosie's head popped up.

"The Ripper." Dawn mouthed the words. "Saw him with those women . . . I remember now . . ."

"Well, well," came a voice from the doorway. "What do we have here?"

Dawn closed her eyes, and Rosie gasped to discover Johnny standing in the doorway.

"Seems our little gypsy has once again defied death. I fully expected to find her expired by now. Instead I discover her whispering secrets into a servant's ear. I wonder what she's saying?"

"Ye'll be stayin' out of this room, Johnny Delacorte. Ye know 'is lordship 'as forbidden—"

"I don't give a damn about what his lordship wants. I'm tired of taking orders from his lordship." He smiled, and the lamplight glinted off his teeth. Rosie whimpered, but though she was shaking terribly, she placed herself protectively between him and Dawn. "Get out of my way," he snarled.

"Lord Rothschild—"

"—has been taken care of, for the time being. As have the others. I'll decide later what to do about them on a more permanent basis. Now, however, I have the little matter of the gypsy to deal with."

As he took a step toward her, Rosie flung her weight against him. With a roar of laughter, he gripped her by the throat and flung her like a limp rag doll against the wall.

She hit with a horrible crack and sank in a heap to the floor.

Fear and pain crushed down on Dawn's chest as she lay helplessly twisted in the sheets, unable even to raise her head. Johnny moved up beside her. He bent over her, his smile exposing his teeth. "You remembered at last, didn't you?" he said softly. "These idiotic buffoons believed that I attacked you from a weakness for fresh blood." He watched a flicker of confusion pass over her features. "So. You really don't remember that it was I who was the cause of your being brought to Rothston Hall. But then, you were unconscious when I happened on you. What sweet luck that was. I'd been searching for you since the night I took the Eddowes woman. Suddenly there you were, lying on the ground as beautiful as some sleeping fairy-tale princess. I might have finished you then had those laborers not happened by. But then . . . we wouldn't have had the opportunity of getting to know one another, would we?"

He touched his fingers to her neck, and she flinched. Johnny laughed deep in his throat. "How amusing it's been to watch these moronic police search futilely for me. They believe the Ripper's reason for butchering those women is some horrid hatred for whores. They've claimed I'm a doctor, a butcher, a barber, and even a member of royalty. The truth is, my mutilation of them has no more reason behind it than my desire to hide the fact that the ladies were murdered by a vampire. Cutting their throats hid all trace of the punctures put there by my teeth. Brilliant, wasn't it?

"But what about you?" he continued." I don't dare kill you here—too many of the *others* know you reside at Rothston Hall. Besides, what fun would there be in that? No, I think London deserves another Ripper slaying. It'll give them something to yammer about in their newspapers and whisper about behind their locked doors. We'll have to think of something special for you, even grander than what I did to Mary Kelly. I disemboweled her, you know.

"I think . . ." His tongue crept out and flicked the sharp tip of one fang. "First we'll return you to the East End. Can't do with having a Ripper's victim discovered anywhere else. Might spoil the pattern. Yes . . . I think we'll go to

Miller's court. That's where I killed Mary. It'll be like thumbing my nose at the police, won't it?''

He slid his arms around Dawn and lifted her from the bed. Unconsciousness dragged her under as she heard him whisper:

''Sweet dreams, dear heart.''

Dr. Leland Bradley stood in Rothston Hall's foyer and listened to the quiet. ''Hello!'' he shouted, getting no response. He peered up the staircase.

Having heard from several sources, all of whom had been dining at Romano's the night before, that Rothschild had shown up at the restaurant with the gypsy woman, and that he had been forced to leave suddenly with the apparently stricken girl some half an hour later, Dr. Bradley had thought to drop by the hall to check on her condition. He found this silence disturbing. Even if Byron and his cohorts had taken to the streets—which he doubted due to the girl's illness (unless, of course, she had died, in which case Rothschild would hardly be in a mood to celebrate)—Rosie would still be there to guard the hall against trespassers.

A noise brought his head around. There it was again, coming from the nearest drawing room: a tinkling of glass.

He strode to the door and discovered Ruth waddling around the table with a serving tray of blood-filled goblets. Dr. Bradley plucked his pocket watch from his waistcoat and frowned. Ten past ten.

''A bit late for supper, isn't it?'' he asked.

Ruth continued to fret about the table, arranging and rearranging the glasses. ''Ahem,'' Dr. Bradley said. When she still ignored him, he walked over and tapped her on the shoulder. She squealed and jumped.

''My good woman—'' She cupped her hand behind her ear and gave him a snaggle-tooth smile. More distinctly, he repeated, ''My good woman, hasn't his lordship come up for his supper?''

She shook her head.

He frowned again. ''Where is Rosie?''

Ruth shrugged.

"I don't like the looks of this." Spinning on his heels, he headed for the stairs. Upon reaching the bedroom, he stopped short in surprise. The bed was empty. Rosie lay sprawled on the floor, her head bleeding as she moaned.

Dr. Bradley and dropped to one knee beside her and waved smelling salts under her nose. "What's happened here, woman? Talk to me, I say!"

Blinking and trying her best to sit up, Rosie glanced toward the bed. "Oh, lud!" she cried. " 'E's taken 'er. Johnny's done taken the poor lass!"

"What's this about?"

" 'E's the Ripper!" she declared with bulging eyes. "The lass recognized 'im. She tol' me just before 'e . . ." Grabbing the doctor's lapels, she said, " 'E's done somethin' to 'is lordship."

"Good heavens!"

They stumbled to their feet and hurried from the room, dashing as fast as they could to the secret entranceway, waiting impatiently as Dr. Bradley yanked on the lever and the door opened at a snail's pace. Down into the darkness they plunged, their footsteps echoing along the marble floor and walls, deep, deeper into the ground until a roar of unbridled fury made them hesitate and question their sanity for braving the perilous moment.

They discovered Rothschild's coffin shackled by great lengths of massive chains. In that instant, however, the iron encumbrances split apart as Rothschild surged with his last ounce of power against the lid of his coffin. His hands and arms bloodied and bruised from attempting to escape during the last hours, he rose up from his bed with an ear-splitting howl of rage.

Rosie collapsed in a faint.

"Johnny's taken the girl!" Dr. Bradley shouted.

"Then she's still alive," Rothschild declared.

"She was . . ." As Rothschild leaped to the floor, the doctor added, "Dawn recognized him as the Ripper."

"See that the others are released. Then I want word sent out to every vampire in this city: search every stinking alley, building, or crypt, but find Johnny no matter what."

* * *

By midnight, a dense fog had slid over London, chasing the city's inhabitants from the streets. Only the occasional drunkard or prostitute braved the bleak, foul-smelling mist. But even they cowed in the shadows as strangers passed by. Eyes wide, bodies trembling, they watched the parade of pale-skinned men and women move silently up and down the walks, occasionally pausing long enough to tip their heads as if listening for some sound amid the unnatural silence. Then, looking neither right nor left, they moved on, disappearing like specters into the dark.

As the hours dragged on and the threat of morning pressed in on them all, Rothschild, Mercutio, Brutus, and Sir Varocher met at the end of Buck's Row, where Polly Nichols had been murdered.

"Nothing," Brutus said.

"The sun will rise any minute," Sir Varocher added.

"This fog will beat it back," Rothschild informed them.

" 'Tis true enough." Mercutio wagged his cap in front of his face. "But not for long, I fear. If we're not careful, we're liable to find ourselves potting soil for Rosie's periwinkles."

Sir Varocher laid a hand on Rothschild's shoulder. "Sire, you know the lass may well be dead already. If not by Johnny's hand—"

"She's not." He shrugged away the hand and looked off into the swirling gray mass. "She's alive. I feel it. There's a soft drumming in the air that seems to call out to me. Yet . . ." He sighed. "I cannot discern from what direction it comes." Leaning back against a damp brick wall, he wearily shook his head. "Cursed life that I should go through eternity as a vampire—cursed even more that I should be forced to endure it without her."

"This is getting us nowhere," Brutus announced.

"Right you are," Sir Varocher agreed. "I believe—"

"Rothschild!" came a cry from the far end of the street. "There is something going on at Miller's Court . . ."

Another voice called out. Then another, sounding up and down the alleys like the sharp and persistent yowls of tomcats. Rothschild broke into a run, using his senses to feel rather than see his way up one street and down another. By the time he reached Dorset Street, the first hint of dawn had broken through the mist. The heat of the morning bore down on him.

The vampires had converged near a group of shabby flats near Miller's Court. They watched Rothschild's face expectantly as Dr. Bradley stepped forward. "Someone saw a man enter Number Nine with what appeared to be an ill woman in his arms. That was some hours ago. He hasn't left the house since."

Rothschild walked through the crowd as it parted before him. His friends' faces were flushed with heat, as was his own. Little by little, the strength was draining from him. Pausing, he looked back into the strained features of his companions. "Save yourselves," he told them. "The daylight—"

"Daylight?" Mercutio scoffed and crossed his arms over his chest. "Pish posh. 'Tis only the gaslight illuminating the dark, my lord. No sun."

"No sun," the others repeated.

Rothschild glanced toward the bluing sky, then turned for the door of Number Nine. He wrenched it from its hinges with little effort, flung it to the far end of the alley, and stepped inside.

Johnny Delacorte threw himself from the bed. His mouth was bloody. His expression revealed amusement, then fury, then terror in the space of a second as he recognized Rothschild.

With the swiftness of light, Rothschild moved against him, took Johnny's throat in his hands, and squeezed. Johnny fought him with surprising strength, hissing and growling and sinking his nails deeply into Rothschild's arms. He grabbed for the knife on the table by the bed and brought it down sharply into Rothschild's shoulder.

"Idiot," Rothschild sneered. "Have you grown so accustomed to murdering humans with that knife that you forget you cannot harm a vampire with it?" Again and again Johnny lashed out with the weapon, and though the blood spilled freely, Rothschild didn't flinch. Instead, he lifted Johnny from his feet and threw him as hard as he could across the room.

"My lord!" came an urgent cry. Someone took him by the shoulders, and as his companion vampires rushed into the room and fell upon Johnny, he did his best to focus on Dr. Bradley's face.

"My lord, you must flee! The morning is upon us—"

Rothschild shoved him aside and stumbled for the bed. "Save yourself," he told his friend. "I won't leave her."

Dawn, her face white and still, her throat bleeding, lay on the bed with her soft black hair strewn over the mattress.

"She lives still," the physician said. "You've time, my lord, but I beseech you to act quickly. Her pulse is practically nonexistent!"

Rothschild eased onto the bed, and with hands that were already blistering before his eyes, lifted her into his arms. "Oh, dear heart," he whispered. "Were I brave enough, I would remain here and we would both die with some dignity. But I've only just found you, and by God, I will not lose you again. My only hope is that I haven't waited too long, or that you won't come to hate me for my selfishness in the years to come. I beg your forgiveness, my darling."

He sank his teeth into her throat, felt the first rush of that sweet elixir spurt over his tongue. It sang through his body and flared like fire through his veins. It filled him with euphoria and sent him hurling beyond the boundaries of life and death. He drank deeply, exalting in the lush ecstasy, all the while honing his every sense on her heartbeat, which grew fainter and fainter with each stroke. If he didn't time it right, she would slip over the edge into death, and he could never bring her back.

There! That instant of hesitation as her heart struggled for one last beat—

He slashed open his wrist with his teeth, and as his blood poured forth, he pressed it to her lips. "Drink!" he cried. "Drink, damn you!"

Her lips moved. Her eyelids flickered. He held her head as she suckled the nourishment like a babe at a nipple, and little by little, the color returned to her cheeks. Then her eyes opened. Her features froze as she stared up at his sweating face.

Oh, God, please don't let her turn on me now.

"My lord?" She touched his face with her hand. "Byron!" she cried in relief and threw her arms around him. "I knew you would save me."

He rocked her against him, only vaguely aware that there were shouts coming from behind him. At last he smiled down into her eyes. "Did you think that after waiting a lifetime to find you I would allow you to leave me? I love you," he said.

"Forever?"

"For always, dear heart."

"This is really asking too much," Brutus announced. "For heaven's sake, you'll have eternity for all this drivel."

Hands closed about the couple's shoulders and lifted them from the bed. They hurried from the room, into the last swirling remnants of fog which would continue to hold the sunlight at bay until they reached their coffins.

"I'm going to bloody well fry in this blasted armor," Sir Varocher announced. "All for the love of a woman . . . by gosh, how very romantic!"

"Ah me," sang Mercutio. " 'For aught that I could ever read, Could ever hear by tale or history, The course of true love never did run smooth!' "

Katherine Sutcliffe

KATHERINE SUTCLIFFE's favorite author is Stephen King.

The Passion and Romance of

KATHERINE SUTCLIFFE

SHADOW PLAY

75941-1/$4.95 US/$5.95 Can

A lusty adventurer whose courage was renowned, the handsome Morgan Kane was in truth a rogue and a charlatan. Beautiful Sarah St. James left the glitter of London behind to seek justice in a lush and savage wilderness. Bound by ties of vengeance, together they found a passionate ecstasy beyond dreams.

A FIRE IN THE HEART

75579-3/$4.50 US/$5.50 Can

She fled the horrors of a British workhouse, seeking refuge with a dark, moody aristocrat. Begrudgingly he sheltered her, fighting the fascination of her saucy innocence. But never did she imagine she would force his surrender to the exquisite torment of a love that denied all reason.

RENEGADE LOVE   75402-9/$3.95 US/$4.95 Can

Avon Romances—
the best in exceptional authors and unforgettable novels!

DEVIL'S MOON Suzannah Davis
76127-0/$3.95 US/$4.95 Can

ROUGH AND TENDER Selina MacPherson
76322-2/$3.95 US/$4.95 Can

CAPTIVE ROSE Miriam Minger
76311-7/$3.95 US/$4.95 Can

RUGGED SPLENDOR Robin Leigh
76318-4/$3.95 US/$4.95 Can

CHEROKEE NIGHTS Genell Dellin
76014-2/$4.50 US/$5.50 Can

SCANDAL'S DARLING Anne Caldwell
76110-6/$4.50 US/$5.50 Can

LAVENDER FLAME Karen Stratford
76267-6/$4.50 US/$5.50 Can

FOOL FOR LOVE DeLoras Scott
76342-7/$4.50 US/$5.50 Can

OUTLAW BRIDE Katherine Compton
76411-3/$4.50 US/$5.50 Can

DEFIANT ANGEL Stephanie Stevens
76449-0/$4.50 US/$5.50 Can